A
Not So
Foreign
Affair

A Not So Foreign Affair

Fascism, Sexuality, and the Cultural

Rhetoric of American Democracy

■

Andrea Slane

■

Duke University Press

Durham & London

2001

© 2001 Duke University Press
All rights reserved
Printed in the United States of America on acid-free paper ∞
Typeset in Monotype Garamond by Keystone Typesetting, Inc.
Library of Congress Cataloging-in-Publication Data
appear on the last printed page of this book.

For Eva

For all the promises

she holds and keeps

Contents

■

Acknowledgments

■

Like most authors of books that take a long time to write, I have many people to thank. Like most first-time authors, I don't know how far back to go with my thanking. But there are a few people without whom this book simply would not be: these are easy. My grandmother, Elisabeth Friedrich, taught me how to listen carefully to stories, no matter how many times they are told. Without knowing it, she taught me the complexity of memory, and of politics and the family. My uncle, Henning Friedrich, helped to educate me more overtly in the layers of meaning that accrue to history. He has, through the years, supported me in many immeasurable ways. Cynthia Walk, my friend and mentor in graduate school, nurtured me and this book through the first major phase of writing it, as a dissertation. Jennifer Terry, with whom I shared my life for most of the years I was writing, advised me on nearly every phase of the process. There is not a single idea expressed in these pages that was not in some way influenced by my discussions with her.

Many more people helped me work through portions of the book in its various stages of development. Lauren Berlant gave me important suggestions for chapter 6 and pointed me toward Preston Sturges for chapter 2. Eric Smoodin lent me his copy of the Disney version of *Hitler's Children* and talked with me about chapter 7. Sharon Willis and the other editors of *Camera Obscura* helped me shape parts of chapter 5. This earlier version of the chapter appears as "Pressure Points: Political Psychology, Screen Adaptation and the Management of Racism in the

Case History Genre" in *Camera Obscura* 45. Rachel Schreiber, Ellen Flanders, and Donna Barr were generous with their time and ideas, talking to me extensively about their work. These interviews, and indeed friendships, are a vital part of chapter 8. Rebecca Isaacs and the staff at People for the American Way made their clippings archive available to me, without which I could not have written chapter 3. Page Dubois oversaw the halting progress of the chapters that originated in my dissertation. My other committee members, Steve Fagin, Vince Rafael, Alain J.-J. Cohen, and Pasquale Verdicchio, also offered valuable suggestions at that early stage. Sandy Flitterman-Lewis, my undergraduate honors thesis adviser, introduced me to film studies in general and put me on the path that years later led me here. Friends and colleagues at Old Dominion University and elsewhere have provided both scholarly conversation and myriad forms of support, especially Sujata Moorti, Dana Heller, Tim Seibles, Diane Davis, Judith Mayne, Bill Horrigan, Bob Moeller, Renee Olander, Manuela Mourao, Ed Jacobs, Steve Carpenter, Zoubeida Ounaies, and Jeff Richards.

There are a lot more thanks to give, for all the little ways in which people have helped me to think or work. People at the UCLA Special Collections archive, the Margaret Herrick Library, the Musée Félicien Rops, and the Museum of Modern Art, for instance, have been very accomodating. Erika Bach and Regine Sylvester helped me to locate Hans-Georg Gaul, who was, once found, quite forthcoming with a print of his photograph that starts off Chapter 4. And Leigh Anne Couch at Duke University Press has been a wonderfully attentive editor, always quick with a response to my many small and large questions in the course of the publishing process.

I've received emotional support and the opportunity to talk about the issues raised in this book from lots of great and wonderful people. Among them are my parents, my brother Peter, my cousin Elke Hunstock, and my great aunt Annemarie Friedrich. Friends who have been close to me and this project over the course of its evolution include Lisa Johnson, Kim Dillon, Renee Coulombe, Charline Boudreau, Berta Jottar, Adriene Jenik, and Janice Conard.

Finally, although I've only known her through the latter stages of this book's revision and production, I'd like to especially thank Eva Röser for building a world with me wherein anything, including finishing a book and thinking about new ones, is possible. To her and to everyone else both mentioned and implied I'd like to say, with all my heart, thanks—for everything.

A
Not So
Foreign
Affair

Introduction

■

The non-analysis of fascism . . . enables [it] to be used as a floating signifier, whose function is essentially that of denunciation. The procedures of every form of power are suspected of being fascist, just as the masses are in their desires.
—Michel Foucault, "Power and Strategies" (1980)[1]

"Democracy" is defined not by the positive content of this notion (its signified) but only by its positional-relationship identity—by its opposition, its differential relation to "non-democratic"—whereas the concrete content can vary to the extreme.—Slavoj Žižek, *The Sublime Object of Ideology* (1989)[2]

Legacy

Outside the 1996 Democratic National Convention, a lone white man in a suit and tie staged a one-man antiabortion protest (fig. 1). Holding an American flag, he clutched a white baby doll to his chest and waved a black one over his head. As a father figure in a domestic tableau, the man likely wanted to be seen as protecting babies from their bad mothers, who, with the approval of the government, would kill them. The protester stood behind a placard that makes this extended wish clear, as the right side touts the antiabortion movement's favorite slogan, "Abortion: America's Holocaust." On the left side is the primary Nazi-like agent of this "holocaust," the "feminazi," the word painted vertically along the tie she wears as part of a brown-shirt uniform along with a button from

Fig. 1   An antiabortion protester outside the Democratic National Convention, 1996. (Associated Press photo.)

the National Organization for Women (NOW) and a "Keep Abortion Legal" hat. Her broad smile echoes that of her painted Siamese twin, a skeleton in a Nazi ss uniform.

This performance, while not particularly successful as a marker of mass support, illuminates some of the specific contours of the ways in which "family values" rhetoric has been deployed by conservative political pundits over the last twenty-five years (i.e., since *Roe v. Wade*). That this rhetoric is so tangled up in images of Nazi Germany, however, calls for a somewhat longer history, one that goes back at least as far as World War II and the critiques of fascism that were formulated in the face of actual Nazis. The logic of the parallel between Nazi Germany and the United States surely draws in large part on a metaphor of the gigantic

Fig. 2. Genocide Awareness Project pamphlet, Center for Bio-ethical Reform.

human costs of the Holocaust, where state-mandated, scientifically-executed killing is equated with the state-sanctioned legality of elective abortion. This argument of course depends on the equation of the embryo or fetus with the adults and children exterminated in Nazi death camps—a widespread practice in the antiabortion movement. In the informational brochure describing its Genocide Awareness Project, for instance, the California-based Center for Bio-Ethical Reform graphically forges such a link by placing images of concentration camp victims, lynching victims, and segmented limbs from an aborted fetus side by side (fig. 2). But the equation of abortion rights with Nazi practices also draws on a much more complicated set of perceived continuities going back to wartime rhetoric not on Nazi racism per se but on Nazi reproductive politics, gender relations, sexuality, and family life.

Among the perceptions of Nazism that operate in socially conservative political rhetoric, the Nazis' overrationalization of reproduction takes center stage. In conservative anti-Nazi rhetoric, overrationalization leads to the replacement of the traditional family with state institutions, the scientific encouragement of sexual promiscuity, and the undermining of the morals of young people. Nazi Germany is cast as an aggressively secular state, which, in the logic of the Christian Right, means an abandonment of Christian morality to secular reason. Despite the regime's rigid gender divisions and the reduction of the role of women to motherhood, it is often gender inversion, exemplified by the uniformed feminazi in the protester's placard, that characterizes this image of fascism. "America's Holocaust" is thus a slogan that carries a much denser confluence of issues concerning sexual morality and social norms than is at first apparent.

Family values rhetoric as it is used in the United States today draws heavily on the historical association of the bourgeois nuclear family with liberal democracy, which has persisted since the eighteenth century. But the current conservative perception of an imaginary family struggling in an adversarial relationship with the state draws from both this ongoing, rhetorically constructed tradition and the more recent history of antifascist (and subsequently anticommunist) rhetoric, both liberal and conservative, from the mid–twentieth century on. It is through this combination that family values rhetoric in current conservative American political discourse is able to claim that the state has abandoned its core traditions and has become excessively powerful. Through the assertion of a narrowly defined notion of the family, which the state is meant to protect and be mirrored in, the state's protection of the rights of sexual beings in extrafamilial relationships (be it with regard to birth control, abortion, pornography, divorce, sex education, or gay and lesbian rights) is cast as threatening to the family and hence the democratic nation. While the state's comparatively liberal stance on these latter matters should logically make the equation of the American government with the Nazi regime patently absurd (since most of these liberal policies, including abortion, were *illegal* under the Nazis), the prominent anti-Nazi conventions of imaging Nazism that have persisted since the end of World War II effect a reversal of the Nazis' historical policies. As such, Nazism is a fascinating trope through which to examine the ongoing rhetorical contours of the process of defining democracy.

Nationalism, Democracy, Fascism

The conservative uses of antifascist rhetoric deployed by antiabortion protesters reflect one prominent way in which images of Nazism continue to shape political debate in the present day. But accusations of Nazism, deployed as the ideal nemesis of both the American nation and democracy, can indeed issue from just about any political orientation. What this flexibility indicates is the definitional undecidability of both the terms at issue, *fascism* and *democracy*, which the epigraphs at the head of this introduction address. For if, as Žižek claims, democracy is primarily defined by what it is *not*, then in much of the Western world it is fascism (or totalitarianism more generally or Nazism more specifically) that has occupied the primary place of democracy's opposite. Yet, as Foucault asserts, *fascism*, too, has been variously defined—in large part, I would say, *because* it rhetorically occupies a negative space in relationship to democracy. This book is a study of some of the ways in which images of fascism have served efforts to define democracy for a range of political visions. My primary interest, however, is with democracy, for it is the interpretations of fascism that issue from democratic debate that make it so variable a concept. Democracy is by nature more of a process than a fixed entity. Rhetorical deployments of fascism, then, reveal the cultural workings of the democratic process through the myriad and ongoing efforts by political actors to define democracy in a way that serves the speaker's political ends.

The longer history of democracy's development in relation to modern nationalism is clearly the greatest force propelling efforts to both understand fascism and cast it as the opposite of what democracy aims to be, for nationalism is the primary form of social and cultural integration out of which democracy originally could be forged. As Jürgen Habermas writes, the nation-state "laid foundations for cultural and ethnic homogeneity on the basis of which it then proved possible to push ahead with the democratization of government," to which he adds, "this was achieved at the cost of excluding ethnic minorities."[3] The exclusion of ethnic minorities indeed provided the national identity that bridged class and other status differences among "the people" that democracy addressed. Tensions between the universal language of individual rights upon which democratic citizenship stands and the limits placed on the political participation of not only ethnic minorities but women, immigrants, and those without property or education are, then, also subsumed under the common bond of nationhood.[4]

Fascism arises from within these historical tensions, privileging a highly restrictive, racially defined, national membership over the rights of individuals. Fascism is thus not democracy's *opposite* per se; it is instead a distortion of this larger nationalist logic, which exposes some of democracy's own deeper historical contradictions by taking them to extremes. The process of casting fascism as democracy's opposite often tries to deny these structural commonalities by either emphasizing those democratic ideals that are indeed dramatically opposed to fascism (i.e., democratic pluralism) or fabricating an opposition through the selective imaging of fascism. The persistent invocation of fascism as democracy's Other in post–World War II cultural rhetoric is symptomatic of these deeper tensions, part of an otherwise noble effort to assert that political agreement rather than ethnic homogeneity is the glue that holds a multicultural democratic society together. When this notion of political agreement becomes an effort to assert political and social homogeneity, however, the definition of *democracy* is once again open to interpretation and conflict.

According to literary theorist Raymond Williams, *democracy*, while having its roots in Greek philosophy, was largely considered a negative term, in the sense of the "tyranny of the masses," until the nineteenth century.[5] In the course of the Enlightenment and ultimately the bourgeois revolutions, the concept of representative democracy emerged wherein the threat of this "tyranny" was tempered by the circumscription of eligibility for voting and office. The history of democratic political theory thus reveals anxiety about "the masses," which were often figured as consisting of devalued groups (especially women and members of the working class, who were often imaged as sexually debauched and morally bankrupt).[6] Nazism, as a populist movement, reinvigorated some of these fears and their correlate rhetorical practices. In some anti-Nazi rhetoric, it was and is Nazi women (both fantastic and actual) and sexual "deviants" (homosexuals and sadomasochists) who are imaged as characterizing the fascist masses. In order to achieve such characterizations, the terms of the opposition between fascism and democracy have to be selectively interpreted. For instance, Nazi policies that severely limited the public role of women were seldom cited by mainstream critics during the war, suppressing the opportunity to assert the equality of women under a democratic system. Dominant wartime and postwar anti-Nazi rhetoric also often selectively ignored fascism's overarching prudery, preferring instead to cast an image of sexual decadence that served the American national/democratic image of purity and moral rectitude. American racism, meanwhile, was typically not connected with Nazi racism.[7] Again, while fascism is rightly cast as ideal democracy's Other, the history of democracy itself comes to the surface in these anxious images in ways that tend to try to preserve the internal hierarchies that have historically troubled democracy and the concept of the nation.

Postcolonial theorist Arjun Appadurai's notion of an "ideoscape" asserts that contemporary political rhetoric is "composed of elements of the Enlightenment worldview, which consist of a concatenation of ideas, terms, and images, including 'freedom,' 'welfare,' 'rights,' 'sovereignty,' 'representation,' and the master-term 'democracy.'" He sees colonialism as having "loosened the internal coherence that held these terms and images together," with "a loosely structured synopticon of politics" left instead, with each term subject to variable definition.[8] While certainly more directly applicable to the contemporary variations in the concept of "democracy" as it is manifested across the globe today, I would argue that American political rhetoric, too, is decidedly loose with regard to the above terms and images, a looseness, which can be read in the many ways, in which fascism continues to be brought to bear on the definition of *American democracy*.

Indeed most of anti-Nazi rhetoric in use since Germany's defeat in 1945 has addressed *domestic* issues. Many of these domestic uses center on the assertion of a democratic ideal by encouraging pluralism—or hoping to mitigate it. Whether it be the Cold-War-era importation of World War II political psychology to explain poverty, racism, feminism, and homosexuality or contemporary rhetorical uses like those of the antiabortion protester in figure 1, fascism's rhetorical function as that which is denied within democracy is further confirmed in this domestic return. In this sense, the rhetorical uses of images of fascism are perhaps informed by the more recent history of Western democracy, wherein pluralism of various sorts and a consonant weakening of traditional forms of national homogeneity inspire new forms of democratic defini-tion. The fact that many of these domestic uses of antifascism focus on issues of family, gender, and especially sexuality then opens up a more specific question: why are these issues so central to the post–World War II definition of *democracy*?

Why Sexuality?

In attempting to answer this question, again both long and recent rhetorical histories come into play. On the one hand, the concept of "sexuality" developed as a consequence of the formation of modern nations and might have been integral thereto, in that a focus on individ-ual behaviors and bodies connected each citizen to the notion of the body politic. On the other hand, the late-twentieth-century political focus on sexuality has unique features that speak to more recent global and national political changes. Both these long and recent histories of national imagery rely on the homology between the individual citizen and the nation—a process that goes a long way toward explaining why sexuality might be such an emblematic terrain in the political imagina-tion of contemporary nations.

Postcolonial theorist Homi Bhabha elaborates the process of homol-ogy by arguing that the imaginary construct of the nation parallels the illusory unified image of the self produced in Jacques Lacan's notion of the mirror stage: for Bhabha, the nation is a "differentiating sign of Self, distinct from the Other or the Outside," where members identify themselves with the perceived collective qualities of the nation through the establishment of an "Other" (other nations, other cultures). As with the trajectory of these individuation processes for the child, however, the resulting divided self is inherently unstable because "The ambivalent identifications of love and hate occupy the same psychic space; and paranoid projections 'outwards' return to haunt and split the space from which they are made."[9] The belief in stable images of nationhood is thus undermined by the need to continually re-create them so as to reinforce the boundary between the self and the Other, this nation and another.

This instability of the identification of the self with the nation and of both the nation and individual subjectivity is what makes sexuality central to the national imaginary on a number of levels. On the one hand, as cultural historian George Mosse has noted, the modern nation has been centrally defined by middle-class notions of respectability, making sexual conduct and imagery (including images of chastity) key to the concept of the liberal democratic nation.[10] But middle-class notions of respectability themselves, as Foucault has written, beg the questions "how, why, and in what forms was sexuality constituted as a moral domain?"[11] To answer these questions, Foucault asserts that ethics are conceived as operating not just through behavior but more fundamentally through "practices of the self." Sexuality operates in this mode of ethics as a privileged arena of personal conduct, acting, as he writes elsewhere, as "a great surface network in which the stimulation of bodies, the intensification of pleasures, the incitement to discourse, the formation of special knowledges, the strengthening of controls and resistance, are linked to one another, in accordance with a few major strategies of knowledge and power."[12] The four "strategic unities" that Foucault names as specific mechanisms of knowledge and power in operation since the eighteenth century (the hysterization of women's bodies, pedagogization of children's sex, socialization of procreative behavior, and psychiatrization of perverse pleasure) can then be linked to Mosse's notion of national respectability and Bhabha's formulation of the national self. Indeed, if sexuality is a privileged arena for the exercise, articulation, and negotiation of power, then Mosse's thesis connects Foucault's observation to the formation of modern nations. Combined with Bhabha's perspective, then, the instability of these "practices of the self/nation" is often expressed *through* sexuality.

Fredric Jameson similarly argues that along with the "mechanistic fragmentation" of subjectivity wrought by the development of capitalism "came a belief that what was released thereby was more primitive, feral tendencies in human conduct: namely a groundswell of anxiety-induced theorizing around sexuality and violence."[13] Jameson links this with the designation of the family as constituting the private sphere against the nascent public sphere of bourgeois society whereby child-hood and the family situation are elevated over other biographical experiences. This privileging of the family results in the isolation of the sexual from other forms of experience and makes it a marker of the separation of public and private spheres—a historical development that enables sexuality's features to carry a wider symbolic meaning, including, I would say, characterizing the nation and the political system with which it is melded.

This brings me again to the ways in which fascism, and especially Nazism, has functioned as democracy's troubled Other. In the most straightforward way, all that is split off from the national self is projected onto the Nazi Other, so that much antifascist rhetoric continues to align democracy with middle-class respectability and Nazism with decadence and perversion. As the split-off projection of the democratic national self, however, Nazism returns to characterize issues of domestic concern. Indeed Nazism, as an object of knowledge, cuts across most of the major strategic unities that Foucault names about the norms of procreative behavior (anti-Nazi responses to Nazi family policy and eugenics), the indoctrination of children (anti-Nazi outrage at state intervention into family domains), and especially the development of psychiatric theories of perversion (with a particular anti-Nazi focus on promiscuity, homosexuality, and sadomasochism). Together with the books, magazines, and movies that deploy these theories as narrative devices, popular and elite forms of invoking Nazism thus reflect the larger mechanisms whereby sexuality serves as a determinant of political viability in liberal democratic culture at the crossroads of knowledge, pleasure, and politics.

In order to determine the ways in which these practices instantiate more recent developments in the history of efforts to define *democracy*, we must return to the central place of sexuality as a domain over which the boundaries between the public and private spheres of liberal democracies are maintained. For, indeed, one of Nazism's primary violations of liberal democratic principles attacked in anti-Nazi rhetoric is the violation of the private sphere—more so with Nazism than with any other form of fascism. Traditional liberalism, dating from early social contract theorists such as John Locke and Thomas Hobbes, valorized the private sphere and saw as "private" the realms of economics, family, and religion, which should, in a broad sense, be protected from interference by the state. But, according to the nineteenth-century political analyst Alexis de Tocqueville, democratic society nonetheless requires the social mores cultivated in the private sphere in order to secure the wider political culture of the nation. As "it is woman who shapes these mores," de Tocqueville writes, "everything which has a bearing on the status of women, their habits, and their thoughts is, in my view, of great political importance."[14] With this statement, de Tocqueville points to the paradox within liberal democracy that would eventually make Nazism a cause for sexual alarm. For while the private spheres of family and religion are ostensibly outside of the realm of public politics—in other words, not political—it is the private sphere that is thought to secure public political life.[15] Nazism's intervention in the private sphere of family and religion, then, was thought to upset all levels of morality—a fear expressed in condensed form in the portrayal of Nazis as sexually amoral.

Leftists' concerns about fascism's violation of the private sphere at times bore a resemblance to liberal critiques by focusing on its destruction of social morality. Their emphasis, however, was primarily on fascism's damaging impact on political subjectivity, and leftists paid less attention in general to defending, as many liberals and conservatives did, traditional sexual morality per se. Hannah Arendt, for instance, saw totalitarianism as differing from tyranny precisely in its insinuation into private life. Under tyranny, she wrote, "the whole sphere of private life with the capacities for experience, fabrication and thought are left intact," while under totalitarianism "the self-coercion of totalitarian logic destroys man's capacity for experience and thought just as certainly as his capacity for action."[16] Arendt's concern about fascism's violation of the private sphere is thus primarily alarmed by the ways in which political agency would be adulterated, preventing the sorts of public debate that the traditional bourgeois public sphere offered. Members of the Frankfurt School voiced similar critiques, noting that mass events and the presence of political symbols in everyday life (the primary images of Nazism) concretely changed and corrupted the experience of political participation. In their view, fascism marked a radical departure from the experience of the bourgeois public sphere (which revolved principally around debate and reason) and instead ritualized political life (i.e., what Walter Benjamin refers to as the "aestheticization of politics"). This shift toward ritual was thought to further waylay the crises in the liberal capitalist social order by channeling resentments and uneasiness into national forms.

Those leftists who embraced Freudian psychoanalysis as a means of understanding fascism, however, again tended to describe the fascist subject in terms of sexual perversion. The fascist subject's rational political agency, as noted above, had been adulterated by fascism's incursion into private life, resulting in an ego structure plagued by the form if not the actual practice of sadomasochism, narcissism, and homosexuality. Thus, while leftist critiques of fascism tended to be less literal in their equation of sexual immorality with fascism, they developed psychosexual models for understanding political subjectivity that bemoaned the loss of the public sphere by joining conservatives and liberals in focusing acute political attention on the private sphere, namely, family and sexuality, and by deploying the discourse of sexuality to meet political ends.

This focus on the problem of fascism's role in private life, approached from different political perspectives, is thus the primary means whereby Nazism becomes democracy's favorite Other and then returns as central to late-twentieth-century discussions of the political role of private life in democratic society. The enduring usefulness of Nazism as a rhetorical figure in the democratic imagination can perhaps be linked to an acceleration of the "privatization" of democratic citizenship in the United States. Cultural critic Lauren Berlant marks the characteristics of this privatized citizenship as centrally including a penchant for sentimentality on a national level, especially what she calls the "non-political political" of family values rhetoric in political discourse. Berlant sees this acceleration as a product of there being no public sphere proper but instead a public scene occupied by "a cluster of demonic and idealized images and narratives about sex and citizenship which obsess the official national public sphere."[17]

The difference between the liberal public sphere and what Berlant calls the official national public sphere helps clarify the diverse functions that the figure of fascism serves today. According to Habermas, the historical public sphere, located between civil society and the state, was the arena wherein critical public discussion of matters of general interest occurred. This public sphere developed in tandem with the capitalist market economy, which produced the middle class as the democratic power base. But the contradiction between the universality of the "rights of men" and the exclusionary realities of representative democracy occasioned, along with the further development of capitalism, the expansion of the public body. Consequently, the state and society became intertwined in the late nineteenth and twentieth centuries, leading to the end of the liberal public sphere.[18] Under this line of thinking, fascism, as described in leftist critiques, is the ultimate example of an entirely vanished liberal public sphere.

 I would argue, however, that the notion of a declining liberal public sphere in the United States is less about the expansion of the public body than about the expansion of the private one. As Hannah Arendt writes in *The Origins of Totalitarianism*, the liberal division between private and public "had nothing to do with the justified separation between the personal and public spheres, but was rather the psychological reflection of the nineteenth century struggle between bourgeois and citoyen, between the man who judged and used all public institutions by the yard stick of his private interests and the responsible citizen who was concerned with public affairs as the affairs of all."[19] Enlightenment thought originally held that public values were superior to private values of home and hearth and stressed the role of "enlightened self-interest" in transforming private interests into civic responsibility. In this logic, women were to be guardians of morality not only within their homes but in society at large by taming male lust and reproducing morally responsible future citizens. For their part, men were to be guardians of women and children both at home and in the larger public sphere. But, as historian Stephanie Coontz writes, "As enlightened self-interest gradually gave way to immediate self-interest in the economy and polity, the nuclear family was made the sole repository for standards of decency, duty, and altruism. In this role . . . private family relations became less a preparation ground or supporting structure for civic responsibility than a *substitute* for such responsibility."[20] The decline of the liberal public sphere thus reflects a privileging of middle-class private interests over communal public affairs. Consequently, when Berlant talks about an acceleration of the "privatization of citizenship" brought about by the economic and social policies of Ronald Reagan and George Bush in the 1980s, she draws their foregrounding of private economic issues together with the elevation of private life to a public discourse—again, what she calls the "non-political political."

This shift is not only due to private economic interests being foregrounded over public ones, however. Berlant notes elsewhere that, although many scholars see the traditional categories of public and private as archaic formations, the continuing attraction to this division exists in part because it organizes and justifies other forms of social division (male and female, work and family, friend and lover, hetero and homo, and "unmarked" personhood versus racial, ethnic, and class-marked identities). Berlant writes, "This chain of disassociations provides one way of conceiving why so many institutions not usually associated with feeling can be read as institutions of intimacy." In other words, privatized citizenship is also characterized by understanding public institutions in private, "intimate" terms, a rhetorical practice that I find reflected in the uses of anti-Nazi rhetoric that center on family and sexuality.[21]

Berlant's assessment of the current climate comprises the more recent history of the centrality of sexuality and family to current political rhetoric. Much of what Berlant marks as the "pseudopolitical citizenship rhetoric of U.S. political culture" indeed employs antifascist rhetoric to produce a "political" effect. If, however, as Berlant says, "Citizenship is a status whose definitions are always in process—continually produced out of political, rhetorical, and economic struggle over who counts as 'the people' and how social membership is measured and valued," then, as my study of the uses of images of Nazism shows, there are a variety of ways in which this "private" realm currently constitutes a "public" sphere of sorts.[22]

This study of fascism, sexuality, and the cultural rhetoric of democracy indeed supports Berlant's assessment of the character of the post–World War II public sphere, where democracy is very centrally understood in terms of personal dramas (both domestic and psychological) and is particularly preoccupied with matters of sexuality. This does not mean, however, that the process by which democratic citizenship is defined has reached an impasse. Instead, the centrality of sexuality to political discourse has necessitated a rethinking of the terms *public* and *private* in ways that continue to intervene and participate in democracy's inherently unstable, and hence ongoing, project.

Cultural Rhetoric

In examining how it is that democracy is understood through personal dramas and is preoccupied with sexuality, I have chosen to focus on anti-Nazi images of fascism that circulate in primarily American democratic political culture and have privileged film texts to do so. The choice is determined by my conviction that film is uniquely positioned in the mid–twentieth century as a medium that hopes to both educate and entertain and pretends to larger cultural relevance. I thus examine a variety of texts alongside films, all of which interpret and present Nazism for democratic ends: academic scholarship, government reports, journalistic reportage and essays, and other kinds of fictional narratives in literature, stage performances, or video. Sometimes these texts are examined as "cotexts" to the films with which each chapter is engaged, illustrating a discursive resonance between the fictional projects of the films themselves and the larger cultural milieu in which they circulate. Often, I further analyze texts peripheral to the films' production and distribution in order to bridge these discursive domains, examining scripts, letters, and publicity materials, for instance, which reveal the ways the people involved in the making and marketing of a film saw their product engaging in precisely this sort of dialogue with the larger culture.

With this eclectic method, I hope to establish the cultural intertextuality through which different sorts of public arenas (whether popular or elite) mine the private sphere for political significance. The "images" or figures upon which I focus are visual (or visualized) depictions of Nazism as well as the narratives spun around them. I argue that "images of Nazism" form a significant part of the image vocabulary—the democratic imagination—through which an array of political issues (both foreign and domestic) are articulated and understood, especially the political connection between public and private life. I have tried to ensure that my focus on anti-Nazi images takes account of the material effects of discourse (not simply relegating them to phantasmatic or tangential matters), as I understand this process of image making and sustaining as in itself constituting a significant aspect of political life.

Similar methodologies have been taken up by historians, who have linked individual and collective subjectivities to textual representations and who understand historical documents in literary terms; in other words, there is a mutually constitutive loop between lived experience and textual representations in part due to the unavoidability of narrative and image in all representations, even those that claim only to document.[23] My use of the term *cultural rhetoric* in the subtitle of this book hopes to acknowledge the nature of this loop, where, as Aristotle says, there is an essence of things and then a rhetoric used to deploy an interpretation of this essence into an argument. I take *rhetoric* as being able to account for both this sort of conscious argumentative use of the available image vocabulary for a variety of ends as well as identifying the dominance of certain types of uses that reveal naturalized structures within political culture. As rhetoric, images of Nazism can be deployed in the service of an array of political arguments, but there are also conventions in these images that tend toward dominant, often socially conservative definitions of political legitimacy.

Bhabha articulates a theory of how the nation rhetorically manages its split between an idealized self and a demonized Other that helps to anchor these dual functions of cultural rhetoric. The national imaginary, in Bhabha's view, enacts a double narrative movement in an effort to stabilize itself: a nationalist "pedagogy" (teaching "the people" to be the types of national subjects desired) and a nationalist "performative" (addressing the people as already embodying national subjectivity). He writes: "The scraps, patches, and rags of daily life must be repeatedly turned into the signs of a national culture, while the very act of the narrative performance interpellates a growing circle of national subjects. In the production of the nation as narration there is a split between the continuist, accumulative temporality of the pedagogical, and the repetitious, recursive strategy of the performative. It is through this process of splitting that the conceptual ambivalence of modern society becomes the site of *writing the nation*."[24] The pedagogical aspects of "writing the nation" correspond more closely to conscious rhetorical efforts, while the performative aspects tend to consist of the unexamined and hence naturalized assumptions or rhetorical conventions. The splitting process that Bhabha describes is revealed in the anti-Nazi uses of Nazi imagery: on the one hand Nazism is cast as the Other to democracy—in "pedagogical" terms, teaching what democratic subjects cannot do or be—while the return of these images as mitigators of domestic differences (e.g., efforts by conservatives to name pro-choice feminists as Nazis) signals a "performative" aspect of national narrative that attempts to project a homogeneous "people." Homogeneity is not ultimately sustainable in contemporary national culture. And so the flexibility of uses to which antifascism has been rhetorically put (feminists can and have accused Christian conservatives of Nazism as well) makes the figure of anti-Nazism a useful one through which to examine the processes through which the definition of American nationhood has been spoken through the concepts of democracy—and especially how it is that this debate has taken the family and sexuality as its primary ground.

The different sorts of texts that I examine contribute to different aspects of democracy as a discourse. Popular editorial journalism is often broad in its claims, simplifying and exaggerating its interpretation of current events in order to distinguish the writer's opinions or instigate debate. This is often the case with wartime anti-Nazi journalism, which tended toward hyperbole (to be distinguished from fully warranted reports of Nazi atrocities) and also existed in a textual environment of conflicting interpretations. Academic scholarship, while often also building on similar interpretations, instead mobilizes elaborate scholarly apparatuses to lend authority to interpretations, which, when they rhyme with the dominant political beliefs of their moment, can then influence the opinions of politicians and ultimately government policies. This creates a loop between an official government position (e.g., on the psychological foundations of the minds of political dissidents) and the proliferation of (often government-funded) research, further substantiating these claims. Popular films, the privileged texts of this study, then, give the interpretations of fascism available in political culture a fictional narrative form, often complicating the journalistic and academic variants of interpretation in the interests of either telling an interesting story or conforming to various generic conventions.

Film theorist Noël Carroll suggests that Aristotelian rhetoric might be a useful way to approach film, as he writes that "While narrative films are not arguments per se, they are rhetorical in that they are structured to lead the audience to fill in certain ideas about human conduct in the process of rendering the story intelligible."[25] This use of *rhetoric* is akin to the notion of ideology elaborated by A. J. Greimas, as it functions through the logically controlled unfolding of possibilities within a given narrative structure.[26] I would add, however, that this approach is useful not only with literary or filmic texts but with academic and journalistic texts as well. This expansion also applies to film scholar Dana Polan's approach, for he says that close analysis of film narratives should examine "not what narrative accomplishes but what work it engages in (representations, containment, transformation) to achieve its aura of accomplishment."[27] A "cultural rhetoric," then, admits to the broader narrative tendencies that would make the "accomplishment" of narrative coherence possible in a range of texts, but the concept also permits the image vocabularies and narrative conventions of which various texts avail themselves to be quite variously employed.

The historical specificity of each of these texts helps to position the argument it makes with respect to the larger political climate wherein the definition of democracy transpired and continues to transpire. This is, then, the main benefit of having the various texts I examine—journalistic, academic, and filmic—speak to one another in my analysis, since it is my conviction that they spoke to one another when they were first produced and that the shelf life of the image vocabularies and narrative conventions they employ is long.

The Organization of the Book

While the process of defining democracy is dynamic and the production of political discourse creative, the history of anti-Nazi rhetoric has produced certain well-defined rhetorical devices that continue to serve American political culture today, albeit in new ways. The book therefore is divided into three parts, each of which examines one major rhetorical practice as it developed during the conflict with fascism in World War II, evolved in the decades after the war, and continues to be employed in American political culture. These rhetorical practices produce the sexual opposition of Nazism to democracy (part one), give form to the importation of theories of Nazism to explain domestic politics in a democratic society (part two), and serve as available tropes for a wide range of uses within democratic political culture (part three). The centrality of sexuality to the "cultural rhetoric of democracy," in its multiple forms, is thus revealed in the myriad uses to which Nazism was put during most of the twentieth century.

In part one, "The Democratic Family," I examine the conventions of what I call nationalist melodrama, a genre that uses the narrative conventions of melodrama to narrate threats to the nation. Unlike the others, this part begins by staging a comparison between the Nazis' uses of melodrama during the war and American uses of it as an anti-Nazi rhetoric. The point of this comparison is twofold: first, to illustrate the ways in which nationalist melodrama narrates foreign threats as threats to the family, regardless of the political system being defended; and, second, to more sharply characterize the American variant of the genre, which subsequently passed into the image vocabulary of the American political imagination. Broadly speaking, Nazi and Hollywood wartime melodramas were engaged in nationalist projects, though, to be sure, they differed substantially as to the nature of the enemy and the function of the family in the political culture each system asserted. In Veit Harlan's *Die Goldene Stadt* (1942), my primary example of fascist melodrama, the complications of both internal and external threats to the German family lead to the elevation of race and gender to national myths of the German *Volk*, or "people," whereas in Edward Dmytryk's

Hitler's Children (1942), my primary example of the democratic melodrama, these complications instead channel broad political issues into the protection of the private sphere.

The American variant of wartime nationalist melodrama typically defined the private sphere in highly normative terms, using the narrative conventions of melodrama to align conservative sexual morals with democracy while casting fascism as antithetical to traditional family life. This social conservatism reflects the ideological mechanism within liberal democracy, which banishes contradiction from the public-political to the private (ostensibly "nonpolitical") realm, all the while making "private" matters of love, family, and sexuality central grounds for a political difference from fascism. This rhetorical function continues to characterize the uses of anti-Nazi rhetoric by social conservatives in contemporary American political debate. The final chapter of part one examines the rhetorical practices of three conservative videotapes, one made to argue against a national health plan, another to oppose gay rights, and a third to criticize federal law enforcement agencies. All three invoke the imagery and narrative conventions of anti-Nazi nationalist melodrama to characterize their "liberal" political opposition.

In part two, "The Democratic Psyche," I consider another prominent kind of national narrative project, the definition, creation, and nurturing of the central democratic citizen through the diagnosis and treatment of American fascists and other political dissidents. Following directly from the wartime theories of the Nazi mind that served the strategic needs of the armed forces, American psychologists and sociologists imported their conclusions to address domestic issues throughout the Cold War period. The inner workings of the family continue to be the key to this project, as psychoanalytic theory dominated wartime and Cold War American psychology. I argue that the ascendency of psychoanalytic political and social psychology produced a new genre of national narrative, the American version of national psychobiography. In the three chapters of this section, my focus is on psychological case histories dealing with the struggles of politically wayward "patients" to achieve proper democratic political subjectivity, that is, an independent ego, social confidence, an ability to accept difference, and often conformity to gender, sexual, and class norms. In the first two chapters, I take Alfred Hitchcock's *Notorious* (1946) and Hubert Cornfield's *Pressure Point* (1962) as central examples, illustrating the ways in which wartime and Cold War variants of national psychobiography work to address a broad array of domestic issues over time. Again, the last chapter focuses on contemporary examples, for, like nationalist melodrama, national psychobiography continues to serve the project of defining American democracy, as it does democracy in other countries with European-dominant populations. Unlike my chapter on contemporary uses of nationalist melodrama, however, which focuses on right-wing uses of fascism as a political trope, this one looks at non-Nazi depictions of actual neo-Nazis, especially skinheads, in order to argue that present-day Nazis also serve a significant rhetorical function in democratic political culture: to both define the limits of political legitimacy and model a reparative therapy for Western democracy's traditional dominant subject, the white heterosexual male.

In part three, "Democratic Sex," I aim to build on the delineations of normative "democratic" sexuality embedded earlier by examining the iconography of "Nazi" sexuality, especially the figure of the sexy Nazi woman. For, along with documentary images of mass rallies from Leni Riefenstahl's *Triumph of the Will* (1934) and the horrible images of concentration camp victims that became widely available after the war, a common visual shorthand for fascism is fictional images of "Nazi" sexual decadence, a fetishized iconography of uniforms and perverse sexual display. By focusing on the iconography surrounding Marlene Dietrich's star persona, I assert that the sexy "Nazi" woman came to serve as a dense marker of political ambiguity. Dietrich's role as Lola Lola in the German production *The Blue Angel* (Josef von Sternberg, 1930) became an icon of fascism in the course of the war years, substituting the spectacle of female performance for the spectacle of Nazi power, her song for the oratory of Hitler. The complexity of the Lola Lola figure as both dangerous and desirable—and portrayed exquisitely by Dietrich as an icon of illicit sexuality/fascism while she is herself an ardent antifascist—is illustrated in her first screen role as an explicitly Nazi femme fatale in Billy Wilder's *A Foreign Affair* (1948). Thus, even as the icon was being forged in the 1940s, the Dietrich/Lola Lola icon could be put to a variety of political uses: as an emblem of the allure of fascism and as a misunderstood, sexually open champion of democracy. The last chapter of part three follows the ongoing uses of this icon and the association of fascism with illicit sexuality more broadly up to the end of the century. Unlike the previous two contemporary chapters, in which I mostly remark on the socially conservative uses to which the genres explored previously have been put, this last chapter considers how the figure of Nazi sexuality has served a widely varying array of rhetorical functions, both conservative and progressive, in contemporary efforts to define democracy through sexuality.

The evils of the Nazi regime—its murder of millions of people on religious, ethnic, political, and sexual grounds—certainly makes fascism a powerful trope in the democratic imagination. Invocations of fascism are consequently able to mobilize strong sentiments, both political and personal. Indeed, the crux of my argument is that one of fascism's less straightforward rhetorical functions in democratic political culture has been to articulate the relationship between the private and public and personal and political realms. While fascism should continue to be cast as that which democracy strives against, this book takes as its object these more ambiguous strains of antifascist rhetoric as they have influenced and continue to influence democratic political culture today. My aim is by no means to diminish the power of antifascism but rather to illuminate how the conflicting conceptions of what democracy is and should be are expressed in these anti-Nazi invocations of fascism. As such, I hope to provide a usable history that can help us understand the changing contours of the mutual project called democracy as we continue to strive to fulfill the concept's high expectations.

I

The Democratic

Family

1

Nazi Nationalist Melodrama:

Science, Myth, and Paternal Authority

in *Die Goldene Stadt*

■

Private and Public, past and present, the psyche and the social develop an interstitial intimacy. It is an intimacy that questions binary divisions through which such
spheres of social experience are often spatially opposed. These spheres of life are
linked through an "in-between" temporality that takes the measure of dwelling at
home, while producing an image of the world of history.—Homi Bhabha, *The
Location of Culture* (1994)[1]

Like ordinary melodramas, nationalist melodrama is characterized by
plots in which the nuclear family is threatened by an external force, the
life or chastity of an innocent is endangered, or the family is potentially
destroyed from within by the bad behavior of its members. Unlike other
melodramas, however, nationalist melodrama explicitly codes these
plots in political terms: in which threats to the family are threats to the
nation, the life and chastity of innocents represent the nation's future
and ideals, and internal dissonance must be quelled in the name of
national unity. The close relationship between the psychological and the
social, the public and the private, which Bhabha names in the epigraph,
is nowhere more clearly narrated than in nationalist melodrama. Nationalist melodrama is thus a primary narrative form through which the
"image of the world of history" is produced in national cultures.[2]

The unusual cover of a clever anti-Nazi pamphlet entitled "Unbelievable" plays on the tradition of nationalist melodrama in its appropria-

Fig. 3. Cover of "Unbelievable," an anti-Nazi pamphlet (1940). (UCLA, Department of Special Collections.)

tion of the conventions of pulp magazines: a prominent image of a cowering young woman stands in for the threat to America, both from abroad and within, of "Hitlerism" and anti-Semitism (fig. 3). Meanwhile, in Nazi Germany, Guida Diehl, leader of the New Land Movement, was writing the following poem: "Mit eisernem Besen / Aus Herzen und Haus / Das undeutsche Wesen / Zum Lande hinaus!" (With iron broom / From hearts and house / Drive un-German creatures / Into the wilderness!).[3] Because its primary aim is by nature nationalist, the conventions of nationalist melodrama are useful not only to liberal democracy, as in the eighteenth-century bourgeois tragedy, but to nations with widely differing political systems.[4] Fascists deployed the genre, as did the Allies, and each side employed its own version of a politically useful binary opposition: fascism versus democracy in the Allied nations and Germans versus "non-Germans" among Nazis. These binary oppositions provide the grid upon which nationalist melodrama can proceed: the democratic family threatened by fascism's efforts to destroy it and the German family threatened by those who would taint its blood.

In addition to this simple coding of binaries, nationalist melodrama suits the needs of the nation by inspiring national fervor. For, despite the fact that melodrama is a culturally devalued genre in its more general forms, nationalist melodrama, because of its political valences, legitimates the "feminine" emotionalism for which the genre is often otherwise condemned. Political rationality may have created the concept of modern citizenship, endowing the enfranchised citizen with liberal reason, but political irrationality, nationalism's recourse to ideals and myths, binds together the "imagined community" of citizens across differences of class and other forms of entitlement.[5] Bhabha comments on the cultural representation of this ambivalence, which can be read in the "wavering vocabularies" through which the nation is described, including, as he puts it, "the heimlich pleasures of the hearth" and the "unheimlich terror of space/race of others."[6]

Historically, much of the melodrama's political importance revolves around the genre's support of hierarchies of gender, race, and class in the political culture of the nation. According to the dominant tenets of early democratic nation-states, women, slaves, and the poor were originally thought not to possess the rational faculties needed to qualify them for citizen status, and hence, like children, they were in need of the political "protection" of their superior governors.[7] The concept of pater familias gives form to the process whereby white landed men are charged with the governance and protection of all subordinated citizens, whereby the term *domestic* comes to apply to both the household and that which is internal to the nation. The "interstitial intimacy" between public and private that nationalist melodrama stages thus aligns order and reason with traditional middle-class family structure and morality, often emblematized in the body of a chaste young woman.[8]

This is indeed the case with *Die Goldene Stadt*, directed by Veit Harlan, who was arguably Nazi Germany's most overtly ideological feature film director. On first glance, however, *Die Goldene Stadt* appears to be a fairly conventional melodrama. The story centers on a young woman, Anna (Kristina Söderbaum), whose father (Eugen Klöpfer) is too strict and controlling for her high-spirited nature. It begins as a love story in which Anna is courting a man named Christian (Paul Klinger) who comes from the "golden city" of the title, Prague, and so represents for her both love and adventure. Her father has other plans and connives to have Christian fired so that he must return to the city without her. Anna eventually defies her father's wishes through the prompting of their Czech housekeeper (who has her sights set on the widowed father's fortune) and goes to the city looking for Christian. Unfortunately, he is already married to someone else when she finally gets there. Before she is able to return to her father's farm, she falls for the manipulative seductions of her shady half-Czech cousin Tony, who also has designs on her inheritance. Her father, meanwhile, has disinherited her for leaving at all and has become engaged to the housekeeper. Anna stays in Prague and becomes pregnant, and Tony abandons her. Desperate, she returns to the farm, is rejected by her father, and drowns herself in the marsh.

Like most films produced by the German national film studio, Ufa, during the Nazi period, *Die Goldene Stadt* does not address Nazi politics directly. As Eric Rentschler writes in his book on the Nazi cinema, "If one is looking for sinister heavies garbed in ss black or crowds of fanatics saluting their Führer, one does best to turn to Hollywood films of the 1940s" instead of German films of the period.[9] Still, entertainment films like *Die Goldene Stadt* do contain ideological messages. Indeed, while in some ways the film is a quite ordinary "woman's film" with a tragic, ill-fated heroine, it is also a nationalist melodrama. The film is structured through the central conventions of the genre, under which the German family is faced with both an internal and external threat, and the tragedy at the end is meant to stir nationalist sentiment—in this case, against Czechs and toward internal German unity. As a mitigator of the "interstitial intimacy" Bhabha names between the public and the private spheres in national narratives, nationalist melodrama places primary political importance on domestic dramas. As in nationalist melodramas more generally, *Die Goldene Stadt* makes the romantic and sexual conduct of a young woman serve as the focal point for the enunciation of a broad range of Nazi political imperatives.

One factor that has complicated the analysis of Nazi nationalist melodrama, however, especially for leftist critics, is that fascism itself has often been characterized as sentimental and indeed melodramatic. Wilhelm Reich, for instance, built his theory of fascism in 1933 out of his observation that Hitler "repeatedly stressed that one could not get at the masses with arguments, proofs, and knowledge, but only with feelings and beliefs."[10] Nazism thus came to be seen as a hypermasculinized reworking of eighteenth-century sentimentalism melded with twentieth-century populism, making its rhetoric of personal sacrifice and dedication to community synchronized with these tendencies in the melodrama.[11] Some analysts of Nazi film, Siegfried Kracauer and Lotte Eisner, for instance, consequently do not identify nationalist melodrama as a genre in its own right (a genre found in other nations as well) but rather see the tendency toward melodrama and sentimentality in films of the pre-Nazi and Nazi period as precisely what marks them *as* Nazi.[12] While this characterization of the tone of Nazi rhetoric is valuable, I suggest that it is also important to understand nationalist melodrama as a genre that serves a variety of nationalist causes. Recognizing the features of nationalist melodrama makes specifying the particular form of the genre's conventions within a given political system (fascism here) more precise.

Film scholar Stephen Lowry has something like this in mind when he makes a case for the emblematic nature of Nazi melodramas and romances, arguing not only that the melodramatic form is typical of Nazi cultural expression but also that the genre's emphases on family issues and women's place therein lie at the core of Nazi ideology.[13] This is a useful move toward recognizing both the centrality of the private sphere in nationalist rhetorics and the particular political use to which the private sphere was put by Nazi rhetoricians. In this move, Lowry joins feminist historians like Gisela Bock and Claudia Koonz in making Nazi family policies central to understanding the regime.[14] Indeed, it is both of these elements, melodramatic tone and content, that make a film like *Die Goldene Stadt* a Nazi nationalist melodrama. The film is a nationalist melodrama on two fronts: (1) the German family is undone by conniving Czechs (an exterior/racial threat), and (2) the German family is undone either by the daughter's waywardness or by the father's unwillingness to modernize (interior threats), each of which mobilize strong emotions calling for the protection of this family, which are to be channeled into nationalist fervor.[15] The specific content of the film is decidedly particular to the ideologies of the Nazi regime; the general form, however, conforms to the shared generic conventions of nationalist melodrama.

First, let me elaborate the shared social conservatism of the genre, which is put to political uses in its nationalist form. The social conservatism of the outcome of most melodramas (nationalist or not) organizes narrative tensions in that social transgressions indulged in during the course of the film are typically punished by its end. In nationalist melodrama, sexual transgression, a staple of the genre more generally, becomes a transgression against the state. In the course of the 1930s, this formula became institutionally solidified in both Hollywood and Germany through the respective policies of the Production Code Administration and the Ministry of Propaganda. While the similarities between these two institutions should not be overstated, there are at least formal similarities in the aims of both the American and German censorship bodies of the time, which hence encouraged the production of national-ist melodramas on both sides of the conflict. Both specified that trans-gressions must not be made to look attractive to viewers, and both specified that institutions of authority must be positively portrayed, their efficacy uncompromised.[16]

What is also similar, however, is the limited success of this sort of guidance. In both Nazi Germany and Hollywood, censors were, as Rentschler says of the Nazi case, "neither omniscient nor omnipo-tent."[17] Nationalist film melodramas, then, are especially interesting not only in their conformity to the genre's conventions but in their defiance of the ideological simplicity called for by their nationalist function. In a superficial sense, Anna's triple punishment for her moral weakness in *Die Goldene Stadt* (she is abandoned, disinherited, and finally commits suicide) satisfies the genre's insistence on punitive narrative closure for stories that represent sexual practices that defy traditional morals; in nationalist melodrama, however, her death is not merely punitive but also a cause for stirring national feeling. In the melodramatic genre generally, the punitive conclusion typically embodies an element of trag-edy that *modifies* the ending as justified moral retribution. Nationalist melodrama tries to capitalize on the ambivalence between the justice and injustice of the punitive ending by scripting the justness of the punishment to address internal dissidence and the injustice of the punishment to address external enemies. It is, of course, not always successful at directing emotions to this extent.

Here the intervention of Nazi propaganda minister Joseph Goebbels in the alteration of the story is important, in that in the original drama on which the film is based (Richard Billinger's *Der Gigant*) it is the father, not Anna, who dies in the end.[18] The father is meant to be the tragic figure who misses the opportunity to learn from his mistakes, while Anna suffers with the knowledge that she helped to speed his death. In the criticism surrounding the film, I have encountered different versions of the negotiation between Goebbels and Harlan over changes to this ending. In one version, Goebbels insists that Harlan make it clear that Anna's death results from her abandonment of her *Heimat* (homeland), which is, on one level, what indeed came to pass in the final film. In some versions of this exchange, Harlan is said to have suggested the alternative of Anna's father successfully intervening in her suicide at-tempt, concluding with their reconciliation and resolve to raise her child on the farm. This ending would have rhetorically asserted an image of the strong and reconstituted German family able to endure external threats through internal unity. Goebbels, however, is said to have rejected the idea because it would have allowed Anna to bear an "inferior Czech bastard" (ein minderwertiges Tschechenbalg).[19] Whatever truth there is to either of these legendary exchanges, Goebbels is always scripted to insist on Anna's punishment—whether it be for the consequences of racial pollution (her extramarital relations with Tony) or for having had any independence at all (going to the city in the first place). Harlan's reputed alternative would have been a more radical departure from the genre's conventions, for without a final tragedy the required deployment of national feeling is potentially diminished.

As it was finally released, *Die Goldene Stadt* is a prime example of the complexities of nationalist melodrama generally and Nazi nationalist melodrama specifically. For, as in Hollywood variants of the "fallen woman" genre, the young and innocent girl is led astray not only through her own weakness but by forces greater than her. She consequently suffers excessively, her punishment being far harsher than her transgressions deserve, and hence she receives a kind of martyred absolution.[20] Whatever Goebbels's intentions, Anna's death only partly reads as just punishment for a transgression. While nationalist melodrama would hope to specify that whatever injustice there is in her death is the fault of the shiftless Czechs who conspire against her, it is also the rigidity and heartlessness of her father's behavior that garners her (gendered) sympathy. Certainly, the nature of Anna's transgression as it is specified by Goebbels signals concerns specific to Nazi ideology and not shared by Hollywood's tragic heroines. But these transgressions also signal the more abstract distinction between Nazi and American variants for which I will argue, for, unlike the liberal democratic formula, wherein conventional narrative resolutions fortify a notion of a privatized political sphere, the Nazi melodrama subordinates private dramas to national ones.

Indeed, gender and race, embodied in the German woman, adhere to one another and solidify Nazi gender and racial ideology *through* sexuality. Hence, Anna's sexual/reproductive body performs the myriad iconographic and narrative functions of nationalist melodrama, as she is simultaneously mythic (as a Nazi ideal), irrational (as a woman), and rationalized (by Nazi racial science). The film's invocations of racial and gender national myths comprise the primary ways in which Nazi nationalist melodrama appropriates the private sphere. But as these myths at times conflict with the more general melodramatic genre's typically flawed central characters (both Anna and her father) the nationalist logic of the genre tries at least to deploy paternal authority and racial science as the "rational" support of the potentially compromised myths. A closer examination of racial myths, science, and paternal authority as they each operate in this Nazi nationalist melodrama will clarify *how* the Nazi melodrama subsumes the private sphere. This, then, will further distinguish Nazi nationalist melodrama from its liberal democratic counterpart, as I will go on to discuss in the next chapter.

Myth

Kristina Söderbaum, the actress who portrays Anna, was discovered by Harlan for his film *Jugend* in 1938, and she continued to star in every one of his films thereafter. She was also his wife. As film scholar Friedemann Beyer notes, Söderbaum embodies one version of the Nazi ideal, as she is light blond, blue-eyed, and portrayed as clearly inferior to men in most things. She is, in both the roles she plays and her offscreen persona, typically loyal, sensible, simple, and self-sacrificing.[21] But Beyer argues that she is also a "femme fragile" rather than the strong women called for by the Reich's propaganda. The characters Söderbaum plays display an irrepressible gusto for life, but they also end up dead by the end of nearly every film. While this is in keeping with the moralism that characterizes much of the genre, such endings are also always tragic in the Nazi sense. Her death is contrasted precisely with her embodiment of "life," for Söderbaum's characters are frequently figured as closely linked to "Nature." Like Nature, she is idealized and exalted (hence the capital *N*) while at the same time she is cast as lacking reason.[22] The Nazi variant of the larger Western tendency of associating women with Nature emphasizes their contiguity in expressly racialist terms: German women are strong, hearty, and healthy and thus present an image of the long future of the race while also requiring the reasoned guidance of men.

In terms of the Left's critique of fascism, the Nazi recourse to myths of Nature precisely exemplifies the kind of antirational thinking that allows for the emergence of the larger myth of the Aryan race. Marcuse, for instance, saw "total-authoritarianism" as initially a reaction to liberalism "launched against the hypertrophic rationalization and technification of life," which posited the idealized Germanic mythic hero (usually male, but in this case female) as an antidote.[23] The idealization of Nature is a means through which to idealize the German race—and the representation of the mythic German woman (joined by the mythic German man)—takes on a new function layered on top of an already pervasive association of women with Nature in Western culture more generally.

Hence, it is both despite and because of Anna's embodiment of an ideal of German womanhood that she ends up dead at the end of *Die Goldene Stadt* through the confluence of three not entirely reconciled reasons: she is manipulated by Czechs, she is subjected to the deadly consequences of her father's stubbornness, and she is ultimately flawed as a woman. The Nazi mythic ideal at work in the love story portion of the film elaborates the second cause of her death, as the objections of Anna's father can be seen as unreasonable—indeed, a failure of his role as a reasoned man—precisely because he forbids the forming of a "Natural" union. Just as Söderbaum is iconographically associated with life and Nature through the course of her various film roles, Anna's choice of Christian as a partner is multiply valorized throughout the first half of the film, as he, too, is the picture of youth and health.

Such valorization echoes tenets central to the Nazi mythic exaltation of racial purity as it was based on the privileging of robust and hygienic romance between men and women of superior heredity. In American and British journalistic accounts of Nazi ideals of mythic Nature, pagan rituals like solstice night celebrations were favorite sensational subjects, wherein, as one writer reports, hundreds of young men and women from sixteen to twenty-five engaged in sports by day and danced naked around a blazing campfire by night. This writer casts nudism in the Nazi context as being used "without concealment as a short-cut to 'free unions' and a higher 'Nordic birth rate.'"[24] In this line of anti-Nazi thought, the Nazi idealization of Nature, aesthetic emphases on robust, healthy, young bodies, and Nazi doctrine about the need for an ever growing population combine to encourage reproduction between able-bodied and racially pure Aryans—like Christian and Anna in the film.

The call of the Natural in *Die Goldene Stadt*, however, is not to the orgiastic coupling of scientifically verified youths but rather to the neo-Germanic myth of the naturalness of sexual attraction and romance that a too-rigid social order might wrongly prohibit. In the film, Anna hopes to *marry* Christian against her father's wishes, thereby reflecting the much more pervasive insistence on conventional morality that in fact characterized *most* Nazi policies.[25] Clifford Kirkpatrick, in his 1938 study of Germany and its family life, for instance, quotes "the official organ of the ss men" as saying, "It seems to us honorable when two young people come together in love and when they stand by their love. It seems to us dishonorable when, for example, a teacher or employer misuses his power, when an old money-sack undertakes to lure needy youth, when an experienced petticoat chaser uses his arts of persuasion, or when some rascal brings into play the influence of alcohol."[26] The objections of more morally conservative minded parents such as Anna's father to "two young people coming together in love" were, at least in the circles of the ss, considered backward-looking. But overall, even in ss circles, a certain conventional sexual morality prevailed. Thus, although indeed the Nazi court might decide against a father filing for legal injury for the seduction of his daughter (just such a case inspired the definition of the ss position), traditional sexual propriety in most cases was maintained. Thus, it is only after Anna's efforts to marry Christian fail that she succumbs to "an experienced petticoat chaser" (Tony) and so is to be pitied by the end of the film.

Insofar as there is indeed a contradiction between traditional morality (sometimes named "Nazi prudishness" in the foreign press of the 1930s) and the abandonment thereof, it arises less from a violation of traditional sexual morality than from the irreconcilability of Nazi myth and Nazi science. While Anna represents the eternal life force and the healthy German feminine ideal, she is simultaneously subordinated to a flawed nature (i.e., prone to moral excesses) by her genetic inheritance. In this way, she is close to nature in two senses of the term, in the sense of Nature as mythic *and* the sense of her hereditary nature (with an *n*) determining her behavior. Her father's misguided repression of her healthy sexual urges sets in motion the tragic, generationally repetitive behavior that proves her sexual (and finally fatal) undoing.

That Anna could embody both the exalted ideal of Nature as well as possess a flawed nature is one of the central narrative tensions of the plot—a way in which nationalist melodrama appropriates the conventions of the woman's film (i.e., its dramatization of the contradictions in women's lives) to its own ends. Two strands of narrative logic absolve Anna from responsibility for her downfall, both of which can be scripted to the nationalist cause: her hereditary predisposition toward moral lassitude (along the maternal line), which exacerbates her need for paternal guidance; and her father's failure to provide that guidance. Thus, Anna is able to remain the Nazi racial ideal despite her flaws, as the same plotlines that make her a sympathetic heroine according to the rules of the genre also ultimately serve the nationalist narrative of a gendered social order.[27]

Science

In the course of the film, Anna's preternatural affinity with her dead mother can be seen as the source of both her mythic embodiment of the "life force" and her behavioral flaws. She is prone, like her mother and aunt, to moral laxity and suicide. The motif of the dead mother is introduced early on in the film, in the course of Anna's flirtatious afternoon with Christian, when they stop to visit the tombstone that marks the spot where her mother drowned herself when Anna was a child. Much has been made of the undeniably potent association of Anna and her mother with the marsh/swamp, a figure determined by Klaus Theweleit to be indicative of the anxieties of the Freikorps "soldier male" about his own dissolution in the bodies of women.[28] This point is well taken in understanding the overriding masculinism of Nazi ideology. But *Die Goldene Stadt* also uses this locale to favorably inflect the heterosexual union of choice between Anna and Christian. The marsh is not initially ominous and is only revealed to have the potential to be so after it has been depicted as the site of a playful, and hence Natural, meeting between them.

The tombstone scene in fact visually dramatizes this dual character of the marsh, which will also come to be reflected in the German women in the film, symbolized by Anna and her mother. The tombstone is first imaged as standing in the middle of the marsh with a narrow path leading to it, very much like the first shot of Christian, which pictures him surveying in the middle of the marsh as well. The three of them—Christian, Anna, and her mother, signified by the tombstone—stand together in the marsh as Anna tells her story: she was only four when her mother died, not old enough to really understand what was going on, and still she confesses to a sometimes "uncanny longing" for her (eine unheimliche Sehnsucht). In this way, the connection between mother and daughter is established as either instinctual (natural) or mythic (Natural) rather than social.

The marsh has so far been positively portrayed as housing an abundance of wildlife, which is illustrated in otherwise gratuitous intercut shots of birds, a salamander, and a water snake in the course of their conversation. The dead mother, however, lends a darkness to the marsh, just as her "uncanny longing" speaks to Anna's affinity for a potentially destabilizing primordial femininity. The mother will later be further associated with a tainted genetic nature, not only through her tendency toward suicide but through the questionable moral character of her sister, the mother of Anna's no-good seducer. Anna is thus caught in a double bind: she is at once strongly associated with mythic ideals of Nature and potentially brought down by her inherited weaknesses. It is in this sense that she is the Reich's "femme fragile": close to Nature but in need of paternal guidance and protection, the lack of which makes her vulnerable according to the genre's melodramatic conventions.

Nazi beliefs in heritable behavioral characteristics are a key ideological arena where the mythic Aryan "race" and gender come into conflict. Paternal authority will ultimately be invoked to mitigate the inferior moral capacities of the film's women as a tradeoff for the film's apparent condoning of defiance of paternal authority permitted in the name of mythic Nature. Along these lines, Lowry's passing comments on the genetic beliefs embedded in *Die Goldene Stadt* occur in his exploration of the narrative's Oedipal dynamics, mainly because the Oedipal model is inadequate to explain the position of Anna's mother. He writes, "Following beliefs in the genetic inheritance of characteristics especially promoted under Nazism, spectators likely understood Anna's unrest, longing and 'moral laxity' as an inheritance from her mother. As it says in the press packet for the film: 'This longing was probably already embedded in the girlish heart at her birth, because her mother was out of this "golden world" and also carried this unrequited longing for her entire life.' "[29] Anna, in Lowry's appraisal, falls victim to these inherited desires as well as to the external forces that conspire against her. These forces include not only the conniving Czechs but her rigid father, whose stubbornness is at least partly to blame for her mother's death. Hence, the drama revolves in part around his failure as the voice of paternal reason, a narrative strategy that ultimately reinstates the father, not Anna, as the tragic figure who should have known better. Ultimately, both Czechs as a race and women as a gender are inherently flawed. But, while the father is expected to provide rational guidance to Anna in one prominent plotline, he is also victimized by Czech manipulations and so is allied with Anna in a common racial bond.

In *Die Goldene Stadt*, the conflict between nature and nurture in Anna is visualized by way of the recursive figure of the portrait, which is first introduced as Christian and Anna talk about her mother at the tombstone.[30] Anna pulls out a necklace she wears bearing her mother's image, which, shot in extreme close-up, illustrates that the physical resemblance between them is indeed uncanny (Söderbaum actually posed for it). The figure of the photograph or portrait will from then on out be used to emphasize cross-generational behavioral heredity: portraits are only associated with Anna and her mother and Tony and his scoundrel Czech father. Later, Anna offers Christian a photograph of herself, which she must take out of its frame—she cannot give him the frame since it was a gift from her father. Through the recursive figure of the portrait's association with her mother, her *image* is what represents her nature, while the frame her father has provided (the nurture side of her upbringing) is signaled to be thereby superseded. This empty frame will later recur after Anna has gone to Prague against her father's will. When he finds the empty frame, he opens it, again emphasizing that the photograph is no longer inside, and proclaims on this piece of physical evidence that "Just like her mother . . . she is lost" (Wie ihre Mutter . . . Sie ist verloren). Significantly, this scene is intercut with Anna's seduction by Tony: she succumbs immediately after her father's proclamation.

A belief in the heritability of personality characteristics, which is shared in the history of both German and Anglo/American eugenics, helps to manage both gender and racial prejudices in complicated ways. The German eugenicist Fritz Lenz, for instance, wrote that "characteristics of the mind, no less than those of the body, are rooted in the human hereditary equipment, and that environmental influences (including education in the narrower sense of the term) can do nothing more than help or hinder the flowering of hereditary potentialities."[31] In general, the consensus of historical writing on Nazi policy is that it appealed to biology to provide support for the general belief that nature rather than nurture was key to the advancement of human talents and institutions. This belief in the genetic heritability of an expanding array of human characteristics laid the groundwork for later Nazi sterilization, euthanasia, and genocidal policies.[32]

But in nationalist melodrama the inevitability of a genetically determined behavior is mitigated by the possibility that the story *could have* ended happily. Indeed, as film scholar Thomas Elsaesser notes, family melodrama "often records the failure of the protagonist to act in a way that could shape the event and influence the emotional environment, let alone change the stifling social milieu."[33] While the primacy of nature over nurture in many ways does underscore Nazi science, the Nazis' extensive attention to child rearing clearly also gives credence to their perception of the need to provide an ideologically appropriate environment. As the family melodrama hinges on the protagonists' failure to take a course of action that the audience is encouraged to believe would have improved the situation, *Die Goldene Stadt* is staged in many ways as a struggle between the potentially dangerous forces of nature and the possibilities of the successful intervention of paternal authority.

Paternal Authority

To mitigate the potential contradiction between Anna's flawed nature and her status as the mythic German ideal, the melodrama employs the father as responsible for guiding her, for aiding the "flowering" of her racially superior potential and hindering the flowering of her gendered flaws, as Lenz puts the process. In that he fails to do so, the father is *tragically* rather than genetically flawed. Along with his wrong-headed repression of a Natural union, the father's mistake lies in the extension of his prohibition on visiting the city from his wife to his daughter. Originally decreed because of his disapproval of his sister-in-law's debauchery, Anna's father proves unable to distinguish between those elements of city life that should be shunned (moral depravity among them) and those that shouldn't—namely, technological progress. It is the fact that Christian is from the city that most irks him in his prohibition of a union with Anna, and this is doubly reinforced by his opposition to Christian's project of draining the marsh and turning it into farmland.

While Nazi ideology certainly elevated the purity of the country over the decadence of the city, it simultaneously valorized the industrial militarism of total war and so required some efforts at reconciliation between these two locales. Anna is figured as the natural purity and innocence of the countryside, while Christian, as a surveyor, is figured as the embodiment of modern knowledge and technology from the city. The two other romantic possibilities for Anna, Thomas (the nice but boring farmhand who is the father's choice) and Tony (the creepy cousin), are both unsatisfactory in part because neither can traverse the divide between the country and the city as Christian can. A comparison between Thomas and Tony of course continues to ensure that the country on its own is superior to the city on its own, but in fact it is the crossing over of the two domains that is most highly endorsed. Anna's desire for the city, both literally and through Christian, thus represents the hope of a traditionalist modernism that Nazi ideology strove to evince, where technological progress is brought to the countryside without a loss of the heartiness and purity for which it is valorized. Anna's eventual downfall at the hands of Tony, meanwhile, underscores her feminine inability to distinguish between the city's promise and the city's threat.[34]

The romance between Christian and Anna therefore represents the possibility of reconciliation, a union of rural innocence and urban knowledge, as much as it reflects the kind of union of robust and healthy youths that is associated with both the mythic and scientific aims of the Nazis. Thus, Anna's inherited longing for the city is not to be listed among her flaws but might signal another way in which her mythical Nature might help guide the future of Germany. The father's stubborn blocking of this union has to do with both his repetition of prior behavior toward his wife and his backward-thinking unwillingness to accept modern technology, which would make the marsh both farmable and no longer dangerous. The tragic elements of the film center on the father's inability to learn from his previous mistakes and the daughter's consequent destiny to endure her mother's fate. The gendered embodiment of a dual Nature/nature in both mother and daughter is structurally central, just as the father is narratively inscribed as fully capable, by contrast, of stopping the cycle by rationally changing his behavior. The father therefore is not so much condemned for his prudishness—although some measure of evidence for this can be found—but for his stubborn unwillingness to act in a way that would both save his daughter and signal the most formidable future for Germany.

The father's central placement as the tragically responsible party for matters within the German family differs substantially from his role in those elements of the plot dealing with the wily efforts of various Czechs to undermine this family. Unlike the German women, whose gendered flaws might be mitigated by proper (male) guidance, thereby allowing their feminine variant of a heroic Nature to flourish, the Czech characters' racial flaws are endemic and incorrigible. While certainly less definitive than anti-Semitism, Nazi racial beliefs in general extended to carving up of the world into superior and inferior races—with Czechs, to a certain degree, belonging to the latter. The drawing of lines of alliance by way of racial categories is most evident in *Die Goldene Stadt* through the second set of changes to the original play: in addition to changing the ending, all the villainous characters were made Czech in the film, while all characters in *Der Gigant*, both villains and heroes, were German. The fact that Harlan had directed several other melodramas with racist plot motivations—most famously *Jud Süss* (1940)—also supports this reading.[35]

In *Die Goldene Stadt*, father and daughter, who are opposed to one another during the first half of the film, are tellingly parallel, tragically and hence sympathetically so, in the second half. Anna is seduced by her half-Czech cousin Tony just as her father is seduced by his manipulative Czech housekeeper Maruschka. The former plotline revolves around Tony's similarity to his morally corrupt father and the fact that he was born of an illegitimate union between this man and Anna's morally lax aunt. As Anna's mother's sister, the aunt embodies what will happen to German women who are not properly guided: her ruin is visually marked by her slovenly appearance, cigarette smoking, and drinking.

The two plotlines are literally crosscut in the film to underline their equivalence. Just as the opening sequence featured a crosscutting series establishing the Natural connection between Anna and Christian against the father's wishes, so Anna's extramarital involvement with Tony is crosscut with her father's engagement to Maruschka. While the first crosscut sequence establishes an opposition between father and daughter, this one effectively forms an alliance between them as parallel victims of racial manipulation. Anna's father should, according to Nazi legal doctrine in racial matters, be held responsible for this.[36] Anna's father is, however, ultimately absolved through the plot's melodramatic formula. Maruschka emerges as a cunning villain, responsible both for encouraging Anna to defy her father (and hence helping instead of hindering her morally weak behavioral predispositions) and for insinuating herself into the breach left by the father's stubborn misuse of paternal authority.

Tony's behavior thus needs to be seen in relation to Maruschka's as they both conspire to destroy the integrity of the German family. It is a narrative logic dominated by the myth of racial purity endangered by contaminating influences, although gender remains key. Tony's inherited behavioral flaws differ from Anna's in that Tony's flawed moral inheritance descends primarily along the paternal line: he has no access to legitimate male authority. Maruschka, as both Czech and female, displays none of the positive potential the German women embody. Instead of requiring proper male guidance, she acts alone and never to positive ends.

On Anna's arrival in Prague, she is introduced to Tony by way of her aunt's account of his illegitimate origins, wherein portraits again play a significant role. The aunt points to the officer's portrait, rushes over to a photograph of Tony that stands on a coffee table beneath it, and exclaims, "Wie seinem Papa herabgerissen ähnlich" (the spitting image of his father). This comment will soon be echoed by Anna's father in the proclamation "Genau wie ihre Mutter" (just like her mother) as he handles the empty picture frame back at the farm. The locale of the couch, beneath the portrait and next to the photograph, will soon be the site of Tony's seduction of Anna, a wily behavior that the aunt acknowledges as the second way in which he is just like his father. Tony, in other words, resembles his father both physically and behaviorally. The portrait of the absent father is invoked a final time when Tony refuses to marry the pregnant Anna as he stands next to it, reminding his mother that he, too, is an illegitimate child. The physical resemblance between these two parents and their respective children underscores the hereditary determination of their behaviors, with the important distinction being the emphasis on the lines of gendered descent.

Two significant strains in eugenic thinking are revealed in this narrative logic: that degenerate characteristics combined with social factors within the family contaminate an otherwise good family tree and that the mixing of races brings out the worst in both. With a different orientation toward racial mixing it could have been possible to conclude that the melding of races guarantees that the best of both will survive in the offspring. In keeping with the particularly pronounced German variant of the eugenic belief that humanity is on a dangerous downward slide into degeneracy, however, such faith in the natural wisdom of biology is forsaken for a belief in the need for active human intervention.[37] The aunt's feminine flaws were clearly brought to the fore by a lack of proper guidance, just as Anna's feminine weakness is now about to be exploited. Anna's dual function as Germanic ideal and feminine subordinate is thus revealed not to be so contradictory after all, as it is only after the coupling of Anna and Christian, mythic Nature's first choice, is thwarted that nature's degeneratable feminine underside emerges. The wrongful intervention into Nature and the wrongful nonintervention between Tony and Anna are thus played out both within the confines of the family and outside of it, in heredity and in social hierarchy.

Anna's seduction by Tony is not, however, an exact repetition of their respective parents' behaviors. Tony's father, after all, seduced Anna's aunt, not her mother. But this seduction was the cause of the father's prohibition on the mother's freedom, which eventually led to her suicide. While Tony and his father and Anna and her mother are joined in the vortex of fate, the significant figure at the center of it all is still Anna's father, who will repeat his rigid prohibition on mixing the city and the countryside *before* he even knows of Anna's sexual transgression. In this portion of the plot, Tony is genetically irredeemable (a mix of a flawed German woman and a Czech man), while Anna, though certainly susceptible to behavioral flaws along the maternal line, suffers mostly because of her genetically robust German father's inability to act reasonably in the face of the evidence before him. His blindness extends to his inability to protect his family from the manipulation of Czech seducers (both Tony and Maruschka). He fails in his paternal responsibility and is punished by *Anna*'s death rather than his own. He lives beyond the end of the film in order to reinstate paternal authority after her death, as he finally agrees to modernize and have the marsh converted to farmland.

In nationalist drama, conflict between enemies is the straightforward narrative framework, resting on a clear opposition between allies and foes. In women's melodrama, as Laura Mulvey writes, "Ideological contradiction is actually the overt mainspring and specific content of melodrama . . . its excitement comes from conflict, not between enemies, but between people tied by blood or love."[38] Nationalist melodramas like *Die Goldene Stadt* combine both kinds of conflict in an effort to alloy family drama with the nationalist cause. Thus, in the Nazi text the family drama both elevates the German family to the status of national/racial myth and reinforces the patriarchal family, as it is the latter that insures the former as long as the father is reasonable. Rather than being privatized, family life and the personal dramas it entails become political in the Nazi melodrama: personal drama is collective drama, the drama of the German people/Volk.

Conclusion

The problem *Die Goldene Stadt* uniquely stages is a more specific version of the convergence of Nazi Romanticism and melodrama, a combination of Nazism's heroic "death erotics," as Jan-Christopher Horak theorizes, and the investment Tania Modleski theorizes for women readers/spectators who enjoy the tragic deaths of their heroines.[39] In order for Anna's death to be heroic, in both the nationalist and melodramatic senses, she needs not to be solely to blame for her fate. Her genetically inherited spirit, longing, and desire are manipulated by others driven by greed, who see her suffer under the already proven to be tragic rigidity of her father. She is, in a sense, *sacrificed* so that her father may more wisely carry Germany into the future. Simultaneously, as a melodrama the film illustrates some complexities similar to those identified by feminist critics who have examined Hollywood melodramas of that time, in which women's complaints, their chafing against the constraints of patriarchy, are not entirely contained. Consequently, it is not so easy to classify Anna's suicide as simple punishment for racial pollution or abandonment of the Heimat, as a more straightforward reading for Nazi content might allow.

In an overarching way, however, I would argue that these complexities do ultimately serve the nationalist narrative. While the woman's film does indeed open up a panoply of complaints about the plight of women in the patriarchal family, paternal failure itself reinstates patriarchy as the necessary means of ensuring the optimal success of the German race. The possibility of subversion continues to exist, of course, evidenced most strongly by the way in which Anna's blamelessness might actually encourage a reading that advocates at least some greater measure of female freedom. But for the most part nationalist melodrama uses even this ambivalence to enact what Bhabha has named a tension between the pedagogical and performative elements of the production of the nation. The text's recourse to racial myth is part of the larger pedagogy whereby the Nazis produced the German race as a vehicle for national consolidation, while the myriad moments of social/racial injustice serve as recursive performances of the need for Germans to band together in racial solidarity.[40]

To the extent that these performances fall short of the pedagogical goal, the dual strategy of national narrative is revealed to be always incomplete. It requires just the sorts of repetitions and partial resolutions of potential contradictions that this film stages. Nationalist melodrama as a genre both gives form to the nation and exposes potential rifts around the subordination of gender and sexuality to the national project. Relying on both myth and science, Nazism manipulates its internal contradictions in the service of patriarchy, however, and as a case in point the film for the most part fortifies the regime's normative conclusions.

These are the complex politics of melodrama that will also be found at work in the American political scene but with a crucial difference. While in Nazi nationalist melodrama personal dramas are elevated to the status of political myth and are ideologically untroubled by internal contradictions, in American nationalist melodrama personal dramas are substituted for public politics in ways that hope to fortify a belief in the primacy of private life and so to "depoliticize" domestic complaints. As we shall see, this liberal-democratic variant of nationalist melodrama, forged alongside and against fascism, was highly influential in Western European and American domestic politics in the postwar period.

2

American Nationalist Melodrama:

Tales of *Hitler's Children*

■

If the whole world I once could see
   on free soil stand and the people free,
Then to the moment might I say,
   Linger a while, so fair thou art!
—Johann Wolfgang von Goethe, *Faust* (1833)[1]

In the 1942 Hollywood melodrama *Hitler's Children*, the lines by Goethe quoted above are repeatedly spoken as a love poem between the film's central characters, Karl and Anna. The lines are introduced by an American professor, Nichols, the film's most stalwart spokesperson for democracy in the face of Nazi tyranny, in the early part of the film when Anna and Karl are adolescents. Anna, a German-American living in Germany, is immediately smitten by the lines and repeats them dreamily, while Karl, a Hitler Youth, is uninterested and mistakenly attributes the poem to an American author. The second recitation of Goethe occurs much later in the film, as Anna, who has been claimed by the Nazis and chafes at their population growth strategies, refuses to bear a child for the state. Karl embraces her, proclaims his love, and they alternate in speaking the poem to one another (fig. 4). Karl offers to father her child but not to marry her, an only partial conversion to the love-driven politics Goethe is made to represent. In other words, Karl has not yet made the conversion the film works toward, when he must come to understand that romance and national Romance are only truly possible in marriage and under a democratic system. In the Romantic tradition, Goethe's lines address the beauty of political freedom; in the film, a nationalist melodrama, Goethe serves instead to blend Romantic love and romantic love.

Romantic ideals of liberal democracy used the language of personal relationships to characterize the bonds between citizens of the young republics—and Goethe's verse typifies these Romantic notions. In the last 150 years of liberal democracy, however, the relationship between the public and private spheres has turned in the opposite direction: instead of Romantic friendship characterizing citizenship, citizenship has come to be defined by the conduct of citizens in the private sphere. Fascism subordinates this private, individualized existence to a fictional, mythic, construct of "the people" or Volk. Unlike the Romantics, who envisioned a nation of friends, and unlike the subsequent liberal-democratic notion of a nation of private citizens, fascists envision the nation as a unified whole in which all relationships, including those within the traditional private sphere, become part of the public political vocabulary of the Volk. Antifascist rhetoric, then, redeployed the private sphere against this notion of the "private made public" German family—sometimes, as in *Hitler's Children*, using a substitution of romance for Romance to do so.

In American wartime nationalist melodrama, fascism is cast as both the external and internal threat from which the democratic family must be protected. In the more socially conservative variants, Nazism is cast as encouraging a moral degeneracy that stems less from racism or the larger political philosophies of totalitarianism than from sexual misconduct that violates conservative Christian moral codes. Sensational anti-Nazi rhetoric in both journalism and Hollywood films thus often cast the danger of Nazism as a threat to women—tellingly, almost always non-Jewish women—a threat to chastity, love, sexual propriety, and family. In this move, gender is foregrounded and race effaced, with sexuality serving as the volatilizing medium. In *Hitler's Children*, then, the verse by Goethe belies the qualitative difference between the Romantic project and the melodramatic anti-Nazi project, as the language of Romantic political ideals is transformed into the valorization of private dramas of family and romance *as,* as Lauren Berlant has put it, a nonpolitical political arena.[2]

My analysis of this negotiation begins with a brief survey of antifascist thought, proceeds to a discussion of the most prominent melodramatic

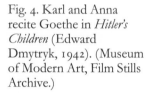

Fig. 4. Karl and Anna recite Goethe in *Hitler's Children* (Edward Dmytryk, 1942). (Museum of Modern Art, Film Stills Archive.)

figures of anti-Nazi rhetoric, and finally arrives again at the example of *Hitler's Children*. This chapter lays the groundwork for the rest of the book, wherein I examine the process whereby the political relationship between private and public spheres, extant in especially American uses of antifascist rhetoric, ensures sexuality a central place in contemporary political culture.

Family, Sexuality, and the Critique of Fascism

The rhetoric of enemies typically consists of the delineation of absolute distinctions, in this case between Nazi Germany and American democracy. As Nazi ideologies of the family consisted of a complex and internally contradictory set of beliefs, however, so critics of fascism's attitudes toward family and sexuality could selectively focus on individual components of the ideology to the exclusion of others. Nazi rhetoric and politics were conservative but utilitarian. Sexual conservatism and the encouragement of reproduction in marriage were the most prominent and preferred strategies for both portraying the respectability of the "new Germany" and encouraging population growth (a strain essentially identical to conservative Christian morality), while the imperative to raise the birthrate eventually led to some softening of the means of attaining it (a distinction from Christian morality, but still no closer to women's emancipation). Anti-Semitism and the myth of the Aryan race were key motives to both. Depending on the definition of democracy a speaker espoused, anti-Nazi rhetoric could choose any point among these policies to cast against the democratic ideal.

The liberal response to fascism cast it as destroying individualism and subsuming the individual into the fascist mass.[3] The middle-class, nuclear family, the home base of liberal individualism, was threatened by fascism insofar as the state took over the family's crucial functions of child rearing and moral education. In short, fascism violated the public/private divide on which capitalist democracies rely. Liberal Protestant churches, while sometimes also taking a stand against Nazi racism, most often complained of the displacement of the church by the state. This meant that the Christian, middle-class, nuclear family was often cast as a democratic antidote to fascism, despite the fact that fascism also relied centrally on this version of the family for the implementation of its ideological programs and had garnered the support of 60 percent of Germany's churches.[4]

Conservative critics were often rather temperate in their criticism of the Nazis until war compelled them to become more pointed.[5] In wartime, conservative responses took liberal anti-Nazi strategies further, casting fascism as destructive of the traditional family and hence of Christian morality. Fascism was seen as encouraging sexual promiscuity, out of wedlock births, and various sorts of perversion. While there is some truth to these accusations, they are more tellingly selective the more conservative they get. While the imperative to encourage racially "pure" population growth included some leniency among the Nazi elite about the issue of illegitimacy, by and large population growth policies were carried out *within* traditional families, as illustrated by policies that forgave a percentage of the state-sponsored "marriage loan" with the birth of every child.[6] Indeed, Nazi programs intended to increase the Aryan population for the most part consisted of extremely conservative measures. The same eugenically minded committee was charged with the prosecution of both abortionists and homosexuals, for example (the Reich's Central Agency for the Struggle Against Homosexuality and Abortion).[7] In many ways, the Nazi regime enforced a kind of prudishness that was in step with conservative Christian morality rather than diametrically opposed to it, as much U.S. and British wartime rhetoric would have it.

The Left's critique of fascism, on the other hand, considered it to be an extreme outgrowth of the contradictions of capitalism and liberal democracy, wherein the rhetoric of freedom and equality masks the reality of economic enslavement and social inequality. Members of the Frankfurt School hypothesized that fascism arose in part due to a crisis in the bourgeois family, in which the authority of the father had been undermined by changing economic relations. They postulated that this had led to a search for paternal authority figures outside the family (such as the Führer) and consequently to the loss of an internalized superego and the creation of an amoral "mass man."[8] This person was thought to have traveled so far into the contradictions of liberal reason as to become irrational, to have reached the point where contradictions no longer appeared as such.[9] Without this recourse to contradiction, this person could never hope to attain critical reason, through which he or she could see the errors of capitalism and liberalism's ways and embrace socialism. As the Left's critique was not often concerned with gender, however, it implied that a return to a model of family wherein the father had genuine authority over both his labor and his political participation would be an antidote to fascism. Hence, leftist critiques, too, encouraged a view of fascism as destructive to a "democratic" family wherein traditional gender roles are basically observed.

Until the United States joined the war in 1941, American attitudes toward Nazism waffled over exactly what might be objectionable about this new regime. Early on, some were outright supportive, even in mainstream publications. Others were vociferously opposed.[10] As late as 1941 (just before the United States entered the war), the Senate held hearings on "Motion picture screen and radio propaganda," wherein right-wing, anti-Semitic senators like Gerald Nye (R-N.D.) *accused* members of the entertainment industry of antifascism, an anticommunist ploy later modified to be called "premature antifascism" during the McCarthy hearings after the war. Once war was declared, efforts to articulate the radical difference between German fascism and American democracy of course occupied much of the mainstream media. These efforts included the rearticulation of the American version of the secular/spiritual balance of liberal democracy and Protestantism against the perceived imbalance of these domains perpetrated by fascism. They included efforts to forcefully assert democratic ideals of liberal reason against repressive fascist dictates (individuality, political freedoms, and equality). And, finally, they centrally included the assertion that Nazi Germany was actively destructive toward the "traditional" family, which democracy was explicitly instituted to uphold. Rhetorical elisions masked similarities between Germany and the United States, including the fact that some Christian churches supported fascism and many more did not take a strong stand against anti-Semitism, that American racism also took institutionally supported forms, that Nazi antifeminism made the nuclear family the core of Nazi racist policies, and that gay men, lesbians, abortionists and leftists were also persecuted under the Nazis.

While certainly there are concrete ways in which Americans felt a part of the collective struggle against a recognizable moral and political evil, the assertion of a unified national collective elided the contradictions within the practice of American democracy concerning race, gender, class, and sexuality. In Homi Bhabha's terms, nationalist melodrama comprises a pedagogy of the democratic family, teaching the American public a national norm by asserting, in repetitive fashion, the purity of the opposition between fascism and democracy in the private sphere.[11]

Embedded in anti-Nazi rhetoric are indeed three melodramatic figures that characterize the elisions of continuity between fascism and democracy, enact the privatized politics of conservative liberal democracy, and potentially expose the fictions of the melodramatic conceit: the combination of antifeminism and a belief in eugenics in the service of a tempered anti-Nazism, the casting of German women as victims of Nazism, and the invocation of "democratic" Christian moralism against Nazi sexual decadence. Each of these figures has a central place in the ongoing political life of anti-Nazi rhetoric.

Antifeminism/Pro-eugenics

As with all melodrama and most political rhetoric invoking the family, the proper position of women was crucial to discussions of family life and also revealed some of the contradictions within the varying strategies that hoped to declare a fundamental difference between the "democratic family" and the Nazis' projected "antifamily" agenda. These contradictions can be traced back to conservative journalistic reporting before the United States entered the war and the way this rhetoric shifted afterward.

Popular journalistic reporting on Nazi family policy in the 1930s was by no means clear on whether these policies should be supported or criticized. Initially, the Nazis' "back to the home" policies were often met with support, especially from writers who believed that women were taking jobs away from men and that working women had contributed to a perceived deterioration of family life. This perception included eugenically inflected complaints about what was often called an "anti-baby strike" by educated, emancipated women, with commentators citing Weimar Germany as a case in point. Rodney Collin, for instance, wrote in the *Living Age* in 1934: "Hitler, by removing women from industry, is giving to men new fields of employment and a greater certainty of livelihood. With renewed opportunity and his direct encouragement, they are entering more easily into the permanent marriage relationship. In the long run, human instincts, however warped in a single generation, should find fulfillment and stability therein. In twenty years the psychological sickness of Germany may have given way to new health. The madness will then be passed."[12] Collin's support of Nazi policies returning women to their primary role as mothers is not entirely unusual, even among writers who otherwise protested the Nazis' totalitarian aims.

Sociologist Clifford Kirkpatrick's 1938 study of Germany's family life, for instance, stresses the complexity of Nazi family ideology and is generally critical, but he stumbles over the similarities between German eugenic policies and American ones. Kirkpatrick says, matter-of-factly, "For two decades or more the German population was sick. The life tides in the German folk organism flowed more and more feebly."[13] He sees Nazi attempts to raise the birth rate as reasonable and necessary and the situation as not unlike that in the United States. He asks "Why did the mothers go on a strike in Germany as in most parts of western Europe and America?" to which he surmises, "Economic hardship, insecurity, mobility, 'keeping up with the Joneses,' ambition to get ahead in the world and perhaps simply a change of fashion in regard to motherhood prompted use of birth-control methods as they became known. In Germany, as in America, the so-called higher occupational groups are most inclined to reject parenthood."[14] Antifeminism is thus embedded in Kirkpatrick's pro-eugenic stance.

As the study progresses, Kirkpatrick complains of the negative effect the association of Nazism with eugenics has had on public opinion in England and the United States. He writes, "In the liberal world where the critical scientific point of view still has positive prestige, National Socialism with its wedding of politics to science has a negative prestige. This negative prestige tends to be drained into the applied science of eugenics. There is nothing logical in such a process of emotional association."[15] Kirkpatrick blames sensational reporting for this "emotional association," whereby "The average American newspaper reader conceives of German women driven out of offices by Storm Troopers and herded back to the home and enforced motherhood. . . . Many Americans are firmly convinced that the conceiving of illegitimate children is applauded by all Nazis and that polygamy is about to be established."[16] By considering these charges to be distortions, Kirkpatrick can both distinguish the "applied science of eugenics" from the Nazis' "wedding of politics to science" and also claim that even in the Nazi case reports of eugenic aims leading to sexual immorality are overblown. Eugenics, for Kirkpatrick, is a perfectly reasonable science. Under his logic, antifeminist support of eugenic policies is not tantamount to support for totalitarianism, just as it is not eugenics per se that should form the basis of a critique of fascism.[17]

Nationalist melodrama appears in two forms in this debate. First, there are the sensational reports of German women "herded back to the home," which invoke a classic variant of domestic/female victims to state/male tyranny. Second, there is Kirkpatrick's anti-Nazi but pro-eugenic counterargument that feminism (among other things) threatens the family from within. Just as Kirkpatrick names Nazi practices as an improper "wedding of politics and science," so he claims that his own antifeminism is *not* such a "wedding"—in other words, it is "not political."

This move is indeed shared by both Kirkpatrick and the sensational journalism he decries insofar as both cast Nazism as a revolutionary movement threatening destructive change rather than as a conservative movement itself bent on turning back the clock on the unfavorable changes wrought by modernity. By employing what rhetorician Albert Hirschman describes as "jeopardy" logic, the encouragement of women to bear children can be praised as in itself good while blaming the "revolutionary" forces of fascism for taking the directive too far.[18] In wartime rhetoric, this sort of reasoning prevailed in the interests of maximizing the distance between American democracy and fascism while preserving aspects of the American social order that were in fact continuous with Nazi culture. In the melodramatic mode, the victimization of German women and the moral compromise of German youth were the two primary narrative patterns for asserting this dual ideological task.

The German Woman as Victim: Sensationalism/Feminism

The melodramatic specter of the intervention of the state into matters of the family routinely cast women as the sexual and reproductive victims of the scientism of the Nazi regime. In keeping with the eighteenth- and nineteenth-century thematization of the nation through virtuous womanhood, these narratives updated the symbolic importance of women to twentieth-century nationalist melodrama. In this type of narrative, the German woman was seen to have been reduced to her reproductive capacity and treated like a stock farm animal or "breeding mare."[19] These images of forced breeding are often coupled, symptomatically, with reports of Nazi nature worship, resulting in a two-fronted argument that Nazism was primarily anti-Christian, both overly secular and pagan. The conceptual closeness of religious primitivism with its counterpart of scientific interventionism are both conceived to violate the sanctity of private family life. Together they illustrate the conflation of Nazi "irrationality" with "overrationality," which was so pervasive in British and American wartime nationalist melodramas.

Several types of stories appeared in American magazines that narrated this sort of conflation. One favorite featured a middle-aged mother who is abandoned by her husband for a younger woman (i.e., one capable of bearing him more children).[20] Another, more sensational variant claimed to describe camps where "thousands of fair-haired and blue-eyed girls, drafted for 'special duty' are mated with ss-men picked for physique and intelligence" along with forced "breeding camps" for German women, where "Sexual relations were not only permitted but compelled. Those who balked faced severe punishment, and several committed suicide."[21] While these reports on the mistreatment of women might offer an opportunity to assert a feminist critique of the Nazis' masculinism, this was by and large not the direction in which these reports went. Instead, the aim was to reinforce the notion that true democratic freedom for women was found in church-sanctioned marriages, which, according to these reports, the Nazis were actively trying to discourage.

There were some feminist journalists whose analysis of fascism also invoked the victimization of German women, but generally these lacked the same sort of recourse to nationalist melodrama. The difference between these accounts and nationalist melodrama is that they make connections between patriarchal societies and Germany and/or they foreground women's oppression in other realms alongside the sexual and reproductive.[22] Even some who criticized Nazi policies toward women on multiple fronts, however, continued to characterize democracy in terms of the private sphere. Quentin Reynolds, writing for *Collier's* in 1933, for instance, writes, "Woman's place in the Germany of the future is in the home. She must scorn night clubs, she must scorn frivolity, she must ignore all artificial pleasure and intellectual pursuit, and she must be happy in serving only the state."[23] Reynolds's critique of fascist policy decries women's disbarment from intellectual pursuits but also decries the politicization of the family and the deprivation of women's private pleasures, both of which contribute to the notion that fascism's primary difference, and hence its threat to democracy, is the obliteration of the private sphere.

British writer Katharine Burdekin's 1937 novel *Swastika Night* (published under the pen name Murray Constantine) similarly posits the destruction of the family as her primary source of critique, projected as the end result of the confinement of women to their reproductive function. While the novel is an interesting example of a gender-based critique of Nazi family policies, Burdekin, too, posits an alternative ideal in Christianity (where women and men are equal before God) and heterosexual marriage (as opposed to fascist homosexuality). A German knight, burdened with the knowledge that women were once not treated like animals kept for breeding, confesses that Christians live more like Germans did before the Nazi success: "Christians in their communities don't live like we do, men and women separately. They live in *families*, that is the man, the woman, and their children, sons and daughters, all together."[24] Burdekin thereby asserts, despite her feminist impulses, that what must be protected from the Nazis is the private sphere. Efforts to maintain the family as private and to uphold traditional marriage, gender roles, and normative heterosexuality are thus cast as antifascist, and hence "nonpolitical political" activities.

Christian Moralism

Liberal and conservative critiques of Nazi family policies sometimes converge around the issue of Christian morality, although certainly there were significant differences between denominations, especially concerning the role of the church in the secular world and the kinds of social responsibilities required of believers. While certainly progressive Christian churches were among the most vocal opponents of Nazism, most of these churches focused on the adulteration of spiritual freedom and, in their best moments, on the immorality of Nazi racism.[25] Conservative churches, meanwhile, which had a history of focusing on personal conduct over social charity, saw the most grievous sin to be a sexual one. This line of argument neglects the fundamental sexual conservatism of

Nazism very much in keeping with a history of conservative Christian moralism to instead make much of the perceived departure from these norms through a departure from Christianity more generally.

Historian William Martin marks World War I and the Bolshevik Revolution as significant turning points for American Protestant fundamentalism in that these events gave rise to what would become one of its major features: religious nationalism. In the second decade of the twentieth century, fundamentalist preachers claimed that Satan was behind the German war effort, spurred on by the introduction of historical criticism of the Bible in German universities. Meanwhile, they described Jews and communists as similarly undermining the nation's moral fiber through their alleged desires to dominate the world.[26] By the end of the 1920s, however, the momentum of this first wave of religious nationalism subsided due in part to its sometime support for anti-Semitic, anti-Catholic, nativist, and other assorted right-wing agendas, including the assertion that only Christians could be true Americans.[27] While anti-communism—and often anti-Semitism—continued to be a unifying cause for the most conservative of Christians and led some to support fascism, more moderate conservatives linked communism and fascism as enemies of God and nation in a rhetoric of new religious nationalism that emerged with World War II. As part of a vision wherein the United States stood for the hope of a biblical promised land, Germany again came to be seen as representing the epitome of moral decline—not so much due to its racism and suppression of nonreligious freedoms but because of its assault on Christian sexual morals.

A major preoccupation of anti-Nazi journalism, then, was the violation of Christian morals. These articles combined the sensational reports of rampant promiscuity and illegitimacy with either Nazi paganism or a concept of the "state as religion." Journalists reported that "The eugenically qualified female would choose at her leisure six mates who would in turn father one of her brood of six or more"; that "Ideas about the unwed mother also have changed. She is officially lauded as having performed a heroic and praiseworthy act"; and, finally, that "Platonic friendships are not popular among Nazi men: marriage, unfortunately, often isn't either." All of these are fantastic exaggerations of life in Nazi Germany.[28] This casting of the terms of opposition to fascism as one of sexual morality leads to the assertion that support for traditional morality—having a baby *in* wedlock, for instance—is an anti-Nazi act.

The rhetorical tactics for countering Nazism included the deployment of sentimentalism and religiosity to claim that Nazis were inhumane, cold, calculating, and soulless or the deployment of a Christian moral order to claim that Nazis were psychologically disturbed or morally depraved. A 1942 article entitled "Sex Is a Nazi Weapon," for instance, illustrates a blend of the latter, with combined appeals to psychology and Christian moralism, "Many psychiatrists have tried to explain Hitler's own career by the abnormality of his sex life. There is impressive support for the theory that the whole Nazi movement arose in large measure out of the sexual frustrations of some groups in the German population. Certainly, distorted personalities have been prominent among the leaders of the movement and orgiastic 'paganism' has been encouraged among the Nazi youth. A telltale hatred for the morality of the Western Christian world runs through the writings of Nazi leaders."[29] The role of psychology in the enforcement of this moral dichotomy, and indeed the management of democracy itself, is vast. Part two of this book further elaborates its pervasive influence during and after the war against fascism. But the claim to a "hatred for morality" with which abnormal psychology is here paired sets up a series of oppositions most common to conservative Christian anti-Nazism, where Nazi "paganism" and sexual perversion (defined by means of psychological aberration) go hand in hand. Psychological health and Christianity are thus also logically paired, as with the statements, "The Norwegian clergy has had the courage to challenge the Nazi attempts to dominate youth" and "despite heroic resistance by Catholics and Calvinists, the Nazi invaders pursue their program of systematic sexual infiltration of the Netherlands."[30]

While there were obvious acts of Nazi brutality that deserve the utmost moral condemnation—the treatment of Jews and other political, ethnic, and sexual "undesirables" most glaringly—the reports that tended to focus on sexual transgressions also tended to diminish the centrality of racism. The Nazis' own grievous practices of casting Jews as sexually perverse in anti-Semitic propaganda are invoked not to decry their racism but as evidence of the Nazis' own lasciviousness, thereby shifting the focus from Nazi racism to issues of sexual morality. Herald, in the article cited above, calls Nazi films "'arty' pornography" and describes Veit Harlan's *Jud Süss* as an "anti-Semitic tract . . . centered on the rape of an Aryan girl in her bedroom and . . . presented with shocking realistic detail."[31] The rape of Dorothea (the Aryan girl) is clearly a moment of anti-Semitic exploitation, but the "shocking realistic detail" Herald objects to is highly exaggerated, as the scene cuts away before Süss and Dorothea have any physical contact. Herald symptomatically does not pursue the egregious problem of Nazi anti-Semitism further. As a result of this rhetorical strategy, it appears that Herald is more concerned with the breakdown of Christian sexual morals than direct ethical questions about Nazi racism and eugenic policy, both of which appear in this way to be just an excuse for sexual excess.

Overall, theologians, whether conservative or liberal, had a more complicated relationship with appeals to reason and rationality, given their own investment in the irrational. Moderate theologians who became anti-Nazi had historically supported the establishment of two humanist spheres: the secular (which was meant to be governed by a state ruled by liberal reason) and the spiritual (which was meant to be the province of a complementary Protestant church). Once the Nazi state demonstrably violated its commitment to liberal reason, these theologians felt compelled to reclaim the secular realm by way of accusing the Nazis of having "spiritualized" it (by way of nationalism) for their own political ends. The Pope, too, condemned the Nazis for elevating race, nation, and state to divine status, thereby also implying that these domains should remain secular. Due to the long-standing equation of democracy and national identity with middle-class respectability, the appeal to Christian moralism was mostly a call to reestablish this spiritual/secular balance and so maintain the liberal democratic bargain of the public/private divide. This is the common thread, then, of the various Christian critiques of Nazism both within Germany and outside of it: that Nazism represented a disturbing blend of rational and irrational logics that muddied the distinction between public and private and consequently violated the established order.

The forms of nationalist melodrama deployed in the three figures common to wartime journalism thus for the most part characterize the conflict between fascism and democracy in terms of the sanctity of the traditional private sphere. This characterization foregrounds sexuality as the primary *political* arena in the ideological battle between democracy and fascism while claiming that the private sphere should be free of state/political appropriation.

Prurient Interest and Sexual Propaganda

Much of this journalism, while claiming to be speaking from the standpoint of wounded morals, also surely held prurient interest. It is difficult to discern how much of the reportage on Nazi sexual practices was printed to help sell magazines as much as it speaks to genuine moral outrage. At its most disingenuous, sensational journalism uses the logic of exploitation to claim moral indignation as a ruse (whether fully consciously or not) for discussing moral transgression. This is an example of Michel Foucault's concept of the "incitement to discourse" in its most obvious form, often scarcely hiding its intentions beneath the veneer of prohibition.[32]

In addition to sensationalist journalism, exploitation films also took on Nazi sexual transgressions in the course of the war. With stricter enforcement of the Production Code in Hollywood after 1934, prurient material of the more explicit sort was driven to cheap B movies, which claimed, often facetiously, to be outraged by what they portrayed. Set up as a means of circumventing the establishment of a national censorship board (among other things), the code was written in cooperation with conservative clergy who had spearheaded a campaign against the film industry for degrading American morals.[33] The code thus explicitly disallowed the portrayal of illegitimacy, extramarital sexual relations, and perversion but allowed some handling of these topics as a means of moral education as long as characters were ultimately punished for their sexual misdeeds. The plethora of B movies that sprang up in the 1930s thus claimed to decry the hazards of drugs, alcohol, and loose women (either associating with them or becoming one). Their formulaic outrage was staged mostly, if not entirely, for the sake of voyeuristic indulgence.

Two exploitation films made by the B movie company Monogram during the war illustrate the anti-Nazi variant of the genre. Alfred Zeisler's *Enemy of Women* (1944), a loose biography of Joseph Goebbels, makes the case that Goebbels' personal life was a major drive behind his politics and hence the Nazi system in general. As film historian Jan-Christopher Horak writes of the film's portrait, "Goebbels is a small, unsuccessful playwright who compensates for his inferiority complexes and physical insufficiencies through power hunger, brutal violence against his enemies, and an unrestricted sexual life." Hence, as in the journalism example, fascist politics is condensed into personal dramas and becomes a matter of sexual misconduct.[34] Steve Sekely's *Women in Bondage* (1943) enacts a similar displacement. It concerns a German woman living abroad who returns home and is appalled by Nazi policies encouraging reproduction out of wedlock and sexual promiscuity. Horak states that in general the disruption of the family is the most unique characteristic of the anti-Nazi genre in Hollywood, supporting my claims about the centrality of nationalist melodrama to American antifascism.[35]

The original and most successful anti-Nazi B movie, however, was *Hitler's Children*. *Women in Bondage* was in fact originally titled *Hitler's Women*, an attempt to capitalize on its success.[36] *Hitler's Children* likewise began as a B movie and follows the exploitation formula, making up for its lack of big stars and lavish sets with sensational content. As with all of these films, *Hitler's Children* was closely regulated by the Production Code Administration (PCA), an influence that, both in its prohibitions and in its proscriptions, shaped the anti-Nazi genre.

Besides forbidding or at least constraining most sexual material, the Production Code also proscribed the positive portrayal of American institutions of government, justice, and church as well as any foreign nation with which the United States was on friendly terms. This meant, as noted above, that films expressing anti-Nazi sentiment prior to the declaration of war were *accused* of being antifascist rather than praised for it. After the declaration, however, Hollywood developed a cooperative relationship with the Office of War Information (OWI), partly out of sincere patriotic sentiment and partly as a way to revamp the negative moral image of the film industry.[37] Thus, wartime anti-Nazi films like *Hitler's Children* passed the review board with few objections despite the fact that the film dealt with taboo sexual issues that violated the code. As long as it was the nation's diplomatic enemy that was perverse and immoral, the code's logic went, these normally disallowed topics could be openly discussed and portrayed.

The PCA files on *Hitler's Children* show minimal problems with state censorship boards and indeed very little wrangling over the script in the course of the production, with only minor suggestions such as "There must, of course, be no unacceptable exposure of Anna's person in this scene where the blouse is ripped off her back while she is being lashed."[38] One member of the review board wrote that "This film must be horrifying and frightening but apparently 'our side' comes through with 'flying colors,'" a statement that makes clear the code's wartime bottom line.[39] *Hitler's Children*, as I'll go on to substantiate, is consequently a prime example of more general rhetorical tendencies in American wartime political culture.

Hollywood's Anti-Nazi Melodrama: *Hitler's Children*

A combination of the rhetorical tendencies described above inform the imagery and narrative structure of Hollywood's anti-Nazi narrative films, which in turn reinforced the overall tendency to narrate the conflict between fascism and democracy melodramatically. In keeping with these rhetorics, Horak provides a chart of antinomies to characterize anti-Nazi film as a genre, wherein love, monogamy, and democracy stand opposite sexuality, promiscuity, and fascism.[40] Through sensationalized stories, Horak writes, a picture of German fascism emerged in film and journalism "that pulled moral rather than political value judgments to the foreground," a rhetorical move that sidesteps other central social issues such as racism, class struggle, and sexism.[41]

Hitler's Children is particularly useful in a discussion of the relation between Hollywood film and American journalism as they colluded in this sort of displacement, as the film is based on a nonfiction book, *Education for Death: The Making of the Nazi* (1941), written by Gregor Ziemer, who was the director of the American Colony School in Berlin. Ziemer published journalistic accounts of the Nazis' social institutions throughout the 1930s and 1940s, based on his experiences in prewar Nazi Germany. These accounts culminated in the book, which was also published in condensed form in *Reader's Digest* in February 1942.[42] The book was quickly optioned by the low-budget production company University Film Productions, with a tentative releasing agreement with RKO even before the film was scripted. In trying to secure a scriptwriter, Edward A. Golden, the film's producer, wrote to the PCA asking for advice. The letter quotes the preface of the book as a means of heralding its virtues, which reveal "how unbridgeable is the gulf between the Nazis and ourselves. Here you can see exposed in all its cruelty and horror the system of perversion with which, since their advent to power, the Nazis have deliberately degraded the minds and morals of the rising generation in Germany."[43] Once the film was made, the book was featured prominently in its promotional materials and is imaged in the opening credit sequence before all else, burning on a pile of other indistinguishable books. This opening image implies that the book, and indeed the film, is fundamentally antithetical to Nazi ideology.

Edward Dmytryk came on board in the summer of 1942. A B movie director at Paramount at the time, his surprise box office success with *Hitler's Children* catapulted him to the A list. Dmytryk calls his wartime films "necessarily oversentimental and chauvinistic," thereby pointing to the particular blend of melodramatic convention and political propaganda that wartime films helped craft.[44] Dmytryk was an interesting character in Hollywood history in that he later became one of the Hollywood Ten, and served his year in prison for contempt of Congress with the others. Later he turned coat and named names when faced with being blacklisted once he got out. Unlike many members of his cohort in Hollywood who had had contact with communism or progressive politics, he was able to make many more films throughout the 1950s and 1960s under his own name, although he was not particularly well liked by anyone. The main reason for raising the issue of Dmytryk's political history, however, is that, unlike two of his other films of the 1940s, *Tender Comrade* (1943) and *Crossfire* (1947)—both of which were authored by scriptwriters who were eventually blacklisted—most of Dmytryk's films do not substantively reflect his short-lived leftist politics. Instead, films like *Hitler's Children*, and its anti-Japanese sequel *Behind the Rising Sun* (1943), conform much more closely to the sort of socially conservative journalism discussed above than to a progressive social agenda.[45] As the Left's critique of the family was also limited at this time, however, the film's antifascism could be said to reflect a more widespread brand of moral conservatism wherein the "democratic family," in "oversentimental and chauvinistic" form, emerges as an antidote to fascism to meet the needs of wartime nationalist rhetoric.

Hitler's Children in fact overtly narrates Ziemer's accounts by way of a fictional romantic melodrama—a strategy that literally emplots the structurally melodramatic tendencies of the journalism itself. The book is an extremely unsubtle description of Nazi youth organizations from before conception through university. The fictional story of the film carries the viewer through some of the same institutions reported in Ziemer's book, but it builds these visits around the multiply thwarted romance of Anna (Bonita Granville), who attends and later teaches at the American school, and Karl (Tim Holt). In the book, Ziemer constantly maximizes the uniform fanaticism of each child or young person with whom he claims to have come into contact: for instance, one schoolboy exclaims "I want to shoot a Frenchman!" and a young, unmarried pregnant woman threatens "Better tell America to get ready for something."[46] In the film, however, the conflictual romantic narrative underscores undecidability: we are meant to be at least nominally uncertain whether Anna will become a Nazi or Karl will forsake his Nazism.[47]

The film concentrates on institutions, depicted in the early part of the book, that manage and implement Nazi eugenic beliefs: *lebensborn* camps where promiscuous coupling between the racially pure is facilitated, "mother and child homes" where unmarried pregnant women go to be cared for by the state, and sterilization centers where the genetically (or politically) impaired are prevented from passing on their bad genes and democratic ideas. While briefly touching on schooling and youth organizations, the film mostly focuses on issues of reproductive policy, privileging the body of the film's heroine as the site of struggle between fascism and democracy. This nationalist melodrama thus ultimately involves two interrelated threads: the threat to Anna as a representative of American democracy and the various barriers to the successful union of the heterosexual couple, a union the film casts as undermined by the Nazis' putative conspiracy against the traditional family.

The Threat to the American Woman/Democracy

Hitler's Children was met with lukewarm reviews when it was released. Bosley Crowther, always vocal on a film's political content, complained in the *New York Times*, for instance, that the script provided "but a superficial survey of some of the more familiar methods of enslaving Nazi youth and resolves the whole moral conflict in a pat and unconvincing boy-girl plot."[48] Still, the film went on to become one of the most popular successes of the following year.[49] *Variety*, in its characteristic jumble of business prospects and criticism, proclaimed that the film should "lend itself aptly to exploitation" and "should not be difficult to sell." *Variety*'s writer suggests exactly how such selling might take place: "While the more bloodthirsty devices of Hitlerism, such as mass executions and the terrors of the concentration camp, have been wisely kept out of the action, the cruelties of the Germanic regime now in power are effectively keynoted. For instance, the scene where the girl (Miss Granville) is about to be flogged, receiving a couple of strikes of the lash before being released, and the shots from a distance of the hospital room where women are being sterilized."[50] This account of the exploitable aspects of the film makes explicit the "wisdom" of the avoidance of the Nazis' more egregious acts of political and ethnic persecution in favor of their displacement onto the bodies of women. Melodramatic sentiment is thereby mobilized for the nationalist cause.

In the film, this displacement is dramatized in a scene marking the first major turning point of the narrative. While the beginning of the film establishes the adolescent conflict/friendship between Anna (a patriotic American) and Karl (a Hitler Youth), the pivotal scene occurs after Anna has grown up and become a teacher at the school. The scene follows immediately after a montage of documentary footage describing the Nazis' war mobilization, a common practice in Hollywood films of the period, lending factual authenticity to the fictional elements of the story.[51] Professor Nichols (the Ziemer stand-in) announces in voice-over that it is Memorial Day, which affords Anna the opportunity to extol the virtues of democracy to the assembled students by reciting a slightly modified form of the Gettysburg Address. Like Lincoln, she exhorts her students to "highly resolve that this nation, under God, shall have a new birth of freedom, and that government of the people, by the people, and for the people shall not perish from the earth."[52] Anna and Nichols then proceed to lead the group in singing the American nationalist tribute "My Country 'Tis of Thee." Anna quite literally appears here as the voice of democracy.

A group of uniformed Nazis pulls up and attempts to quiet the singing, which, in a show of patriotic resistance, the students refuse to do until they have finished. One of the Nazis announces that they are there to dismiss Jews, Poles, Lithuanians, and "all persons of German blood" from the school. Nichols protests that this is an American school (i.e., one that is multiethnic, a point also obliquely referenced by the Gettysburg Address allusion), but the head Nazi ignores him and proceeds to announce the names of a series of slightly "ethnic-looking" students—and finally Anna. Unlike the students, Anna verbally protests on her own behalf, saying that she may have German parentage but she *is* an American. She and Nichols proceed to try to make a case for her citizenship but are unsuccessful. Anna is claimed for Germany.

From this point forward, the plot revolves exclusively around Anna, dramatizing Nichols's efforts to free her from Nazi indoctrination, then persecution, and Karl's confused efforts to indoctrinate and protect her. Despite the invocation of the American Civil War as perhaps a parallel struggle over racial justice, this brief mention of ethnically persecuted groups is thenceforth subsumed under Anna's ensuing trials. This scene in fact contains the only mention of Jews in the film, mitigated as it is by the lumping together of Jews, Poles, and Lithuanians. Largely, and tellingly, this is a consequence of a general wartime queasiness in the Hollywood industry about "overemphasizing" anti-Semitism due to the fact that the same conservative Christian moral campaigns that succeeded in pressuring the industry to adopt the Production Code had frequently invoked anti-Semitism to imply that since Jews "ran Hollywood" they were the cause of the "moral degeneracy" the industry allegedly espoused.[53] The industry as a whole was thus decidedly less vocal about Nazi anti-Semitism at this time than other aspects of the regime, despite the fact that many people working in Hollywood were personally addressed by this egregious issue. *Variety*'s praise of the "wise" decision not to highlight racial and political persecution thus performs two functions: it masks the American racism just beneath the surface (if that) of American domestic politics and reveals the function of the substitution of "domestic politics" in the second sense, wherein the family stands in (pedagogically) for the homogenized nation as a whole. This is how Anna, not the Jews, comes to be the threatened entity whose drama the film pursues.[54]

The battle over Anna is both political and sexual. On the political front, it concerns whether or not she, as an ethnic German, can be indoctrinated, swayed from the beliefs she espoused in the democratic anthems she spoke and sang in the moments before she was taken away. But in the course of the film the marker for whether or not she will be swayed becomes almost exclusively whether or not she will succumb to Nazi sexual immorality.[55] In other words, race and gender are volatilized by sexuality in a way that foregrounds gender and effaces race in the Amercian nationalist version of democracy.

The next time we see Anna she is working on the staff of a labor service camp, a job secured for her by Karl. Contrary to actual Nazi practice, the film blends this camp with a mother and child home. While both institutions existed under the Nazis, one involved a general one-year work detail that women carried out as a parallel to men's military service and the other was a race-policy-induced, social welfare institution. The film brings them together to imply that German women were literally conscripted to bear illegitimate children. In a pivotal scene, Nichols has arranged for a visit to the camp and asked for Anna to be his guide. The tension in the scene lies in whether Anna may have succumbed to Nazi ideology, signaled by whether she is bothered by the sight of so many unwed mothers untroubled by their condition.

The sequence features a triangular structure in which Anna is torn between Nichols and Karl. She seems to be closer to Karl both in her physical positioning and in the political rhetoric she speaks. Through a series of meaningful hesitations between words and some carefully placed reaction shots, she does, however, indicate that she is bothered by the same central moral objections to illegitimacy and state parenting that Nichols voices. At the beginning of the scene, the audience is meant to fear that she may have lost her (sexual) moral compass, while at the end she again emerges as a spokesperson for democracy. Anna verbally informs Nichols that the mothers, as in the Ziemer book, receive the finest of care, as "nothing is too good for those whose children will belong to the state." Nichols responds indignantly, "Even if they're illegitimate?" thereby implying that in a democratic state the mothers of illegitimate children should *not* be entitled to the finest care. A bit later on, Nichols asks, "Does the state offer them the alternative of a home and a husband?" In response, Anna asks Magda, a pregnant woman, who replies that it is "much nobler" to have a child for the state and the Führer than "having a child just for a home and a husband." In this way, it is once again implied that Nazism discouraged heterosexual marriage, a basic historical untruth.

In the script, as in the book, the replacement of the sentimental nuclear family with state-supported promiscuity is resoundingly brought home by an image of sexual perversion: at the end of her glassy-eyed speech, Magda confesses, while leaning forward suggestively, "Do you know what I am hoping? I hope I shall have much pain when my baby is born." With this, the film cuts to a medium shot of Anna, responding ambivalently, as Magda continues, "I want to feel that I am going through a real ordeal for our Führer."[56] This is the breaking point for Anna, as the statement signals the Nazis' ultimate perversion of maternity, already strained by the apparently outrageous suggestion that children born out of wedlock should be treated well. Under the Nazi system, Magda's speech suggests, childbirth has become an opportunity for the expression of masochistic desire for Hitler.

In the face of this general sexual "immorality," it turns out that Anna has not succumbed. After Nichols leaves, she tells Karl that she hates everything the Nazis stand for, claiming to have put on a show for Nichols in order to prevent him from endangering himself on her behalf. With this repugnant incident, however, she has lost her ability to put on such a show, and she goes on to resist more and more vocally, compelling Karl to go to greater and greater lengths to protect her. Thus, while the scene in the mother and child home in the book serves as an opportunity for Ziemer to display the same kind of moral outrage against illegitimacy and perversion, the film smoothly narrates it by way of a struggle over the political beliefs of an American woman. The Nazis' retaliation against her inability to even feign support for the system of sexual immorality is then likewise sexual in nature: she is threatened with either her own illegitimate pregnancy (brought on by coerced promiscuity) or sterilization.

The threat of sterilization and its projected single alternative under the Nazi system (i.e., illegitimate pregnancy) are the two ultimate political indignities to which the democratic female body can be subjected, since, through the logic of nationalist melodrama, the nation is represented most centrally by way of the woman's role as the bearer of legitimate children. In fact, it is precisely at the moment when the threat that Anna might be sterilized is articulated that Karl shows the first glimmer of dissent from the Nazi order. As he sits side by side with a Nazi colonel and Nichols in an observation balcony overlooking a mass operating room, he is not initially disturbed by the five simultaneous sterilizations being performed below, nor by the colonel's comment that the reasons for sterilization "range from eliminating hereditary color blindness to dangerous political thinking." Nichols is outraged, calls them barbarians, and leaves, at which point the colonel makes explicit to Karl what has already been implied: that he is talking about Anna. Karl, clearly shaken, asks if he can stay, claiming, "I should like to watch a while longer." The shot reverses, once again showing the operating room, now with Karl's face reflected in the glass.

The effect of this is to stage the moral reckoning of Karl through his sense of responsibility for Anna. Karl's hoped-for conversion to a properly moral, love-driven, melodramatic subject is closely aligned with his objection to Anna's potential sterilization, which further translates into a potential for American, democratic, anti-Nazism. Rhetorically, Anna's ongoing ability to reproduce is crucial to the logic for which she was the spokesperson earlier in the film: the pledge that "this nation should have a new birth of freedom." While Karl is not yet completely won over to the American democratic side, his hesitation reads as a sign of political hope.[57]

Sterilization was in fact not the cut and dried issue in American political rhetoric that it would appear to be here, as sterilization of the criminalized, the mentally ill, and the "feebleminded" was carried out under official decree in many U.S. states with broad political support.[58] Poor and Black women were most often sterilized, exposing again the more specific class and racial focus of nationalist melodrama.[59] It is the threatened sterilization of a white middle-class woman that is so outrageous and antidemocratic, belying the use of the practice on poor and Black women on American soil. *Hitler's Children*'s moral trigger is thus not the practice of sterilization per se but the specter of the sterilization of a woman who is white and middle class, espouses the dominant views of democracy, and has come to represent the nation. This is nationalist melodrama at its contradiction-suppressing best.

In the B movie, however, exploitation and melodrama are perhaps closer than in the A movie melodrama, enough so that the melodramatic convention of making the threat to an innocent girl stand in for a threat to the nation lapses into the more overt deployment of this threat for the purposes of sexual titillation. The review of the film in the *New York Times* points to this dynamic when Crowther, always politically astute, writes, "Bonita Granville performs through the picture in a state of defiant outrage as the girl for whom the threat of sterilization is rather luridly described."[60] Recalling the *Variety* account of the "wise" deflection of large-scale Nazi barbarities onto Anna's flogging and the threat of sterilization, the film's luridness highlights the way in which promiscuity, perversion, and sterilization are companion threats/incitements to democracy's soul and body—narrated through the specter of defiling Anna through either preventing her from bearing children or, as a correlate, forcing her to do so out of wedlock, as the next scene of the film goes on to show.

For the Love of Democracy: The Romance of romance

At the end of the scene just described, Karl's contemplation of Anna's potential sterilization cuts directly to a long shot of a dance at the labor service camp where Anna is now confined (and where she previously held a staff position). The voluntary nature of the camp, which Anna previously championed to Nichols, is revealed, like her feigned commitment to the Nazis, to be a lie. The scene begins with Anna refusing offers to dance with various ss men, a scenario that is immediately legible through Anna's earlier explanation that in this camp "recreation is limited to a Saturday night dance. There lovers may meet and decide to share the experience that makes them worthy of the Führer." Anna's refusal to dance, her subsequent coercion at the direction of a woman leader, and her slapping of an ss man who tries to kiss her, are thus interpreted as resistance to fascism and hence are emblematic of democratic feminine virtue. While there will soon be a montage of shots of Anna speaking passionately to small assemblies of young women, the content of her words is never heard. It is again her refusal to be promiscuous more than anything else that constitutes the "dangerous political thinking" for which she might be sterilized.

The story thenceforth shifts from a primary focus on Anna (who's democratic essence is now secure) to a central focus on the couple in a series of moves that dramatize Karl's conversion from Nazism to liberal democracy. Karl intervenes at this moment, conflating the classic patriarchal gesture of protecting his lover's virtue with political subversion in his tacit support of Anna's democratically inflected abstinence. Again, his willingness to protect her signals the potential for a political change of heart. He warns Anna that if she does not begin to comply she will be sterilized. Their dialogue illustrates, however, what is still a political and moral contrast between them as well as the role love and marriage will play in redeeming Karl. Anna responds to Karl's news firmly, claiming that she would rather choose sterilization than illegitimacy, saying, "No, Karl. Even that holds no terror for me now. If it's a choice between having a baby from a boy from the camp down the road . . ." at which point she breaks off and Karl exclaims, "My darling Anna!" as they embrace. They profess love to one another in the interchange that follows, once again invoking Geothe, with love serving as a direct counterpoint to the hideous specter of mating with "the boy from the camp down the road" (fig. 4).

As Anna considers her fertility put to the service of the Nazi regime, she envisions her sterilization as depriving the Nazis of a child, having already considered her body as not her own but rather an arena for political struggle. Karl tries to persuade her to instead have a baby by him, since, he illogically argues, the state wouldn't inquire who the father is. The logical convolutions of this argument try to assert the unacceptableness of this second alternative as well since Karl does not offer to marry her. Anna's subsequent objection finally makes clear that there is but one democratically acceptable childbearing situation: the romantically based, heterosexual marriage. The stretched logic of the dialogue reveals one of the ways in which *Hitler's Children* expresses internal contradiction rather than merely performing the function of nationalist consolidation. In the final outcome, however, sexuality becomes the exclusive marker of political rightness, as democracy is coded in highly privatized terms.

A second logically shaky exchange occurs following Anna's categorical refusal of Karl's proposition. Karl claims that "each generation must look out for themselves," a statement that is meant to suggest that Nazi parents no longer have responsibility for their children since the state has taken over their tasks. The statement actually runs counter to the communitarian Nazi rhetoric of the Volk, wherein every generation is precisely responsible for the next (and the next and the next) until the vision of the Thousand Year Reich and "racial purity" are achieved. *Hitler's Children* suppresses this racial logic in order to characterize Nazi family policy as requiring the abandonment of children to the state so that Anna can posit family tradition and a genealogical model of patriarchal progress as the democratic alternative. She exclaims, "If our fathers and their fathers before them hadn't all hoped a little, dreamed a little, and worked for the ones that came after them, why we'd still be a pack of savages. That's the kind of world you're working for, Karl. That's the world I won't bring a baby into. I won't give in to them. Then my son and his son won't either. I won't Karl! I won't!" Fathers passing their social achievements down to sons appears to be contrary to fascism, again substituting the private sphere for public political engagement. The speech on one level contradicts earlier scenes that visually posit an opposition between American individualism and Nazi collectivity, where the boys and girls of the American school run freely around the playground while the boys at the male-only Nazi school march together in step. Both versions of the difference between Nazism and democracy, however, revolve around the same distinction. American individualism and patriarchal families are both emblems of the private sphere that liberal democracy (and capitalism) are defined by in the film's logic, while Nazi collectivity and its purported substitution of the state for the patriarchal family are the public alternatives that threaten this privatized vision of "democracy."

Anna's speech also contradicts earlier premises of gender equality presented in the narrative, where American women are encouraged to pursue academics and professions while German women are barely schooled. These distinctions ironically disappear in the course of the film, as American women's ambitions are subsumed under the equation of freedom and family. The contradiction bears out the problem of female autonomy that *Hitler's Children* does not want to overstate, even in the name of democracy. That this antinomy breaks down in this climactic scene is telling. Anna is willing to relinquish her reproductive capacity in protest to a Nazi system that has reduced her to that, but she does so by way of reinscribing herself as the mother of sons and the daughter of a father rather than as an autonomous woman. Here we find a perfect example of the slippery manner in which antifascist Christian moralism can retain a positioning of women as mothers (i.e., within a nuclear family sanctioned by the church and the democratic state) while denouncing the reduction of women to their reproductive function within fascism (i.e., where reproduction outside the nuclear family is condoned and children are wards of the fascist state). Freedom *from* promiscuity and perversion and freedom *to* love and marry become tantamount to respect for political freedom and love of one's country.

This is where, in the spirit of the merger of romance with the national Romance, Goethe is once again enlisted to act as the glue that binds democracy and heterosexual, marriage-bound love. The lines of the poem are repeated at precisely those moments when love and political freedom collide and ultimately combine. The poem initiates Karl and Anna's attraction to one another when they are adolescents and then signals Karl's partial conversion to love-driven resistance to fascist policy in his rescue of Anna from forced promiscuity at the dance. The third exchange of the poem further charts Karl's progress, as they embrace after he has intervened in Anna's flogging. The last exchange of the poem occurs during Karl's final renunciation of Nazism over a live radio broadcast. The camera shuttles between Anna and Karl as he makes his fatal, heroic speech, and she realizes that he has finally declared his love for both her and democracy. Karl is killed shortly after he finishes reciting the poem and falls forward. Anna calls out his name (offscreen), and she, too, is shot. As she falls onto Karl, they build the culminating shot: Anna and Karl, hand in hand in the face of their heroic deaths. The tragic ending thus hopes to channel the emotions it arouses into the national cause.

Conclusion

This substitution of romance for Romance is certainly not the only way Hollywood approached the topics of family, sexuality, and politics during the war. Examples from a variety of genres, including melodrama, did not employ this rhetorical move. Even Walt Disney's 1943 cartoon version of Ziemer's book, which shares its title, "Education for Death," presents another variant of nationalist melodrama, which, while still socially conservative, does not foreground sexuality. The "special cartoon" makes reference to the Dmytryk film in the opening title card, which proclaims that this will be "the story of one of 'Hitler's Children' " and proceeds to use a German child, Hans, as an example of how Germany's women and children are being victimized by the Nazi regime. Due to the conventions of Disney animations, Hans is most sympathetic when he is a saucer-eyed young weakling threatened by the mighty Nazis. The cartoon narrates the tragedy of his molding into an ironclad fighting soldier. This convention produces a potentially interesting subversion of the ideal of masculine strength, which most American wartime films were not willing to compromise, though overall the melodramatic formula continued to narrate fascism as a threat to the private sphere/family.[61]

Some wartime Hollywood melodramas did not invoke the family in this manner. The "prematurely" antifascist Frank Borzhage film *The Mortal Storm* (1940), for instance, also revolves around a family being torn apart by Nazism, but it remains focused on issues of racism and freedom of speech and thought. New alliances are formed in this film on the basis of political sympathies both within and outside of the family rather than insisting on either elevating the family above political issues or equating it with democratic freedoms. Other genres, most notably thrillers and romantic comedies, sometimes even specifically addressed the contradictions within nationalist melodrama, with thrillers exploiting the expectation of familial trust, which turns out to be misplaced, and romantic comedies playing these expectations for parody and humor. Orson Welles's immediate postwar film *The Stranger* (1946) even opens up the possibility that the American family might *harbor* war criminals and Nazi sympathizers instead of standing for democracy. *Once upon a Honeymoon* (1942) requires Ginger Rogers to recognize her husband as a Nazi informant. And Preston Sturges's comedy *Miracle of Morgan's Creek* (1944) specifically lampoons the effort to make the family bear the burden of so much national symbolic sentiment. In contrast to *Hitler's Children*, these Hollywood films either posit a public sphere wherein politics can be debated or question the substitution of the private sphere for this sort of political discussion.

By way of presenting an alternative American anti-Nazi rhetoric, Sturges's film deserves a closer look. *Miracle of Morgan's Creek* revolves around a good-time girl who gets drunk one night and marries a GI about to leave for the war—only she barely remembers him and the "wedding night" that evidently followed. Unfortunately, she finds herself pregnant and needs to confirm that she's married in order to avoid scandal. She enlists the local dweeb (who's got a nervous condition that keeps him out of the army) to pretend to be the foggily remembered GI, "Ratsky Watsky," so that she can quickly restage her marriage and this time have a certificate to prove it. The plan goes awry, and he ends up in jail, while she gives birth to sextuplets. The montage that follows hilariously depicts the news of these births as a national and military triumph, with each of the Axis powers responding in fury at being so trumped by the reproductive profligacy of an American woman. The national spectacle requires that the governor step in to "fix" all the moral loose ends that might not fit the narrative situation to the conventional norms of national imagery: the first foggy marriage is annulled, the second made retroactive, and the previously rejected stooge becomes a decorated officer.

The sequence both criticizes the fascist governments and their population policies and ridicules American attempts to claim the births as an occasion for national pride. The obvious falseness of the accoutrements of respectability that are arranged for the couple all contribute to a farcical critique of "family values" as representative of American democracy. In this way, the efforts of nationalist melodrama to meld sexual morals with both nationalism and democracy are revealed to be entirely fictional, requiring fantastic efforts to cover up the actually more loose and pleasure-loving spirit that sent Ratsky Watsky off to war.[62] Irreverence is, of course, the source of political comedy's power, and contradiction is its fodder. Nationalist melodrama, on the other hand, tries to cover up these contradictions, scripting them into a privatizing logic that tries to suppress the ambivalence the genre more generally stakes as its narrative ground. Ultimately, *The Miracle of Morgan's Creek* critically exposes the political falseness of a rhetoric that would try to equate democracy with sexual propriety and reveals the elaborate forms of specifically political intervention required to produce such a "nonpolitical political" private sphere.

Since the end of the war, there have been innumerable films, books, works of scholarship, and journalistic articles dedicated to depicting, analyzing, or appropriating the confrontation with fascism for the present. Some recent films with melodramatic components, like Italian comic/director Roberto Benigni's 1998 hit *Life Is Beautiful*, continue to set up the family against fascism. This film, however, doesn't waver from its focus on Nazi racism and brutality, nor does it set up the family as the exclusive realm of political resistance. Polish director Agnieszka Holland's *Europa, Europa* (1991) is even able to script the Nazi threat to a young Jewish man by way of sexuality (a fear of exposing his circumcised penis) without resorting to the simple, fictional, moral coding typically found in socially conservative nationalist melodrama.[63]

In the arena of contemporary conservative political rhetoric, however, nationalist melodrama of the sort depicted in *Hitler's Children* continues to be pervasive: in fact, the genre lies at the very core of contemporary American deployments of the term *family values*. In recent conservative videotapes produced not to entertain but to indoctrinate, the genre's conventions are once again employed in an effort to mobilize the equation of the private domain of the family with democracy, and its "violation" with fascism, and to foreground sexuality as a primary marker of "democratic" politics. It is because of this prominent right-wing strategy that the rhetorical practices of wartime nationalist melodrama remain not only relevant today but vital to understanding contemporary American political culture.

3

"Family Values" and Naziana in

Contemporary Right-Wing Media

■

Republicans believe that as the family goes, so goes the nation. Strong families and strong communities make a strong America. We don't need a government-run health care system with costly new entitlement programs. Instead, we need to facilitate efforts to keep families intact.—*Contract With America* (1994)[1]

Hitler's Children Revisited

In contemporary political rhetoric addressing American domestic issues, nationalist melodrama continues to give narrative form to conservative social agendas. The excerpt above, taken from the Republican Party's 1994 policy statement, clearly continues to align the family with the nation. As the authors write, in classic melodramatic form, "Today it seems the values of the family are under attack from all sides—from the media, from the education establishment, from big government. . . . After forty years of putting government first, Republicans will put families first."[2] Most of the issues put forth in the *Contract With America* are indeed cast in this form. The document claims that illegitimate births, for instance, are "ripping apart our nation's social fabric," and its authors vow to make their reduction a national priority, just as they further vow to strengthen parental control over children by allowing parents "to protect their children against education programs that undermine the values taught in the home."[3]

These uses of nationalist melodrama, I will argue, draw on the variants of the genre forged to combat Nazism in the course of World War II. Though not evident in this particular document, anti-Nazi melodrama is often *explicitly* invoked by conservatives who wish to malign liberal social policies. According to a formula very similar to the one implemented in the course of the war, fascism here equals the "big" federal government that Democrats purportedly desire, which encourages "perversion" through the support of gay and lesbian rights and persecutes innocents through legal abortion. Democracy is once again charged, first and foremost, with defending the narrowly defined family.

In this chapter, I will analyze three videotapes produced by socially conservative political groups and explicate their use of the metaphor of Nazism. As in the previous chapter, this analysis will illustrate how conservative American rhetoric continues to equate political participation with private acts of sexual morality, with nationalist melodrama as its primary narrative mode. The centrality of this mode reflects the "privatization of citizenship" bemoaned by Lauren Berlant, the consequences of which include the impeachment of the president for sexual impropriety in 1999 and acts of domestic terrorism like that which destroyed the federal building in Oklahoma City in 1995. The former proceedings enact a melodrama wherein the family/nation is wrecked from within; by equating the first family with the nation, the wayward husband/president becomes the villain who is out to ruin it.[4] The latter act represents the twisted outcome of the actions of a man who cast himself at the center of a melodrama, a "little guy" squashed by the iron fist of big government who saw himself as valiantly retaliating against a threatening political evil.

The shift to domestic enemies does not mean that foreign enemies are no longer subjected to similar sorts of moral coding: Iraqi and Serbian leaders Saddam Hussein and Slobodan Milosevic have both been compared to Hitler repeatedly in the American media. But the threat they pose is most often drawn by way of their imperialism, their megalomania, and their intolerance of difference. In short, it is less of a melodramatic invocation of Nazism than the much more common use of this rhetoric as it is addressed to domestic policy. Some of this turn to domestic affairs follows from the post–World War II Red Scare, which also focused on domestic/internal enemies rather than foreigners. Some has to do with the application of psychological theories of fascism to postwar domestic problems like racism and poverty, which I will discuss at length in part two. New social movements that have emerged in opposition to these normative notions of citizenship—the civil rights movement, the women's movement, and the gay rights movement, for instance—in turn inspired reactionary social movements prone to invoking nationalist melodrama against them, making social change the internal enemy. By the 1980s, the "Moral Majority" had broadly targeted secular humanism as the primary internal threat. In this way, contemporary nationalist melodrama typically casts progressive politics as conspiring to destroy the fabric of the nation through its influence in the public schools, movies, publishers, academia, courts, and finally government.

The three liberal agendas that have attracted the most accusations of Nazism by social conservatives are abortion rights, gay and lesbian rights, and gun control. Within the political movements opposed to each of these agendas, a series of catchphrases and neologisms have crystallized the practice: feminazis, pink swastikas, and the jackbooted storm troopers of the Bureau of Alcohol, Tobacco, and Firearms (BATF). Three videotapes produced by proponents of these views exemplify the narrative process. *Who Lives? Who Dies? Who Cares?* produced by Coral Ridge Ministries, extends the antiabortion cry of "feminazi!" to the now defunct Clinton Health Security Plan. *"Gay Rights": Private Lives and Public Policy*, also a Coral Ridge production, joins the infamous *Gay Agenda* tape of the Antelope Valley Springs of Life Ministry in charging that the gay and lesbian rights movement is akin to Nazi imperialism. And *Waco II, the Big Lie Continues*, by Linda Thompson and the American Justice Federation, equates federal agencies' 1993 siege at the Mt. Carmel compound in Waco, Texas, with the Holocaust. Analyzing these three examples of rightist anti-Nazi video rhetoric will provide some insight into the historical processes that have made what might seem like rhetorical acrobatics possible. For, however preposterous the newly coined slogans of "feminazi," "pink swastikas," and "jackbooted thugs of the BATF" might sound to the more liberally inclined, they are products of the rhetorical legacy whereby the flexibility offered by socially conservative, wartime anti-Nazi propaganda made gender, sexuality, and the family the centerpieces of highly charged contests over how the United States could distinguish itself from Nazi Germany.

Berlant casts many of these contemporary political struggles as drawing their rhetorical power precisely from the ways in which politics is understood, in the context of privatized citizenship, in *intimate* terms. She writes that "across the globe challenges to the public/private taxonomy from feminist, antihomophobic, antiracist, and antipoverty movements have been experienced as an eruption of the most sacred and rational forms of intimate intelligibility, a canceling out of individual and collective destinies, an impediment to narrativity and the future itself."[5] Since the conflict between fascism and democracy was also largely understood in terms of a violation of the public/private balance of liberal democracy, it follows that progressive social movements that critique normative versions of this political division would fit into a similar rhetorical mold.

Historian Stephanie Coonz asserts that efforts to politically center personal and familial morals reflect the "idealization of private life," which she sees as characterizing the late twentieth century, a historical tendency parallel to that of the late nineteenth century. Coonz sees this idealization as a consequence, in both eras, of "reckless self-seeking and conspicuous consumption among the rich, growing insecurity for workers, and a middle-class retreat from previous engagement in social reform."[6] But, as cultural critic Linda Kintz notes, Christian fundamentalists claim that it is "the traditional family, not the individual, which is the core unit that must be protected by the Constitution," and so they feel justified in denying the constitutional rights of gays and lesbians while antifeminist activist George Gilder claims that "All politics is on one level sexual politics" and "the sexual constitution may be even more important to the social order than preservation of the legal constitution."[7] These logics do not reflect a *retreat* into private life; instead, they represent a forceful negation of the public sphere through the substitution of the private. Nationalist melodrama, then, narrates this substitution through the genre's conventions of equating family with the nation and sexual conduct with political activity.

"Totalitarianism," the Collapse of the Left and Right, and Nationalist Melodrama

An emphasis on sexual morality and family life does not deflect attention away from the "real" political issues at hand. Rather, family is a political issue in itself, inspired by varying motives. An analysis of the figure of German fascism as a staple of nationalist melodrama with a traceable rhetorical history helps expose the larger rhetorical processes of contemporary American domestic politics.

The Nuremberg trials of 1945–46 juridically dramatized the Nazis' political crimes—especially "crimes against humanity," which in its very phrasing hoped to assert that what the Nazis had done was an affront to humanity itself. Hence, in the search for explanations and root causes for what had happened in Germany, sexuality and family life played a central postwar role, in part due to the ascendancy of psychology as a field of wartime expertise and in part due to the continued conservative conviction that Nazism represented a radical departure from traditional human social formations and values. The latter especially continued to allow Christianity and patriarchal family structures to be posited as antidotes to Nazi social radicalism, often downplaying the role of racism, antifeminism, and sexual repression in Nazi policies.

The consolidation of the conservative image of American democracy as grounded on strict gender roles and monogamous reproductive heterosexuality after 1945 involved the merging of Nazism with Soviet Communism under the common label of "totalitarianism."[8] Coined in the 1930s and reinforced by the Nazi-Soviet Pact of 1939, the term drew together elements of Stalinism (which stood in for all communisms) and Nazism, and directly opposed them to the concept of democracy. The melodramatic themes of the destruction of the family and the church continued to be dominant focal points, fanned by the flames of perceived trouble in the American family itself. Fear of internal infiltration and weakness extended the power of this conservative image of American democracy to the policing of American families (especially mothers) through the boom advice fields of child psychology and home economics, the purging of homosexuals from government offices, and the persecution of America's domestic critics on the Left. What was "un-American" to social conservatives in the 1950s thus bore considerable resemblance to the selective image of fascism in the 1940s: too-powerful women, anti-Christian socialists, queers, and civil rights activists were seen to threaten the American way of life from within.[9] These villains, according to nationalist melodrama's conventions, assailed "democratic" national subjects: churchgoing, white, heterosexual people organized into traditionally gendered nuclear families.

Anticommunist rhetoric in the postwar period actively sought to extend the equation of Christian morality and traditional families with democracy by claiming that communism's antireligious, anticapitalist policies were a scheme to abolish the family and destroy the morals of young people. Popular preachers like Billy Graham made anticommunism a regular part of their sermons, warning that communist infiltration was making America vulnerable to Satan, with bold equations claiming that communism was "anti-God, anti-Christ, and anti-American."[10] Free enterprise and an opposition to labor organizing were also promoted by these preachers, not the least because they often received financial support from prominent businessmen who liked their socially conservative messages. While some of the most conservative of these rhetoricians were actually pro-Nazi during World War II—frequently mobilizing anti-Semitism in the service of an overarching anticommunism—the more mainstream variant of this rhetoric, like Graham's, actually saw Nazism and communism as of a piece, with little to distinguish them.[11]

There are, of course, some significant distinctions between the rhetorical image of fascism and that of communism, the most prominent for my purposes being that fascism has been more elaborately psychologized and sexualized and hence inextricably linked to debates about gender and the family. Some of this has to do with the efforts of leftist critics and theorists, who were among the most prolific and insightful in their examination of fascism and had a deep investment in psychoanalysis. These critics did not turn the same critical eye on Soviet Communism, and so no comparable set of theories emerged to psychologize and sexualize communism. In addition to this, the most pervasive anti-Communist popular images of the Soviet Union made much of its presumed lack of humor, its sexlessness, and its absence of pleasure. The suppression of consumerism and a perception that the gender equality Communism encouraged masculinized women and reduced passion between the sexes produced images of a drab and loveless existence. Significantly, however, the distinctions between the highly sexualized Nazis and the often desexualized Soviets breaks down when anticommunism is brought to domestic terrain in the United States.

Early-twentieth-century Red Scare rhetoric had already established a legacy whereby communist anti-Christianity and the association of some American leftists with the "free love" movement linked communism to sexual immorality. Some of the rhetoric around the perception that Hollywood was wholly infiltrated by communists—and run by Jews—illustrates another variant of a kind of anti-Semitism/anticommunism that links Jews/Communists with sexual debauchery.[12] This rhetoric was particularly flagrant in the 1930s and became less common as Nazi anti-Semitism took on its ever more horrible cast. But in the Cold War period Communism and homosexuality would be conceptually linked as twin dangers to American political/sexual sovereignty.

With the election of John F. Kennedy and the Supreme Court decisions in 1962 and 1963 that declared Christian prayer and Bible study in public schools to be in violation of the constitutional tenet of the separation of church and state, conservative anticommunists charged that Communist influences in mainstream liberal government were undermining democracy, Christianity, and hence the morals of youth. Clashes over sex education in public schools also often cast sex educators as communist infiltrators intent on destroying the morals of America, which, in the minds of conservatives, was a precursor to making America susceptible to totalitarianism.[13] The entanglement of these themes with conservative white Christian opposition to the civil rights movement likewise resulted in progressive black church leaders (and indeed progressive churches in general) sometimes being accused of being communist as well. The right-wing organizing forces that began to coalesce around the association of the American federal government with what they saw as anti-Christian, morally decadent politics expanded as the 1960s wore on. On the whole, domestic communism was much more often associated with sexual license by conservatives than were their images of the Soviet Union. Nazism certainly faded into the rhetorical background in the face of the "Red Menace" of the Cold War, but the conventions of nationalist melodrama that World War II codified were easily extended by way of the concept of totalitarianism.

Fascism reemerged as a concept with the rise of the New Left in the 1960s. Leftists and liberal progressives rejected the concept of totalitarianism precisely because of the easy collapse of Nazism into leftist politics that had allowed American right-wing politics to be aligned with democracy in the name of anticommunism. By insisting on the specificity of fascism, New Leftists hoped to reclaim true democracy for the Left by drawing parallels between Nazi Germany and both American racial prejudice and the suppression of political freedoms. Feminists extended the parallels to misogyny and sexism and sexual liberationists to fascism's sexual conservatism. Frankfurt School political theorist Herbert Marcuse, who had helped coin the concept of totalitarianism in the 1930s, wrote in the 1950s that sexual repression was a characteristic of fascism and sexual liberation its antidote. Marcuse writes that with the concept of perversion "The same taboo is placed on instinctual manifestations incompatible with civilization and on those incompatible with repressive civilization, especially with monogamic genital supremacy." He proceeds to draw a crucial distinction between destructive forms of perversion (that of ss troops, for instance) and benign forms that may be expressed in "forms compatible with normality in high civilization."[14] This way of thinking about sexual politics gained particular prominence in the late 1960s and 1970s, when a postwar generation that had been raised to believe that Christian sexual conservatism was antitotalitarian rejected this characterization for its opposite. In combination, sexual liberation and the use of fascism as an epithet directed at social conservatives stoked the ire of the New Right, which formed in opposition to these developments. It would soon, in turn, redirect the Nazi epithet back to the Left itself.

Recalling the epigraph by Michel Foucault at the head of the introduction to this book, the accusation of fascism became so widespread that many leftists, and especially historians of the Holocaust, worried about and objected to the dilution of the concept. I will pursue the ongoing influence of this significant shift in the use of fascism for the cultural rhetoric of democracy in part three of this book. For now, my focus turns to conservative uses of the charge of Nazism.

The Rise of the New Right and Its Deployment of the Accusation of Nazism

A turning point in melodramatic narratives of the nation came with the 1976 election of Jimmy Carter to the United States presidency. Carter's campaign hoped to combine invocations of national Christianity with more progressive social politics, but instead his tenure in office proved most formative for the future of a politically active Christian Right. During his campaign, Carter spoke of the American family as being in trouble, citing rising divorce rates, increases in unwed motherhood, and a rise in the rates of juvenile crime, venereal disease, and alcohol and drug abuse as among the greatest problems facing the nation. To wit, he pledged that "There can be no more urgent priority for the next administration, than to see that any decision our government makes is designed to honor and support and strengthen the American family."[15] This stand, along with his declaration that he was "born again," led many conservative Christians to support his election, only to be dismayed by his much more liberal solutions to social problems.

When the National Women's Conference was held in November of 1977 as part of International Women's Year (funded with federal money), the official statements emerging from the conference were feminist in a broad sense. These included positions conservative Christians found particularly offensive, namely, support of the Equal Rights Amendment (ERA) (which they opposed due to their belief that women were meant to be radically different from, not equal to men); abortion rights; and lesbian rights. Social conservatives opposed to what they perceived to be federally supported positions formed new political organizations and organized a parallel protest event, called the National Pro-family Rally, which explicitly melded antifeminism, antiabortion rights, and antigay sentiments into a nascent use of the term *profamily*. Subsequently, evangelists like Jerry Falwell and James Robison would preach vociferously that the National Women's Conference was "antifamily, anti-God, and anti-America" and that its resolutions read "like a summary of the feminist/humanist movement's grand design for destroying the American family."[16] Carter's more progressive hopes for melodramatic narrative were thus effectively hijacked and dismantled in a rhetorical practice that has persisted ever since.

In the wake of this burgeoning rhetorical shift, Carter announced that there would be a White House Conference on the American Family to take place in 1980. Both conservatives and progressives had ample time to prepare, and the huge rift in public rhetoric that was forming over these explosive issues ensured that the conference would be contentious. Conservatives fought social progressives over the definition of *family*, which social conservatives wanted to strictly limit to people related by blood, adoption, or marriage, pointedly excluding unmarried partners, unwed mothers and their children, and especially gay and lesbian partnerships, all of which they did not want recognized as in any way legitimate. As religious historian William Martin writes, conservative "profamily" participants came to resent the fact that "their own view of the family had been marked as narrow and stultifying, a source of inequality and oppression, rather than being seen as a basic and vital foundation for a moral and democratic society."[17]

Political theorist Ellen Messer-Davidow similarly describes social/cultural conservatives as ascribing to a "functionalist" argument, which claims that the conservation of "traditional Western culture" is necessary in order for democracy to be successful. Ironically, she argues, this claim to tradition is on some level a radical redefinition of political life.[18] Reversing the feminist slogan "the personal is political," which offered up the family for political critique, Berlant sloganizes this strategy as "the political is the personal." Berlant writes, "Reversing the direction of the dictum's critique has resulted in an anti-political nationalist politics of sexuality whose concern is no longer what sex reveals about unethical power but what 'abnormal' sex/reproduction/intimacy forms reveal about threats to the nation proper/the proper nation."[19] She argues for a strong distinction between the feminist credo and its rhetorical reversal—a distinction I am likewise dedicated to reinforcing.

As political rhetoric comes to focus more and more often on sexuality and reproductive rights, nationalist melodrama—which had in World War II been but one form of opposition to fascism among many—runs the risk of becoming the only national narrative. Such an ascendancy circumvents efforts to define democracy in more communitarian ways, with more emphasis on public, civil duties. Contemporary invocations of anti-Nazism in nationalist melodrama deployed against progressive social changes (or hoped-for changes) illustrate this shift most dramatically. In the remainder of this chapter, I examine the three instances of this narrative practice: in antiabortion rhetoric, anti-gay-rights rhetoric, and finally the antigovernment rhetoric of the militia movement.

The Feminazi Reign of Terror

The term *feminazi* arose out of the practice among abortion foes of referring to legal abortion as an American Holocaust. The parallel is drawn metaphorically, eliding the historical evidence that abortion was illegal in Nazi Germany (for "Aryan" women) and in fact punishable by death. To finesse this, the "pro-life" argument often collapses arguments against abortion with arguments against euthanasia, which indeed was practiced by the Nazis.[20] By drawing an equation between the murder of millions of Jews and other "undesirables" and abortions, antiabortion advocates hope to succeed in both granting personhood to embryos and casting feminists and abortion doctors as state-sanctioned murderers. The fetus thus replaces the virgin as the "innocent" who is menaced by villains in the bourgeois tragedy, and nationalist melodrama once again narrates a consolidation of the nation with the family.

The term *feminazi*, of course, also calls on older images of feminists as having a sadistic disregard for human life (as opposed to traditional mothers), a primary investment in their own (often sexual) gratification, and a desire to destroy the American family—images also produced, for instance, by opponents of women's suffrage in the second decade of the twentieth century.[21] Its most prominent logic lies, like these earlier images, in the conventions of nationalist melodrama, in which feminists become the genre's primary villains. There are two rhetorical moves required by this deployment of the genre: to argue that feminists are antifamily and then, by way of the metaphor of Nazism, to reassert that feminism is consequently antidemocratic. A further method of aligning feminists with Nazism, as with lesbians and gay men, is to claim that feminists hope to eradicate the difference between the sexes (echoing the images of Soviet men and women). The supreme historical illogic of this will be taken up later. For now, I will pursue the ways in which this "Nazi" eradication of sexual difference is often deeply entangled in antiabortion rhetoric as part of what makes feminists antifamily and antidemocratic.

In a letter to his followers about the U.N. Fourth World Conference on Women, which was held in Beijing in 1995, James Dobson, leader of the conservative Christian group Focus on the Family, characterized the conference as "the most radical, atheistic and anti-family crusade in the history of the world." The feminists who controlled this conference, he claims, exhibited "enormous hostility to the institution of the family." Twisting quotes from various radical feminist critiques of the patriarchal family, Dobson goes on to claim (in this order) that feminists want to eradicate gender; promote safe sex, reproductive rights, and gay rights; and display hostility toward religion. The jumble of claims is not so much incorrect with regard to at least some feminists as that the language used to convey these agendas is melodramatic, and hence serves a broader agenda, as in Dobson's concluding statement: "Imagine the damage that can be done around the globe if the credibility of this wonderful country, with all its resources and power, is used to undermine the family, promote abortion, teach immoral behavior to teenagers, incite anger and competition between men and women, advocate lesbian and homosexual behavior, and vilify those with sincere religious faith. This is Satan's trump card if I have ever seen it."[22] The fundamental links between family, church, and nation undergird the nationalist melodrama Dobson deploys against feminism. As the Focus on the Family website proclaims of the organization: "We believe that God has ordained three basic institutions—the church, the family and the government—for the benefit of all humankind. . . . The government exists to maintain cultural equilibrium and to provide a framework for social order." The destruction of this social order is what feminists (and sexual minorities) are thought to desire. Beverly LaHaye, founder of the Christian conservative group Concerned Women for America, similarly writes in her 1984 book, "In Brazil, the subversives called themselves

Communists; in America, they may call themselves feminists or humanists. The label makes little difference, because many of them are seeking the destruction of morality and human freedom."[23]

The antecedents for this casting of feminists as totalitarian date back to World War II. The rarity of women in the highest Nazi ranks did not dissuade U.S. wartime and postwar sensational writers and filmmakers from imagining them everywhere and making much of their leadership roles in the upbringing of girls, in women's groups, and especially as concentration camp guards. Their dominion over other women is often inflected with sadism, rightly in the case of guards but also frequently conflated with lesbianism as well, despite the fact that much of the function of women's organizations was to encourage motherhood as a national duty. The convergence of simultaneously developing theories of the workings of dominance and submission in human behavior then found an unsubstantiated but handy echo between lesbianism, sadism, and Nazism. By way of claims that feminists were all "man haters," and hence lesbians, the tangle of associations is solidified.[24] While most feminists would not recognize themselves in these images and would rightfully claim that their efforts have largely been directed toward strengthening human ties and working toward a more equitable and just basis for the formation of families of various sorts, antifeminist rhetoric typically claims that feminism seeks to destroy the family. Since social conservatives typically recognize the patriarchal family as the only form of family worthy of the name, it follows that since feminists seek to rescript gender roles and encourage alternative child-rearing arrangements this could be read as destroying *the* family.

Abortion rights is a key issue in the contemporary characterization of feminism by the Christian Right insofar as the right to a safe abortion changes women's relationship to motherhood. Kintz says, in her study of "the emotions that matter" to the Christian Right, that the two primary concerns of the movement are "the reconstruction of motherhood and the reconstruction of masculinity" and that these "come together in the issue of abortion."[25] She notes that the reconstruction of masculinity requires an image of women that is threatened by their freedom to control their reproductivity—and it is also threatened by lesbianism. As male homosexuality likewise disrupts this project, abortion rights and gay rights "constitute deep symbolic threats to the men and women who live by this world view."[26]

The American Life League's *Pro-Life Activist's Encyclopedia* frequently equates abortion with the Holocaust, and feminists with Nazis, along these lines. Feminists are cast as persecuting the unborn in the same way that Nazis persecuted Jews. The parallel is made most explicit in a chart entitled "Newspeak employed by the Nazis and pro-Abortion Movement" in which direct comparisons are made between Nazi doctors and contemporary American abortion doctors, the mass murder of Jews and abortion, concentration camps and abortion clinics, and German "conscientious objectors" and antiabortion activists.[27] Elsewhere gay men and lesbians are likewise targeted, including the claim that "There are very strong connections between the right-to-die groups, abortion rights organizations, and homosexuals. The sodomites commonly work in abortion mills and often lesbians and homosexuals act as clinic escorts. These are the most unpredictable and violent people of all; they do not tolerate anyone opposing them in any way."[28] The Holocaust parallel on the one hand musters sympathy for the innocent victims of Nazism/abortion, calling for defense of these innocents in melodramatic form; on the other hand, it casts the proponents of abortion rights as fascist.[29]

Indeed, Berlant has noted that "pro-life rhetoric has seen the relation between nature and nation as central to it sacred logics," which she sees as similar rather than opposed, as the Christian Right would have it, to the "conversion of gender to nationality in the conscription of German women to reproduce citizens for the Third Reich." Berlant sees these logics as reflective of what she calls "national sentimentality," where "complex political conditions are reduced or refined into the discourses of dignity and of the authority of feeling."[30] Politically and emotionally powerful images are invoked in order to garner this authority of feeling, as with the common parallels of the antiabortion movement between images of starving children in Ethiopia, African American victims of lynching, Jewish victims of the Nazi Holocaust, and the aborted fetus or embryo.[31] The strong sense of injustice called up with images of victimized children and adults also speaks to an *identification* with them, as both Berlant and Kintz have noted. Thus, feminists and gay rights advocates are threatening to both family and *self*. As Kintz writes, "In an era in which feminists, gays, and lesbians are engaged in the irreversible project of dismantling traditional masculine identity, many men, even those sympathetic to those attempts, may find the experience of uncertain ego boundaries to be very traumatic, and it appears that it is man's increasingly uncertain status that is reflected in the uncertain status of the fetus."[32] Thus, the feminazi is cast as threatening not only to the fetus and the family but to the difference between men and women and hence the self-definition of men. National sentimentality gives political force to these fears, which are then given form through nationalist melodrama.

The Health Security Plan proposed by the Clinton administration in 1992 met its political demise partly through the successful deployment of nationalist melodrama to these ends. The rhetoric around the feminazi and the casting of the fetus as the central character of contemporary nationalist melodrama extended the associations of Nazism to liberal health agendas in general. In uses of nationalist melodrama to defeat these health care agendas, the fetus is joined by the elderly and the handicapped, who together play the role of the threatened innocent in the melodramatic mode.

The Coral Ridge Ministries' videotape *Who Lives? Who Dies? Who Cares?* employs this logic. One of the largest, wealthiest churches in the country, Coral Ridge is led by its founder, Presbyterian minister D. James Kennedy, who was also an original member of the Moral Majority in the 1980s. Kennedy broadcasts a weekly blend of religious and secular sermons on *The Coral Ridge Hour*, which is carried on more than five hundred television stations across the country.[33] *Who Lives? Who Dies? Who Cares?* is hosted by Kennedy and was broadcast repeatedly while the Clinton Health Security Plan was being debated. The rhetorical strategies of the tape include the implication that the Clinton administration's reform plans were both socialist and fascist and hence antidemocratic. The tape is a prime example of national sentimentality and the contemporary use of nationalist melodrama.

Who Lives? Who Dies? Who Cares? features a Christian *Rescue 911* format in which life-threatening scenarios are invariably resolved through divine intervention brought on by prayer. The tape consists of four vignettes, each followed by a minisermon by Kennedy. The first is an abortion vignette in which a young and recent grandmother rejoices in her decision twenty years ago not to have had an abortion. Kennedy follows this by admonishing the "liberal media" for its supposed proabortion-rights bias, asking, "When did you last see an aborted baby on the nightly news? The media certainly doesn't mind showing graphic and bloody pictures of crime victims and the Holocaust, but they know that just one look at the reality of a dismembered child would break the hearts of most women and probably bring an end to this *abortion* holocaust altogether" (his emphasis).

By invoking the familiar trope of the abortion holocaust early in the tape, Kennedy sets in motion the string of associations with Nazi medicine that he rhetorically collapses into the invective of "socialized medicine." The Clinton Health Security Plan subsequently is characterized as providing financial incentives to encourage abortion and the early termination of disabled, terminally ill, and elderly citizens. The already standard practice of referring to legalized abortion as a holocaust (and hence supporters of abortion rights as Nazis) thus prepares the viewer for the further extension of this association to the health plan more generally by way of an invocation of the concept of "lives not worth living" as part and parcel of the "quality of life" doctrine the Clinton plan is seen to endorse. Kennedy thus forges his rhetorical bond between Democrats, Socialism, feminism and Nazism, all seen as conspiring against the weak and powerless, who represent the nation's sacred innocence.

Kennedy does this by setting up an opposition between the "sanctity of life" position (which he characterizes as considering every life precious) and the quality of life position, which he claims amounts to believing that "human life is cheap and disposable." With this definition in place, another vignette follows, wherein the parents of a police officer shot in the line of duty have refused to pull the plug on their son, even when doctors claim that he might be brain damaged (which in the end, of course, he is not). Kennedy asserts the claim that the Clinton plan would deny medical treatment to people deemed not worth rescuing, in effect causing the death of all less than hopeful cases. With heart strings strumming after the story of the paralyzed Christian officer, Kennedy once again slides down the slippery slope of his binary opposition, claiming that the Health Security Plan would deny medical treatment to people like the officer, not just by refusing extravagant life support treatments but by "denying them basic care like food and water to hasten their death." Mental images of starving concentration camp survivors and victims are invoked, retaining the thread from the verbal reference to the abortion Holocaust in the previous segment. Again, using melodramatic conventions and the association of liberal agendas with Nazism, Kennedy attempts to convince his viewers, many of whom are elderly, that democracy is in peril.

What follows is the most didactically direct portion of the tape, that dealing with a summary of complaints against the Health Security Plan. Featuring a series of white, middle-aged men in suits and ties, the tape makes its most "inside the Beltway" pitch against Clinton's proposed reforms. Ed Haislmair of the conservative Heritage Foundation complains of the bureaucracy the plan would build, claiming that it is an elaborate way for the government to increase its control over our lives. Burke Balch, the state legislative director of the antiabortion group National Right to Life, illogically argues that the plan will encourage abortions, as they will be less expensive than family planning measures. And U.S. congressman Christopher Smith (R-N.J.) claims that the plan will allow "abortion on demand at any time during pregnancy" while American taxpayers foot the bill. The tape's early focus on abortion insures the persistent link of antifascist rhetoric to the health plan in general by way of threats of an expanded bureaucracy and increased government control over "our lives." Berlant's "authority of feeling" and Kintz's theory that the fetus stands in for all adult insecurities thus combine, granting the fetus a unifying role as the universal threatened democratic entity, built on these melodramatic conventions.

To cement this move, the next sequence of the tape begins by panning across a series of elderly people in wheelchairs. Syndicated columnist Cal Thomas describes the "short move" from the euthanasia of extreme cases "to the government deciding your life is no longer valuable," which he claims we've already seen "with abortion and increasingly infanticide." The tape shifts from abortion to an exposé of the "involuntary euthanasia" of the elderly in the Netherlands and England, claiming that socialized medicine and doctor-mandated murder go hand in hand.[34] All of the spokesmen in this tape harp on the fears of the elderly that, as in the case of "unwanted" pregnancy, they too might be unwanted. The argument very centrally relies on an equation of "socialized medicine" with Nazi science, and the implication throughout the tape that, like Nazi doctors, doctors in America kill people who wouldn't otherwise die. The antidote to this governmental threat is both Jesus and the traditional family, which, in the classic melodramatic mode, are pictured as standing up to evil doctors and politicians.

By the time the tape proceeds to a second nonabortion vignette, about a child with spina bifida, the audience is primed to feel empathy for the sonogram footage of an embryo presumed to be the child who will eventually sing "Jesus Loves Me" for the TV audience and also to see the threat of her doom as a threat to themselves and the nation. The audience is well prepared to hear another comparison with Nazi medicine spoken by the child's mother, who claims that "our society is getting more and more like what Hitler wanted to do—sifting out all the unwanteds in our society."

The utilization of a melodramatic formula ensures the smooth substitutability of various vulnerable representatives of the iconic family/nation. By replacing the young marriageable woman with the fetus as the central victim to democracy's foes, however, the Christian Right's use of the genre is able to both cast feminist women as national enemies and banish some of the genre's usually characteristic ambivalences, such as those evident in *Hitler's Children* (1942).[35] Bhabha's notion of the pedagogical function of national narratives still works in recent examples to fortify a foundational family unit. The nature of the repeated performances that hope to reiterate this pedagogy, however, have multiplied and at the same time become more narrow. As women are no longer able to bear the symbolic burden of potential victimhood to those who seek to destroy *the* family—since many have learned to speak for themselves—the embryo/fetus, the elderly, the infirm, and the handicapped have taken their place. Political rhetoric, of course, always tries to banish ambivalence, but rarely is it completely successful in doing so. Until these latter populations are able to infuse some ambivalence into their casting, as many progressive disability-rights and elder-rights advocates are trying to do, this new variant of nationalist melodrama will continue to be convincing to people held in its sway.

The Domestic Imperialism of Sexual Minorities

When conservative TV and talk radio personality Rush Limbaugh publicly coined the term *feminazi* in the early 1990s, he made the primary logic of the term relate to pro-choice feminism, but soon it was extended to any woman who holds any sort of political power. He writes, "I often use the term to describe women who are obsessed with perpetuating a modern-day holocaust: abortion. . . . Nothing matters but me, says the feminazi. My concerns prevail over all else."[36] The "intolerance" of opposition to the selfish views of "militant feminists" allows the extension of the term to conservative campaigns against "political correctness." Through the invented dominance of feminists on college campuses and in the Clinton White House, the feminazi is associated with established channels of power, and opponents of feminism become freedom fighters in the face of the totalitarian "thought police," an obviously self-serving move on the part of antifeminist men like Limbaugh.

First Lady Hillary Clinton is often invoked as the ringleader of the current feminazi rule. In one extreme example, the dust jacket of a 1994 book about the political influence of feminazis reads: "They are like [sic] anything the world has ever experienced. They're ruthless, shrewd and calculating—and they've got a stranglehold on the White House. Recruited and empowered by their boss, Hillary, these are the women who tell Bill Clinton what to do. Get ready, America, for the rise of the FemiNazis! *Big Sister is Watching You* unmasks the coven of brutally correct women who now rule over us. Hillary's regiment of hardened, militant feminists include lesbians, sex perverts, child molester advocates, Christian haters and the most doctrinaire of communists. They possess awesome Gestapo powers. One heads the FBI, another the IRS."[37] While this example is considered extreme even among right-wing ideologues, the rhetoric of feminist sexual debauchery is not at all uncommon. In the right-wing rag *American Spectator*, for instance, Hillary Clinton has been variously reported both to have had an affair with Vince Foster (the former Clinton associate who committed suicide in the course of the Whitewater investigation) and to be strictly lesbian.[38] On the one hand, she is projected to embody the heterosexually promiscuous woman and on the other the rejection of men entirely. Both involve an equation of her political and personal strength with sexual "immorality." Despite the fact that Hillary Clinton is a very public wife and mother in the most heterosexually defined public position in the country (that of the first lady), she clearly challenges the pedagogy of *the* national family with which the conservative Right would like the nation to be equated.

Lesbianism is, along with "baby killing," a favorite image of Nazi villains in contemporary nationalist melodrama. This contemporary image of lesbians draws on an iconographic tradition in which, as cultural historian George Mosse has noted, the nineteenth-century equation of respectability with nationalism began to see lesbians as a threat to "women's role as patron saints and mothers of the family and the nation," a threat also embodied in women who have abortions.[39] In keeping with Kintz's observation that the second major motivation of contemporary right-wing politics is the defense of traditional masculinity, the lesbian is joined by gay men (or any other practitioner of sexual variation that doesn't fit the narrow mold). Anti-gay-rights activism has indeed been *the* major fundraising issue for the Christian Right since the early 1990s.[40] In keeping with Berlant's astute reversal that in conservative, and increasingly mainstream, American logic "the political is the personal," sexuality is, as it was in wartime nationalist melodrama, a central marker of political allegiance.

Like New Right movements opposing New Left gains in abortion rights and gun control, the contemporary anti-gay-rights movement was originally organized to oppose the victories of local antidiscrimination ordinances in the late 1970s (e.g., Anita Bryant's antigay crusade in Dade County, Florida, in 1977). The campaigns to repeal these laws, prevent their future passage, and further to expel gays and lesbians from positions of influence (especially over children) relied heavily on charges that homosexuals are child molesters who pose a threat to the family and that gay rights is part of a "national gay conspiracy," all components of the antigay variant of nationalist melodrama.[41] Drawing on the association of Nazism with sexual perversion, which has formed part of the anti-Nazi rhetorical tradition since the 1930s, anti-gay-rights rhetoricians of the 1990s claimed, as the title of chapter 117 of the *Pro-Life Activist's Encyclopedia* proclaims, that "The True Objective of 'Gay Rights' [Is] Total Domination."

Gay rights is a particularly potent issue for "profamily" rhetoricians since conservative Christians, unlike their more spiritually generous liberal religious counterparts, have been completely uncompromising in their opposition to the granting of social legitimacy to gays, lesbians, bisexuals, and transgendered people. Once again, as a matter of foundational logic, homosexuality is deemed inherently antifamily, even when gay and lesbian couples effectively mirror the structures of matrimonial monogamy and love. While usually invoking images of gay male promiscuity as primary evidence that homosexuality in general is contrary to Christian morals and family life, antigay rhetoric has also consistently tried to cast gay families as illegitimate and not subject to constitutional and legal protections. Once again, the melodramatic formula of protecting *the* family frequently invokes Nazism as a rhetorical device to imply that gays and lesbians—and especially the gay rights movement—are both antifamily and antidemocratic.

The Oregon Citizens Alliance (OCA), one of the most vociferous state organizations working against gay rights, exemplifies the dominant strain of social conservative organizing when its statement of principles proclaims that "we affirm that the traditional family unit is the foundation of society. Government policy should be to safeguard the traditional family unit against those forces which tend to undermine it."[42] The OCA opposes welfare, gun control, higher taxes, gay rights, and abortion and supports "traditional family values" and the free enterprise system. Stated in nationalist-melodramatic form, the public sphere of political activity is entirely occupied by the personal and private matters of family life, while the public arena of commerce is treated as a private matter. The group discourages government regulation and intervention in matters of business but encourages it in matters of personal conduct. The original public/private divide of liberal democracy is modified, all the while claiming a foundational logic whereby *the* family is the nation. Rallies in support of the OCA's antigay ballot measures thus prominently include patriotic displays of red, white, and blue and feature the singing of "God Bless America."[43]

The Antelope Valley Springs of Life Ministries, another conservative Christian antigay group, used similar strategies in its more successful campaign to prevent the repeal of the ban on gays in the military in its videotape *The Gay Agenda*. The tape, which was distributed to the Joint Chiefs of Staff as the repeal was being debated in Washington, repeatedly invokes the idea that the gay rights movement is waging "an aggressive offensive at every segment of society."[44] This claim finds ready supporters among "patriots," who likewise claim that the open presence of gays and lesbians would assist in the destruction of the military and hence the surrender of the nation to the "New World Order."[45] Like feminists, gay rights advocates are cast as seeking to disrupt biblical and cultural traditions and are hence akin to both communists and fascists.

Antelope Valley's publication *The Report* (later renamed the *Lambda Report on Homosexuality*) makes explicit its equation of the gay rights movement with Nazi imperialism, even though *The Gay Agenda* does not explicitly make this claim.[46] Antelope Valley indeed displays the more common strategy of saving the most inflammatory rhetoric for in-house publications and toning down that which is meant for wider public consumption. The OCA, on the other hand, did make public use of the Nazi parallel in its voter information materials in support of its antigay ballot measures. The arguments for the 1994 Measure 13 (the OCA's second attempt to limit the way governments and schools address issues relating to gay men and lesbians) were submitted to the voter's guide by a group called the Jews and Friends of Holocaust Victims, but the campaign was paid for by the Stop Special Rights political action committee, which is connected with the OCA. The materials read: "Who's a Nazi? Americans are watching history repeat as homosexuals promote the BIG LIE that everyone who opposes them is harmful to society. It's nothing new. They used this tactic in Germany against the Jews. Yes, some anti-Nazi homosexuals were persecuted by the Nazis, but the persecutors were homosexuals themselves. In fact, Nazism was largely an outgrowth of Germany's gay-rights movement." The argument goes on to provide "evidence" that Nazism was really a homosexual movement. Happily, voters did not respond well to this historical distortion and the ballot measure was defeated.

The strategy of accusing the gay rights movement of Nazism is both an outgrowth of the centrality of nationalist melodrama in narrating conservative American politics and a reaction to the prominent strategy of deploying the pink triangle (the symbol used by the Nazis to mark non-Jewish homosexual inmates in concentration camps) as a symbol of the gay rights movement. Since the advent of the contemporary movement (commonly marked as beginning with the Stonewall Riot in 1969), gay rights activists have embraced the pink triangle as a symbol connecting the Nazis' oppression of gays with current U.S. policy. Gay rights advocates, like other proponents of social movements emerging from the New Left, often invoke anti-Nazi rhetoric to characterize the opposition. Historian Barry Adam writes, for instance, "A new Holocaust now seemed possible to many when, after a tumultuous year and a half, Harvey Milk, the best-known openly gay public official in the United States, was assassinated."[47] The strategy deployed by the Christian Right to counter the pink triangle, then, is a pink swastika, a historically fictional symbol that asserts, as the OCA materials do, that homosexuals masterminded the Nazi movement. The OCA, Colorado for Family Values, Coral Ridge Ministries, and Pat Robertson's 700 Club have all at some point disseminated this theory, with the express aim of thereby associating the gay rights movement in the United States with the persecution of Christians (as above), with the undermining of democracy (by challenging the constitutionality of antigay ballot measures), and, further, with a frightening image of a country ruled by power-hungry, amoral, sadistic pedophiles. The most listened to talk radio personality of 2000, "Dr. Laura" Schlessinger, warns listeners to take action against a militant gay conspiracy, saying "You people have to get off your duffs, or you're going to lose your country to fascism."[48]

As Dr. Laura's statement shows, while the strategy of invoking the Holocaust and Nazism for moral arguments about sexuality is predominantly a conservative Christian strategy, Jewish members of antigay groups and Jewish antigay scholars are also active producers of this rhetoric and as such are often invoked by Christian rhetoricians to lend legitimacy to their claims. Hence, the front organization for the OCA, Jews and Friends of Holocaust Victims, appeared in the voter pamphlet described above. The pamphlet includes a statement by Amy M. Feinberg (OCA member and daughter of a Holocaust survivor), complaining,

"How dare these homosexual political activists compare their selfish agenda with the experience of the Jews. How dare they accuse me, as an OCA member, of being Nazi-like because I refuse to endorse their lifestyle. . . . We should all be alarmed when we see self-defined 'victims' accusing their opponents of doing what they themselves are doing. They accuse others of hatred, with voices full of hate. They accuse others of imposing their will on society, while imposing their own will on society." The first part of the complaint is fair enough, as the rhetorical uses of antifascism for progressive agendas does gloss over significant historical differences. But Feinberg's statement then reverses the logic and prepares for the more overt accusations that centrally characterize the pamphlet: that the American gay rights movement is a Nazi movement.[49] The parallel is established by sentiments more equivocally expressed by Feinberg: that gay rights advocates "hate" their opposition (i.e., hate religion) and that they are imposing their will on others.

Scott Lively, the membership director of the OCA at the time, went on to coauthor a book, *The Pink Swastika: Homosexuality in the Nazi Party*, with Kevin Abrams, who writes for an Orthodox Jewish newspaper, the *Jewish Press*.[50] For Abrams, the antigay crusade is about setting the record straight (literally) on who was victimized by the Holocaust, as it was for Feinberg. Abrams's Jewishness is useful to Lively in that it continues to lend authenticity to the claim that Nazism and homosexuality go hand in hand. Gay rights is then more easily claimed to be antidemocratic.[51]

In a 1994 article entitled "The Other Side of the Pink Triangle," Abrams rehearses the same litany found in the 1994 OCA pamphlet, that "there was far more brutality, rape, torture and murder committed against innocent people *by* Nazi deviants and homosexuals, than there ever was *against* homosexuals."[52] Abrams does not deny that there were homosexuals imprisoned and mistreated by the Nazis, but he claims that these were effeminate, nonpedophilic homosexuals, while the Nazis consisted of butch or "masculo-homosexuals," who were propedophilia. While this dubious distinction might imply a willingness to recognize the role of patriarchy in Nazism, Abrams avoids this and quickly slides into generally characterizing Nazis as homosexuals and claiming that it is this type of homosexual that is behind the gay rights movement in the United States. Of course, the prolific use of images of drag queens in both images of Nazi Germany and in antigay videotapes belies this characterization. There are thus two simultaneous threads in operation, one that stresses the hypermasculine forcefulness of gay rights advocates and one that capitalizes on their symbolic threat to a strictly ordered, gender-dimorphic universe. In other words, like feminazis, the gay rights movement essentially is the forerunner to a neofascist American government because of its dual threat to the family/nation and the symbolic gender order that the family represents. The two threads do not necessarily weave together all the time.

In fact, as with antifeminism, the specter of gender inversion that threatens the conservative pedagogy of family is precisely what trips Abrams up in his futile effort to be considered a respectable historian. Christine L. Mueller, a real professor of history, wrote an article in response to Abrams, refuting his claims in an article entitled "The Other Side of the Pink Triangle: Still a Pink Triangle."[53] She begins with a quote from the leader of the Nazi ss, Heinrich Himmler, noting that he "escalated the war on sexual behavior that did not conform to male heterosexual supremacy, an ideal he linked to winning the world race war of survival," and proceeds with a lengthy point by point dismantling of Abrams's case. While not denying that there were some Nazi homosexuals, she makes the cogent point that Abrams ignores the fact that homosexuals appear in all other walks of life, too. She also notes that much of Abrams's evidence comes from the Nazis' own politicization of the issue of homosexuality—their efforts to blame the party's brutality from 1930 to 1934 on the "homosexual" sa (as opposed to the ss) after the Roehm purge.

Abrams, like many pseudointellectuals of the Right, jumped at the chance to enter into a dialogue with a professional historian, and the *Lambda Report* published the two articles side by side as a "debate."[54] Abrams responds to Mueller's point that he used the Nazis' own words, despite his original argument about "masculo-homosexuals," by sliding illogically into a gender inversion argument, claiming that Mueller is "correct about Hitler being labeled the vain operetta queen in Munich by Goebbels. Vanity, as Ms. Mueller may know, is a negative female characteristic and Hitler's character has often been described as effeminate." Clearly, the statement was also meant as a sexist reproach to Mueller herself. Abrams's fear of homosexual domination (his original finessing of the oppression of effeminate homosexuals by masculo-homosexuals) is here interchangeable with his anxieties about gender inversion and domination by women. Contrary to his statement "The record clearly shows there is no such thing as an irrational fear of homosexuality and its consequences," he clearly fears being "unmanned" by gay men and feminist women as he leaps between characterizations of masculine and feminine men.[55]

The strategy of invoking some variant of the pink swastika argument in the service of nationalist melodrama has become a fairly common practice among members of the Christian Right, sometimes overtly and sometimes in more coded forms.[56] One prominent strategy for coding this message is to visually equate gay rights advocacy with the Nazi movement, rather than to say so as openly as these groups do in the pages of *The Lambda Report* or in their closed door meetings.[57] A common strategy of antigay videotapes meant for wider public persuasion presents decontextualized images of gay and lesbian pride events and footage from political protests, visually connecting sexual "decadence" and the moral and political imperialism of the gay rights movement without actually mentioning the parallel to Nazism. *The Gay Agenda*, as noted above, while it was produced by the same people who published Abrams's pink swastika claims, doesn't explicitly mention the parallel either. Still, as with other tapes produced by the movement, the inflammatory images, scripted in a nationalist melodrama format, are meant to invoke the same emotional association.

As these tapes are made primarily for propaganda purposes, images and passages are repeated within and across the various versions; the same footage of a protest, march, or parade—in fact, the same interview footage with some of the antigay movement's favorite "experts"—turns up in several of them.[58] While *The Gay Agenda* was circulated on Capitol Hill to dissuade legislators from lifting the ban on gays in the military, Coral Ridge Ministries repeatedly broadcast its version, *"Gay Rights": Private Lives and Public Policy*, to its television congregation. Along with much of the footage, the two tapes share the common message that the gay rights movement uses spurious claims to disguise its intention to take over the country.[59]

In keeping with D. James Kennedy's "rational" approach to conservative social values evinced in Coral Ridge's "pro-life" tape, *"Gay Rights"* sets out to refute the common claims of the gay rights movement one by one. The opening sequence of the tape presents an outline of this refutation against a backdrop of images that visually associate gay rights marches and protests with Nazism. The tape begins with footage of the fire setting and window breaking that occurred in pockets of protest in San Francisco when California governor Pete Wilson vetoed Assembly Bill 101 in 1991, a statewide antidiscrimination bill that would have included sexual orientation in its language. The bill is described in the tape as promoting "special minority rights for homosexuals," thereby undermining the legitimacy of the protests and underscoring the rhetorically persistent claim that gay rights agendas are *aggressive* and cunning rather than formulated in defense of civil rights.

The footage, which prominently features burning storefronts and smashed windows, visually evokes Kristallnacht, the infamous night in 1938 when marauding Nazis carried out a "spontaneous" anti-Semitic putsch. This parallel is reinforced when the footage is repeated later in this introductory sequence. The talking head of a woman appears in an inset box over the flaming images as she describes how the protesters "broke our bedroom window." The assumption is that a heterosexual couple was invaded in their family home, evincing a parallel between Jews and heterosexuals and Nazis and homosexuals by way of nationalist melodrama.[60] To further blend gay rights politics and melodramatic villainy, *"Gay Rights"* cuts together footage from the Assembly Bill 101 protests with footage from gay pride parades and the 1993 gay rights march on Washington. The pride parade footage primarily emphasizes the "perversion" and "obscenity" of the parade participants, as nudity and slogans on T-shirts and banners are frequently digitized, indicating that the contents are too obscene for broadcast television. The strategy behind including these shots *as* digitized shots hopes to convince the viewer that gays' efforts to "force the acceptance and approval of their chosen lifestyle" (as the voice-over declares) means condoning lewd and vulgar language and behavior. Thus, the intercutting of these images with the 1993 march and further protest footage establishes, in the first two minutes of the tape, that the gay rights movement consists of the forceful attempt to disseminate perversion as official government policy. At this point Kennedy makes his first appearance, saying "what you've just seen isn't just confined to San Francisco, but is playing out in towns and cities across this nation—and its shaping up as one of the most important moral battles of our time."

Kennedy's battle metaphor is immediately taken up in the next shot, as gay and lesbian marchers chant "We're young, we're queer, we're gonna rule the world!" The obvious camp value of this chant is completely lost on the video makers of Coral Ridge, as the statement "We're gonna rule the world" is clearly taken literally. Over another series of shots of angry protesters and flamboyant gay pride events, a lesbian activist makes the meant-to-be alarming claim that the Clinton administration has opened a "window of opportunity" for gay rights. A gay man then makes the ominous-sounding threat that "if the government does not respond, we are going to *make* the government respond." And finally marchers supporting the rights of gay and lesbian teachers are juxtaposed with a parent saying "This destructive lifestyle is being forced on young minds, and parents are being held hostage." Each time, the forcefulness of gay rights rhetoric and the passionate shouts at demonstrations are translated as assaults on heterosexual Americans, families, and the nation itself.

In this way, peaceful political protest, a mainstay of democratic society, is handily equated with Nazism and efforts to destroy, rather than extend and exercise, democracy. Recall the heading from the *Pro-Life Activist's Encyclopedia*, "The True Objective of 'Gay Rights'—Total Domination!" In a sidebar to the Abrams/Mueller debate, entitled "Gay Naziism Today," the editors write that the connection between gay rights activism and Nazism "should not be surprising, given that some homosexual activists have employed undemocratic tactics that trample on others' freedoms," by which they mean ACT UP's practice of disrupting church services and the like. As with most of the anti-gay-rights rhetoric I've discussed so far, the strategy here is to deploy the rights of the mainstream against the quest for rights by sexual minorities. The former are democratic rights based on tradition, the latter a radical assault thereon, and hence antidemocratic.

Progressives' own overuse of the concept of fascism comes back to haunt them here. When a founder of the Washington, DC, chapter of ACT UP, for instance, wrote in the *Washington Blade*, a gay newspaper, "I have helped create a truly fascist organization that I now believe to be among the greatest threats to our freedom and the healing of our people," the article was subsequently often cited by antigay rhetoricians as concrete evidence of gay fascism, all the more convincing since it issued from the pen of a gay activist himself.[61] In the Coral Ridge tape, literal readings of statements like this connect the chant "We're gonna rule the world" to the mass demonstration footage from the 1993 march. With the Capitol in the background, gay and lesbian marchers evoke the fascist masses, akin to images of the Nuremberg rallies so familiar from Leni Riefenstahl's 1934 film *Triumph of the Will*.[62] As the introductory segment comes to a close, a hoarse-sounding voice shouts "We will not stop until we have achieved OUR freedom, OUR justice, OUR pursuit of happiness!" Laid over more images of burning storefronts, this voice finally evokes Hitler's own memorable oration, an association that is underscored by the eventual unveiling of the speaker as a man at a podium with a mustache—a modern-day Hitler in a pink polo shirt.

By employing a more subtle visual rhetoric within a rhetorical field in which such parallels are already widely established, Coral Ridge aims to manipulate broader public opinion by pretending *not* to resort to historically dubious assertions like the ones that backfired in Oregon. Instead, these less overt uses of the parallel, easily legible to viewers well versed in antigay rhetoric, hope to camouflage some of the extremism often found in less publicly available media products. As a counterstrategy, Parents, Families, and Friends of Lesbians and Gays (PFLAG) subsequently produced a pair of paid television advertisements, which they hoped to air during prime time programming, that featured extreme antigay statements made by televangelists Pat Robertson and Jerry Falwell on Christian television programs. The ads linked these statements with both the high rate of suicide among gay and lesbian teens and the murder of gays and lesbians during hate-inspired gay bashings. Robertson, in footage taken from his *700 Club* broadcasts, says, "Homosexuality is an abomination. Many of those people involved with Adolf Hitler were satanists, many of them were homosexuals. The two things seem to go together." Robertson's Christian Broadcasting Network immediately threatened lawsuits against stations that aired the spots, and they all eventually succumbed. As PFLAG points out in the newspaper ad it subsequently ran in *USA Today*, Robertson apparently doesn't mind saying these things in the course of his own TV show, but he objects when they are broadcast for a general audience and "linked to the climate of intolerance they help create."[63]

In order to illustrate the wider reaches of melodramatic logic, binding together a broad range of conservative agendas, I would like to explicate one final example of conservative thinking: the antigovernment rhetoric of the militia movement. As this example is less explicitly tied to sexuality, it serves to conclude this part of the book by pointing to the general ubiquity of nationalist melodrama and its powerful ability to mobilize sentiment not only against political minorities but against the government itself.

Storm Troopers in Your Living Room

The OCA voters' guide accuses the gay rights movement of perpetrating "the BIG LIE that everyone who opposes them is harmful to society. It's nothing new. They used this tactic in Germany against the Jews." The term *big lie* most often refers to the projection of destructive intentions onto a persecuted group, most commonly the belief in a Jewish conspiracy. Here, the term is appropriated to implicate gay rights activists' use of the accusation of bigotry when it is "really" they who "hate" Christians and want to destroy democracy.

The metaphor of the big lie functions prominently throughout conservative political rhetoric, perhaps most centrally in the anti-federal-government rhetoric of the militia movement. Two videotapes, *Waco: The Big Lie* and *Waco II: The Big Lie Continues*, both produced by the American Justice Federation and directed by Linda Thompson, are about the alleged cover-up of the real motives behind the federal siege of the Branch Davidian compound in Waco, Texas, in 1993. The "Big Lie" this time is supposed to be the government's claim that the Branch Davidians posed a threat (to children, as reports of sexual abuse emerged, and to their neighbors, due to their stockpiling of weapons). The truth, according to these tapes, is that it is in fact the government itself that poses the greatest threat to the well-being of families and neighborhoods. This is the manner in which nationalist melodrama and its common companion, conservative antifascist rhetoric, once again perform in domestic political speech.

The antigovernment rhetoric of the "patriot movement" and citizen's militia groups is frequently crafted from a series of accusations aligning the federal government with Nazism, Soviet Communism, and state-sanctioned criminality.[64] While it is more secondary than the rhetorics surrounding abortion and gay rights, anti-gun-control rhetoric often invokes nationalist melodrama. The logic stems in part from the selective equation of gun control in Nazi Germany and Soviet Russia with gun control in the United States, with the BATF often imaged, in melodramatic form, as violating not just rights but homes. One full-page ad put together by the National Rifle Association (NRA), for instance, features an image of helmeted, faceless, BATF agents, with weapons drawn, under bold capital lettering that reads "Tell the Clinton White House to Stay out of Your House" (fig. 5). Beneath this image is text arguing against President Clinton's proposed crime bill, claiming that "there's good reason to fear that broad new powers under the Clinton Crime Bill could lead ATF to intensify its reign of storm-trooper tactics," thereby implying, in nationalist melodramatic form, that gun control laws are a Nazi-like threat to the sanctity of the American home and family as the symbolic stand-in for the nation.[65]

There are several ways in which nationalist melodrama extends to the rhetoric of the anti-gun-control and militia movements, but the most prominent is by way of the great degree of crossover between the social

TELL THE CLINTON WHITE HOUSE TO STAY OUT OF YOUR HOUSE.

THE BUREAU OF ALCOHOL, TOBACCO AND FIREARMS HAS NOT ONLY LOST PUBLIC TRUST, BUT DESERVES PUBLIC CONTEMPT.

From news media and our 3.5 million members have come reports of ATF abuse that range from intimidation and harassment to confiscation or destruction of property, entrapment, fabrication of criminal charges, even deadly assault.

This threat to civil liberties is compounded by the President's proven willingness to condone warrantless search and seizure, and by the Attorney General's proven willingness to use lethal force against innocents.

Worse yet, there's good reason to fear that broad new powers under the Clinton Crime Bill could lead ATF to intensify its reign of storm-trooper tactics.

The ATF's tyrannical record of misconduct and abuse of power under the Clinton Administration reveals a contempt for civil rights, especially firearm ownership, that should alarm every American.

No freedom-loving person can condone a bureaucracy whose mission is to make gun ownership by

definition a suspicious act, and gun owners by class suspected criminals.

We call upon the Clinton Administration to **1:** regain control of the ATF; **2:** expose and prosecute those guilty of civil rights abuses, and **3:** institute strict policies that honor the Bill of Rights.

If the Clinton Administration does not rein in this rogue agency, then Congress should step in and abolish it altogether.

Only the loud voice of honest citizens separates a free state from a police state.

A PROTEST IN THE SPIRIT OF PATRIOTISM FROM THE MEMBERS OF THE NATIONAL RIFLE ASSOCIATION OF AMERICA.

Fig. 5. Advertisement placed by the National Rifle Association in the *Washington Post*, 1 March 1995

agendas of the Christian Right and militia groups (although not exclusively so). Most "patriot groups" claim to uphold traditional notions of family and liberty against an intrusive and/or destructive government. Women in militias in particular most commonly name their interest in these groups in melodramatic terms. Helen Johnson, who along with her husband leads a patriot group in Columbus, Ohio, says that women who are mothers have a greater sense of urgency about the country's direction. For Johnson, looking out for her children involves distrust of the feds, reverence for the Constitution, and opposition to abortion, gay rights, and feminism.[66] The commonness of this form of argument has led journalists to coin the term *militia mom* for women in the militias, reflecting the role they image for themselves alongside the "militia men" in their own version of nationalist melodrama.[67]

In keeping with this logic, many militias argue a variant of the family values melodrama, as when Samuel Sherwood, an official with the U.S. Militia Association (located in Blackfoot, Idaho), said that during his term in office President Clinton "will have killed more babies than Hitler, put more homosexuals in government than Sodom and Gomorrah, [and] had the schools teach your children [this] is right and forced you to accept it."[68] And Michigan Militia member George Matousek, sponsor of an antigay initiative that failed to qualify as a 1994 state ballot initiative, has said that gays and lesbians are a key element of the New World Order, the alleged conspiracy hatched by international bankers and the United Nations to take over the U.S. government. Matousek says that "The homosexual movement will destroy the military. . . . Soon half the troops will be gone. They don't want to serve next to the queers. And the half that's left will be useless—women and homosexuals, people who can't fight their way out of a paper bag." From this, he concludes that "we'll be doomed. Clinton, or whoever's in office, will turn all our troops over to the United Nations. And this country won't exist anymore."[69]

The feminazi variant of nationalist melodrama is also prominent in militia rhetoric, as when NRA board member Harry Thomas said, "Miss Reno, I say to you: If you send your jackbooted, baby-burning bush-whackers to confiscate my guns, pack them a lunch. It will be a damned long day."[70] Gender inversion often surrounds Clinton's Attorney General Janet Reno in these texts, as in a videotape offered through a catalog published by the Militia of Montana entitled *Janet (Butch) Reno*, which claims that she is a "flaming lesbian."[71]

These images of Reno figure prominently in the more indirect invocations of nationalist melodrama typical of discussions of the militia movement's outrage at federal mismanagement of the gun-control-inspired sieges at Waco in 1993 and Ruby Ridge, Idaho, in 1992. Again, common tactics associated with these two incidents label the federal government as the Nazi-inflected, melodramatic villain. In the Waco incident, the government is cast as having staged an assault on a religious organization (the Branch Davidians), which tragically concluded in the deaths of children. In the Ruby Ridge incident, the government is cast as having staged an assault on a family (the Weavers), resulting in the deaths of Randy Weaver's wife and son. In the latter case, the two Weaver victims are almost always referred to in terms of their familial relationship with the man charged with the violation of gun laws, although Vicki Weaver, like her husband, was an active white separatist. Once again the image of Nazism implies not only excessive force—a justifiable complaint—but the melodramatic argument that the government is anti-Christian and antifamily. While there are certainly significant issues to be dealt with concerning the practices of the BATF, including the fact that government agencies like it have long engaged in illegal and unconstitutional activities directed against U.S. citizens on both the Left and the Right, the accusations of Nazism that invoke nationalist melodrama hope to additionally consolidate support for conservative social agendas about religion and the family that are unrelated to gun control.

Most of the American Justice Federation's 1994 tape *Waco II: The Big Lie Continues* constructs an elaborate conspiratorial argument detailing the many ways in which the federal government has covered up illegal acts committed during the siege at the Davidians' compound, which lasted from February to April 1993.[72] Like the first tape, the sequel most centrally features the close analysis of videotaped news footage shot by various television stations and sometimes SWAT, FBI, and BATF team members themselves.[73] The melodramatic twist to the conspiracy theory the tape espouses most dramatically invokes the threat to home and family in the last few minutes. Featuring footage, pirated from C-SPAN, of its coverage of the dedication of the U.S. Holocaust Memorial Museum in Washington, the ninety-minute catalog of complaints culminates in Thompson's rhetorical comparison of the Clinton administration with the Nazis and the Branch Davidians with Holocaust victims. Over this footage of the dignitaries, officials, prominent anti-Nazi activists, and large crowds of people gathered to hear Clinton's dedication, Thompson draws out her conspiratorialist time line. She says, "Ironically, that night, as Mt. Carmel still smoldered, President Clinton spoke in Washington, DC, at a dedication of the Holocaust Museum, dedicated to the people tortured and murdered by the Nazis in Germany. It is especially ironic that the Branch Davidians were attacked the same day fifty years later that the Nazis had attacked the Warsaw ghetto in Germany [*sic*]. And it was fifty years to the day after the Nazis burned the Warsaw ghetto that Mt. Carmel was burned to the ground." Thompson then lets the audio of Clinton's speech proceed, leaving C-SPAN's superimposed title, "Holocaust Memorial Museum Dedication Ceremony," on the screen to help prolong the rhetorical parallel. Clinton says, "The Holocaust began when the most civilized country of its day unleashed unprecedented acts of cruelty and hatred, abetted by perversions of science, philosophy and law . . . [by] the merciless hordes who themselves were educated, as others who were educated stood by and did nothing. Millions died for who they were, how they worshiped, what they believed, and who they loved." The image of Clinton freezes, and Thompson's voice-over abruptly interrupts, asking, "Was he talking about Nazi Germany? Or was he talking about Waco, Texas, in 1993?" The frozen image of Clinton slowly dissolves into an image of the compound burning; the sound of flames bridges the president's image with Mt. Carmel in flames and extends over the closing credits.

Thompson is surprisingly suggestive here, abandoning her usual exhaustive dogmatism to send the audience home to mull over the exact parallels that she implies. The Justice Department's investigation might be akin to the Nazis' "perversion of science, philosophy, and law." The educated people who "stood by and did nothing" might be those of us who have not done enough about the government's mishandling of the siege. These suggested parallels are fairly straightforward. But the last part of Clinton's speech implies another series of parallel substitutions. Clinton's statement that people were persecuted for "who they were, what they worshiped, what they believed, and who they loved" is capitalized on due to its vagueness, forcing the statement to refer not to gypsies, Jews, Jehovah's Witnesses, socialists, and homosexuals but to Christian families. The "irony" that Thompson hopes the viewer will see is that Clinton, the featured speaker at the Holocaust Memorial Museum ceremony, is the potential leader of this new "Nazi" nation. In an interview she gave to the conservative magazine *Rutherford*, Thompson said that the United States is "virtually in a totalitarian state," which she warns Americans will miss if they focus on the targets of the Nazis instead of their tactics. When asked whether Americans "need to go through a holocaust before something happens," she replied, "I don't think you follow me. We're going through a holocaust now. People are so stupid. They say, 'Oh, it couldn't happen here. They're not going after Jews.' The targets aren't the issue, it's the tactics. Give the public an enemy, and you can pass any fascist legislation that you want. People will turn their heads as they're loaded on the cattle cars and taken off."[74]

While critics on both the Left and Right might agree with Thompson's naming of tactics that brutally suppress opposition as antidemocratic, it is precisely the choice of *targets* that marks their difference. While leftist critics of government approaches to political opposition have focused on such things as the suppression of leftist radicals and disregard for the health of American citizens in nuclear testing, rightist critics focus on the right to bear arms, the perceived persecution of

Christians, and threats to a limited notion of the family. While totalitarianism is envisioned as the goal of every conspiracy (whether the conspiracy theorists are leftists, rightists, or neither), the conspiracy theories of the militias often link their primary concern with gun rights to other rightist agendas like opposition to abortion and gay and lesbian rights.[75] In the broadest sense, the melodramatic mode is invoked in militia rhetoric to place not the fetus, the elderly, or the disabled in the role of nationalist melodrama's threatened innocent (as in antiabortion rhetoric) but rather the white, often working class, heterosexual male, who metonymically stands in for "the family."

Mostly, the antigovernment rhetoric of the militia movement relies on a similar nationalist melodrama, even when the position of the family in this rhetoric is more submerged. The invocation of the parallel of the Clinton administration to Nazism helps expose the weaving together of conservative agendas, however, which this flexible and selective use of history achieves.

Conclusion

Certainly, there are important distinctions to be made between different groups and different agendas. "The Right" does not exist as a unified front, and there is much disagreement between various factions. But they each consistently invoke nationalist melodrama in order to assert the foundationalist view of democracy they share—that is, the idea that democracy rests on the basic foundation of Church and Family. From this foundation, the conventions of nationalist melodrama deployed in the course of World War II cast fascism as fundamentally anti-Christian and antifamily instead of racist and sexist. This wartime practice was resuscitated with the redeployment of the term *fascism* in the political debates of the 1960s as a means of answering the New Left's use of the term to criticize American political and social conservatism.

In the wartime uses of nationalist melodrama, women's sexual and reproductive bodies tended to serve as the terrain over which the forces that threatened the nation were played out. The contradictory place of women in Western political thought—under both fascism and democracy—ensured that these melodramas would betray some level of internal contradiction and ambivalence. In the course of the resuscitation of the conservative anti-Nazi nationalist melodrama in the last thirty years, however, the woman has for the most part been replaced as the key melodramatic figure. Instead, the embryo or fetus, the elderly, the infirm, the physically handicapped, the child, the white working man, or, more abstractly, "the family" and "the church," have taken her place.[76]

This series of substitutions hopes to banish the ambivalence of the figure of woman, most obviously by fortifying the limited definition of the Church/Family foundation. Feminists, therefore, are often cast as the genre's favorite villains, as they represent the component of ambivalence that disrupts the original melodramatic formula. As with many melodramas, contemporary nationalist melodrama tends toward hyperbole in its depiction of villains, be they feminists, queers, or liberal government, hence the use of images of Nazism to characterize these groups. But this use of Nazism in the service of nationalist melodrama also reflects the historical trajectory that shrunk the public sphere and replaced it with highly privatized political conduct, wherein the "nonpolitical political" (family, church) substitutes for all other types of civic responsibility. D. James Kennedy, for instance, argues with his characteristic brand of Christian logic that illicit sex "is not only a sin against God . . . but also has societal effects. Taxpayers pay billions to clean up the consequences of that sin for illegitimate children and AIDS."[77] The "costs" are both material and symbolic. In this way, the long-standing cooperation between conservative social agendas and free enterprise in fact insures, as Coonz has said, that the private sphere—the one that includes family, religion, and economic practice—overtakes any efforts at more communitarian politics.

Direct and indirect associations between liberal agendas and Nazism, making their way back and forth from extremist channels to more mainstream Rightist media and political rhetoric, work to *pull together* many disparate threads of antiliberal sentiment and align them with this highly privatized notion of democracy. The rhetorical power garnered from invoking Nazism as the privileged counterpoint to American democracy is deployed specifically in order to make the melodramatic mode central to nearly every political issue. As the uses of the Nazi trope proliferate, the pedagogical object of this national narrative narrows to a highly circumscribed notion of nation, church, and family. The variations on nationalist melodrama in the various arenas of debate explored above (abortion, health care, gay rights, gun control, and the extent of the powers of government) are thus creative, deceptive, and repetitive performances that endeavor to point to this pedagogical goal.

Berlant suggests that the effect of this sort of persistent narration is to make it difficult to imagine the characteristics of a different story, a move that "effectively siphon[s] off critical thought about the personal and the political," critical thought that would inspire a person to realize that "social forces and problems of living that seem not about the private 'you' are, nonetheless, central to the shape of your story."[78] While the examples I have been exploring in this section represent some of the more extreme efforts to limit the vision of democracy and the type of behaviors it allows, this limited vision is actually pervasive. The practices of the Right are thus instructive of a wider cultural tendency, the contours of which they chalk in bolder lines. The next part of this book, then, explores a more subtle variant of this vision of a limited, private form of democratic and national engagement, still wrought through the family and sexuality but finding its primary form in the psychological case history.

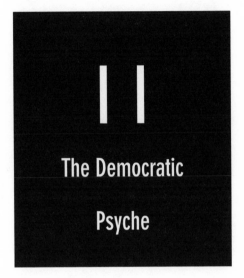

II

The Democratic

Psyche

4

Nazism, Psychology, and

the Making of Democratic Subjects

■

Brutal Nazi excesses against Jews, justified on the basis of a phony racial science, are easily recognizable as a species of sadism. In the same way, Nazi sexual excesses in occupied countries, explained officially in terms of 'Nordic eugenics,' are clearly a species of moral perversion. The story of the Nazi aberration will have to be told, after its final eradication, not only by historians, but by psychiatrists.—George W. Herald, "Sex Is a Nazi Weapon" (1942)[1]

The slender man with thin lips and haunted eyes had the kind of childhood one longs to escape from. His mother left him when he was 10, moving away to Texas and then Flordia. A quiet, scrawny boy, he was picked on by schoolmates who called him 'the Wimp.' His nickname, at his Pendleton, N.Y. high school, was 'Chicken McVeigh.'—"The Plot," *Newsweek* (1995)[2]

In 1991, a mother was photographed in Eisenhuttenstadt, a German town near the Polish border, as she grabbed her skinhead son and dragged him away from the hostel for asylum seekers that he and his friends were attacking with rocks (fig. 6). The image, published in a Berlin daily, called upon classic images of mothers as the moral conscience of the family. A variation on nationalist melodrama, this image hopes to suggest a similar centrality for the family, this time in the service of reining in and guiding the behaviors of politically wayward sons.

Fig. 6. A mother and her skinhead son. (Photo by Hans-Georg Gaul.)

The national narrative behind this image continues to cast the setting for the nation in the family. Instead of a foreign threat, however, the problem has developed *within* the family, which is held to be responsible for the production and maintenance of democratic subjects. Failures to do so invite scrutiny, and the story turns to the process by which this family has produced a fascist. In the image of the mother intervening in her son's behavior lies the hope that, unlike the many other residents of Eisenhuttenstadt, who stood by and watched or cheered, this mother could still exercise her role as guardian of the nation's conscience and morals.

In this case, however, the image of the political mother was only held up as long as she remained an image and did not speak. In an interview with the family conducted by journalists Max Thomas Mehr and Regine Sylvester, the story of the subjects of the photograph that served nationalist melodrama so well took a turn to the second type described above. The mother, it was revealed, did not possess particularly strong convictions about her son's skinhead activities, nor about the rights and plight of the asylum seekers he and his friends had targeted. Instead, she had grabbed her son and dragged him away because he was late coming home. She and her husband were embarrassed by the picture not because their son was caught in a racist act but because it gave the impression that they could not control him.[3]

This revelation is the first narrative turning point in a genre I call national psychobiography: the stone thrower's story becomes a story of how the family contributed to its son's political views rather than serving, as in nationalist melodrama, as the bedrock on which antidemocratic politics is defined. The epigraph drawn from *Newsweek*'s early profile of Timothy McVeigh, who was eventually convicted of the 19 April 1995 bombing of the Murrah Federal Building in Oklahoma City, reflects a similar narrative effort. The explosion, which killed 168 people, focused the nation on the specter of internal political dissidents, inspiring, both in the popular media and in academic circles, impromptu psychobiographies of McVeigh and his political cohort.

The central question these narratives ask is what would drive a red-blooded American man—white, ostensibly heterosexual, and a former soldier—to such a brutal act of treason or more generally to the antigovernment politics that brought him there. One thread, like the Eisenhuttenstadt example from Germany, begins to question family life and formative childhood experiences. A second thread, also focused on personal history, scrutinizes the dissidents' personal failures. The profile of the extremist that emerges almost always marks these men as "losers" of one kind or another, their failures as men serving in popular political psychology as the reason for their hostile politics. Real men, in this version of the story, are democratic, centrist, and loyal to the current system. As the bomber's association with a larger network of similarly disaffected Americans became well known, the model of America's losers quickly expanded to members of the citizen militias across the country—with, of course, loud objections on the part of militia members themselves.

A historical antecedent to these contemporary profiles of politically wayward mothers and sons can be found in Hollywood screenwriter Ben Hecht's original treatment for what became Alfred Hitchcock's *Notorious* (1946), wherein two of the film's main characters, Alexander Sebastian and his mother, are described in detail. Sebastian is described as a "debonair type of a master-race exponent" who "was once a botanist of standing" and "has graduated from these minor accomplishments into a German hero." The description emphasizes that Nazi racism has given the character an overblown sense of superiority built on relatively shaky ground. His mother, an Englishwoman in the treatment (she is German in the film), is "outwardly a more dominant personality than her son. She adores and rules him, possesses him through a fanatical attentiveness, and guides him with a lover's awareness of his weaknesses." Sebastian, for his part, is "gentle and whimsically obedient to her."[4]

These characterizations reflect popular theories of the psychology of the Nazi mind developed by anti-Nazi psychologists in the course of the conflict with fascism: the overgrown ego of the man of "minor accomplishments" and the overbearing mother who treats her son like a lover. Hecht would draw the psychobiography of these characters more starkly in the course of working with Hitchcock in that in the film Sebastian's sense of superiority is subsumed under Madame Sebastian's domination. Sebastian is no longer "whimsically obedient" to his mother, as in the treatment; he either defies her or obeys her, and in the end obedience rules. By the final version of the script, the theory that fascism results from unresolved Oedipal dramas thoroughly governs the logic of the characters' interactions.

These examples mark the terrain that this second part of the book explores: the domestic drama of the (politically) troubled family, the internal drama of the (politically) troubled man, and finally the extension of this narrative of individual turmoil to a larger (politically) disaffected population. These national psychobiographies reflect on the one hand a continuation of the equivalence of family and nation that is central to nationalist melodrama; on the other hand, more recent versions reflect a reversal wherein the nation itself is suspected of having mistreated its wayward sons. I offer the thesis that popular applications of political psychology, originating in the conflict with Nazi Germany, have paved the way for this reversal of accountability.

The declaration in the George Herald epigraph that the "story of the Nazi aberration" will have to be told by psychiatrists appeared in the pages of the popular magazine *American Mercury* in the middle of World War II, indicating the degree to which psychiatry had already been enlisted to explain the political phenomenon of fascism. Indeed, the growth of the professional fields of psychology and psychiatry in the course of the twentieth century indicates the ascendency of a way of thinking about personal, social, and political problems that privileges psychological and interpersonal dynamics. As Ellen Herman writes in her book on the history of this ascendency, "It no longer suffices to think of psychology as merely one category of expertise among others. Psychology in our time is a veritable worldview."[5] Certainly, the story psychiatrists and psychologists told has centrally molded the American understanding of political phenomena: its characters and their motivations centrally inform how political events have been reported, filmed, and otherwise narrated in the postwar era.

Herman's book begins with World War II because, she says, "No event illustrates better how military conflict offered psychologists unprecedented opportunities to demonstrate the practical worth of their social theories, human sciences, and behavioral technologies in making and shaping public policy."[6] Military psychologists aligned the profession with patriotic concerns, leading to a postwar legacy that saw psychology as the privileged mode of knowledge through which we can come to understand national security, domestic conflict, and social welfare. A strong link was thus forged between the concepts of mental health and democracy.[7] National psychobiography is a favorite genre through which to narrate this ubiquitous link.

Much like nationalist melodrama, national psychobiography expresses a desire to align a normative notion of family, gender, and sexuality with a "healthy" democratic psyche but with more willingness to acknowledge the tenuousness of this project (a tenuousness that ensures the job security of psychiatrists). This kind of psychobiography can therefore as easily issue from conservative, liberal, or leftist thinkers, each of whom sees the tenuousness as a cause for alarm. While their solutions vary, these different political orientations have historically shared a surprisingly similar support for a normative social order—at least until the intervention of feminist, postcolonial, and queer theorists. This chapter examines the wartime variant of this story, with particular attention to the gendered expectations for democratic subjectivity that ensued. Hitchcock's *Notorious* will serve as a premiere example of national psychobiography, whereby the normative characteristics of the genre's central characters are defined and given a family history. These characters and their motivations became central to postwar political rhetoric, a legacy still very much at work today.

Profiles in Fascism: Political Psychology in World War II

Some of the melding of social and political anxieties evident in the substitution of normative personal for political actions certainly can be traced through the history of the ascendency of the psychological worldview. Consisting of parallel developments in psychology, sociology, and anthropology, the field of political psychology grew out of nineteenth-century efforts to characterize cultures and subcultures and to explain social behaviors in psychological terms. Sociologist Max Weber's work at the turn of the century, for instance, offered cultural insights into northern and western European culture by way of his analysis of the psychology of Protestantism.[8] Psychoanalyst Sigmund Freud, of course, simultaneously developed his elaborate system of analyzing individual psychology, eventually also turning to group psychology and cultural analysis, in large part by generalizing insights gleaned from individual case histories.[9] Developments in both social psychology and anthropology in the 1920s and 1930s were also influential in the development of the notion that personality and culture were closely interrelated.[10]

With the rise of fascism and the approach of another world war, social analysts, many of whom were émigrés fleeing Nazi persecution themselves, took on the task of characterizing and explaining the motivations of fascists, proposing theories of German (and Japanese) national character and the psychology of Nazi leaders and followers. They scrutinized the processes of socialization in enemy cultures, focusing on how tendencies toward dominance or submission and independence or dependence resulted in a collective personality structure. Based on such assessments, psychological insights shaped policy directives. American theories of culture and personality thus came to reflect the growing conviction that political beliefs (especially hostile ones) should be combated with psychological remedies by extrapolating individual psychiatric diagnoses to characterize social movements.[11] Whether or not German fascism was *more* psychologically based than any previous political phenomenon (as Herald asserts in the epigraph) is open to debate—but this is nonetheless how it was approached.

Freud's theories of social and individual psychology have been by far the most influential on the body of work analyzing the fascist mind. His theories of frustration and repression are especially crucial to these theories, many of which greatly simplify and literalize them. The fundamentalness of the Oedipus complex, and the various perversions possible when it remains unresolved, were also extremely central.

In a broad sense, Freud posited that there was a fundamental conflict between instincts and civilization. The former must always in some measure be frustrated so that the latter can develop. Indeed, Freud believed that the suppression of sexual instincts is necessary in that it provides the energy for the other tasks civilization requires.[12] The suppression of instincts of aggression on the other hand, also necessary to civilization, *requires* energy. Hence one of civilization's tasks is to channel aggression to appropriate targets, and mitigate it with affectional bonds: the bonds of group identification (i.e., nationalism) and the bonds of familial love.[13] As to nationalism, Freud writes, "It is always possible to bind together a considerable number of people in love, so long as there are other people left over to receive the manifestations of their aggressiveness. . . . [It is not] unaccountable chance that the dream of a Germanic world-dominion called for anti-Semitism as its complement; and it is intelligible that the attempt to establish a new, communist civilization in Russia should find its psychological support in the persecution of the bourgeois."[14] For Freud, there was always aggression beneath the bonds between people, both within families and in larger national formations. Nationally condoned aggressions like the scapegoating of minorities and war inspired powerful national bonds by channeling these underlying aggressions. Freud did not believe that these bonds were sexual, however, as the psychic energy required to channel this aggression was being drawn, if anything, *from* sexual instincts.

For socially conservative psychiatrists and psychologists influenced by Freud, however, this theory justified those aspects of the national psychiatric story that stress the necessity of sexual normativity to democracy. Most conservative followers of Freud who came to theorize fascism consequently lost sight of the fact that the repression of sexuality would also be the source of fascist affectional/national bonds. Instead, fascism was theorized as perverse through the invocation of sadism, masochism, homosexuality, and unresolved Oedipal dynamics.

Freud's influence on American social psychologists is evident in the latter's common tendency to characterize German fascism as a movement that appealed to emotional insecurities, most of them forged in childhood through strictly gendered German family dynamics, which in turn structured the sexuality of fascist political subjectivity. Erik Erikson, for instance, was a Committee for National Morale consultant during the war who analyzed Hitler's speeches with a view toward suggesting effective prisoner of war interrogation techniques and anti-Nazi propaganda. Erikson read Hitler's *Mein Kampf* as a projection of the image of an adolescent who never gave in, who refused to surrender to the domineering father and insisted on protecting the weak, loving mother. As Hitler's early family experiences mirrored the most common characterizations of the German family in general, so he was able to appeal to unconscious desires inspired by these widespread family patterns.[15] In another article, Erikson reiterated that "It is as if the German nation as a whole could be likened to a not uncommon type of adolescent who turns delinquent."[16]

This model of psychic immaturity led directly to the Freudian theory of homosexuality for many social theorists. Psychoanalyst Ernest Jones, for instance, saw Nazi collaborators and followers as identifying with Hitler as a father image to whom they submitted. Jones theorized that their alliance with Hitler was a regressive homosexual solution to the Oedipus complex. Jones writes, "The people who are most subject to the wiles of Nazi propaganda are those who have neither securely established their own manhood and independence from the father nor have been able to combine the instincts of sexuality and love in their attitude towards the mother or other women. This is the psychological position of the homosexual."[17]

The designation of Nazism as (male) homosexuality stems from the more general theory that fascism derived from a kind of mass cultural immaturity—with homosexuality being seen, in this theory, as an immature form of sexual expression compared to heterosexuality. Hence, democracy was figured as a more mature political form than fascism in a formula that aligned fascism with homosexuality and democracy with heterosexuality.[18] This version of the fascist psychobiography made its way into popular journalism as well, with Rodney Collin writing in British and American magazines that "Distorted sex showed itself in Jew baiting, persecution, ultra-Puritanism, and . . . homosexual sadism. More innocuously, these frustrations were in many cases sublimated into extreme patriotism, loyalty, and a certain disciplined idealism."[19]

The most influential military study of Hitler's personality reveals another kind of normative bias. In 1943, Gen. William J. Donovan, chief of the Office of Strategic Services, recruited a team of psychoanalysts to analyze Hitler through his speeches and writings. The book reporting their findings, written under the direction of Walter C. Langer, was printed in limited quantities during wartime, classified as secret, and distributed to Allied leaders.[20] The analysis, like Erikson's, casts Hitler's father as a sadist, "brutal, unjust, and inconsiderate," while his mother was "an extremely conscientious and hard-working individual whose life centered around her home and children." While the latter description would seem to exonerate the mother from blame for her son's fascist proclivities, it instead becomes the source of them in that "every scrap of evidence indicates that there was an extremely strong attachment between herself and Adolf. . . . In view of her husband's conduct and the fact that he was twenty-three years her senior and far from having a loving disposition, we may suppose that much of the affection that normally would have gone to him also found its way to Adolf."[21] This combination of circumstances places the Oedipus complex at the center of Hitler's development, with the mother's own purported desire for her son responsible for pushing this "normal" psychic drama to the extreme. While the dominance of fathers is a major factor in the studies of German families (including Hitler's), it is more often the overattachment of sons to mothers (and vice versa) that became the primary causal motivation in American national psychobiography after the war, as is exemplified in Hecht's treatment for *Notorious*.

In Langer's study, Hitler's writings about "women as seductresses responsible for men's downfall" are read as "probably the outcome of his early experiences with his mother who first seduced him into a love relationship and then betrayed him by giving herself to his father."[22] Langer's reading consequently duplicates the misogynist sentiment of Hitler's own statements by perpetuating a belief that women (especially mothers) are to be held responsible for the downfall of men. Because the dominant American version of Freud did not include a critique of the patriarchal family, this practice of blaming mothers for the faults of their children would reach its peak in the postwar United States, when an adulterated American version of Freudianism—one very keen on the fortification of the male ego—was at its greatest height of influence. An outcome of growing anxieties about changing gender roles and the history of nationalist melodrama, fears about motherhood came to grip American popular and social scientific thought in the conflict with fascism.

The background to this concept of the bad mother derives from the same forces in the formation of the new democratic republics in the late eighteenth and nineteenth centuries that centered nationalist melodrama. As historians Molly Ladd-Taylor and Lauri Umansky write in their anthology on the subject, "The ideology historians have dubbed Republican Motherhood defined women's place in the new nation and tied 'good' mothering to nation building." Women were, they write, responsible for "the moral education of their citizen-sons," a role considered essential to a democracy.[23] In the course of the early nineteenth century, the belief in original sin was replaced with a faith in childhood innocence and susceptibility to influence, and so mothers could be blamed for their children's failures. In the 1920s and 1930s, the momentum behind this concept of the mother's blame for the actions of the child steadily increased along with the influence of neo-Freudian thought. In the course of World War II, the cultural concept of the bad mother thus informed much of the political psychology of fascism.[24]

The two-pronged social conservatism of theories of the psychology of fascism (concerning sexuality and gender), while certainly to be found in Freud's theory, was highly exaggerated in the application of his theories to the analysis of fascism, making them just as expressive of anxieties about American sexual relations as about fears concerning Germany. While somewhat contradictory on this account, Freud himself sought to distinguish erotic "perversions" from their mass manifestation. The pleasure that is potentially derived from the aggressive activities of a group is not sexual in nature; rather, "the satisfaction of the instinct is accompanied by an extraordinarily high degree of narcissistic enjoyment, owing to its presenting the ego with a fulfillment of the latter's old wishes for omnipotence."[25]

The same is true of masochism, another condition commonly attributed to the Nazi subject. Freud saw in a more general way that civilization required the directing of some portion of the aggressive instincts inward to back up the harsh superego, which "obtains mastery over the individual's dangerous desire for aggression by weakening and disarming it and by setting up an agency within him to watch over it, like a garrison in a conquered city."[26] The superego actually longs for punishment of the subject for its forbidden desires through guilt. Freud focuses here on the Oedipus complex but concentrates less on forbidden sexual desire for the mother than on murderous desire directed against the father. He writes, "Since civilization obeys an internal erotic impulse which causes human beings to unite in a closely-knit group, it can only achieve this aim through an ever-increasing reinforcement of the sense of guilt."[27] Freud's distinction is subtle, and so, although Freud himself denied that Nazism (or other totalitarian movements) had the specific character of sexual sadism or masochism, it would not be difficult for those selectively influenced by Freudian theory to carry on as if he had never made that distinction.

On the Left, there were several efforts to further psychoanalytic theories of fascism that respected Freud's distinction. These theories, by and large, reveal the sexual conservatism in Freud's conceptual structure, even after the concepts are desexualized. Erich Fromm, for instance, a prominent member of the Frankfurt Psychoanalytic Institute from its founding in 1929, sought to understand why so many people embraced authority with such ardor by theorizing a desexualized "sadomasochistic character" at the core of the "authoritarian personality."[28] In his work of 1937, Fromm grounded this sadomasochistic character in the sexual complexes explored by Freud, but in his later work, *Escape from Freedom* (1941), he, like Freud himself, would drain the concept of its sexual content as he extrapolated his theory to include not just Germany but all societies in which the "authoritarian personality" could be found.[29]

Fromm's idea of the pleasures derived by the sadomasochistic character included a feeling of negative relief from the anxieties of individual choice in modern life and the positive illusion of participation in power. Fromm argued in 1937 that this pleasure included a disinclination toward sexuality focused on genitals (i.e., heterosexuality) and featured instead a regression to pregenital (especially anal) libidinous stages. Once this explicitly sexual portion of the theory was excised, the conceptual structure still characterized authoritarianism as both sadomasochistic and homosexual, again by way of a model of psychic immaturity. In Fromm's work, just as in Jones's, there is a direct connection between homosexual desire, regression, sadomasochism, and authoritarianism, even if by "homosexual" Fromm did not mean people who actually practiced homosexuality, as popular images often did. Like many leftist thinkers at the time, Fromm critiqued the patriarchal social structure that had spawned the brutality of totalitarianism, but he did not critique the heterosexuality that lies at its core. Instead, he joined those who conceptually posited a more egalitarian heterosexual genital sexuality as a precondition to rational, democratic politics.

Fromm was ultimately rather hostile to sexuality in general, however, spending much of the 1930s contemplating the merits of a matriarchal theory that idealized a desexualized, maternal love. Unlike Freud, he did not believe the Oedipus conflict was universal. Instead, he thought that matriarchal, maternal love proved that love was not at all dependent on sexuality (a great departure from Freud), and that, as historian Martin Jay writes, "In fact, sex was more often tied to hatred and destruction."[30] Other members of the Institute for Social Research would disagree with Fromm, and as his vision for the sexual character of democracy became more and more restrictive (and less and less sexual) he fell out of favor with institute members Max Horkheimer, Theodor Adorno, and Herbert Marcuse, albeit for different reasons. Jay discusses an unpublished essay Adorno wrote in 1946, in which he reportedly argues that revisionists like Fromm were wrong to take sexuality out of Freud, seeing such desexualization as a denial of the conflict between essence and appearance. Jay says that "Fromm, Adorno argued, was very wrong to deny the sexual basis of sadism just when the Nazis were displaying it so blatantly."[31] Marcuse, on the other hand, would come to advocate "polymorphous perversity" as *anti*-authoritarian sexuality in his 1955 work, *Eros and Civilization*. Marcuse's work stands out as a prescient, sexually progressive counterexample to both Adorno's and Fromm's variants of sexually conservative leftist analyses of fascism.[32]

Wilhelm Reich represents another effort to incorporate Freudian insights into an analysis of fascism from the Left. Reich, too, developed a matriarchal theory as an antidote to fascism in *The Mass Psychology of Fascism* (1933). Like most theorists influenced by Freud, Reich posited the Oedipus complex at the center of fascism, but rather than blaming mothers for the role they play in a constrictive patriarchy he hypothesized an idealized matriarchal society in which maternal love would be the model for freedom. In this way, Reich sees patriarchy as producing sadism and fascism, while "natural" and nonperverse sexuality is the product of the "original matriarchal work-democracy" he posits as historically preceding patriarchy.[33] Reich's theories would later be modified by Marcuse to become an important element of the New Left's approach to sexual liberation in the 1960s, but in the 1930s and 1940s his theories were not very influential on the popular perception of the psychology of fascism.

The Frankfurt School's concept of the authoritarian personality, formulated not only by Fromm but by Horkheimer, Adorno, and other members who worked on the *Studies on Authority and the Family* (1936), would influence the postwar transposition of the psychology of fascism to the psychology of American prejudice.[34] The theory of the authoritarian personality that they formulated basically held that under liberal capitalism the father satisfied economic needs and so "naturally" led the household. In capitalism's monopolistic phase, the father lost his autonomy as head of his own business, and so paternal authority became only ideological and irrational and hence fragile. This change allowed for the transfer of the "aura" of paternal authority to be transferred to external institutions like the state. The 1936 study aimed to discuss men in general, without specific reference to Germany or a specific social class, stressing instead that the authoritarian personality can develop in all classes in a capitalist society.[35]

As with many leftist theories that connected fascism with capitalism, Nazism loses its specificity and they become more broadly applicable—a trend that would accelerate after Germany's defeat, especially in the

United States, to which many of these theorists had emigrated.[36] During the war, Frankfurt School members Otto Kirchheimer, Franz Neumann, and Marcuse, for instance, were among the social scientists who worked for the Office of Strategic Services, and Leo Lowenthal worked for the Office of War Information. Like other social scientists who had served the wartime cause, the authority they gained from the conflict with fascism carried over into the postwar era.

This concept of the authoritarian personality posits a privileged place for the family—understood in Freudian terms—whereby it becomes the site not only where fascists are potentially produced but where resistance to fascism can originate. In the Frankfurt School's postwar elaboration of the theory, *The Authoritarian Personality* (1950), the Oedipal family produces authoritarian subjects, but *as* subjects, at least; when the family is superseded by the state, the possibility of resistance is eliminated since individual subjectivity is lost.[37] Adorno and his colleagues' theory of resistance to a totalitarian Oedipus (the state) is therefore Oedipal (reinstating the paternal authority of the father). Cultural critic Andrew Hewitt notes that consequently homosexuality continues to stand for incomplete subject formation and hence authoritarianism.[38] This is the intellectual Left's version of nationalist melodrama, where democracy and the traditional family are made equivalent and alternative sexualities are cast as antidemocratic. While certainly oversimplifying these theories, it is these characteristics that they share with other, more conservative theories of political psychology, and with most popular appropriations thereof, that inform national psychobiography. This form of psychoanalytic political psychology is to be further distinguished from Bhabha's much later formulation, via Lacan, of the split nature of the national subject, which I elaborated in my introduction. Lacan's notion of the subject is *not* unified by design, while Freudian-derived American ego psychology imagines an ideal, sexually normative, "healthy" subject and indeed imagines that most Americans have achieved such subjectivity.

Feminist historian Elaine Tyler May notes how in a more general cultural sense the conflict with fascism served as a high point for anxieties about sexuality, especially about the place of women in the social structure. She writes, "Although wartime did contribute to intimacy, romance, and sexual encounters with or without marriage, there is no evidence that these relationships led to the dire consequences that were widely feared. In fact, more families were formed than torn asunder during the war."[39] Still, she notes, the wartime and postwar periods can be characterized by a fear of all forms of nonmarital sexuality. This observation supports historian Carroll Smith-Rosenberg's point that "when the social fabric is rent in fundamental ways, bodily and familial imagery will assume ascendance . . . [and] thus sexuality and the family, because of their primitive psychic and social functions, serve as reservoirs of physical imagery through which individuals seek to express and rationalize their experience of social change."[40]

A focus on sexuality and the family in times of crisis and change arises fundamentally from the ways in which, as George Mosse writes, the rise of modern nationalism represented a triumph of middle-class respectability over aristocratic "decadence."[41] As Michel Foucault has said, sexuality is not to be understood here to be a thing in itself, which "power" tries to subdue, but rather as "an especially dense transfer point for relations of power." It is not the most uncontrollable aspect of power relations but "one of those endowed with the greatest instrumentality: useful for the greatest number of maneuvers and capable of serving as a point of support, as a linchpin, for the most varied strategies."[42]

Thus, while critics of fascism who invoked psychology (especially psychoanalysis) certainly varied across the political spectrum, the surprisingly uniform aspect of the "cure" that they desired almost universally involved a normative, familial model, with heterosexuality and paternal leadership as its basic features. Popular narratives in journalism, fiction, and especially Hollywood film gave narrative form to this hoped-for cure through the depiction of characters whose psychobiographies matched their theories of political motivation.

Political (Oedipal) Dramas: Hitchcock's *Notorious* and the Psychobiography of the Democratic Subject

Siegfried Kracauer's *From Caligari to Hitler: A Psychological History of the German Film* (1947) applied many of the above characterizations of the fascist psyche to characters found in German film, not so much in the Nazi period itself but during the Weimar Republic that preceded it.[43] Like other national character studies, Kracauer searches these films for common motifs that can reveal the disposition of the German people and what made them susceptible to Hitler. He finds repeated Oedipal themes, suicidal tendencies on the part of protagonists, and abuses of power and authority. His portrait of the "German soul" is hence masculine, masochistic, torn between rebellion and submission, and prone to homosexual, paranoid, narcissistic fantasies, all conclusions that underscore a consensus about the nature of the fascist psyche. This consensus expanded remarkably in the postwar period.

As with most theorists who analyzed fascism, Kracauer saw his study as having value not only for film studies, nor even only for the analysis of specifically German fascism, but for postwar American politics as well. He writes, "I have reason to believe that the use made here of films as a medium of research can profitably be extended to studies of current mass behavior in the United States and elsewhere. I also believe that studies of this kind may help in the planning of films—not to mention other media of communication—which will effectively implement the cultural aims of the United Nations."[44] Kracauer's "psychological history" thus stands at the crossroads between the uses to which psychology, and psychoanalysis in particular, were put in the cultural as well as actual battle against Nazism in World War II and the dawning challenges of the Cold War.

Postwar films indeed enacted the variants of national psychobiography laid out by social scientists, as they continued to characterize Nazi antagonists and model the desired democratic psyche in heroic protagonists as well as playing out repetitive performances of characters struggling to achieve the latter. Italian director Roberto Rossellini's postwar films, especially *Rome: Open City* (1946) and *Germany, Year Zero* (1947), fairly straightforwardly characterize their Nazi characters along these lines. *Rome: Open City* features two Nazi antagonists, one an effeminate male and the other a masculine, lesbian-inflected female. *Germany, Year Zero* features a defeated Nazi antagonist with a sexual interest in young boys. These films are instructive by negative example, organizing their stories around one character, who struggles to resist the pull of Nazi decadence and perversity in the face of economic need (Marina in *Rome* and the unnamed boy in *Germany*). Rossellini's films are more sociological than psychological in this regard, but they do reflect the general psychological profile of Nazi characters.

Most films portraying the struggle of a character to resist or to extricate himself or herself from fascism staged performances of conversion, cure, or failure, which served the pedagogical project of national psychobiography directly. Often, this type of project not only involves distinguishing the fascist from the democratic psyche but explores the potential weaknesses of the democratic subject (economic need in Rossellini's case), which were thought to need careful management in the postwar period. This type of national psychobiography—soon to be more common in anti-Communist plots—brings together wartime studies of the fascist mind with postwar efforts to use these insights to manage domestic populations, especially in the United States.

Of all the filmmakers working in Hollywood in the immediate postwar period and into the 1950s, Alfred Hitchcock made the most explicit use of the kinds of psychoanalytic political characterizations forged by the theorists above. Film scholar Robert Corber considers Hitchcock's postwar films to have staged the production of (and indeed helped to produce) what he calls the "postwar settlement": the management and containment of the political claims of organized labor, women, and racial minorities through the offer to participate in the postwar culture of consumption. This strategy was in part effected by an exaggeration of the influence of the Popular Front on New Deal liberalism (playing on escalating anti-Communist sentiment) and a commensurate effort on the part of anti-Communist liberals to substitute socially conservative psychological remedies for Popular Front class politics. Corber sees Hitchcock as just such a Cold War liberal who, like his intellectual cohort, exploited hysteria about the purported infiltration of Communists and homosexuals into the federal government to prevent competing constructions of social reality from mobilizing popular support.[45] Rossellini, it should be said, aimed to do something similar *for* class politics. Hitchcock, however, mobilized psychoanalytically influenced theories of political psychology to incite spectators to the postwar vision of proper political subjectivity based upon gender conformity and heterosexuality, *not* on economic considerations.

Hitchcock's conscious deployment of the American version of psychoanalytic theory needs to be understood within its milieu, working as he was at creating political thrillers in a historical moment that saw politics as a larger scale version of interpersonal dramas. Of course, as a filmmaker and not a social scientist Hitchcock also took considerable liberties with the specifics of psychoanalysis, even in its popularized form.[46] Hitchcock's particular uses of psychoanalysis, however, still reflect the ways in which, as Teresa de Lauretis notes, psychoanalysis has been historically malleable in terms of its core fantasies (in her case the function of lesbianism, in Hitchcock's, the function of fascism), and its commensurate understandings of subjectivity.[47]

In Hitchcock's political thrillers, the romances that almost invariably parallel the espionage plots make normative gender identity and political loyalty mutually constitutive. Hitchcock's overt use of psychoanalytic principles of subjectivity formation, based on strict categories of sexual difference, ensure that normative gender and sexual behavior are aligned

with a democratic political orientation, while gender-inappropriate behavior and sexual variance (especially homosexuality) are aligned with
totalitarianism. In keeping with the more conservative uses of psychoanalytic theory put to the service of political psychology by military
strategists, *Notorious* serves as an emblematic text in that it thematizes
the struggle between democracy and fascism and the United States and
Nazi Germany as a struggle over proper Oedipal resolution. In the
course of the film, the gendering of political subjectivity reveals the
social conservatism beneath much of the theorizing of what might constitute a "democratic" psyche.

As the film's American heroine, Alicia Huberman (Ingrid Bergman),
struggles to differentiate herself from her Nazi father, so the central
Nazi character, Alexander Sebastian (Claude Rains), must struggle to
gain autonomy from his domineering mother. Alex grapples with the
classic model of Nazi Oedipal failure, and, in keeping with the peculiarly
American form, it is his mother, Madame Sebastian, who represents the
only truly fascist woman. By contrast, Alicia's own unresolved Oedipal
dramas with her fascist father, while initially casting her as politically
suspect, serve as the proving grounds for her commitment to American
democracy. Her ultimate submission to male authority is not a sign of
her questionable political leanings the way Alex's submission to female
authority is, but rather it becomes a sign of her democratic loyalties. The
two Oedipal trajectories involved in these projects are both interdepen-
dent in the project of socially conservative antifascism. By the end of the
film, Alicia succeeds, and, though reduced to a mere shell of her spirited
former self, she is firmly allied with the fight against political evil and for
democracy. Alex, meanwhile, loses his battle and is condemned to the
brutal fate of the Nazi/mother-dominated order from which he will
never be extricated.

The relationship between politics and patriarchy is central to the
analysis of both Alicia's and Alex's trajectories. This relationship underscores the uneasy difference the film attempts to manufacture between
the unresolved Oedipal dramas of Alex (which are posited to be at the
root of his fascism) and the unresolved Oedipal dramas of Alicia (at the
root of both her initially perceived lack of political commitment and her
promiscuity). In the case of the latter, the opening sequence of the film
illustrates the substitution of Alicia's "notoriety" for her father's conviction for treason in a number of ways. John Huberman, the father, is seen
first, shot from behind in long shot from the point of view of a news
photographer waiting outside the courtroom. The defendant's crime

and lack of repentance are immediately made clear in his threats that the Nazis will return to avenge their defeat, thus launching the rest of the film's espionage plot. But because his back is toward the camera there is no face with which to connect these seditious statements. As Alicia exits the courtroom, it is she who is pursued by the waiting journalists and so provides the face. When another man says, "Let us know if she tries to leave town," it is unclear what Alicia's politics are: she is treated like a traitor and, more specifically, is suspected of being like her father.

In the course of the drunken party scene that follows, Alicia remarks that she's being watched "because I'm a marked woman, you know? I'm liable to blow up the Panama Canal any minute now." A marked woman in this scheme is both sexually and politically disreputable, her sexual impropriety interchangeable with sedition. To underscore this inter-changeability, Devlin (Cary Grant), the American undercover agent who infiltrates Alicia's party and will become her love interest, is initially introduced as the force of sobriety. Graphically matched with her father in the opening sequence, he is initially imaged in silhouette, with his back to the camera, visually both cementing his eventual role as the appropriate object choice with which to resolve her Oedipal conflict and standing for a direct opposition to her father's politics. When he accepts Alicia's offer to go for a drive, her suggestion is sexual, not romantic, the continuance of a seduction begun over a bottle of liquor. But, as the agent of both the government and sexual judgment, he ties a handkerchief around her bare midriff, toning down her attire and indicating his own more prudish, American-government-sponsored intentions. While Devlin, too, will need to resolve his ambivalence toward Alicia in order to rescue her (and hence democracy) from the clutches of Nazism, at this point in the film his propriety establishes the classic contrast of sexual propriety/democracy versus sexual wantonness/fascism, a schema familiar from nationalist melodrama.

In the scene that follows, Alicia is pressed into service for the American government through a combination of calls to her latent patriotism, a deployment of her guilt over her father's fascism, and finally her growing interest in Devlin. Her task will be to spy on a group of Nazis who are engaged in an unknown clandestine activity in Rio de Janeiro.[48] Again, political allegiance is voiced in Oedipal terms, for the logic behind choosing her for the job lies precisely in her connection to her Nazi father, through the exploitation of which she could, as Devlin says, "make up a little for [her] Daddy's . . . peculiarities." The pause before *peculiarities* strengthens the association of abnormal behavior and political deviance, lending a sexual connotation that will be underscored by Alicia's subsequent rejection: "No thank-you. I don't go for patriotism—or patriots." The juxtaposition of "Daddy's peculiarities" and patriotism is a version of the binary demarcation between fascism and its sexual "peculiarities" and democracy and its supposed lack of them. Of course, Alicia does fall in love with Devlin—she goes for a patriot after all—but the narrative twist that prevents their simple union requires her Nazi-inflected sexual wantonness first to be put to work before she can be redeemed through matrimony. As feminist film theorist Tania Modleski writes, "it is only through allowing this sexuality to be placed in the service of a harsh and unbending law (that is, through becoming a Mata Hari for callous American agents) and nearly dying the same death as her father—death by poison—that Alicia can expiate her own sins and those of the father."[49] Alicia's sexual sins and her father's political sins are, in other words, one.

The connection between her father's politics and the formation of her sexuality is overtly entangled with the Oedipal resolution she has not yet fully achieved. In an illicitly obtained recording of a conversation between Alicia and her father, Alicia's disgust for both her father's treason and touch cross over as she screams, "Don't ever come near me or speak to me again about your rotten schemes!" Her rejection of her father, on both political and incestuous grounds, is not normatively resolved, however, in that she does not transfer her desire to a single heterosexual, politically acceptable, love object—the only democratic solution to just such an Oedipal/political drama. Instead, Alicia's rejection of her classically overbearing Nazi father has resulted in her promiscuity—indicating that even if she has at least nominally rejected his politics she will not have truly rejected them (nor him) until she is able to replace him with a husband.

The continued entanglement of Alicia's sexuality with her father's politics leads to her being characterized as overbonded with her father, despite her statements in the recorded conversation. This overbonding is exemplified by her monologue on the plane to Rio after being informed of his prison suicide: "I don't know why I should feel so bad—when he told me a couple of years ago what he was, everything went to pot. I didn't care what happened to me. But now I remember how nice he once was. How nice we both were. Very nice. It's a very curious feeling. It's as if something had happened to me and not to him. You see, I don't have to hate him any more—or myself." The speech provides an explanation for Alicia's drunkenness and promiscuity in her despair over her father's Nazism, her letting her image of her nice self go to ruin along with her image of her once-nice Daddy. Again, Alicia's being sexually "not nice" is bound up with her father being politically "not nice," a melding that leads her to hate both her father and herself and prevents her from truly resolving her Oedipal/political conundrum. The father's death does not provide the relief she feels for a few moments and in her blossoming love for Devlin. Rather she must be put through the ordeal of restaging the whole drama, sleeping with and marrying a Nazi, a friend of her father's, in the course of which she must be subjected to constant reminders of her sexual notoriety before she can be "rescued" by the supposedly "good" object choice of Devlin, a democratic partner who will separate her from her Nazi father once and for all.

The anxieties about female promiscuity and heightened sexual desire in wartime described by Tyler May reveal a vested interest in the equation of female sexual propriety and service to the democratic nation. Social commentators like Victor Robinson and Philip Wylie, for instance, had published wartime books proclaiming female promiscuity a home front crisis.[50] This connection is shown to be highly complex in *Notorious*, however. The fact that the film's narrative forces Alicia to continue an overly close association with her father in the service of her conversion into a reputable and truly patriotic woman ultimately points to the contradictions inherent in a sexual coding that tries to make fascism distinct from patriarchy. In fact, Alicia's romance with Devlin ends up being more sadomasochistic than anything the Nazis in the film ever exhibit, an interesting result of the degree to which a sexual woman must be controlled in order to be tamed for the properly passive female sexuality of "democracy."

National psychobiography is engaged not only to pedagogically model the ideal object of traditional family roles and sexual normativity but to enact performances of the mental torment that accompanies deviations from these norms. Alicia is in fact doubly tormented in that she torments herself (i.e., she is not really happy when she is promiscuous) and is tormented by Devlin (i.e., she is not so easily forgiven). As Alicia moves toward independence from her father, she moves toward the kind of autonomy democratic rhetoric endorses, but, as she is female, her autonomy must be subordinated, making her achievement of democratic subjectivity equal or indeed secondary to her acquiescence to normative heterosexuality. Alicia's torment signals the contradiction at the core of both anti-Nazi melodrama and anti-Nazi psychobiography, namely, that both Nazism and this conservative form of democracy are fundamentally patriarchal.

Modleski criticizes *Notorious* on similar grounds, claiming that the narrative collapses the distinction between the public and private realms and so displaces the political onto the personal, denying the classic feminist credo that the personal is political. She notes that film critics without a feminist approach have celebrated the political drama as a MacGuffin (Donald Spoto, for example) but notes that the substitution comes at the expense of the woman, as she, instead of the uranium the Nazis are dealing in, becomes the object of the story's epistemological quest.[51] Certainly, as Modleski goes on to note, even Sophocles' original drama *Oedipus Rex* presents a political enigma (what is the origin of the plague?) that is answered in Oedipus's personal history, and Hollywood narratives have long privileged the personal over the political. But, in the postwar and Cold War psychobiography, this move from political to personal is exacerbated by the larger liberal and conservative political project that hopes to contain the complaints of the economically and socially disempowered by individualizing their "problems"—complaints raised to a higher pitch by the highly idealized rhetoric of democracy inspired by the conflict with fascism. Indeed, it is the response to this sort of effort to depoliticize the complaints of women (and ethnic minorities, as I will discuss in the next chapter) that second-wave feminists originally coined the phrase "the personal is political" in the 1960s.

Corber takes issue with Modleski, arguing that her point does not take into account the extent to which the personal was precisely political in the postwar scene, writing, "Devlin and Alicia's inscription within the discourses of national security enables the American government to regulate and control the most personal aspects of the construction of their subjectivity, including the organization of their sexuality."[52] Corber, however, seems to miss the specifically feminist point of Modleski's critique, even as he is right to point out that the personal had long been political, indeed. Modleski, however, is saying that it was not recognized as such. What feminist critics like Modelski call for is an explicit recognition of this type of transhistorical political move, which masks its efforts to substitute patriarchal gender relations for more generalized democratic humanism or the recognition of oppressed social categories. Together, Corber and Modleski both point to the ideological perpetuation of normative gendered subjectivities carried out specifically in the service of postwar national identity fortification and most prominently by calling on persistent narrative conventions that make women bear the primary burden of patriarchy's reinforcement.

This both specific and more long standing move is staged not only in Alicia's Oedipal drama but in the male Nazi Oedipal drama played out in the triangle created by Alex, his mother, and Alicia. Unlike most characterizations of the typical Nazi household, Hitchcock erases the father figure (there is no mention of Alex's father), intensifies Madame Sebastian's power over her son compared to the way it was described in Hecht's original treatment, and thus installs Madame Sebastian in the position of domineering mother/Nazi, a move characteristic of American wartime and postwar gender anxieties.

Philip Wylie is the most famous popular purveyor of this image of the domineering mother who, among a host of other things, prevents her son from achieving autonomy and hence causes his Nazism. In his 1942 treatise on the psychic state of the union, *Generation of Vipers*, he rails against the global concept of the domineering "mom" who destroys the men of the nation. His demonization of the mom is informed by popular images of Nazism in a number of significant ways: "Like Hitler, she betrays the people who would give her a battle before she brings up her troops. Her whole personal life, so far as outward expression is concerned, is, in consequence, a mopping-up action. Traitors are shot, yellow stars are slapped on those beneath notice, the good-looking men and boys are rounded up and beaten or sucked into pliability, a new slave population continually goes to work at making more munitions for momism, and mom herself sticks up her head, or maybe the periscope of the woman next door, to find some new region that needs taking over. This technique pervades all she does."[53] Domineering mothers might not only cause their sons to become fascist but in fact act like fascists themselves. Madame Sebastian is a fascist by virtue of her suffocating mothering in Wylie's sense as much as she is a suffocating mother by virtue of her fascism. While Wylie's views are clearly more extreme in their rhetoric than any of the more liberal-centrist and leftist psychologists cited above, his hyperbolic prose was extremely popular, his books bestsellers, and his exaggerated version influential to a pervasive belief system that put bad mothering at the core of all the nation's ills.[54]

Prominent psychiatrist Edward Strecker gave Wylie academic credibility when he incorporated the theory of momism into his 1946 book, *Their Mother's Sons: The Psychiatrist Examines an American Problem*. Expanding and inverting Wylie's characterization of moms as Nazis, Strecker characterized Nazism itself as a "mom surrogate with a swastika for a heart," a kind of twisted matriarchy (a momarchy) in which "The Fuehrer had all the qualities and ingredients which go into the making of a super-mom. He even had the feminine note of hysteria which may be heard in the voices of moms when they are battling for their children and, if need be, are willing to give their lives for them. . . . Here indeed was a mom who never forgot his children."[55] In Strecker's formulation, the feminization of Hitler blends with construing moms as fascists. With a new twist, "Hitler's children" (recalling the title of the film discussed in chapter 2) are again seen, as was the case with the more moderate psychological analysts, to be suffering from mass immaturity.[56] Strecker would take these analyses, gleaned in large part from his work as a psychiatric adviser to the Armed Services in World War II, and bring them home to the United States in the postwar period. Delivered first as a lecture in April of 1945 entitled "Psychiatry Speaks to Democracy," Strecker cautioned specifically against moms and their detrimental effects on democracy. More than a critique of fascism, then, these beliefs were projected into the postwar period, bringing along a tenacious fear about the tenuousness of democracy. This tenuousness is seen by Strecker to be symptomatically readable in mental illness, alcoholism, feminism, and homosexuality—all conditions that he saw as threatening the fortitude of American democracy and that he reported were on the rise. The symptoms of democracy's weakness, the blight of the Cold War's internal enemies, are all traceable to mom.

In *Notorious*, aspects of one of Wylie's ideas, that frustration gives rise to gender-inverted behavior, manifests itself in Madame Sebastian's masculinization.[57] Thus, while Alexander Sebastian is initially introduced by way of Alicia's Oedipal problems (he is a friend of her Nazi father), Alex is ultimately not allied with the position of the Nazi father at all. Instead, Alex (or Sebastian, as Devlin refers to him in the film) is the victim of his masculinized, domineering mother Madame Sebastian, a title that, in its echo of the family name, reinforces the power of the bonds that plague him. Madame Sebastian, as a quintessential Nazi mom, serves as the pedagogical object against which democratic women should model their mothering. As a result of this emphasis, Alex emerges as surprisingly sympathetic for a Nazi character in 1946, precisely because he is less to blame for his politics than his mother is. The contemporary saga of the "damaged male," the subject of chapter 6, thus finds a powerful precursor here. The entanglement of Alicia's and Alex's Oedipal dramas, then, involves a dual project of proscribing political and sexual behavior in gender-appropriate (and hence politically favorable) terms.

On their second meeting, Alex invites Alicia to dinner at his house, where his mother is giving a dinner party. Madame Sebastian immediately comments on Alicia's resemblance to her father, and Alicia returns the observation to link Alex and his mother. Having established the Oedipal lines in question, Madame Sebastian's tone shifts abruptly and she accuses Alicia of filial negligence: "You did not testify at your father's trial—we thought that unusual." The connection between Alex and his mother becomes a royal "we," which might include the whole host of Nazis in the next room. Alicia attempts to allay these suspicions by claiming that her father didn't want her to testify, but a close shot on Madame Sebastian highlights her suspicion as she coldly asks, "I wonder why?" At this moment, Alex interrupts with an offscreen hello, his presence first registered in his mother's reaction as she glances offscreen. This link between Madame Sebastian's line of questioning and her son's warm welcome introduces the mother's dual suspicions of Alicia as both a political ally and a mate for her son. As he enters the room, the first of many visual triangulations between the three of them occurs, with Madame Sebastian positioned directly between her son and Alicia. The scene has now been set for Alex to spend much of the second act engaged in defying his mother through his romance with Alicia, a nearly successful Oedipal separation that will fail when his mother resumes a dominant role after Alicia is discovered to be a spy.

Alex will ultimately become most sinister, in a pathetic, dependent way, when he accepts his failure to differentiate from his mother and gives himself over to her domination, the point at which he most clearly becomes the antidemocratic subject Wylie and Strecker warned against. Alex's somewhat pitiable weakness is first revealed in a scene at a racetrack, the second time the triangle is visually depicted, as Alex and his mother have a quintessentially Oedipal conversation: Madame Sebastian says she feels displaced by Alicia in her son's life, as Alicia's empty chair sits between them. But after he spots Alicia talking to Devlin his normal separation from his mother falters, as he jealously accuses, "I presume that's why you left my mother and me; you had a meeting with him." The fact that he mentions his mother at all, and before himself at that, is an indication that Oedipal separation has not yet been successful and in all probability never will be. Alex is and remains, underneath it all, regressive and hence a Nazi. The political impact of this pattern of partial separation followed by stronger melding is then most dramatically demonstrated by the locational parallel between the scene in which Alex argues with his mother about his plans to marry Alicia and the scene in which he confesses to her that she's an American agent. In the latter, his mother wreaks revenge on the woman who supplanted her. Both take place, rather obviously, in Madame Sebastian's bedroom.

In the first scene, the opening shot features Madame Sebastian prominently in the foreground right, large and looming as she sews (a recursive gesture on her part, which comes to signify the sinister maternal) with Alex in the background left, smaller and less powerful until he stands and walks around the bed that initially separates them to announce that he will marry Alicia with or without his mother's approval. When Alex gains the upper hand, Madame Sebastian becomes less sinister and more mundane in her suspicions. Instead of questioning Alicia's political loyalties, as in the first encounter, she now asks, "Are you quite sure she didn't come down here to see you? To capture the rich Alex Sebastian for a husband?" As Alex rights the improper inversion of the gender hierarchy his subservience to his mother allowed, the mother shifts her focus from political/sexual to merely sexual suspicion, a positive development as far as the sympathetic portrayal of Alex is concerned. At the beginning of the second scene, Madame Sebastian again first suspects only Alicia's sexual loyalty to her son. As her son admits that something is wrong, she smiles, self-satisfied, and says, "I have expected it. I knew. I knew. What is it? Mr. Devlin?" Alex's partially successful attempts to properly displace his mother with his wife resoundingly fail, then, as he confesses that the infidelity is even worse: she is an American agent. The trajectory of depoliticization is thus reversed, bringing back the dynamic of Oedipal irresolution with an even greater vengeance.

In the scene in which Madame Sebastian is displaced, she sits next to her bed when Alex confronts her; in the scene in which she returns to her position of dominance, she is actually lying in it. She does not at first respond to him verbally but reaches in a gesturally "masculine" fashion for a cigarette. As she sits up in bed, the image dissolves to a shot of Alicia asleep, then dissolves back again to Madame Sebastian. The mother's psychic displacement of the wife is evinced in this graphic match. The mother, who has never before been shown to smoke, bullies her son while talking through a cigarette as it dangles from her mouth. At the end of the scene, she stands next to the now thoroughly regressed Alex as he sits on her bed with his head in his hands. Her body language iconographically presents the visual comportment of stereotypical fascist women: one arm tightly held around her own waist, the other elbow also tight, and the cigarette smoldering at an acute angle near her mouth (fig. 7). Everything about her is contained and exact as she says, "You are almost as impetuous as you were right before your wedding. You barred me from that episode—let me arrange this one."[58] Madame Sebastian's masculinization signals her renewed ascent to the status of mom.

The problem for the film narrative now is that the mom's loyalty to her endangered son must take precedence over her loyalty to the Nazi cause. Mother and son from here on stand together in their efforts to eradicate Alicia's threat before the other Nazis find her (and hence him) out. The perverse Oedipal drama has effectively superseded the political drama that originally organized the narrative, lending credence to the idea that the political plot is a MacGuffin not only for Alicia and Devlin's romance but for the Nazi family plot as well. This substitution does not, however, mean that politics has been evacuated from the drama. On the contrary, the Oedipal drama itself is offered up *as* a political problem. The next time the Oedipal triangle is pictured, it is of course no longer a battle *over* the son but a plot *against* the wife. In the scene that follows, innocuous household conversation flits over the heaviness of the camera's slow pan from Alex and across Alicia as she takes her first sips of poisoned coffee. It finally comes to rest on Madame Sebastian, doing needlepoint. Alicia does not come between them anymore but is *caught* between them in a deadly grip. This same visual arrangement is reproduced in the third poisoning sequence, in which Alicia finally realizes she is being poisoned. Alicia's point of view is first focused on her coffee cup, then on Madame Sebastian, who stares unwaveringly back at her as the camera zooms in. The shot is followed by another zooming point-of-view shot of Alex, who is *not* looking at Alicia. Like previous shots of other Nazis in the film, Madame Sebastian controls by means of the gaze. Alex does his part simply by *denying* his connection with his wife by not looking at her. This economy of gazes implies that the Nazism the film (and indeed the postwar American climate) is *really* interested in is the Nazism of dominant mothers: no less political, only *apparently* so. As Alicia's realization of the plot to poison her comes crashing in, she rises, and begins to faint. From her point of view, again, mother and son become silhouettes and their shadows merge, visually literalizing what we already know to have taken place on a psychic level.

Corber, too, points to the problematics of Nazi parents (Alicia's father and Sebastian's mother) in the film. He claims that these parents are demonic in part precisely because they have explicitly politicized the

Fig. 7. Madame Sebastian and her son in *Notorious* (Alfred Hitchcock, 1946). (Museum of Modern Art, Film Stills Archive.)

nuclear family by attempting to prevent their children from achieving political autonomy and so have eroticized their relation to their children. Corber claims that Madame Sebastian has made her love for her son contingent on his commitment to the Nazi cause and so he is unable to detach himself from her.[59] Corber's reading, however, overstates Madame Sebastian's political motivations: it is not so much that her love for her son is *contingent* on his dedication to the Nazi cause, but rather that his overattachment to her *is* the essence of Nazism. The bond between mother and son actually exceeds Madame Sebastian's commitment to Nazism, which is why she doesn't turn her son in after he makes a politically dangerous mistake with Alicia. This type of substitution echoes the kind of domestic political psychology put forward by people like Strecker, who claimed that moms thwart their children's efforts to attain erotic autonomy and hence proper political subjectivity.

While wartime and postwar American psychology also politicized family relations, it claimed to do so in the service of creating autonomous, ego-fortified citizens—in other words, claiming to de-eroticize family relations. This rhetorical effort uses sexual normativity to handily undermine women's attempts at political agency. While Alex Sebastian's overattachment to his mother signals a dangerous eroticism that destroys his chances for proper male political subjectivity, Alicia's efforts to demonstrate her commitment to democracy's cause instead requires her to rehearse her too-close bond with her father by marrying one of his friends. In the course of this roundabout way of absolving her political/sexual sins, Alicia is nearly killed. Finally, when she can no longer stand or see straight, she is rescued by her appropriately patriotic love interest, Devlin. The claim that this move de-eroticizes the family is specious, as is any claim that the deflection of the plot about Nazis onto personal dramas in any way depoliticizes Hitchcock's story. Modleski writes, "After setting the woman up as an object of male desire and curiosity, the film proceeds to submit her to a process of purification whereby she is purged of her excess sexuality in order to be rendered fit for her place in the patriarchal order." To this, I would add the patriarchal *democratic* order.[60]

Conclusion

Dana Polan notes that wartime Hollywood films often grappled with the contradiction between their overriding tendency to foreground the personal and the war situation's imperative of sacrifice to the greater political cause, a tendency that Modleski notes is particularly potent in the "impossible positions" in which Hitchcock places his heroines.[61] But what these impossible positions reveal is a fundamental problem in the conceptualization of postwar democracy. The effort to substitute personal, psychological explanations for public, collective action made the question of the proper political subjectivity of women a particularly sticky and central problem. While the wartime nationalist melodrama tended to idealize the culture of American democracy against its fascist Other, the already strained opposition between democratic and fascist family dynamics increasingly broke down as attention turned to racial and gender trouble in American culture itself. Women in general thus came to absorb the lion's share of anxious narrative attention along with men who seemed to challenge the norms of white patriarchal manhood (homosexuals and Black men).

Virginia Wright Wexman argues in an article on Hitchcock's *Vertigo* that the collapse of the political onto the personal reflects the way that Cold War political anxieties were projected onto women as a catchall locus of male fears. She complains that feminist film theory, by focusing on issues of sexual difference, perpetuates this collapse—a point with which Modleski takes issue. Modleski argues that this criticism "presupposes an older hierarchy of values that feminists have been concerned to call into question—a hierarchy in which the political (consisting of World Historical Events) is opposed to and privileged over the personal, conceived of as the realm of sexuality."[62] Modleski suggests that the Hollywood tendency to personalize the political *must* be interrogated on these terms, especially by examining why it is that women (Alicia and Madame Sebastian in *Notorious*) bear so much of the burden of political signification. What films like *Notorious* contribute to the postwar national political project is a story line and set of character motivations that reiterate the wartime formulas of socially conservative family structure, gender roles, and sexuality as key to democracy and transpose them into terms that instruct the American populace in the practice of recognizing and correcting their own "dangerous" personal impulses. Wayward women and political dissidents made good object lessons for reeducation.

In the next chapter, the case of one such dissident, an American Nazi, illustrates the ways in which male political subjectivity was likewise managed through a parallel process of making the political personal. Criticism of this process offers a way, if I may modify Modleski's claims for feminist psychoanalysis, of "continuing to politicize the personal realms . . . *not* of personalizing politics."[63] The distinction is crucial in that the phrase "the personal is political" *counters*, as Lauren Berlant has said, a practice that instead claims that the political is the personal. It is this latter type of logic that makes sexual conduct a primary marker of political loyalty in a socially conservative democracy rather than more communitarian acts of civic responsibility in a more socially progressive one.

5

The American Nazi:

Cold War Social Problem Films

and National Psychobiography

■

Oh I see, you're studying me. Want to get a closer look? Maybe you want me to take my clothes off?—The Patient in *Pressure Point* (1962)

In 1962, Sidney Poitier and Bobby Darin acted the parts of a prison psychiatrist and an American Nazi in *Pressure Point*, a not particularly successful "social problem film" that by the time of its release could not be considered groundbreaking. With the approaching Black radicalism of the late 1960s and the rise of stronger Black realist voices in American filmmaking, movies like *Pressure Point* would soon seem tame, their politics outdated. But as a text whose multiple versions characterize the political narratives of its era, *Pressure Point* is instructive in unpacking the work of national psychobiography in the postwar and Cold War United States.

Pressure Point is actually the last version of a story that, like many Cold War narratives, finds its genesis in World War II, when psychoanalyst Robert Lindner worked for a federal penitentiary and had an American fascist in his care. While the story behind the film begins here, the final film version exhibits the journey that political psychology will have taken in the years since the end of the war. The ethnic and social identity of the analyst is changed from Lindner to Poitier, from Jewish to African-American. The production history of the film spans two decades of American efforts to consolidate national identity through narrative conventions that pedagogically model proper democratic subjectivity through the treatment of American domestic problems—in this case, racism. As with the wartime version of the project of delimiting a democratic against a fascist subject, normative notions of family, gender, and sexuality serve as a political guide to private life.

The shift toward psychological theories of political behavior that had begun during the war picked up momentum in the postwar period and expanded with two developments interrelated with the defeat of fascism: the ascendency of the concept of totalitarianism, which combined Communism with fascism and so extended wartime theories into the Cold War; and the turn to questions of domestic politics and the social management of conflicts internal to the nation, especially racial prejudice and political dissidence.

By the end of the war, as one historian has noted, " 'Democracy' had become the major slogan of the period."[1] As with any slogan, however, the substance of the term proved to be malleable, and much of the next two decades would centrally feature efforts to delineate precisely what democracy looked like. One strong version of this debate concerned the fate of citizens whose political views departed from the liberal-democratic norm—whether these departures issued from the Left or the Right. As discussed in chapter 3, the concept of totalitarianism that emerged in the 1930s suited this national project of limiting democratic legitimacy to the "center" of the then popular concept of a political continuum. While American anticommunism historically predates antifascism, their conflation under the concept of totalitarianism ensured that despite communism's longer history post–World War II theories of its contours would be profoundly tied to theories of fascism developed during the war.

Numerous factors contributed to the forging of this conflation, many of which have to do with domestic politics of the 1930s (New Deal liberalism, the influence of Popular Front politics, and various forms of conservative opposition to these currents).[2] While for the most part these various tendencies in American political thought were unified in their opposition to fascism, with fascism's defeat at the end of the war the hearts and minds of the American public again were thought to be up for grabs, with the definition of American democracy hanging in the balance.

Indeed, the effort to constrain what counted as democratic was already part of the wartime national project. Liberal social analyst Walter Lippmann, for instance, in his influential book *The Good Society* (1936),

Fig. 8. Publicity materials for *Pressure Point* (Hubert Cornfield, 1962). (UCLA, Department of Special Collections.)

devoted a chapter to "Totalitarian Regimes" by which he meant both communism and fascism.[3] Terms like *Hitler* bolshevism, brown communism, and red fascism, and direct comparisons between Stalin and Hitler were common in popular journalism. The identification of these regimes as antidemocratic (and rightly so) was soon extended, however, to cover many forms of domestic dissent. When Congress established the Special Committee on Un-American Activities (later known as HUAC) in 1938, the committee was originally charged with investigating domestic fascists. As it was chaired by Martin Dies (D-Texas), who abhorred Roosevelt's social recovery programs, the committee soon turned its focus nearly exclusively to flushing out American communists.[4] The term *totalitarianism* was a useful way to effect such a shift in the name of wartime patriotism.

The volatile relationship between Nazi Germany and Stalinist Russia in the course of the war of course complicated rhetoric that tried to keep the two systems closely aligned. For American Nazi sympathizers, fascism's overt anticommunism was often used to explain why Hitler should be supported. When the Nazi-Soviet pact was signed in August of 1939, this argument clearly had to change. Meanwhile, the pact cemented the blending of communism and fascism in more mainstream rhetoric. When the Nazis broke their pact with the Soviets and attacked the USSR in June of 1941, it was mainstream rhetoric that had to be redirected, especially once the United States joined the war at the end of that year. *Time*, for instance, had named Stalin its Man of the Year in 1940, claiming that he "matched himself with Adolf Hitler as the world's most hated man." After Hitler broke the pact, the magazine made Stalin one of several not entirely satisfactory Men of the Year again in 1942, equivocally praising him as "the only leader who has yet to face a major German drive without a military disaster."[5] As support for the Soviet Union was always rather tenuous, conflicts over the division of captured German territories at the end of the war easily fanned anticommunist flames, and totalitarianism once again became the conceptual opponent of U.S. democracy. The rhetorical conflation of fascism and communism, despite the wartime changes of alliance, held sway in the postwar era.

When it came to applying psychological theories of fascism to domestic problems within the United States, this conflation of fascism and communism allowed for the establishment of a notion of normative democratic psychology set against a fairly uniform template of antidemocratic psychology. American sociologist Talcott Parsons, for instance, like most American army psychologists, thought that Germany needed to be de-Nazified by leading the German people to a norm that for him was represented in U.S. democracy.[6] Although most wartime and immediate postwar rhetoric stressed this sort of opposition of the United States and Germany, the effort to delineate a template for the democratic psyche grew just as much out of psychiatrists' doubts about the political psychology of *Americans*. While largely convinced that most Americans possess the capacity to internalize authority and hence exercise political reason alongside nationalist passion, official initiatives and research projects begun during the war show that democracy was not regarded as an inevitable outcome but as something that needed to be inculcated and managed. Psychiatrist Julius Schreiber, for instance, found that it was much easier to get soldiers to hate fascism than it was to get them to show genuine enthusiasm for democratic institutions, concluding that American nationalism did not differ significantly in form from the German version.[7] And Frank Capra's "Why We Fight" series, commissioned as an effort to explain why the war effort should be supported, illustrates one tactic that tried to diminish popular ignorance and apathy. In other words, popular support, even among soldiers, was not thought to be automatic despite rhetoric to the contrary.

In this regard, the postwar ascendancy of political psychology can, on the one hand, be seen as an extension of Progressive Era concerns over the scientific management of social welfare. But its more universal application signals an expansion of the notion—formerly restricted to primarily immigrant and working-class families—that traditional social institutions were not adequately socializing citizens for the tasks of modern democracy and capitalism. Studies of fascism were thus not thought to apply only to German national character; rather, they simultaneously raised concerns about the American population.

One area in which such concern was surely justified was the problem of racial prejudice. During the war, the degree of emphasis put on the centrality of Nazi racism—especially anti-Semitism—to the characteristics against which democracy would be defined varied depending on the speaker, but images of the American populace as a multiethnic "melting pot" were at least nominally set against the forced homogeneity of Nazi Germany. By and large, however, the realities of segregation in southern states and the Armed Services, the internment of Japanese-Americans, and pernicious anti-Semitism made this clear-cut opposition so messy that it was often avoided entirely. These contradictions ultimately provided a unique opportunity for the advancement of racial equality in the United States in that wartime rhetoric allowed liberals and leftists concerned about American flaws to turn prejudice into a postwar national issue. The burgeoning movement for the civil rights of African-Americans especially mobilized wartime antifascism in the service of eliminating racial barriers within the United States. The NAACP's wartime Double V campaign, for instance, hoped to turn public attention toward the problem of American racism in the face of a war against a racist nation by suggesting that the victory should be over both foreign and domestic prejudice.[8]

Here, too, political psychology hoped to intervene. Concerns about American "morale," in terms of both intergroup conflict and the morale of minorities (especially in the face of the Detroit and Harlem race riots of 1943), was a concern of wartime psychological experts. In 1944, Gunnar Myrdal's influential study of American racism, *An American Dilemma*, combined liberalism and behavioral science, considering Black-white race relations in the context of democratic principles and against fascism.[9] Racism for Myrdal was caused by defense mechanisms built on white guilt about the contradictions between democratic principles and the practices of racial discrimination. Since the causes were psychological, so was the cure. After the war, William Menninger, chief psychiatrist for the army, subsequently named racism "America's number-one social neurosis."[10]

These theorists and their Cold War descendants were deeply influenced by the era's dominant school of psychological theory: psychoanalysis. The application of the American version of psychoanalysis to domestic racial conflict, like the management of political dissidents, tended toward highly normative, privatized solutions. The American Left's involvement in the noble project of uncovering the sources of prejudice, while generally dissenting from the facile collapse of fascism and communism, colluded with liberal and conservative tendencies to posit normative social solutions to the problem of racial prejudice.

Three major studies of American prejudice that appeared in 1950 told this type of story: Bruno Bettelheim and Morris Janowitz's *Dynamics of Prejudice*, Erik Erikson's *Childhood and Society*, and Theodor Adorno et al.'s *The Authoritarian Personality*.[11] All reached similar conclusions as to the psychological processes behind racial prejudice, which they believed were focused for the most part on the deflection of various personal frustrations onto the hated group, and all grew out of theories of German fascism drawn up in the course of the war. All had personal contact with fascism: Bettleheim was a concentration camp survivor and Janowitz, Erikson, and several members of the Frankfurt School were psychological advisers to the Armed Services, most of the latter being German émigrés (both Jewish and gentile).

By shifting the theory of the root of social and political problems away from issues of economic equity and class-based disaffection, this collection of liberal, conservative, and leftist social theorists endorsed psychological analyses and solutions that would not require the redistribution of material resources or wholesale economic reform.[12] Instead, the focus would be placed on the individual psyche and its capacity to achieve a healthy balance between freedom and independent-mindedness, on the one hand, and conformity to community norms on the other. This dominant rhetoric in the aftermath of World War II thus drafted the new genre of national psychobiography. This narrative genre ultimately sought to achieve, by different means, a similar national image as nationalist melodrama does, wherein the patriarchal family both regulates and stands in for the democratic nation. Individual citizens, like family members, are fundamentally gendered in these stories, as sexual difference and the regulation of normative sexuality that it hopes to ensure is employed to manage the disruptions that racial difference presents. As the national "family" cannot resort to the racial homogeneity generally pictured in nationalist melodrama, the focus turns to the individual.

The pedagogical goal of national psychobiography is to model a normative democratic subject for the nation's citizens through the treatment of a representative individual who has strayed from the ideal/norm. The audience for these dramas is interpellated in a performative fashion as people who have either already achieved the centrist norm or certainly could by following the therapeutic scheme laid out before them. The domain of this sort of drama is the democratic psyche and the "practices of the self," to use Foucault's concept, out of which it would be constituted.

The Popularization of National Psychobiography

The case history that comprises the narrative of *Pressure Point* went through a series of media in its journey from couch to screen. The case itself occurred in 1942 and first appeared in popular print form as "Destiny's Tot" in Lindner's collection of "psychoanalytic tales" called *The Fifty-Minute Hour*, which became a national best-seller in 1954.[13] The next version was a one-hour *Public Affairs* presentation, which was aired on a Sunday afternoon in January 1960 by NBC News.[14] And finally there was the feature film, starring Poitier as the psychiatrist and Darin as the fascist patient, directed by Hubert Cornfield. Both the television and film versions were produced by a prominent producer and director of liberal social problem films, Stanley Kramer. The course of this case history's multiple-media journey spans the twenty-year heyday of psychoanalysis in American culture—on the level of both influence on social policy and popular familiarity and support.

Robert Lindner was not a large player in the psychiatric profession and was not among the many psychiatrists who were paid by city, state, and federal governments to advise policymakers on social issues. He was, however, one of the many psychiatrists who was able to garner a popular following, which went hand in hand with this official good favor. Professionally, Lindner was chief of the Psychiatric-Psychological Division of the federal penitentiary at Lewisburg, Pennsylvania, and then a professor of psychology at Lehigh University. It was at the penitentiary that he treated "Anton," whose case history is dramatized in the multiple media described above. Lindner is best known for his popular books, especially *The Fifty-Minute Hour* and *Must You Conform?* (1956).

Lindner's cachet as a popular figure is evidenced by the fact that most of the publicity materials for *Pressure Point* include references to him, sometimes even when Cornfield, the director, is unnamed (Kramer is the other person who is virtually always mentioned, aside from the actors). Some of the posters for the film even include the line "Some men and some motion pictures just won't conform," and Kramer is consistently referred to as a nonconformist in press releases, all of which points to the assumed familiarity of the public with Lindner and his writings.[15]

The road to the popularization of psychoanalytic theories was such that even by 1940 people who read newspapers and magazines would have been familiar with a number of psychoanalytic concepts, all of them rather oversimplified from their original conception, including the idea of the unconscious (its expression in dreams and psychosomatic behavior), the importance of early childhood and sexuality, the power of repression, and a basic continuum between normal and abnormal behaviors. In a summary of popular magazine articles, historian Nathan Hale found that psychoanalysis was treated seriously, typically portraying analysts as both highly trained experts and ordinary Americans, while patients were people with whom readers could identify. These articles tended to downplay Freud's emphasis on sexuality and make the curative potential of analysis more hopeful.[16] These are the basic narrative characteristics of the genre of national psychobiography as well—the conventions of which hope to achieve a model democratic subject by the end of the story.

Max Lerner, an intellectual historian and cultural commentator, wrote the introduction to *The Fifty-Minute Hour*, in which he praises Lindner's book as a high point of the new psychoanalytic case history genre. He characterizes the five patients who are central characters in each of the "tales" as a representative cross section of American society at that moment, as he writes, "Here they are then—the young criminal, the neurotic girl, the Communist organizer, the fascist adventurer, the brilliant young physicist living in a science-fiction world of the imagination. They form almost a portrait-gallery of the characteristic figures of our era."[17] Each of these cases, disparate as they may seem, presents a very similar narrative in which the ailing individual—whether homicidal, obese, communist, fascist, or schizophrenic—is brought back in line with dominant beliefs about normal subjectivity despite Lindner's championing of nonconformity elsewhere.

In its narrative conventions, Lindner's book resembles other popularizations of psychoanalytic therapies like those surveyed by Hale. In their print and movie forms, these therapies are inevitably successful, illustrating simplified Freudian concepts like the effectiveness of catharsis and the interpretation of psychosomatic symptoms as caused by traumatic experiences. They illustrate the importance of dreams, which invariably turn out to be the expression of an inappropriate sense of Oedipal guilt. They often feature psychodrama, the literal acting out of scenes from the patient's past between the doctor and the patient.[18] Popular psychoanalytic cases deemphasize the complexities of the sexual and instead endorse rigid male and female gender roles, jettisoning Freud's theory of bisexuality for a conviction that heterosexual object choice is the innate norm. In general, they reflect how, as Freud's theories became more widespread in both popular and professionally practiced forms, they were increasingly reconciled with conventional American moral and religious values, normative sexual practices, and a firm belief in the ideal of an ego-fortified, autonomous individual.

Like other theorists who posited totalitarianism as psychic immaturity, Lindner reads both communism and fascism as psychically rooted problems that analysis can cure. Like Arthur Schlesinger's *The Vital Center* (1949), Lindner postulated that communists are lonely and frustrated people who seek social, intellectual, and sexual fulfillment by joining a group. These people are attracted to the rigidity of the party's demands for loyalty, its offer of a way to feel good about themselves by helping the weak and getting back at the wealthy. In Lindner's case, the symptom that the communist patient, Mac, is in analysis to cure is impotence, a psychosomatic manifestation of his insufficiently individuated male ego, which results in his apparent need for a group to give meaning and guidance to his life. As Lindner's diagnosis concludes, "Mac learned that the Party was his neurosis. When he concluded his analysis, it went with his symptoms. About six months after we had terminated, Mac quit the Party. He no longer needed it."[19]

Lindner is ultimately far more sympathetic to Mac than he is to the German American Bund member, Anton, in that in Lindner's schema communists are diagnosed as neurotics (harmful mainly to themselves) while fascists are psychopaths (harmful to others). Anton, indeed, comes into Lindner's care rather involuntarily, as he seeks help with blackout spells he experienced while imprisoned for sedition during the war. As with the communist, however, Lindner sees his patient as politically ill and will not consider him cured, despite the alleviation of his symptoms, until he changes his beliefs. Both cases bridge wartime theories of the psychology of German fascism and postwar applications of these theories to the problems of American political dissidence. Anton's case further bridges these studies and postwar studies of American prejudice, a central variant of national psychobiography in both the academic and popular realms.

Popular variants like Lindner's, much like their academic counterparts, claimed to perform important social work in healing the nation's rifts caused by prejudice. At the end of the broadcast of the 1960 teleplay based on Anton's case, the announcer explains that the program is NBC's tribute to the American Jewish Committee's Institute of Human Relations, which had been dedicated a few days earlier.[20] Herbert B. Ehrmann, president of the committee, addresses the television audience, explaining that the institute is intended to serve as a unique center for the study and treatment of group prejudice and bigotry in all of its manifestations. He says, "Only recently have we begun to understand how and why it is possible for the Antons of the world to play upon the fear and discontent of their fellow men, to convert private anger into public danger, and quiet prejudice into violent and explosive clashes among men and even among nations. This is vital knowledge for our time."

In keeping with these large-scale ambitions for national psychobiography, Anton's story dramatizes in print and television form how an American suffering from anti-Semitism might be brought back into line with appropriate democratic male subjectivity. In the filmed version, then, Kramer modifies the case to extend its pedagogical function to address white/Black racism. This extension, and the revisions to the logic of the analysis it required, exposes some of the contradictions embedded in national psychobiography more generally, where, as in Hitchcock's *Notorious*, a deep investment in preserving conservative social norms of gender and sexuality ultimately undermines the democracy that this sort of subjectivity-defining drama claims to ensure.

The Social Problem Film as National Psychobiography

Kramer was a major player in the new social problem genre, which comprised the cinematic variant of the studies of domestic social and political problems cataloged above.[21] He would either produce or direct films with Poitier three times, beginning with *The Defiant Ones* (1958), then *Pressure Point*, and finally *Guess Who's Coming to Dinner?* (1967). In the midst of this, he also produced and directed *Judgment at Nuremberg* (1961), which like *Pressure Point* had originally been a teleplay for the CBS television network. Taken together with Kramer's first film, *Home of the Brave* (1949), *Pressure Point* represents an effort to repeat and combine already well established genre interests. As Poitier himself said at the Berlin Film Festival, where the film was screened, "I found it devised strictly for box office potential. . . . In many American films, even those we're doing now, there is a singular lack of truth and we seek the wrong things. Basic truths often get lost in our paying court to values that propel us into vacuums."[22] Poitier could so clearly articulate this insight precisely because the film's narrative conventions had already become so well worn that their liberal solutions of interpersonal management were increasingly unsatisfying even to mainstream audiences. Kramer, too, has said that in retrospect the project was a failure, although at the time he hoped that his casting of Poitier might help the film achieve "greater explosive qualities through the switch."[23]

At the end of the 1940s when the Hollywood film industry began addressing racism in a cycle of social problem films, the fact that racism was being addressed directly was indeed significant.[24] Even the anti-Nazi films made during the war tended to shy away from anti-Semitism as a topic, often avoiding utterance of the word *Jew*.[25] This squeamishness was likely due to the power of American anti-Semitism, including the fact that the censorship battles of the late 1920s and early 1930s, which finally resulted in the establishment and ongoing diplomacy of the Production Code Administration, had often deployed anti-Semitism against the film industry, claiming that Jews were responsible for the lack of morality in Hollywood. Opposition to anti-Semitism was consequently not a central feature of prodemocracy rhetoric, and wartime anti-Nazi films tended to stress more socially conservative threats to democracy, like those given form in nationalist melodrama, rather than singling out Nazi anti-Semitism, which might make Hollywood appear too self-interested. After the defeat of the Nazis, however, liberal and leftist producers felt emboldened by both the momentum gained through wartime antiprejudice rhetoric and the track record of the industry in assisting the war effort. The first films in the social problem cycle reflected the shift to concerns over prejudice on American soil already being debated in academic circles, with two films that specifically addressed American anti-Semitism: *Crossfire* in 1947 and *Gentleman's Agreement* in 1948. By 1949, however, the social problem genre, like American political/social psychology and policy, turned to white racism against Blacks, with *Home of the Brave*, *Lost Boundaries*, *Pinky*, *Intruder in the Dust*, and *No Way Out*.[26]

Two of these films, *Home of the Brave* and *No Way Out*, are important precursors to the project that finally became *Pressure Point*. The former was the first Kramer production to deal with the psychology of racism, and the latter was the breakthrough film for Poitier, which began the lifelong series of roles—including *Pressure Point*—in which he played restrained Black men who endure the indignities and injustices of racism with cool strength and patience. These roles represent the type of Hollywood liberal vision that held sway throughout the 1950s and into the early 1960s, a vision that even at the time was considered to be limited by those who hoped for more realistic and radical portrayals represented by the roles played by other, less "Hollywood," Black actors like Paul Robeson and Harry Belafonte.[27] Poitier's repetitive roles were highly successful, however, in signifying progress toward racial harmony for consensus-driven, centrist America, even as they lagged behind the actual events of the civil rights movement.

Home of the Brave, like *Pressure Point*, is a national psychobiography, except that it deals with the management of a Black patient's racism-induced psychological problems. In the film, a psychiatrist treats a Black soldier named Moss for the symptoms of partial amnesia and hysterical paralysis, of which he is miraculously cured, as was the norm for the popular genre, through analysis. The origin point of the paralysis lies with the death of a buddy and his feelings of guilt associated with it. His guilt derives from the fact that, because his friend nearly called him a "nigger" just before he was shot, he feels in some measure glad that his former friend and platoon mate is dead. The cure lies in Moss realizing that his gladness instead issues from the quite universal feeling of relief that it was not he who was killed. The issue of Moss's sense of betrayal at his friend's utterance is thus never adequately addressed. Instead, the conclusion holds out the liberal hope that underneath it all there are really no differences between men. As with other psychological theories of social problems, the progressive intentions of the antiracist sentiment are somewhat tempered by a deflection of attention away from an analysis of systematic racism in both the army and white society at large by focusing instead on personal and/or universalist solutions.

Much like the casting choice that would later alter the course of Lindner's case history, *Home of the Brave* is an adaptation of Arthur Laurents's play by the same name about anti-Semitism, but here the patient's identity is changed from Jewish to Black rather than the doctor's, as in *Pressure Point*.[28] The perceived ease with which a Black patient was substituted for a Jewish one reflects the focus of postwar studies of racism, which either left "prejudice" unspecified, implying a generalizable phenomenon, or were primarily concerned with Black-white relations but extrapolated them from studies of Nazi anti-Semitism.

Psychoanalyst Franz Fanon, working in colonial and postcolonial France contemporaneously with the upsurge of psychoanalytic work on the effects of racism in the United States, has addressed the specificity of white racism against Blacks and how this differs from anti-Semitism. He has argued that to the prejudiced white man the Black man's threat is not intellectual, as the Jewish man's is, but sexual. He notes that "when a white man hates Black men, is he not yielding to a feeling of impotence or of sexual inferiority? . . . In the case of the Jew, one thinks of money and its cognates. In that of the Negro, one thinks of sex." A bit later, Fanon puts it most directly: "The Negro symbolizes the biological danger; the Jew the intellectual danger."[29] Most studies of prejudice in the United States, however, did not make distinctions between different forms of racism, even though the categories Jewish and Black were culturally rather rigidly separated at the time.

As part of the effort to generalize rather than specify forms of prejudice, antiracists in the 1940s and 1950s endeavored to make race a more central issue by claiming that racism was not only something that detrimentally affected Blacks, as in *Home of the Brave*, but was also something that prejudiced white people "suffered from." As historian Ruth Feldstein puts it, "This dual focus helped to redefine racism as undemocratic and un-American. In particular, focusing on how prejudice hurt whites helped to make race relations a national problem, and issues of race more central to liberal discourse generally."[30] Lindner's case reflects this sort of strategy in that Anton's symptoms—his nightmares, blackout spells, and insomnia—are painful manifestations caused by the same psychic factors as his political bigotry. When Kramer had his scriptwriters adapt this case in order to accommodate his casting of Poitier in the doctor's role, this focus on the suffering of the racist white man is retained, but it is also significantly augmented by more overt efforts to claim equal levels of psychic damage done to Black and white men in a racist society, in part by addressing Black hatred of whites as a parallel to white hatred of Blacks. Exaggerating tendencies already present in Lindner's case and echoing Kramer's strategy in *Home of the Brave*, *Pressure Point* makes masculinity the primary ground over which this drama unfolds. But it is ultimately a narrative logic that has difficulty reconciling the material and theoretical differences between Black, Jewish, and dominant white male subjectivity in its efforts to equalize the causes and experiences of racism.

In my analysis of the two most significant versions of this case history—Lindner's print version and Kramer's screen version—the alterations required to accommodate the change in the doctor's ethnicity (from Jewish to Black) are the most revealing of the normative agendas embedded in the national psychobiography and the textual failure of the liberal project of generalizing prejudice as a problem experienced similarly by everyone. The changes made to the script after Poitier was cast significantly modify the logic of the patient's analysis, mainly because the new script has difficulty fitting Black masculinity into the same template into which Jewish masculinity was inserted in Lindner's original version.[31] A second change then adds a narrative frame that provides a parallel case of a 1962 contemporary Black patient with which to compare Lindner's 1942 Anton. A third category of change, wherein Anton's political/sexual pathology shifts from sadistic bisexuality to failed heterosexuality, then underscores the thoroughgoing centrality of normative masculinity to the liberal antiracist project, albeit in a surprising fashion. These three sets of changes together chart some of the more compelling ambivalences nestled in the logic of national psychobiography as it attempted to expand its narrative salience to an ever wider range of domestic political issues.

The Doctor's Mantle: Anti-Semitism, Racism, and the Issue of Transference from "Destiny's Tot" to *Pressure Point*

The interpretive strategies of psychoanalysis scrutinize both the patient's past and the dynamics of the present dialogue between the analyst and analysand.[32] It is clearly the second narrative that is most affected by the casting of Poitier in the doctor's role. In Lindner's published version of the case, "Destiny's Tot," the Jewish doctor's and the anti-Semitic patient's mutual struggles over transference lay the groundwork for Lindner's theory of the relationship between sexuality and racism. Lindner discusses his own understandable disgust, as a Jew, for his patient and the patient's views, while the patient in turn wields his anti-Semitism at his Jewish doctor, merging it with his hatred for his father. This connection is exacerbated by the patient's sense of the doctor's disgust, making it parallel his sense of rejection by his own father and thereby preventing—for a time—the successful enabling of the process that will allow him to see the root of his actions: his homosexual identification with his father's brutality covering over his homosexual desire for his father's affection.

Understanding the ambivalence of his hatred for his father is thus akin to Anton's reckoning with his racialist hatred for the Jewish doctor. In Lindner's account, the process for achieving this (and the crucial incident through which it is achieved) has everything to do with the correlation of paternal authority with the authority of the prison hierarchy, the doctor's profession, and ultimately the perception of Jewish alignment with science and knowledge. This latter component is clearly not available to the doctor played by Poitier because science and knowledge are generally not associated with Blackness, as Fanon points out. Racist conceptions of Blackness instead associate it with irrationality, primitivism, and brute strength.

To keep the two versions of the story straight as I go on to compare them further, I will use the name "Lindner" to designate the doctor in the print version, and "the Doctor" to designate him in the film, where he is unnamed. Likewise, I shall use "Anton" to designate the patient in the book and "the Patient" in the film. This is in fact how they appear in the final version of the script, underscoring the ways in which the film aspires to present a general template for political psychobiography, with the patient serving as an all-purpose bigot rather than a particular case.

First, then, we will consider Lindner's formulation of the role of Jewishness in Anton's therapy. As above, Lindner's theory appears to coincide with Fanon's as to the source of anti-Semitism: an "intellectual" fear. But, as cultural historian Sander Gilman observes, this theory might well mask a deeper cultural logic wherein sexual fears, akin to, though not the same as, those associated with Blacks, are more primary than the theory allows. Gilman notes that Freud's own Jewishness is curiously absent from his theoretical formulations, racial difference being deflected instead onto sexual difference. In this way, race, commonly thought of as neglected in Freud's work, actually resides at its core.[33] Gilman postulates that Freud's deflection represents his own efforts to negate the anti-Semitic alignment of Jewish men not with "money and its cognates" but with femininity and sexual deviance. By elevating sexual difference between men and women to premiere importance, Freud projected qualities formerly projected onto Jewish men onto the category of "woman."[34] As a result, men represent direct figures of authority for Freud as fathers or as the sons who want to become them. Gilman argues that Freud was reacting against the nineteenth-century racialization of Jews—in fact, the development of a medical discourse of race in general—by reorienting explanations for human behavior toward a sexual system that affirmed the patriarchal order of things.

Lindner, trained in the psychoanalytic tradition, retains Freud's focus on sexual difference and sexuality but reintroduces the question of the analyst's Jewishness—a move in keeping with the tenor of political psychology and its postwar focus on racial prejudice. Like Freud, however, Lindner does not acknowledge the anti-Semitic association of Jewish men with femininity and instead overtly names the role of his Jewish maleness in the therapy as dependent on its alliance with scientific, governmental, and ultimately paternal authority. Some of this is conveyed by way of Lindner's description of the patient's brand of anti-Semitism, which identifies a powerful Jewish conspiracy as justification for his views. In the first meeting with the patient (before he actually enters analysis), Anton scoffs at the Jewish doctor for thinking that his opinions are pathological, by way of the following exchange.

> *Anton*: A Jew psychologist! What the hell else can I expect from you!
> *Lindner*: You can go anytime you like. But I'd like to know why you think a Jew psychologist can't give a valid opinion on whether or not you're crazy.
> *Anton*: Because you Jews are all the same. You've wanted to get me for a long time. You put that crippled bastard into the White House and now you think you're in the saddle! Well, all right, so you got me in this joint and there's nothing I can do about it now. You can call me crazy and lock me up. That's just what a Jew psychologist would do— But . . . you can't keep me here forever![35]

This exchange of course reflects the patient's rather common opinions about Jewish conspiracy, which Lindner subsequently tries to use as bait by saying that maybe he could conspire to have Anton committed on the basis of his connections with other "Jew psychologists." But while this sort of pervasive belief in the conspiracy of Jews typically hinges on a "parasitic" vision of Jewish power (achieved via manipulation and other such indirect, "feminine" methods), Lindner ultimately elides this persistent subtext by insisting that the patient perceives Jewish power as paternal power. What Lindner's insistence misses, then, is the way that the "feminization" of Jewish power in anti-Semitic thought is actually a means of defending paternal power for whiteness by associating Jewishness with the insidious corrosive feminine that *undermines* paternal authority through proximity or intimacy.

Instead, the association of Jews with scientific and governmental authority, and thus with paternal/patriarchal power, is central to the logic of both Lindner's theory of the patient's transference and his own countertransference. The patient is meant to identify with the doctor as an authority figure and so work out his neurosis with regard to his father. Lindner, meanwhile, is charged with seeing himself as a father figure in relation to this hostile wayward son and indeed to see himself in him as well. The analysis then bears this out: an analytic breakthrough follows Anton's discovery that his blackouts are precipitated by seeing a shadowy figure—identified first as his father and then as himself. He is subsequently able to understand the Oedipal nature of his symptoms. In typical popular style, the revelation of the patient's never-verbalized hatred for his father (and the buried guilt expressed by his substitution of himself for the murdered body) miraculously alleviates the symptoms. Anton believes himself cured and stops coming to therapy. Lindner, however, does not think his patient is cured. Indeed, he cannot comfortably occupy the father's role nor identify with Anton because the latter still holds his aberrant political beliefs. When asked to comment on his eligibility for parole, the doctor says he will not recommend Anton on these grounds. Thus ensues the conflict between analyst and analysand that occasions the larger connection that the book, and then the film, hopes to make between racism and the Oedipal drama.

After some time, Lindner has occasion to encounter Anton again, when he fills in for a medical officer charged with screening prisoners who have requested medical attention. Anton refuses to tell Lindner why he is there and then yells out in front of other inmates, "You know damn well what's wrong, you Jew bastard!" and storms out. Lindner recognizes that he has to do something about the breach of discipline by confronting Anton man to man—shedding his "Jewishness"/authority in the process. As Lindner confronts Anton in his cell, the patient initially doesn't respond, saying the doctor wouldn't be so brave if he wasn't wearing a uniform. Lindner takes his insignia off and says, "I don't have any uniform on. There's just the two of us here and I won't call the guards. Will you apologize or do I have to make you?"[36] After some hesitation, Anton backs down and apologizes—and says he wants to start therapy again.

Lindner's analysis of this confrontation stresses his role as a paternal symbol in that Lindner's denied recommendation reminds Anton of rejections he suffered at the hands of his father. Lindner extrapolates from this to the patient's anti-Semitism:

> He wanted to strike back and I, as the living immediate representational figure of the childhood drama, was the aptest subject for his hostility. Further, through me, he could get at larger groups: the Jews, whom I represented, and the authoritarian world that restricted him, of which I was a symbol. My response to his challenge had impressed him not only because it indicated something personal about me, but because by it I had destroyed the illusory links and synapses by which he could connect the paternal image with the wide world: my individualization of the conflict had forced him to face the way he so mechanically ascribed his problems and frustrations to external groups or forces.[37]

In other words, by stripping himself of institutional authority Lindner breaks the theorized link between father/Jews/authority, so that the patient's fury can once again be directed where it belongs—toward his father. This is also a breakthrough moment for Lindner, then, for he is only here able to assert direct masculine superiority—in other words, truly assume the father role.

The longer history of anti-Semitism—and in particular the variant that imagines a Jewish conspiracy—is not typically one that obtains from Jews embodying an "immediate representational figure" of paternal authority. Instead, the male Jewish conspirators/authority figures of anti-Semitic lore are, as Michael Rogin describes it, of a "feline, spidery, parasitic, sexually ambiguous character": in a word, feminine. Thus, the diagnosis of anti-Semitism as an extension of Oedipal desires for parricide are, as Rogin goes on to say, "partly a male Jewish wish for rational authority, a flight from the identification, by assimilating Jews as well as gentile anti-Semites, of the 'infected and infecting' Jewish man with the *ostjudisch*, Black and female body."[38] Lindner, after Freud, plays up his show of threatening masculinity as central to the drama of transference, even as he confesses to being ill equipped for physical confrontation. Lindner's efforts to fortify Jewish masculinity with patriarchal authority thus sublimate the feminine. Tellingly, then, when the doctor's racial identity is changed to African-American, some of this sublimation leaks through.

In the film, the Black psychiatrist does not have the same recourse to institutional power, and so the script alters the initial exchange to reflect Jewish advocacy for Black advancement. The Patient says, "Now that the Jews put that cripple in the White House you people think you've got it made." When the Patient says he can't be kept there forever, the Doctor replies, "Oh I don't know about that—I could team up with some Jew Psychiatrists and have you committed." Black male authority is thus highly mediated—"parasitic" (and hence feminine) in a way that Jewish authority is *not* in both Lindner's and the film's formulations. The Patient's originally scripted transference of hostility from his father to Jews is uncomfortably extended to Blacks—a move that not only leaves unexamined the specifics of white racism against Blacks, the intellectual versus biological danger in Fanon's terms, but ultimately projects the textually sublimated femininity of anti-Semitism's images of Jewish men onto Black men instead.[39]

In the film, the Patient comes to the Doctor's office in order to solicit his support for his parole hearing. The confrontation between them takes place immediately, in the office, with no one else around. The Patient demonstrates his unchanged political views, claiming that when the Nazis take over the United States "they won't have to make Negroes wear armbands," clearly threatening that Blacks, like Jews in Nazi Germany, will be targeted for persecution and extermination. The Doctor demands an apology for the Patient's aggression, and when he doesn't get it he takes off his jacket to encourage the Patient to fight him man to man. As in Lindner's version of the confrontation, it is only at this point that the Patient backs down and apologizes. As in Lindner's version, the Doctor offers an analysis, asserting that when he denied the Patient his parole recommendation the Patient felt rejected, and hence the Doctor reminded him of his father. Again, because he is a doctor and thus an authority figure, the Patient is said to be unable to strike out directly and so attacked him "as a Negro."

But this is the point where the parallel comes apart. The Doctor says that when he took his jacket off he was "no longer a figure of authority, nor even a Negro—just a man. And to one man it is easy to apologize." In Lindner's case, as in the subsequent script versions prior to Poitier's casting, the act of taking off the insignia is seen as disaligning the Jewish doctor from the conspiratorial stereotype he came in that moment to represent: taking off the insignia thus individualizes the doctor, making it possible to get beyond the racial association. But when Poitier takes off his jacket he is no less a Black man than he was with his jacket on, since no similar stereotypical association of Black men with institutional authority exists. If anything, taking off his jacket makes the Black doctor even more of a threat, closer to the bodily danger that Fanon describes above. The Black man's threat to the white man might echo the physically threatening father, but this echo is not dispelled by his taking off the doctor's mantle. Nor would the doctor's problem of countertransference be alleviated by such a convenient, visible gesture.[40]

The relevance of this slip is symptomatically revealed in the press materials used to promote the film. Trying to build on Kramer's success with *The Defiant Ones*, the posters for *Pressure Point* feature virtually the same graphic scheme: a white and Black man facing off as if about to grapple in a physical fight (figs. 9 and 10). In *The Defiant Ones*, Poitier plays against Tony Curtis, and the two are prison fugitives literally chained together and therefore dependent on each other for their escape. Physical conflict does occur in the course of the film, although the final message, like that of many liberal social problem films, is that conflict can be assuaged by kindness and generosity on the part of the oppressed minority. The conflict sells the film, while its dispersal in the course of the narrative illustrates the genre's hegemonic logic. In *Pressure Point*, the Doctor still exhibits exceptional patience and magnanimity (in keeping with Poitier's star persona), although this attitude seems more narratively warranted than in *The Defiant Ones* in that it is part of his role as a doctor.

The ad campaign, however, by exploiting the salability of racial conflict, robs Poitier's character of his status. While viewers could already have come to expect Poitier's character to rise above this sort of brute faceoff of Black and white masculinity, it is precisely because of the excessive brutality accorded to Black men that he must be portrayed as so exceptionally in control. The racist expectation of Black male brutality in the campaign is exacerbated by promotional slogans like "This is what happens when White-hot Rage and Black Fury reach the Pressure Point!" which further equalizes the men's hostility toward one another, balancing white and Black racism, transference and countertransference. The ad materials thus inadvertently reveal the unconscious logic of the scene that actually does appear in the film: a scene in which the Doctor's taking off his jacket if anything *increases* his signification as a potentially brutal, dangerous Black man. No longer a doctor, he is what the racist image imagines: a physical menace. The only reference in these promotional materials to the fact that Darin's character is a Nazi is that their bodies have been arranged in such a way as to suggest a swastika; that it is both of their bodies that comprise this emblem further underscores the parallelism for which liberal rhetorics and popular psychology strive.

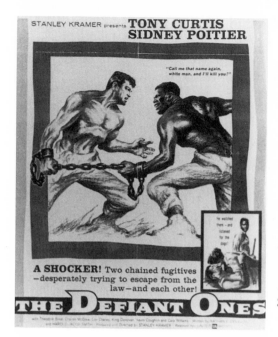

Fig. 9. Publicity materials for *The Defiant Ones* (Stanley Kramer, 1958). (UCLA, Department of Special Collections.)

It is more likely the sexual nature of the unconscious menace of the brutal Black man, however, rather than anything as complex as trouble with countertransference, that is symptomatically banked on in the publicity materials. Sexual menace is further suggested through the graphic placement of a white woman with a tic-tac-toe board on her back, sometimes between the men and sometimes to the side (figs. 8 and 10). On some lobby cards, her image is accompanied by the sensational quote "There are Some Men Worse Than Killers . . . Some Things Worse Than Murder!" The figure references a scene in which the Patient recounts his sexual assault on a woman, one of the plot points where his failed heterosexuality helps to characterize the psychopathology of his politics. The publicity materials, however, leave the question as to who committed these "things worse than murder" unanswered. Given the long history of projecting the rape of white women onto Black men, the ideological work done by this image again completely obscures the actual gender dynamics of the story. The white woman, indeed, plays the role of a marker of the Patient's (political) illness, but on the lobby card she instead appears potentially as a figure to be fought over by the men or perhaps protected by the white man from the Black man's sexual predation.[41] The publicity materials therefore make visible what is actually but a momentary leak in the logic of the film, which otherwise allows Poitier

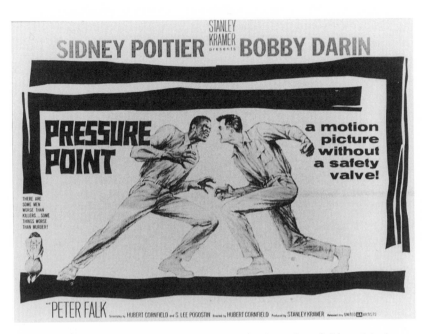

Fig. 10. Publicity materials for *Pressure Point* (Hubert Cornfield, 1962). (UCLA, Department of Special Collections.)

the quiet dignity that his liberal role requires, revealing how the Doctor's Blackness cannot be fully reconciled with the already somewhat phantasmatic paternal part originally written by and for a Jewish doctor.

The second consequence of this substitution builds in a seemingly contradictory fashion on the Black man's perceived sexual menace: Poitier's position as a Black man not only reflects a repressed image of Black male brutality, but it is also *feminized*. Gilman is again useful here, in that he documents the ways in which in the course of the nineteenth century menacing Black male hypersexuality became conceptually aligned with female hypersexuality.[42] Nineteenth-century scientific racism linked "inferior races" to women and children, who were thought to be closer to nature or their "animal" origins, even as women were being divided into hypersexual and largely asexual categories based on both race and class. While it is surely submerged in most racist imagery of the sexually ominous Black man, this connection by way of mental "primitivism" persists in the deep structure of racism and sexism as they are combined. It is also legible by a contrary logic in the liberal convolutions of *Pressure Point* as it attempts to extend Poitier's exceptional gentility to a strictly gendered psychoanalytic schema.

This genteel, feminized Black man is a staple of the literary tradition of antiracism and abolitionism—the most celebrated example being Harriet Beecher Stowe's maternal Uncle Tom, who sacrifices himself for the lost child Little Eva in *Uncle Tom's Cabin* (1851). This image attempts to counteract the image of the hypersexualized (and thus hypermasculinized) Black man by aligning him with the nobler view of feminine "nature." The same strategy might be read in several of Kramer's social problem films in which Black men (Moss in *Home of the Brave* and Poitier's character in *The Defiant Ones*) are portrayed as caring for their white companions. Both films even contain scenes in which the Black man cradles the dying white man in his arms. But this combination of tendencies—the unconscious conceptual association of Black masculine hypersexuality with feminine hypersexuality and the attempt to counter the image of Black hypermasculinity with an image of the maternal Black man—results in two converging iconographic codes that associate the Black man with femininity and femininity with long suffering, selflessness, and weakness.

The first instance of feminization in *Pressure Point* occurs after a scene in which the Patient has recounted a scenario in which his often drunk father brings home an equally drunk woman and torments his mother with his infidelity. The boy is imaged as struggling not to succumb to his mother's "seduction," but he ultimately gives in to caring for her, stoically receiving her cloying and clingy embraces after the father has left. The Patient describes these moments as times when he did not feel sorry for his mother, even as he appeared to soothe her. The Doctor consequently intervenes to ask why not, to which the Patient responds that he doesn't know. The Doctor presses forward, asking, "Don't you feel sorry for people who are weak?" which affords a topical segue to a discussion not of the Patient's feelings toward his mother but of his racism toward Blacks.

The Patient responds that he admires a weak man who competes. He says he thinks "Negroes are inferior" but admits, on the Doctor's prompting, that he admires them on the basis of their efforts to compete regardless. The Doctor then asks about Jews, whom the Patient says are more dangerous than Blacks because they can pass for white and are smart. Jews are thus again aligned with authority while African-Americans are aligned with maternal weakness. As African-American women are undertheorized in both psychoanalysis generally and in the film's version thereof, what this logical convolution reflects is the film's efforts to offer Poitier's persona as a substitution for the racist image of the brutal Black man, but it does so by aligning him with the Patient's mother. In the narrative logic of the case history genre, this move reflects the interrelation of two somewhat contradictory aims: while modeling the psychoanalytic cure as the production of a proper democratic subject, the film's makers reveal their own anxieties about race, gender, and sexuality.

Thus, attempts to portray the Doctor's subjectivity also emphasize his feminine identification. Ironically, the female assault victim so ambiguously featured in the publicity materials plays a crucial role. The scene, which does not appear in the book or the television versions but was added in the course of rewriting the script for the cinema, portrays a past event in which the Patient and his rowdy buddies wreak havoc on a bar owner and his wife when they are told they can't have anything more to drink. The scene is part of the larger effort to link the Patient's sexual dysfunction (here his cruelty toward women) with his political psychology, but inexplicably the doctor says in his omniscient voice-over, "That was the point at which I became frightened—I wasn't sure exactly what I was frightened of." This uncertainty seems odd. Certainly, there would be something frightening about sitting across from a rapist, but the Doctor claims to feel an indescribable fright, clearly larger than his empathy for the woman who has been victimized, humiliated, and indeed *marked* by her assailants, like the walls of the bar, with tic-tac-toe boards all over her body and face. A more hopeful reading would be that he feels a sense of mutual devaluation in the political world. But in a film that, like psychoanalysis itself at the time, insists so much on gender as a defining characteristic, this progressive read is revealed to reflect the kind of feminization of Black men that is typical of liberal approaches to racism. For it is mainly through this indescribable fear that Poitier reveals his trouble with countertransference—not in direct hostility, as Lindner does in the case history.

The cause of the Doctor's inchoate fright is explained in the film after the Patient has gone through his entire account of how he came to join the American Nazi Party. At the end of this account, the Doctor says that the Nazis have no hope of succeeding because everything they're driving for is a lie (meaning white superiority), to which the Patient responds that the United States is based on an even bigger lie: "all men are created equal." The Patient says that as a Black man the Doctor should know how deep that lie runs. In another omniscient voice-over, the Doctor then states, "Right then and there I knew what I was frightened of"— meaning that the Patient has a point: there is a gap between the rhetoric and the reality of equality in the United States, which might prove to be the reason for his heinous party's success. Going back, however, to the point at which the Doctor's fright originally emerged, it is significant that he would begin to get an inkling of this problem after hearing of the Patient's cruelty toward women and not be able to name what bothers him until later. While largely unexplored as a sentiment, the implication is that the Doctor not only empathizes with the woman but in the end unconsciously *identifies* with her as a sacrificial victim to the disturbed white male psyche. The tic-tac-toe boards written on her body literalize their mutual belonging to marked identity categories against which the white man defines himself. No such parallel identification occurs in any of the previous versions of the script, teleplay, or book, in which the doctor is Jewish, since the counterracist effort in those texts was to assure that Jewish men had direct access to paternal power.

Indeed, the film's script complicates the Black man's access to psychoanalytically understood power further by excising references to the homosexual desire the boy Patient is theorized to feel toward his brutal and emotionally distant father in the book and teleplay. The film's final script instead makes the Patient's relationship to women more prominent in the profile, wherein he either idealizes or denigrates them. Hence, while in all versions of the case it is the mother who most influences the young man's capacity for psychosis/Nazism, further suppressing the psychic role of the father in the film results in the Black man being more sexually ambiguous than the Jewish man was originally scripted to be. The liberal politics that inform the dominant variant of American political psychology thus foreground the reinforcement of patriarchal gender relations as solutions to domestic social problems like racial prejudice. But the underlying anxieties that racial difference presents to this logic of "we're all men here" keep breaking through, revealing that the category "men" is not as representationally uniform as the rhetoric requires.

"You Don't Understand How Deeply He Hates": Racism, Reverse Racism, and the White/Black Mother

This lack of the uniformity is nowhere more evident than in the narrative frame added to the film's script after Poitier was cast. The frame, which takes place in the film's 1962 present, offers the most straightforward presentation of the liberal logic that there are no differences between men that cannot be surmounted by appeals to the common gender characteristics of "democratic" patriarchal manhood—in other words, benign as opposed to brutal paternal authority.

The frame story presents Poitier as an older version of the Doctor. This older Doctor is inspired to narrate the case of the American Nazi and his difficulties with his therapy because of its purported similarity to a case being conducted by a young doctor under his supervision, only in the contemporary case it is a white doctor who is trying to treat a young Black, male patient. The young doctor (Peter Falk) wants to be taken off the case, which he believes is not progressing because of the young man's hatred of white men. As he says, "The boy hates me—you don't understand how deeply he hates." The older Doctor then asserts that the boy's hatred is in fact the root of his problem and that he deliberately chose to put the young doctor on the case because he is better than the rest. The Doctor thereby claims that he both did and did not assign Falk because of his race.

To convince the young doctor not to quit, the Doctor recounts the adaptation of Lindner's case, which comprises the bulk of the film, claiming that he, too, almost quit over a case involving racial hatred many years ago. The most immediate line of identification is thus a professional one (two doctors with patients who hate them), reinforcing the liberal notion that all men are equal, which by extension implies that all racisms are equal as well. The common bond of the Black and white doctors further models the pedagogical object of the male democratic psyche, the benign paternal authority that the elder doctor exhibits toward the younger and that in turn the doctors exhibit toward their patients—a strategy that is meant to bring the wayward male patients' behaviors into line with this model.

However, the rhetorical dependence on race blindness via gender commonality trips itself up here as well. At the end of the film, the story returns to this frame, as the elder Doctor reassures the younger: "I'm not saying that case was as difficult as the one you have now but. . . . I didn't quit." The younger doctor is then inspired by this paternal offering to concoct a most confounding response: "I know how I'm going to whip this case. I'm getting some pieces of burnt cork and I'm going into the next session in blackface." The racial parity offered by the elder Doctor is thus extended to a caricature of "we're all men here." Nonetheless, the elder Doctor simply replies: "Good idea. But don't let me down because you're a white man."

With this exchange, the last in the film, the problematic oscillation between race blindness and race consciousness bubbles to the surface.

The last line, "But don't let me down because you're a white man," echoes an earlier scene in the body of the film when the Doctor tries to have himself taken off the 1942 case. He is talked out of it by his white supervisor, who says that the Patient's needling is in fact one of his symptoms. The supervisor claims that he took some risks in hiring a Black doctor and adds, "Now don't tell me you're going to let me down . . ." The voice-over of the Doctor then finishes the sentence for him, saying " 'Just because you're a Negro' is what he didn't say." The reversal of this statement at the end of the film is thus meant to perform another gesture of parity between men. Coming as it does on the tail of the blackface comment, however, and especially marked as the last line in the film, it instead seems to remind us that, in or out of blackface, Falk's character remains white, a point that contradicts the film's over-arching liberal tenet of the transcendence of gender sameness.

The invocation of the blackface tradition itself might reveal such a contradiction, insofar as blackface hardly makes Black and white men equal. As Rogin has noted, American blackface in its various forms was part of what he calls the project of "engendering white America." It "loosened up white identities by taking over Black ones, by underscoring the line between white and black."[43] Immigrant groups in particular—and especially Jews—used blackface to become (white) American by tapping into America's cultural Other, the African-American, against whom whiteness could be defined. The suggestion that a psychiatrist might improve his relationship to the young Black man who hates him by arriving in blackface ignores this history. As the Doctor's following comment symptomatically reveals, what the practice instead does is reinforce the privilege of whiteness. This privilege, then, has graver consequences for the young Black patient, whose "reverse racism" is by equation made equally as "sick"—and undemocratic—as the Patient's Nazism. Yet the implied parallel that is drawn between the Nazi and Black patients again reflects the larger context of American political psychology within which the film appeared.

The Nazi patient's life history, indeed, quite closely mirrors the numerous efforts to describe and suggest correctives for the prejudiced "personality" in the postwar era. In both the book and the film, the Nazi patient's father is a brute, his mother weak and clingy; he is torn between identification with his father's brutality and desire for his affection, and he is both repulsed and attracted to the "special incestuous character of his relationship to his mother."[44] In the course of the various script revisions, the Oedipal formula is purified, from the original case in which Anton is the youngest of five children to his description as an only child once Cornfield, the film's director, takes over from S. Lee Pogostin, who wrote the teleplay and the first draft of the screenplay. Anton becomes a Nazi because, as Lindner states, "It provided everything for which a psychopath could ask," which includes "a whole world to hate, in extension of his primary hatred of the father."[45] In the film, the connection between psychic life and the Patient's adult identity is most often conveyed aurally, as the adult Patient often speaks in a child's voice. The connection between this life history and the Patient's politics is then both visually and aurally reinforced in the film. The Doctor's voice-over says that "if 100 frustrated individuals line up behind one psychopath then you are essentially dealing with 101 psychopaths" just as the camera zooms in on a portrait of Hitler and then dissolves to a close-up of the Patient's face.

The Black patient in the film version, on the other hand, is characterized through only a very brief summary of his life history: he is thirteen years old, his mother is a prostitute for white men, and his father was hanged by white men for killing one of the white men his mother brought home. The pathological Black family dynamic is psychoanalytically theorized as follows: the Black boy hates whites because (1) white men as a group have usurped his Oedipally desired position as partner to the mother; and (2) a group of white men have usurped his Oedipally desired position as murderer of his father, who in turn was lashing out against his own displacement. In this version of an Oedipal scenario, the Black father is always in the position of the male child, looking on as his wife is coupled with (and degraded by) white men as a category. His lashing out against these men (or a single representative of them) is then punished by the racial/patriarchal law that denies him. The son watches all of this at another remove, where, unlike the Nazi, his primary connection to his father is not to his authority but to his disempowerment.[46] Thus, even though the film's liberal rhetoric encourages a parallel between the experiences of all men, the invocation of the psychobiography to effect this conclusion contradicts its own aim.

In psychoanalytic narratives, the root of these unlikely parallels between all men lies in the structural parallel forged between their mothers: African-American women are seen as responsible for the ostensible social pathologies of Blacks; and, in the Cold War's obsession with (white) momism, the mom is seen as the internal subversive agent responsible for producing sons too weak to choose democracy. While there are significant distinctions, of course, both hinge on the association of dominant women with social and political pathology.[47] Since the relationship between paternal authority and political authority is theorized as nearly identical, it is mothers who determine the success or failure of their sons in navigating both. Surely, the antifeminism voiced in postwar attacks on mom is obvious, but the variant put forward in antiracist rhetoric is similarly antifeminist in more subtle ways (including a lack of research interest in women and girls). Mothers are not seen as political subjects here (in fact, the political views of mothers are never an issue). They are political agents only *as mothers* who may produce sons who will affect the political landscape of the nation, regardless of the mothers' own political philosophies.

Psychological studies of the effects of racism published around the same time as *Pressure Point* was going through its various revisions redoubled their efforts to reinforce Black men's need for access to patriarchal authority so that over time the notion that "we are all men here" could become a more workable rhetorical strategy for the nation.[48] These studies suggested that the primary problem facing Black men was that "matriarchal" gender relations had arisen out of their disenfranchisement and now could be blamed for a wide range of social problems. Sociologist Thomas Pettigrew, for instance, conducted research in the 1950s and early 1960s on the causes and effects of racism toward Blacks and concluded that fatherlessness most typified the Black male personality, regardless of whether or not they had grown up with fathers in the home. Pettigrew notes that 75 percent of Black families included a male breadwinner, yet he proceeds in his analysis of fatherlessness as if it applied to all Black men and their families.[49] The most famous and controversial policy document was what became known as the Moynihan Report, which drew on many of these previous studies to conclude, as they did, that the matriarchal Black family was a large part of the problem of Black poverty.[50]

These theories and the policy decisions they influenced sought to improve race relations by bolstering Black masculinity through patriarchal authority and the reinforcement of sexist notions of traditional gender roles. Black feminists have addressed the sexism embedded in these theories. Angela Davis, for instance, criticizes sociologist E. Franklin Frazier, the first to develop the idea of a Black matriarchy, for having "misinterpreted the spirit of independence and self-reliance Black women necessarily developed, and thus deplored the fact that 'neither economic necessity nor tradition had instilled (in Black woman) the spirit of subordination to masculine authority.' "[51] Hortense Spillers further notes how "the African-American female's 'dominance' and 'strength' come to be interpreted by later generations—both Black and white, oddly enough—as a 'pathology,' as an instrument of castration."[52]

These pathological images of independent Black women, joined by emotionally manipulative white ones, were a staple of both academic and popular political and social psychology throughout the Cold War era. In *Pressure Point*, the Nazi's white mother is figured as extremely needy, and so she prevents her son from adequately separating from her and causes him to reject her (and hence normal heterosexuality) repeatedly. In the framing story, the Black mother is similarly positioned as overly present in the young Black male patient's psyche, since it is over her body (and her presumed defiance of her husband's objections to her prostitution) that the disempowered Black father and the powerful white men enact the displaced Oedipal dynamics of race relations. Ironically, it is because of her "bringing home" white men (note the active verb) that the castrated father acts aggressively toward white men and is punished. The son likewise is aggressive toward white men, a further chain reaction resulting from the Black father's lack of prerogative over the mother's body/will.

The gender dysphoria that was thought to result from disempowerment and the centrality of the mother is thus a further conduit for the theoretical parallel between Black pathology and Nazi psyches. Sex role adoption is named by Pettigrew, for instance, as a problematic area for Black girls and boys, resulting in Black men either exhibiting more "feminine" sensibilities than their white counterparts or overcompensating by way of displays of hypermasculinity—much as in the theory of Nazi males.[53] The central anxiety that this double coding reveals concerns efforts to claim a subjectivity for democracy that strictly observes normative gender roles and associates anything outside of this narrow band of acceptable behavior (whether this be cross-gendered behavior or excessively gendered behavior) as *politically* suspect. This is a particularly craggy project with respect to casting a democratic subjectivity for African-American men and women who have been denied access to political power and whose potential to achieve political power continues to scare the dominant white culture. While it is logically perverse, then, the precursor for this coding of Black subjectivity in the 1950s and 1960s was in fact the psychoanalytic study of the Nazi psyche.

Pettigrew's liberal aims in some ways echo those of the Frankfurt School in its surprisingly normative conclusions in *The Authoritarian Personality*. While this 1950 study remains focused on a comparison of prejudiced and unprejudiced white men and women, its socially normative conclusions lay out a model for the "democratic personality" against which Pettigrew and others can later define the subjectivity of poor urban Blacks.[54] The compensatory mechanism of "hypermasculinity" is read in the Frankfurt School study as a symptom, where "A compensatory display of 'toughness' and ruthlessness is . . . correlated with antidemocratic social and political beliefs." This toughness is theorized to result from the prejudiced man's inability to sublimate his identification with his mother successfully, for which he feels he must overcompensate.

There are crucial differences, of course, between the image of the Nazi and the image of the Black man in psychological theories, but gender dysfunction caused by an emotionally overpresent mother and emotionally (or literally) absent father are common to both. Overall, these studies—especially those of the African-American psyche—never questioned their assumptions that patriarchal gender relations were the most beneficial to the social order. As historian Ellen Herman describes it, "Supporting masculinity was, in other words, a preferred method of tackling poverty, illegitimacy, inadequate housing, poor academic achievement, and a host of other community problems, including rioting."[55] Through the widespread belief that damaged masculinity produced both prejudice (no matter who it was directed against) and the conditions of social "failure" measured by white middle-class standards, the theory of the fascist/antidemocratic psyche gained surprisingly wide applicability.

In this uncanny fashion, a parallel might indeed have been drawn between the American Nazi of *Pressure Point* and the angry thirteen-year-old Black patient so briefly mentioned in the frame story. Myriad studies at the time found the mental states of African-Americans who sought to better themselves by integrationist/assimilationist means far healthier than those of separatists, whose hatred of whites was thought to be connected to a hatred of themselves. This easy reversibility of prejudice in fact sometimes included considering hatred of whites as a characteristic of an African-American version of the authoritarian personality. This personality was in some ways indistinguishable from that of white racists.[56]

Fanon notes another way in which this conflation can occur in his landmark study *Black Skin, White Masks* (1962), wherein Black men and Nazis come to share a mental arena in the minds of white people. He reports on a word association study as follows: "It is interesting to note that one in fifty reacted to the word *Negro* with *Nazi* or ss; when one knows the emotional meaning of the ss image, one recognizes that the difference from the other answers is negligible—in that the other words associated with 'Negro'—words like 'savage,' 'strong,' 'devil,' 'sin,' (as well as the ubiquitous 'penis') were also words associated with the general scheme of ss or Nazis."[57] What this lumping together of very different sorts of "things to be feared" indicates is the underlying logic of a parallel between Nazis and African-American men in political psychology and the popular narratives it inspired, a parallel that arises out of an equivalency wrought out of a *white*, generally male, "democratic" mind whose phobic structures closely associate physical and sexual threat.[58] In a post–World War II political climate in which colonial uprisings and the African-American struggle for greater civil rights seemed to threaten white sovereignty and safety, Nazis and Blacks became one.

Fascism and the Failed Heterosexual: The Enigma of Political Sexuality

Since political subjectivity is primarily configured as a correlate of masculinity in national psychobiography, normative heterosexuality also plays a defining role. The wartime and postwar practice of drawing analogies between vastly different experiences encouraged the homology between fascism and homosexuality, as the theory of family dynamics and identificatory structures thought to produce homosexuals indeed matched the template of social pathologies of many sorts, including those of Nazis and other racists.[59] Through the collapse of these "pathologies," the postwar expansion of fears of momism, and heightened surveillance of both individuals and families, homosexuals came to represent the most publicly vilified "un-American" sexuality, ranking with, and sometimes conflated with, communists in their threat to the Cold War nation.[60]

The notion of the "psychological position" of the homosexual does not necessarily require sexual acts. In this way, both actual and "psychological" homosexuals (who may even be homophobic) can fall into the category of fascist/communist. Sociologist Clifford Kirkpatrick commented in 1938, for instance, that "It is quite in line with the paradox of National Socialism that a party which made Captain Roehm leader of the Storm Troopers has been vigorous in the denunciation of homosexuality."[61] In the course of the war, this neat logical trick insured that despite the fact that Nazi law punished homosexuality this, like the support of traditional gender roles, was not among the things against which democracy needed to be defined.[62] The democratic ideal, as one journalist put it in 1934, is "a satisfying and stimulating sex life for the majority of a nation's citizens, leading in most cases to permanent monogamous marriage with the responsibility of family."[63]

Indeed, it is not only conservative voices that reinforced this belief. The leftist authors of *The Authoritarian Personality* also associated sexual normativity with the "democratic" personality, a variety of deviations from these norms then coming to both cause and characterize the authoritarian personality. Their findings almost exactly mirror the childhood history narrated by Lindner in the case of Anton, with the resulting difficulty again figured in terms of either gender inversion or overcompensation for its possibility. The authors write, "It will be seen to be of rather crucial importance for the social and political orientation of the individual how much passive striving there is in men, and even more important, how much countercathectic defense is built up against it, and how much acceptance and sublimation of masculine identification there is in women. The problem of homosexuality relates to the different ways of failure in resolving the Oedipal conflict and the resultant regression to earlier phases."[64] A tendency toward authoritarianism is therefore figured as a problem of failed or troubled gender identification—"passive striving" (i.e., effeminacy) or the defense against it in men and masculine identification in women—with masculinity mostly understood in traditionally patriarchal, paternalistic, and normative heterosexual terms (as ideally active, decisive, and independent).

As in virtually all of the American variants of Freudian psychoanalysis, homosexuality is seen in this study as part of a panoply of perversions of the "healthy" heterosexual norm. In the interview schedule of the study, the underlying issues concerning the major pattern of sexuality include both whether the subject displayed "mature, heterosexual attitudes" and "if not, what (promiscuity, exploitation of other sex, dependence on other sex, degradation of other sex, or putting other sex on pedestal, rejection of opposite sex, homosexuality, etc.)."[65] A variety of deviations from normative heterosexuality are thus cast as inherently antidemocratic, a list that reflects a larger political consensus. National psychobiography then models this sexually circumscribed, "democratic" subjectivity by diagnosing and curing politically deviant sexuality in the same analytic gesture that regulates normative masculinity.

The place of homosexuality and other forms of "failed heterosexuality" in the various versions of the case on its way to becoming *Pressure*

Point are illuminating on this count. In Lindner's case, Anton's homosexuality is a function of his will to dominate, resulting from his own victimization (by his father and other boys) and hence is connected ultimately to his sadism toward women as well. He is described as having invented an imaginary playmate, a younger boy, in response to his father's cruelties and his sense of being the last in line in a chain of familial aggressions. While the teleplay essentially retains this diagnosis, the first screenplay draft (both written by Pogostin) brings to the fore the implied homosexual content of the imaginary playmate fantasy by connecting it to childhood incidents revealed later in Lindner's case history.

In the first variant of this scene, the imaginary playmate is ordered by the boy Anton to clean his shoes; in the second scene, older boys are ordering Anton to clean theirs. A voice-over explains that "when Anton was five he had been seduced into performing for an older boy, was shamed and embittered by the experience and resolved to turn the tables when he got bigger and stronger. . . . By the time he was twelve, his greatest delight was in forcing smaller boys into his former position—both in fantasies and in reality." Shoe cleaning is thus the visual representation of fellatio, more explicitly named as such in Lindner's account of these events.[66] While the first scene is retained when Cornfield takes over the script—the imaginary playmate does indeed stoop to clean the shoes of the boy Patient in the film—the second version, which made explicit the homosexual content, is dropped.[67] In fact, by the time the last draft prior to Poitier's casting is written, all other voice-over references to homosexuality have been omitted as well.

What substitutes for homosexuality in the development of the Patient's sadism? It is the Patient's treatment of women, culled from other variants on the list of antidemocratic behaviors like the ones cited in *The Authoritarian Personality*. The scene in which he rapes the bar keeper's wife is added as well as a sequence in which he puts a woman "on a pedestal."[68] While this inclusion of brutality toward women can be seen as a step toward identifying the patriarchal structures at the core of fascism, I suggest that the critique is limited: while the expunging of homosexuality from the formula takes some of the heat off actual gay people, the notion of failed heterosexuality continues to posit an idealized heterosexuality as the democratic political ideal.

These two tendencies—to fortify norms and undercut alternatives—work sometimes in a contradictory fashion, as is particularly legible in the figure of the rape victim with a ticktacktoe board drawn on her back who shows up in the publicity materials (figs. 8 and 10). The game board

Fig. 11. The Doctor and the Patient in *Pressure Point* (Hubert Cornfield, 1962). (Museum of Modern Art, Film Stills Archive.)

links the Patient's misogyny with his fascism, as it is linked in the film to its graphic similarity with the swastika. The scene leading up to the flashback of the rape features the Patient drawing overlapping swastikas and tic-tac-toe boards on a pad of paper as he begins to tell the story (fig. 11). Since the event is meant to have taken place before the Patient becomes a Nazi, the scene functions to sketch his failed heterosexuality as a key factor explaining his susceptibility to Nazism.

The second added sequence—in which the Patient puts a woman on a pedestal—even more directly substitutes for homosexuality in the screenplay and elaborates the Patient's profile of failed masculinity/ heterosexuality. The scene, which features the patient's frustrated romance with a Jewish woman, was added later in the revision process, after Cornfield took over the script. It first appears in the same script that cuts out a sequence from the book, teleplay, and earlier screenplay in which Anton is introduced to Nazism (and especially anti-Semitism) by way of a mentorship with a "minister" he meets in prison. Lindner's account implies that Anton found a father figure in the minister, thereby extending the homosexual thesis of Anton's path to Nazism. In the later versions, the failed romance appears to provide an alternative explanation, still highly normative, of the origins of the Patient's anti-Semitism.

In the film, the Patient meets a pretty young Jewish woman while on the street selling apples during the Depression. She buys all his apples, and he tells the Doctor in voice-over that he'd "never met anyone so kind before, or since." He meets her again the next day, and his idealization continues. She is clearly from a wealthy, cultured family not seriously affected by the Depression, as signified by her large house and the classical music playing in the background. The sequence culminates when, on her invitation, he cleans himself up and comes to her house to court her. The woman's father slams the door in his face. At this point, the camera zooms in on a mezuzah nailed to the door frame, which cuts directly to an image of a swastika flag. The Patient's rejection by this Jewish father (echoing his rejection by his own father) results in his becoming a Nazi. His idealization of the Jewish woman, a symptom of troubled heterosexuality and a predilection for prejudice in the psychopolitical analyses examined above, turns immediately to hatred of all Jews.

This very personalized explanation for anti-Semitism is of course a ridiculous way to explain the broader phenomenon of anti-Semitism; surely, it is unlikely that many anti-Semites owe their prejudice to having been at some point rejected in love relationships by Jews.[69] The leader of the German American Bund featured in *Pressure Point* offers a loose economic explanation (that Jews were purportedly not as affected by the Depression), but the film favors a tale of failed heterosexual romance over such complex systemic factors as the mystified workings of capitalism, coupled as they are with the patriarchal expectation that white men should have dominion over their lives and the lives of others. The disassociation of fascism with homosexuality that the film effects (as opposed to the original case history and teleplay) is thus not a sign of progressive sexual politics. Instead, the film continues to express anxiety over normative, politically charged sexuality, thereby illustrating the kind of paradox that arises in the face of a lack of systemic critique, in this case, especially, one that hopes to continue to endorse a patriarchal family structure while fearing for the ability of that structure to produce democratic subjects.

Instead of a critique of patriarchy, then, momism again emerges as the stronger logic behind the Patient's fascism: the fascist son's "homosexual" attachment to his father, submerged in the film, gives way to the incestuous advances of the mother. This emphasis is already evident in

Lindner's case, as he writes, "After therapy had penetrated to the homosexuality and laid bare the sexual core of the psychopathic state, it was but a short step to bring into focus the factor that lies at the very center of the psychopath's personality, so remote, so carefully defined, and so closely guarded that the knowledge of its presence is the very last thing to which he would admit: and that is the special incestuous character of his relationship to his mother."[70] The subsequent versions of Lindner's case, then, amplify the mother's role in this drama even further, making the regulation of gender relations the most prominent anxiety that persists in the later scripts, where references to homosexuality are suppressed and failed heterosexuality is made primary.

In national psychobiography, the family, as in nationalist melodrama, remains the privileged icon of national security, but it also paradoxically becomes the site of highly volatile political anxieties. The film's emphasis on failed heterosexuality represents a focused effort to model "successful" heterosexual masculinity by negative example while at the same time blaming women for creating the problem in the first place.[71]

Conclusion

The most widespread ongoing rhetorical use of national psychobiography continues to be the liberal approach to white male political dissidents like the Patient in *Pressure Point*. The utmost care continues to be given to preserve white male heterosexual privilege in the act of theorizing what could have gone wrong with this still central default model of the democratic subject. The 1978 film *The Boys from Brazil* (directed by Franklin J. Schaffner) aptly illustrates this ongoing negotiation and so serves as a bridge between this chapter and the next one, where I will elaborate the contemporary variant of national psychobiography.

The premise of the film is that Hitler himself has been cloned by Joseph Mengele (Gregory Peck), who has been farming the baby Hitlers out to white families across the globe that share his biographical conditions: overbearing civil servant fathers and doting mothers.[72] With rather dopey literalism, Mengele's plot to create a new Hitler is discovered by a likewise aging Nazi hunter (Laurence Olivier), who takes note of a series of unexplained deaths of the adoptive fathers of thirteen-year-old boys. He puts together the psychopolitical pieces and susses out Mengele's efforts to replicate the timing of the death of Hitler's own father. The climactic confrontation of the film occurs when the Nazi hunter gets to the American clone before the father is killed, a scene that quite dramatically invokes elements of national psychobiography with its careful preservation of white male privilege in the very act of acknowledging its antidemocratic potential.

At the pivotal moment, the young American Hitler clone must decide between the limitless power Mengele offers him and American national ideals of frontier-style autonomy of the "you can't tell me what to do" variety. As he opts for the latter, the Hitlerian glint in his eye suggests that his totalitarian tendencies might be usefully channeled into patriotism and a nascent paternalism as he saves his adoptive father's life. As this conclusion is cast as a triumph of good over evil, the irony of this formulation is somewhat inadvertent: totalitarian tendencies, genetically harbored in the white boy and encouraged by an extremely traditional family structure, are in the end good for the late-twentieth-century American nation.

This type of national psychobiography, modified from its Cold War variant mostly in the urgency and vehemence with which the white heterosexual male is guarded as an ideal democratic subject, will be the subject of the next chapter. As in the Cold War, this narrative (and support for the type of man at the center of it) spans a surprisingly wide range of political perspectives.

6

Skinheads, Militiamen, and the

Legacies of Failed Masculinity

∎

In 1978, William Pierce self-published a novel, *The Turner Diaries*, under the pseudonym of Andrew Macdonald—a book that has had an enduring influence on right-wing groups ever since.[1] It is the fictional diary of Earl Turner, "written" from 1991 to 1993 (or 8 B.N.E.—before the new era), during a revolution that established a fictional white supremacist society on the North American continent. Turner, a rank and file member of the Organization, the group that helped bring about the revolution, has a major gripe with the mainstream American news media, as he frequently complains that they are *biased* against the racist cause for which he stands. He writes: "What's happening now is reminiscent of the media campaign against Hitler and the Germans back in the 1940s: stories about Hitler flying into rages and chewing carpets, phony German plans for the invasion of America, babies being skinned alive to make lampshades and then boiled down into soap, girls kidnaped and sent to Nazi 'stud farms.' The Jews convinced the American people that those stories were true, and the result was World War II, with millions of the best of our race butchered—by us—and all of eastern and central Europe turned into a huge, communist prison camp."[2] The actual atrocities committed by the Nazis, like the fictional atrocities that Turner and his Organization commit in the book, are elided in this complaint and replaced with new ones committed *against* the Nazis—and by extension

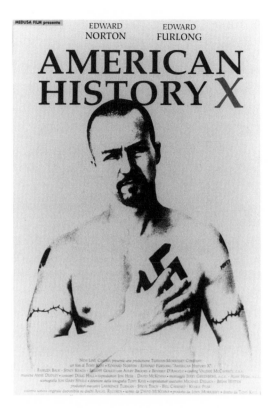

Fig. 12. Publicity poster for *American History X* (Tony Kaye, 1998). (Author's collection.)

against the neo-Nazis of Turner's group—by the anti-Nazi (Jewish-controlled) media.

This strategy turns the tables on the dominant place of Nazism in democratic rhetoric, wherein it is the ideal image of evil and neo-Nazism the guarded-against harbinger of a return that must be prevented. In claiming instead victimhood and oppression, Turner hopes to mobilize the powerful appeal of the American underdog, the outcast-rebel who, as in a Protestant jeremiad, knows the truth and will in the end prevail. Embedded in this twist, however, lies the complex figure of contemporary Nazism as it functions, on the one hand, as the limit point of democracy and as it reflects, on the other, emerging complications in contemporary white male identity. The first function was fundamental to the definition of democracy in the twentieth century: fascism is democracy's rhetorical opposite. The latter, meanwhile, represents a more subtle range of negotiations over American, and indeed global, democracy's always evolving definition, negotiations especially focused on the present and future place of democracy's historical subject, the white man.

The focus of this chapter is not on right-wing strategies themselves but on a critique of a prominent strain of liberal discourse currently making the rounds in many democratic societies with historically white majorities—one that basically buys variants of Turner's claim. Indeed, the public presence that *The Turner Diaries* has enjoyed since its publication provides an interesting introduction to what I see as an increasing tendency to grant credence to Turner's complaint by way of some measure of sympathy afforded to men who feel victimized by multiculturalism, feminism, gay rights, and, a bit more justifiably, changes in the global economy. There are two ways in which this is accomplished, the first being to drain the racism out of neo-Nazism and instead focus on the other positions that such people share with more mainstream social conservatives and, as far as the global economy goes, with some leftists. This strategy fixes on the idea that white men can't get a fair shake, that progressive social rhetorics are biased against them. The second way in which sympathy is garnered is to focus on the psychology behind an embrace of neo-Nazism, which is seen to be caused by the uncertainty inspired by social and economic change. This strategy, the newest variant of national psychobiography, continues to be grounded in normative solutions involving the reinforcement of patriarchal family narratives. Both hope to eke out a narratively valorized position for the white man as victim while still holding his place at the top of the food chain, a move that substitutes sympathy and humanism for feminist/ethnic/queer/class refusal, rage, and, indeed, critique.

Strategy 1: Denazification of a Different Sort

The Turner Diaries was brought to the attention of the American public on two occasions of right-wing political violence: during the criminal investigations of The Order in 1984 and of Oklahoma City bomber Timothy McVeigh in 1995. During the news coverage of the former events, the neo-Nazism of the group and the book that inspired them were central and their rejection categorical. During the coverage of the Oklahoma City bombing investigation, however, the neo-Nazism of the same book was mostly pushed into the background, although its other complaints were given significant airtime.

Some of the difference between these treatments of *The Turner Diaries* surely has to do with the stated causes of the parties involved. The

Order was a splinter group formed out of the neo-Nazi Aryan Nations, which was prosecuted for, among other things, the murder of Alan Berg, a Denver talk show host who publicly criticized its racist politics. The informer who alerted authorities to the group's activities claimed that it had drawn inspiration from *The Turner Diaries*, wherein "the Order" refers to a secret cell within "the Organization," whose members, as Turner says after his selection, "have all proved ourselves, not only through a correct attitude toward the Cause, but also through our acts in the struggle for the realization of the Cause," a cause that is, at core, racist.[3]

The Oliver Stone film *Talk Radio* (1988), which was based on Berg's killing, depicts the members of The Order as sinister, disembodied threats, voices coming through a radio station's call-in line spewing bigotry and promising violence. Barry Champlain (the Berg character, played by Eric Bogosian) refuses to be intimidated by them, spars with them on the air, just as he does with everyone else, and so apparently underestimates their danger. Champlain's producer and station manager repeatedly try to dissuade him from engaging with the neo-Nazi callers, who have also taken to sending him threatening messages, Nazi flags, and dead rats in the mail. In the end, he is shot by a classically villainous character, an ugly, overweight, slightly effeminate redneck with bad teeth. The threats to Champlain take two forms in the course of the film: he provokes the hostility of a wide population of listeners, who frequently express their love/hate for him on air, and he incurs the specific hatred of The Order, which is represented in the end by the lone outcast marked as white trash. Whether racist and homophobic bigotry (Champlain, who is Jewish, is often called a fag, although he's not gay) is exceptional, endemic, or just part of the broad opinion landscape of American democracy is a question left somewhat open—although the final embodiment of The Order in the redneck villain seems to point more toward the exceptional. The class politics of the film's conclusion potentially relegates that which is politically unacceptable to the margins of American society. It is not white people in general who harbor racism, anti-Semitism, or homophobia, but white people who have clearly failed to cash in on their structural privileges. In this cosmology, the loser white man is an exceptionally dangerous antagonist because he feels acutely the loss of his entitlement, which he interprets as having been stolen from him by women, ethnic Others, and homosexuals rather than facing up to his personal failures.

The symbolic marginalization of racism that the conclusion of *Talk*

Radio enacts is a common rhetorical practice in late-twentieth-century American political culture, which in part defines itself by means of a rejection of *overt* racism. More subtle forms of racism—anti-immigration and anti-affirmative-action sentiments, for instance—can then assume more mainstream political legitimacy by claiming not to be racist at all. Neo-Nazis like those belonging to The Order thus symbolically absorb racism in ways that the political mainstream can feel satisfied in rejecting—a move that does not require the examination of racism's less overt forms. One prominent progressive strategy in response to this move has been to expose the connections between the overt racism of neo-Nazis and other white supremacists and the racism of these less obvious agendas.[4]

A media controversy in Australia in 1998, for instance, began when *The Australia/Israel Review* published a list of two thousand members and donors of Australia's recently founded right-wing One Nation Party, hoping thereby to make the party's secret supporters have to defend their support of the party's central anti-immigration platform. One supporter on the list, Gideon McLean, is the lead singer of the Sydney-based neo-Nazi skinhead band Blood Oath. *The Daily Telegraph*, a Sydney tabloid newspaper, promptly published a large front-page image of Blood Oath giving the Nazi salute (an image from their website) accompanied by the headline "Liebler's List: Jews Name 2000 One Nation Members"—referring to Mark Liebler, publisher of the *Australia/Israel Review*, and of course to the 1993 film *Schindler's List*.[5] With this tabloid headline, a firestorm of rhetoric supporting, decrying, and redeploying the figure of the neo-Nazi ensued. One Nation immediately distanced itself from Blood Oath, and Pauline Hanson, leader of the party, made the following public statement: "I am definitely not a racist person. . . . I don't support racist people and I don't want them to be any part of One Nation."[6] Some One Nation supporters even suggested that the publication of the list was like the compiling of lists of Jews by the Nazis, making it analogous to a fascist activity.[7] One Nation Party leaders called for an examination of whether the publication of the names breached the U.N. Charter of Human Rights or privacy and antidiscrimination laws—the irony being that, as one reporter pointed out, One Nation had been "fiercely critical" of these laws in the past.[8]

Taking the two strategies represented in this controversy together reveals the precise ways in which overt neo-Nazism serves as a rhetorical figure defining the limit points of democracy. For progressives, the strategy of associating a right-wing mainstream political party with neo-

Nazism is intended to delegitimate right-wing claims by marking them as fascist and hence antidemocratic. The Right's response is to disavow the association, insisting that they are not Nazi and hence, in their logic, not racist, and then reversing the accusation. The progressive strategy hopes to expand the understanding of antidemocratic racism to include agendas like One Nation's anti-immigration stance, while the Right, in counterpoint, hopes to narrow the definition of *racism* to overt Nazism, and hence deny that their agendas are antidemocratic, and then shift the debate to issues of freedom of speech and opinion.

Political commentator Stanley Fish has noted that in the United States, "Individualism, fairness, merit—these three words are continually in the mouths of our up-to-date, newly respectable bigots who have learned that they need not put on a white hood or bar access to the ballot box in order to secure their ends; rather, they need only clothe themselves in a vocabulary emptied of its historical content and made into the justification for attitudes and policies they would not acknowledge were they frankly named."[9] Australia's One Nation Party supporters employ a similar strategy when they write, for example, that "Pauline Hanson's party does not in any way subscribe to Nazism. . . . It does not subscribe to divisiveness and racism. . . . What the party does stand for is a fairer and balanced immigration system and a government that is representative of all Australians, no matter what their racial background."[10] What terms like *fairer, balanced,* and *representative* mask is that a primary goal of the One Nation Party is to preserve the *current* racial demographics of Australia, namely, a white majority.

The strategy of rejecting the label of racism is, I would argue, not about rejecting the principles of racism. Rather, what is being rejected is the negative political valence of the term. Indeed, even the overtly neo-Nazi character in Pierce's second novel, *Hunter*, rejects the racist label in an illuminating way. *Hunter* features a group of neo-Nazis as they make a racial revolution in a decadent, multicultural world. Among their strategies is the successful establishment of a television ministry by a racist named Saul, who uses religious rhetoric to preach his message, presenting "a racial message without actually mentioning race." Once Saul's ratings rise to 55 percent of the Sunday market share, the other televangelists, Caldwell, Braggart, and Richards, band together. At this point in the book, they have "accused Saul of being a 'racist' and denounced his sermons as 'un-Christian' and 'divisive.'"[11] Pierce thus astutely notes that some members of the Christian Right (the above are references to Jerry Falwell, Jimmy Swaggert, and Pat Robertson) are perfectly comfortable with the ideas behind racism but won't publicly embrace *overt* racism.

The quotation marks around "racist" are peculiar and deserve special attention here, since in fact Saul is an unabashed racist, a fact the book takes to be a very good thing. Quotation marks are used very specifically throughout this neo-Nazi book, as in a moment farther along in the plot when Yaeger, the novel's protagonist, again complains about the coverage of Saul's activities in the media: "Saul was branded as a 'hater' and a 'neo-Nazi,' . . . most readers would not realize they were being lied to when they were told that Saul's broadcast had been filled with 'Hitlerian ravings' and 'anti-Semitic filth.' "[12] The distinction Pierce would like to draw (via his narrator) is between the racist, neo-Nazi beliefs he sees as positive (i.e., as the birthright of race-proud white Christian Americans) and the negative function of the words *racist, neo-Nazi,* and *hater* in public political rhetoric with which he does not identify. In this convoluted rhetorical move, even a self-described neo-Nazi can object to being called one.

The similarities between the American and Australian rhetorical climates stem from the structural similarities between nations with dominant white majorities, a significant ongoing immigrant history, and an oppressed native population. Add to this the more recent globalization of national economies that have brought in an influx of international investment and encouraged both the outsourcing of manufacturing to the Third World and heightened merchant-class immigration. Although they differ in substantial ways, the United States and Australia both feature a central political struggle over the definition of democracy as pluralistic and evolving or as consisting of historically dominant populations and their social traditions.

In the United States, a similar sort of division also exists in socially conservative agendas contained under the umbrella term *family values.* Through the concerted efforts of leaders of the religious Right, racism does indeed tend to play a marginal or nonexistent role in the logic of many proponents of antifeminist and antigay agendas, for instance. The role of the accusation of Nazism is thus more complicated here, in that the socially conservative views that neo-Nazis share with more mainstream conservatives (opposition to abortion, gay rights, and gun control) have not enjoyed the universal rhetorical rejection that racism/ "racism" has. One progressive strategy has been to reconnect racism with other conservative social agendas, as when an Atlanta-based group, the Center for Democratic Renewal, writes: "White supremacy is no longer a 'faction' belonging to the fringe of mainstream America. While the old Klan and new Nazis are still abhorrent to the vast majority of the American people, their sentiments have been embraced by the public when presented in a more sanitized fashion and disguised as nationalism, patriotism, and family values. . . . No longer able to rely on open racism as an effective recruiting tactic, white supremacists have found more socially acceptable targets for hate—lesbians and gays, immigrants, abortion providers, and the U.S. government."[13] The analysis still hopes to capitalize on the general unacceptableness of overt racism by stressing the ways in which it has gone undercover. This strategy's drawback is that making racism a primary motive misses the opportunity to address the specificity that issues of gender, class, and sexuality demand. Indeed, American conservative political rhetoric generally has shifted toward "family values" in the course of the 1980s, and so the shift represents larger preoccupations with personal conduct commensurate with the "privatization" of democratic citizenship that I laid out in the book's introduction. The equation of racism and Nazism by both critics and supporters of social conservatism elides these broader neo-Nazi agendas. Consequently, the same socially conservative groups that invariably express indignation at being associated with neo-Nazism can claim vociferously that while perhaps some antigay, antifeminist, anti-immigrant, antigun-control activists are Nazis the issues themselves are not necessarily racist/Nazi and therefore not antidemocratic. This conservative move hopes to reduce neo-Nazism, which does speak to a broad range of conservative issues concerning nationalism, gender, sexuality, and personal sovereignty as well as race, to a rarified, easily recognizable racism that becomes the only type of truly fascist belief that is unacceptable in democratic society.

Thus, it is not only proponents of racially motivated mainstream agendas like immigration and affirmative action who actively distance themselves from neo-Nazism. In the wake of the Oklahoma City bombing in 1995, for instance, the various spokespeople for the militia movement used their moment in the spotlight to distinguish their activities from those of "the hate groups and the Klan." The *Wall Street Journal* recounted one militia member's claim that "When the white supremacists joined her at a rally against the world trade pact last year and began passing out hate literature, [she] hustled them away."[14] Anti-abortion-rights and anti-gay-rights activists are also quick to distance themselves from neo-Nazi and white supremacist groups, as when a consortium of anti-gay-rights groups took out full-page ads in major American newspapers, claiming in the text that contrary to the claims of their opponents they are "motivated more by love than hate."[15] The issue here is twofold. While a majority of militia members, antiabortion activists, and anti-gay-rights activists are not linked to Nazi and white supremacist organizations, the fact that a substantial minority are (about 20 percent of the over 200 militia groups have such affiliations) reveals the continuity of social conservatism with both historical and contemporary Nazism. Contemporary struggles over accusations of Nazism thus follow from the rhetorical history of conservative antifascism, which very selectively defined Nazism in ways that preserved social conservatism for democracy.

The claim to be "not Nazi," despite shared agendas, indeed characterizes the second major instance of attention to *The Turner Diaries* in the American media. In the weeks following the bombing, investigations into the background of McVeigh revealed that he, like members of The Order, had read *The Turner Diaries*, offered copies of it to his friends, and sold it on the gun show circuit. At his trial in 1997, the novel played a central role in the prosecution's case, for in photocopied passages found in a sealed envelope in the defendant's car "politicians and bureaucrats" are taught by the book's fictional terrorists that "not one of them is beyond our reach . . . [and] we can still find them and kill them."[16] The mainstream media's portrayal of the book and its role in McVeigh's life focused almost exclusively on its antigovernment politics, often not even mentioning its blatantly racist, antifeminist, and homophobic neo-Nazism.[17] Indeed, neither the prosecution nor the defense attorneys mentioned the book's neo-Nazi politics in their closing arguments. This omission begs a question: What is achieved by this shift in focus from neo-Nazi racism to what counts as "other complaints"? The predominant function of neo-Nazism continues to be to emblematize that which cannot be tolerated. This is how the violent crimes of The Order were dealt with as well as those of white supremacists Buford O. Furrow and Benjamin Nathaniel Smith, who each went on racially motivated shooting sprees in the summer of 1999.[18] But McVeigh, though convicted of a heinous crime, targeted government workers rather than members of a particular race or ethnicity, and so his acts, and hence his reading of *The Turner Diaries*, were not considered to be connected *in any way* to racism, sexism, or homophobia.

McVeigh's crime instead offered the opportunity for a different rhetorical project than the violence of white supremacists. While still rejected for his violence, McVeigh was allowed his antigovernment views, and his affection for the neo-Nazi novel, as he was cast as *not* a Nazi but a particularly volatile example of a troubled white man. Indeed, his deed provided an opportunity for the public expression of the phenomenon of white, perhaps particularly working-class, masculinity in crisis. Robert Nigh, one of McVeigh's attorneys, went so far as to suggest that "the motives that have been attributed to Mr. McVeigh are in no way unique."[19] Defense lawyers certainly have a vested interest in portraying their clients as "in no way unique," but the widespread placement of McVeigh as *ordinary*—alongside his other not or not-yet violent anti-government compatriots—makes it rhetorically possible to claim that reading and promoting a work of neo-Nazi fiction is also "in no way unique," which is what his lawyers claimed.[20]

What I'm arguing here is that the concerns of disaffected white men (and some of their wives), despite their association with neo-Nazism, are being accepted as legitimate gripes—or at least "ordinary" or common enough to warrant a lot of careful attention—and not the response of categorical rejection usually afforded to the white supremacist variant of neo-Nazism. What, then, does the claim of ordinariness do? It asserts normativity if not exactly political legitimacy. It tends to default to normative lifestyle images for "ordinary citizens" and posits views like these as something to be *taken for granted*. As such, it calls for a form of redress that turns back the clock on social reform, dismantling affirmative action and voting down gay rights initiatives, for instance.

Mainstream reporting on the 1998 arrest of members of Team Viper (a splinter group of the Militia of Arizona) on charges of plotting acts of domestic terrorism stressed their ordinariness in a way that asserted both of these functions. These reports again virtually ignored the fact that the arrests resulted from information gathered by an undercover infiltrator who posed as a neo-Nazi. An article in *Newsweek*, for instance, insisted that (with my emphasis) "As nearly as one can tell from the evidence now being presented in federal court, the members of Team Viper appear to be *fairly typical* Phoenix suburbanites who played guerrilla games in their spare time—and may have considered much, much worse. They live on streets like Shangri-La Road and West Glendale Avenue; some have kids, and most hold 9–5 jobs. They are neither drifters nor dropouts—not hermits, not commune-dwellers, not religious cultists. How this particular mix of people came so close to the edge of terrorist violence is a mystery for now."[21] The "mystery" of this story stems precisely from the acceptance of an image of democratic citizenship that foregrounds normative lifestyle, prompting the loaded question: How can people with suburban homes, children, and steady jobs be politically deviant? The ordinariness or typicality ascribed to the members of Team Viper tacitly accepts that a neo-Nazi would feel at home in this group—so much so that *Newsweek* does not make an issue out of it. As with McVeigh's trial, the "issue" is elsewhere; in other words, racism, sexism, and homophobia are not thought to be *relevant* here.[22] The coverage of Team Viper's arrest is an example of a broadly liberal approach to democratic debate in which racism, sexism, and homophobia are normalized. Critique is consequently suppressed in the name of incredulity over the failure of the status quo to represent the ideal citizen.

While neo-Nazism continues to define a limit point of democracy, it is apparently not a clear-cut boundary. Instead, neo-Nazism is the topos where the "extremist fringe" meets the "ordinary" and hence mainstream legitimate politics. Racism of an overt and self-proclaimed kind is perhaps the one thing that distinguishes the neo-Nazi from his other antigovernment, antifeminist, antigay and nativist brethren. But the tacit racism involved in hobnobbing with such people is not enough to banish a person from the realm of political legitimacy. Instead, the overt form of racism spoken by neo-Nazis is exactly what is banished from public discourse, only to be sublimated into either less obvious forms (anti-immigration or anti-affirmative-action agendas, for instance) or other forms of intolerance that have not yet been banished from public rhetoric (like homophobia and antifeminism). Neo-Nazis in this regard act as the marker of the boundary between which kinds of racism are acceptable and which kinds are not. The social normativity of the borderline political actors near, but not embracing, neo-Nazism guarantees that their political views—racist, sexist, homophobic, and/or nativist though they may be—and certainly their complaints about being overlooked by the powers that be are taken exceptionally seriously as symptoms of widespread unrest.

Strategy 2: Poor Boys of Another Sort

The second approach to right-wing dissidents that strives for a similar normative aim focuses on the psychology behind a deviation from centrist norms, a psychology that again reinforces the ordinariness of the characters involved but suggests that, unlike the members of Team Viper, who already live a normative lifestyle, a normative lifestyle would be the cure. The ordinariness of someone like McVeigh is more along these lines in that it is his failure to achieve this sort of lifestyle (financial and personal stability measured in terms of career success and family) and his parents' failures before him that account for his deviant actions. This sort of formula continues to assert a model of the life of a democratic citizen that is measured primarily in personal and private rather than public terms. It is a vision that continues to assert patriarchal, white, racial, and middle-class privilege as the primary markers of dominant political subjectivity. While deviations from these norms are common (and hence ordinary in their own right) adherence to them is what defines *legitimacy*.

The path of this latter type of story is generically chartable national psychobiography, with its goal to diagnose, treat, and suggest a cure for the political patient, which brings him back to the democratic center. Through the conventions of the genre, even overt neo-Nazis can be reclaimed for democracy, mainly by complying with the cure's normative visions: establish a (heterosexual) family with male headship, assert enough male and racial privilege to secure a steady job, and hence be secure enough in the spoils of white masculinity not to succumb to the substitute promises of Far Right political rhetoric. While the rise of the civil rights movement, feminism, and the New Left in some measure delegitimated the normative tendencies of Cold War era political psychology and the national psychobiography genre it inspired, the rise of the New Right in response to these movements both gave political psychology a new object of study (Far Right extremists) and relegitimated some of its normative aims by making New Right assertions of the value of social normativity more mainstream.[23]

While globalization of the world economy has increased the degree of multiculturalism in democratic nations (with its redistribution of labor and heightened displacement of people across and within national borders), it has also spawned a new crop of white men (and some white women) who feel displaced in a more figurative sense: displaced from the center of political attention and displaced from the advantages of whiteness and/or maleness they still expect. Lacking a language for a critique of capitalism that might make sense of the experience of disempowerment felt by white, and especially working and lower middle class, populations, right-wing ideologues blame the ethnic, gender, and sexual minorities they feel have benefited from the mobility that has robbed them of their status. Complicit with this lack of class critique, then, is the dominant/liberal tendency to validate feelings of displacement as social or psychological, rather than economic in a large sense, through national psychobiography.

This is how, while for the most part continuing to serve as the limit of acceptable political views in democratic society, even neo-Nazis can be sympathetically portrayed, contrary to Turner's complaint quoted at the beginning of this chapter. Indeed, in the years since *The Turner Diaries* was written, sympathetic portrayals of troubled white manhood, made even more sympathetic when the flawed protagonists are young, have become prominent in many national contexts in which white majorities feel threatened by social and global economic changes. Indeed, the genre's favorite patient in recent years has been none other than the youthful neo-Nazi skinhead. While the "national" part of national psychobiography might seem anachronistic given the international character of this genre, it is deliberately so, for these narratives of the politically wayward, young white man shore up a racialized nostalgia for a nationhood that has been superseded by globalization. An analysis of the conventions of contemporary national psychobiographies that treat the skinhead will ultimately reveal the complex ways in which the dominant rhetoric continues to imagine a democratic subject who is white, male, and heterosexual, despite the ever growing diversity of democratic populations.

In the end, I will return to the central questions begged by these sympathetic portrayals: what does it mean to humanize one of democracy's demons and at what cost is this humanizing achieved?

The Popular Psychobiography of Neo-Nazi Skinheads

Before discussing their newfound place of sympathy, I'd like to stress that neo-Nazi skinheads, with their easily recognizable style and prominent display of Nazi symbols, still most often visually figure the kind of overt "named for what it is" racism that cannot be tolerated in a democracy.[24] While the skinheads began as a youth movement and continue to have both racist and nonracist variants, connections between some skinhead groups and organized Far Right organizations evolved throughout the 1980s, ostensibly following a strategy whereby, as the Center for Democratic Renewal puts it, "Skinheads are the 'urban guerrillas' of the hate movement" while "More seasoned adults have abandoned open violence to sanitize their public images."[25] Exploiting the version of democracy that sees value mostly in political centrism, this strategy broadens and shifts rightward the "center" against which the banished "extremes" are measured. It is a clever mimicry of democratic processes for antidemocratic ends—for even the rest of the racist Right can then seem moderate by comparison. The status as limit is thus earned by neo-Nazi skinheads mainly through their propensity for violence rather than their views alone.

Skinheads entered the media spotlight following the murder of Ethiopian immigrant Mulageta Seraw by a skinhead gang in Portland, Oregon, in 1988.[26] These skinheads were connected to prominent American racist Tom Metzger, who had spearheaded their recruitment to his neo-Nazi organization, White Aryan Resistance (WAR).[27] Public appearances on afternoon television talk shows by other skinhead groups followed. Geraldo Rivera featured racist skinheads and Black leaders on his show, which ended in a brawl wherein Rivera suffered a broken nose. A month later, Oprah Winfrey also did a show on skinheads, during which Metzger publicly insulted her. As skinheads continued to commit hate crimes and occupy the media spotlight, neo-Nazi skinheads, mostly figured as gangs of all-male white youths despite the common presence of women and families in actual skinhead groups, came to serve as classic villains in films like *Hate* (1995, France) and *Skinheads: The Second Coming of Hate* (1989, United States) or as guerrillas of the larger far Right movement, as in *Red Scorpion 2* (1994, United States) and *The Infiltrator* (1995, United States).

The categorical villain role is still a major rhetorical function of the neo-Nazi skinhead. But this outcast position has also made them ideal candidates for the reclamation strategies of national psychobiography. Almost as soon as films with skinhead villains hit the screen, so, too, did films that decried their politics in more sympathetic form. The latter focused on skinhead protagonists who manifested a psychologically explainable—and hence potentially curable—dysfunctionality. These films either examined their family relationships (*The Turning*, 1992, United States), presented their conflicts with each other (*Luna Park*, 1991, Russia; *Romper Stomper*, 1992, Australia), or investigated their psychological troubles (*Cracker: To Be a Somebody*, 1994, Great Britain; *Higher Learning*, 1995, United States; *Speak Up! It's So Dark*, 1993, Sweden). Some films claimed to tell their stories from the skinheads' point of view (*American History X*, 1998, United States), though clearly, since each film claimed to be *antiracist*, it is not really their point of view that is presented.[28] These more sympathetic characterizations surely reflect more sophisticated approaches to the phenomenon than their simple casting as evil villains. But films that psychologize skinheads, derived as they are from Cold War era political psychology, also often "depoliticize" their views, turning them into questions of personal psychological drama in order to assert the ostensibly "not political" solution of normative family and social roles.

As such, skinheads have come to serve as the ultimate psychopolitical patient of the white Western world. They have become the tragic heroes of journalists, social theorists, and filmmakers who do not want these "angry young (white) men" cast out but rather brought back into the *center* of the fold.[29] White men, *as* white men, are consequently reassured in and by these texts that the larger complaints of racist skinheads are not invalid but merely misdirected. They can still be rescued from their politics by way of a promise to remain central to democratic society through the exercise of the privileges of normative masculinity.

Sympathy for skinheads can issue from any number of political orientations: of course, from the Far Right, whose members share their views, but also from the liberal center, which seeks to preserve the racial and sexual status quo (though seldom admittedly so) and even from the Left, which sometimes foregrounds class politics to the detriment of racial and sexual equality. This leniency is mostly a result of a widespread perception of globally embattled white masculinity. Globalization, with its highly decentered and multiple power bases, provides a context wherein a handy, visually consolidated evil like neo-Nazism is rhetorically attractive to the mainstream. But it also provides the conditions of insecurity and mobility that threaten established symbolic hierarchies enough to unsettle a broader population of white people whose position in their home nations seems inexplicably precarious to them. Hence, the skinhead—as both villain and symbolic spokesperson for that which cannot be publicly discussed otherwise—becomes a popular but troubled icon.

The rhetorical strategies of three sympathetic skinhead films—*Speak Up! It's So Dark*, *Romper Stomper*, and *American History X*—reveal the variety of ways in which this clearly international genre reveals a new, more global pedagogy, one that continues to try to reinforce the paradigmatic primacy of the white male to democratic subjectivity even as the demography of national subjects becomes increasingly diverse. These films present strategies of displacement (especially of responsibility), of false solutions, and most commonly of reassurance that not much really has to change about the traditional social position of the white man after all, and in fact that restoration of white and masculine supremacy is necessary to maintain order in "advanced" postindustrial democracies.

Speak Up! It's So Dark

Suzanne Osten's 1993 film *Speak Up! It's So Dark* revolves around the psychotherapy of a neo-Nazi skinhead, Søren (Simon Norrthon), which is initiated after a chance encounter with a Jewish psychoanalyst named Jacob (Etienne Glaser), who came to Sweden as a child fleeing the Nazis.[30] As with all psychobiographies, liberal humanism undergirds the film's therapeutic logic: doctor and patient will transcend their political opposition through the mutual recognition of the experiences they share. This strategy requires that Jacob be extremely generous toward Søren, more so even than Poitier's doctor from *Pressure Point* (see chapter 5). *Speak Up!* in fact seems to suggest that Jews, immigrants, and women must take care of Søren if he is to get (politically) well. It is a strategy established in the first few sequences of the film and carried on to its hopeful end.

In the opening sequence, Jacob is in a train compartment, witnessing a group of skinheads beating up a Black man on the platform. He is startled as Søren suddenly barges into his compartment and sits down. As the train pulls away, Jacob notices that the teen has a small head wound and offers him a bandage—along with his card—telling him to come to the clinic the next day. The link between external and internal "head wounds" functions as a visual pivot between Søren's and Jacob's parallel experiences: as they finally part, Søren calls Jacob a Jew (clearly meant as an epithet), occasioning a flashback to an incident in Jacob's childhood when he bumped his head on a lamppost. In the flashback, a nearby Nazi draws his cold bayonet and lays it on the child Jacob's forehead to ease the swelling. The flashback is shot in high-contrast black and white, a style introduced during Søren and Jacob's conversation, as Jacob is reminded of the Black man's beating. The lines of connection and cross-identification are thus established. Stylistically, the doctor's childhood experience parallels the victimization of the Black man; in content, however, it parallels Søren's similarly placed head injury. The impetus for Jacob politically is his identification with the skinheads' victims; the therapeutic dynamic, meanwhile, relies on the cross-identification of Søren with Jacob. This is essentially the crux of the liberal humanist solution to the neo-Nazi problem: sympathy for both victims and perpetrators and an appeal to an underlying humanity that can bridge all differences.

Søren, by breaking away from the rest of the group, announces himself as a candidate for the individualizing and personalizing strategies of national psychobiography. The profile of Søren that subsequently emerges in therapy closely resembles profiles of Nazis developed by political psychologists during World War II. Søren seems to suffer from an emotionally and physically threatening father and an abdicating mother.[31] An early therapy scene establishes the transference dynamic wherein Jacob stands in for Søren's father. After Jacob asks Søren if his "big, real big" father ever beat him, Søren threatens to kill the rather small Jacob. Emotions really meant for the patient's father are successfully transferred to the analyst, providing an outlet for his Oedipal rage—and, the film hopes, for the expression of paternal/filial love. Søren's expression of aggression, Jacob theorizes, serves two purposes simultaneously: Jacob represents male power (i.e., is like the father); and, being Jewish, he represents the kind of difference that threatens Søren's sovereignty ("They want to take everything away from us/me"), which is then also codified as Oedipal (the father possesses the mother and has the phallus). Søren struggles with the classic formula that posits homosexuality (here psychic rather than enacted) to be at the core of the Nazi mind in that his unresolved love/hate for his father is redramatized in his politics. Thus, while the doctor's Jewishness and maleness serve to make him like Søren's father, they also function as a bridge between Søren and the doctor (the same thesis asserted by Robert Lindner and *Pressure Point*). The doctor's maleness serves as a common bond with Søren, while his Jewishness is a marker of difference that Jacob suspects the young man covets as a way to embody difference from his same-gendered parent.

Søren's most overt uses of anti-Semitism against his analyst reveal these two related functions of the Jewish/male doctor. In one scene, Søren tries to reason that the doctor is not like "lampshade Jews" and other foreigners, which is his way of saying that he has affection for the doctor and identifies with him. When the doctor resists this exceptionalism, Søren unleashes a torrent of anti-Semitic names and asks the doctor to picture himself beaten to death and his wife raped in front of their children. This is clearly a displaced and modified Oedipal scenario wherein Søren can kill the father and have the mother through a lens of racial violence. Søren thus quickly shifts from the politically hopeful connection (my Jewish doctor is like me) to the core of his anti-Semitism (he is like my father).

In order to break this patterned response, Jacob recognizes that he must surmount Søren's hostility toward the father. In a later scene, when Jacob must cancel an appointment (which Søren reads as rejection), Søren accuses him of lying about his family members having been at Auschwitz and then denies that Auschwitz was a death camp. Jews have made all this up, in his account, in order to make people feel guilty. Jacob sees this as Søren's response to his feelings of affinity and affection for his Jewish doctor, which make him feel guilty about Jewish persecution, a feeling Søren doesn't like and wants to deny. The film theorizes this version of anti-Semitism as a displacement of guilt over aggressive feelings toward the father onto racial guilt and compensatory counteraggression. Jacob, as the transfer point for Søren's feelings toward his father, confirms that racism is merely a symptom of Søren's more deeply rooted familial problem.

The film's psychoanalytic theory prominently foregrounds fear as a root cause of Søren's acting out of these Oedipal dramas over racist terrain. Søren says he is often scared that "someone" will get hurt when he and his skinhead friends go out marauding (that "someone" being Søren or a child stand-in for him). The doctor attempts to make him see that his fear is paralleled by the fear felt by "foreigners" when they are threatened by skinheads, again trying to encourage Søren to see foreigners as "like me." But following a scene in which Søren and Jacob cross-identify their fears (in this case of drowning), Søren has a hysterical attack (featuring painfully labored breathing) and again lashes out at the doctor. The film cuts to another high-contrast sequence in which skinheads are diving into a mosh pit, with Søren held aloft by his buddies. In other words, he is figuratively saved from "drowning" in the crowd. This metaphor points to the second root of Søren's psychological shenanigans dramatized in the film, his fear not only of physical or emotional victimization by his father/Others but of *anonymity*. Being convinced of his similarity to Jews and other racial minorities does not assuage this fear; indeed, it exacerbates it.

Fear of anonymity is paradoxical. It is a fear of being in the unmarked category against which foreigners and all racial Others are defined ("I am not special and wish I was") and it is a fear of having the privileges of being in an unmarked category taken away ("I am special and must de-

fend my specialness"). In order to find a concrete solution to this paradox, the film marks its root cause psychoanalytically, this time as a reaction to parental indifference. Søren confesses that he hoped that he
might be feared by his parents, or at least get a rise out of them, with his
skinhead getup, but instead they seem not to take him very seriously.
Hence, Søren's subjectivity is shaped by his apparently failed masculine
self-image, the image of a strong man marred by his inability to stand up
to his father and the image of being an idol to women marred by his inability to reach his mother. He overcompensates for these feelings, the
theory goes, with aggression. Finally, he seeks out a hypermasculine
group identity, conceptually based on race but also on gender, ideology,
and style, in order to bolster an immature ego. My critique of this
psychologizing theory is that it posits a solution in the reinforcement of
the patient's masculine core. In order to combat neo-Nazi racism, these
young men must not be threatened or challenged by men (especially
men of color or Jews), and they must be given more attention by
women. This solution doesn't challenge the skinhead to reach an intellectual understanding of the benefits of multiculturalism and antisexism,
nor does it leave room for women and minorities to express rage or a
more radical critique of the very expectation of privilege and attention to the white heterosexual man that this approach assumes and
reinforces.

The theory of the neglected white man is echoed in journalistic
accounts of the skinhead phenomenon. American journalist Tamara
Jones, writing on Germany's problem with neo-Nazi skinheads for the
Los Angeles Times Magazine, for instance, first asserts that "There is no
typical profile of a violent skinhead or neo-Nazi" but then goes on to say
that right-wing crimes are most often committed by young men "whose
parents are alcoholic, emotionally or physically abusive or too over-
whelmed by their own problems to pay much attention to their kids. The
peer group becomes an ersatz family . . . [and it is] more an expression of
self-identity than hatred of others."[32] The family portrait is not dissimi-
lar from earlier psychological portraits of the fascist mind except that
the emphasis is now placed on the notion that skinheads become Nazis
to get attention in a world where their parents and, they think, multicultural society ignore them.[33] Herein lies the call for their handling with
sympathy and care in the films under review here. Like *Speak Up!* Jones
gives credibility to a solution that requires us all to pay attention to these
"neglected" white men. Søren is required to identify with racial minorities (though not women), and so perhaps understand their experiences

(as being like his rather than like his father's), but he is never required to acknowledge the privileges he *does* enjoy—the expectation that people *should* pay attention to him in the first place, for instance. Indeed, no one observing Søren's behavior is encouraged to recognize any privileges at all accruing to white masculinity. Instead, the audience is asked to identify with Søren's pain. *Speak Up!* as one representative of new national psychobiography thus carefully preserves the privileges of white men in the interests of projecting a society of democratic equals, where my pain, your pain, and a neo-Nazi's pain are all one and form the basis of a common base-level political understanding that does not need to acknowledge historical structural inequalities.

Romper Stomper

The first and most common strategy of the sympathetic skinhead genre, as illustrated in *Speak Up!*, is to recenter the white man in democratic society through attention to and reassurances for the individual white man. A second strategy, working in tandem with the first, is to assert normative heterosexuality as the ideal place where white men can recover their lost sense of self and hence leave behind a destructive life. Sociological analyses of skinhead life, however, often note that their own collective perception of white "victimization" posits idealized notions of family and community as the antidote to their complaints. American Journalist Kathy Dobie describes one skingirl's image of a lost America as "daddy-worship—erotic and childlike; and very wishful. It's a fantasy about strong men, men who are competent and secure enough to protect their families, about sweet, deep job satisfaction."[34] Criminologist Mark Hamm, too, writes that both political and nonpolitical skinhead groups are family oriented and include women who serve a number of important functions: "Women bring to the internal structure of skinhead groups a respect for traditional family values. They encourage attitudes toward childbearing and parenting. And this gives the group a positive outlook on the future, and 'someone they can count on.' "[35] Cinematic portrayals of skinheads, however, almost never include this nostalgia for traditional family structure in their images of skinhead groups. Instead, nostalgia for traditional families is more often shared by the filmmaker.

Most images of skinheads—whether as villains or tragic heroes—portray them as embroiled in the homosocial world of drunken, group-incited violence, where women are simply for sexual use. *Romper Stomper* and *American History X*, which both feature variants on this image, can then posit heterosexual love and a patriarchal family as *alternatives* to the skinhead way of life. These images are built on the legacy of images of Nazi Germany, which similarly posit decadence and homosociality against images of democratic sobriety and conventional family life. Like images of Nazis, images of neo-Nazi skinheads ignore the fact that most large skinhead groups live in rather conventional family units with male heads of households and that they eschew drugs and most forms of alcohol. Indeed "clean living" and "family values" are much more common in skinhead groups than are the lifestyles portrayed in films about them.[36]

Geoffrey Wright's *Romper Stomper*, a film centered on a group of neo-Nazi skinheads in the suburbs of Melbourne, Australia, features this sort of decadent characterization and the "democratic" solution of normative heterosexual love.[37] The film's story revolves around three characters: Hando (Russell Crowe), the skinhead leader and central neo-Nazi ideologue; Davey (Daniel Pollack), his best friend and fellow skinhead; and Gabe (Jacqueline McKenzie), a young woman who is originally taken into the group as Hando's sexual plaything but who forms an emotional bond with Davey. The skinheads' story begins as they violently defend their territory against Vietnamese immigrants. After a run-in with police, however, their primary task becomes avoiding arrest while secretly preparing to escalate the race war. In the course of this, Hando gets tired of Gabe and tries to kick her out. She retaliates by informing to the police. The group scatters, and Davey ends up with Gabe. Hando eventually catches up with them and challenges Davey to choose between them. When Gabe sets his getaway car on fire, Hando tries to kill her but is instead killed at Davey's hand.

The film's narrative structure does not follow that of the most classic psychobiography, wherein a literal case history is brought to the screen as in *Speak Up!* But the intertwining relationships and political dramas similarly serve to chart the psychopolitical profile of the central characters. Wright has said that he "wanted to do a story that revealed the pathetic personal vulnerability of young neo-Nazis and remind them that whatever they think, they are primarily motivated by a profound sense of inadequacy."[38] The skinheads in Wright's film, however, see themselves as underdog heroes pitted against the world, which is out to get them. *Romper Stomper* thus stages both versions of the sympathetic skinhead image that undergird national psychobiography: their ordinary psychological dramas and their somewhat legitimated claims of being victimized.

The white man's victimization in Wright's film is primarily posited in class terms. As working class youths, these young men do not have access to the most prominent forms of economic dominance and are hence vulnerable to the kind of changing economic environment that also brings merchant-class immigrants into their neighborhoods. Leftist critics often assert that working-class young men blame immigrants for their plight because they lack a critique of capitalism that would help them see the larger structures of power that constrain them.[39] Wright, while lending the class hypothesis some visual weight in the film, does not pursue this critique of capitalism and globalization very far. Instead the working-class milieu, which may garner some credence to the under-dog role the skinheads' ideology gravitates toward, becomes the backdrop for the almost entirely interpersonal struggles that occur between Hando, Davey, and Gabe.

In the press materials released with the film's American distribution, Wright cites the recession of the 1980s and early 1990s, high unemployment, and urban alienation as factors that compound white male working-class youth problems, which, he asserts, stem from family dysfunction and a lack of self-esteem: psychological problems, as in *Speak Up!*, ultimately serve as the primary cause of the skinhead phenomenon. Wright claims that, without having to condemn the skinheads overtly, his film teaches the audience that if you follow the skinhead way you will end up arrested or dead. In the final scene of the film, when Davey kills Hando and goes off with Gabe, Wright claims that "the film counterpoints hatred and violence with tolerance and love. In a completely unsentimental way, love wins."[40] Hando, the film's primary Nazi ideologue, is sacrificed as unsalvageable (and hence villainous), while Davey, the follower, and Gabe, the lost girl, rescue one another in a conventional narrative closure (acting thus as the film's protagonists). The purging of the neo-Nazi threat is largely symbolic in this film, and none of the larger structural issues that Wright claims compound the skinheads' problems are cast as really requiring change. Instead, heterosexual romance carries the undue burden of righting the wayward characters' paths.

The film stirred up quite a bit of controversy in Australia, where many critics thought skinheads were depicted too sympathetically and accused the film of being morally ambiguous. Australian film scholar Tom O'Regan identifies the hottest point of controversy as the way in which "the social problems documented in the film—violence, incest, gangs, misogyny, racism—are not treated as the issue. They are simply there to motivate the narrative." Like Alfred Hitchcock's classic Cold War era plots, they function as MacGuffins; as O'Regan writes, "the film turns out to be a love story."[41] But foregrounding a love story has never been a strategy that *actually* evacuates public social problems; instead, they are refigured in the private domain. Indeed, the deflection of these issues onto personal (especially romantic) dramas in the second half of the film reflects the larger post–World War II tendency toward channeling economic or social dynamics onto a program of gender/sexual conformity. It is a process that has politicized the family unit and the heterosexual couple even as it pretends to depoliticize the plot or, as Lauren Berlant has put it, "the political is the personal."[42] The actual shape of the love story, then, like the love stories in wartime and Cold War plots like that of *Notorious*, reveals the significant political work carried out in the name of romance.

O'Regan's analysis inadvertently reveals as much when he describes the central story of the film as "a love triangle with a difference." For, as he notes, it is Davey, not Gabe, who is the object of exchange.[43] By shifting the triangle in such a way that Davey serves as its vortex, Wright's stated aim on the one hand holds true: Gabe can represent a positive alternative to Hando, and heterosexual "love" can be exchanged for homosocial "hate." But this highly normative formula neglects the fact that Gabe, too, is prone to retaliatory violence. In the course of the film, she first enlists her father and his hired thug to beat up the boyfriend she is trying to leave. She then enlists the skinheads to rob her father, a relationship inflected with incest. She further enlists the police to arrest the skinheads when Hando tries to kick her out (in the course of which some of the skinheads get killed). Finally, she sets Hando's car on fire when he tries to persuade Davey to leave her, instigating the fight that results in Hando's death. Gabe's "love" is thus not so clearly of the sort that presents an alternative to the destructive lifestyle the skinheads have been leading. While this might be what Wright has in mind when he claims that love wins in a "completely unsentimental way," it is surely granting heterosexual romance quite a lot of undue credit to suggest that a relationship with this particular woman is an antidote to violence. In fact, Gabe's mind-set is, if anything, somewhat *analogous* to that which Wright claims for the skinheads. She and they both feel that aggression is the only available response to victimization, and neither she nor they ever transcend to any kind of more systemic or humane understanding of their situation. Gabe is surely better off with Davey than she was with Hando, which is signaled mostly by their more mutually pleasurable lovemaking practices. Davey is, in the logic of the triangle, surely better off making love with Gabe than he was marauding with Hando. But their union, like heterosexuality generally, is at best ambivalent. The artificial optimism of the film's conclusion, whether sentimental or not, asserts a mythic role for heterosexuality in democratic society, a role that is unabashedly ideological.

Gabe's character, indeed, serves a complex symbolic function throughout the film that is denied by its ending, in that she models a psychological profile for the skinheads, whose inner life we never really get to see. For, despite Wright's claims that he has exposed the "scared, small people who need reassurance" beneath the tough guy façade, he never gives us much insight into the interior life of the male characters. Instead, we are given quite a lot of evidence that it is Gabe who is a "scared, small" person beneath her temperamental exterior. And although Wright posits family dysfunction as a prerequisite to skinhead leanings in the economically harassed working-class milieu, it is only Gabe, who comes from a wealthy background, whose dysfunctional family we witness. The inclusion of Gabe as *not* working class at least acknowledges, as many strictly class-based understandings of skinhead motivations don't, that there are other factors perhaps more compelling to choosing a skinhead life.[44] Gabe is also presented as just along for the ride, however, and not particularly drawn to neo-Nazi ideology, and so she embodies the "depoliticized" view of skinhead motivations.

This practice of substituting women's subjectivity for that of male skinheads deserves a closer look, for it can also be found in a 1998 American film, *Pariah*, which, as film critic Ed Scheid writes, "develops the backgrounds of the female gang members better than those of their male counterparts, showing how past sexual abuse and low self-esteem has drawn them into the abusive culture."[45] In a variation on national psychobiography, Wright gives us (as does *Pariah*'s director, Randolph Kret) a by-now-familiar psychological portrait of a woman who has suffered sexual abuse: *she* then stands in as a model for the subjectivity of the male racist. Damaged white male subjectivity is thus not only centered and made parallel to the experiences of women and minorities (as in *Speak Up!*), but *Romper Stomper* and *Pariah* actually appropriate women's experiences unself-consciously as an analog (or metaphor?) for male psychic damage.[46]

Just as with the missing critique of capitalism and globalization, an opportunity is sorely missed here to direct Gabe's justifiable anger at the father who abuses her into a critique of male authority—mainly because expectations of male authority continue to be central to the film's "alternative" democratic world. By making Gabe apolitical, the film also misses the opportunity to expose the way in which neo-Nazi rhetoric often mobilizes white women's sexual victimization to recruit both men *and* women into the neo-Nazi movement. Indeed, the mythic/stereotypical threat of rape by racial Others and incest as a sign of the breakdown of the family are central logics to Far Right support for a racialized family values rhetoric. In another neo-Nazi novel released by the same publisher as *The Turner Diaries*, for instance, the romantic partner of the novel's hero became a runaway at twelve to escape a sexually abusive father because "The American family is more than half destroyed, the old values gone." Her story is that she was put to work as a prostitute by a Black gang and sold to a pornographer in Cairo before finally being rescued by one of the neo-Nazi men. When the hero exclaims that she must harbor a lot of hatred, his informant assures him, "No. Not hatred. Not the way some women hate men, with less cause. Not Liese. She is hard and cautious, like a . . . a crab in a shell. Tough, ready to fight . . . but fragile, and inside very soft. . . . She does not hate, but she does want to dismantle the system that hurt her. Replace it with a world in which such horrors cannot exist."[47] What this description seeks to accomplish is to circumvent feminist anger (coded as hatred of men and thoroughgoing hardness) and direct white women's anger toward ethnic Others, liberals, and the cultural decadence that comprises the "system that hurt her," in other words, not patriarchy.

What *Romper Stomper* does is not only fail to acknowledge this prominent Far Right strategy but to enact a similar displacement, without admitting, as the neo-Nazis do, that this move is ideological. In *The Turner Diaries*' author Pierce's second novel, *Hunter*, the hero's girlfriend describes her attraction to and rejection of feminism thus: "Most [feminists] weren't just angry about the way women were treated; they were angry that they were women, instead of men. . . . To put it crudely, they wanted to be the rapists instead of the rapees, the fuckers instead of the fuckees. And since I've always been happy to be on the bottom, as long as there was a good man on top, I couldn't empathize with them." Her racist boyfriend then responds, "I'm grateful for that baby. It would have been a real loss to the race if you'd become a dyke."[48] The liberal-humanist solution to the skinhead phenomenon brought to the screen by Wright similarly circumvents a feminist critique, but instead of directing women's anger elsewhere, as in the political novel, she is appeased to be merely placed back into a more normative heterosexual unit and thereby "depoliticized." For *both* the neo-Nazi novel and the liberal sympathetic skinhead genre, however, women need to be kept from a critique of patriarchy by being strongly scripted into normative heterosexuality.

Wright is surely not aware of these logics at work within right-wing groups, and I am not accusing him, as some critics have, of secretly supporting the neo-Nazi cause. But his deployment of Gabe's history of incest (signaling the dysfunctionality of Australian family life) and his opposition of Davey and Gabe's "love" to Hando's hate reveals a rhetorical conservativeness, which, like actual skinhead groups, posits family dysfunction as the problem and normative heterosexuality as the solution. Like Hitchcock's Cold War era films, then, the love story behind the MacGuffin political plot is actually a political plot as well, speaking to the highly privatized notion of democracy that a socially conservative national narrative like this one creates.

American History X

Tony Kaye's 1998 film *American History X* presents a third variant on national psychobiography along these lines. The film is the story of two skinhead brothers, Danny (Edward Furlong) and Derek (Edward Norton). The film begins primarily as Danny's story, as he narrates an essay on the circumstances that led to his older brother Derek's incarceration. The film is mostly told through flashbacks, initially from Danny's perspective, on the eve of Derek's release. These flashbacks reflect how much Danny idolizes his brother by portraying his racist actions as heroic. Derek, however, has undergone a change of heart in prison and so becomes committed to pulling his younger brother out of the skinhead life. The film shifts to Derek's story midway, as he comes to tell Danny about his change of mind.

In terms of national psychobiography, *American History X* is again not a literal case history. But it is the story of the social and psychological influences that led to Derek and Danny's attraction to skinhead life as well as the factors that "cured" Derek of his misguided politics. Indeed as scriptwriter David McKenna says, "the question that intrigued me is: why do people hate and how does one go about changing that? My premise was that hate starts in the family. . . . I wanted to write an accurate portrayal of how good kids from good families can get so terribly lost."[49] McKenna wrote two story elements into the script that suggest this thesis: the major precipitating factor to Derek's becoming a skinhead is his father's murder (apparently by Black men); and a later flashback reveals the father as having held racist views, as arguing, in fact, with his then more liberal son. Despite these familial "causes," however, the most visually and narratively reiterated factor for Derek's becoming a skinhead, seen in both the flashbacks and the present of the film, seems to have been the omnipresence of scary Black gang members. Indeed, nearly all the young African-American men who appear on the screen are menacing (there are no Black women). Derek and Danny become skinheads as a defensive move, it seems, justified in the face of such an ominous, clearly murderous threat.

In the diagnosis of Derek's problems, *American History X* is troubled by two factors: (1) as the film is originally told from Danny's perspective, it glorifies the skinheads and makes them the principal site for audience identification (a problem shared by *Romper Stomper*); and (2) in sympathizing with the young men's more ordinary needs and fears, it shifts the burden of stemming the tide of white racism mostly away from white men themselves (much like in *Speak Up!*). As to the first problem, the film boldly aligns the viewer with Danny's heroic view of Derek even in the opening scene, which depicts the murders that sent Derek to jail. Shot in high-contrast black and white, Derek's chiseled, swastika-emblazoned physique, photogenic face, and the slow motion of his movements make him appear strong and beautiful. His murder of these men, while certainly excessive, seems in some measure justified: they were armed, they were on his property, and they were trying to steal his truck. This problematic strategy is exacerbated in subsequently narrated flashbacks. In a wildly improbable basketball game that Derek instigates between the Black men who dominate the Venice Beach court and the white men who want it, Derek, shirtless, his swastika-tattooed chest again beautifully photographed, leads the white team to victory. Heroic music accompanies the scene, as the audience is invited to cheer for the skinhead side. Their victory—underscored by the fact that one of their teammates is seriously obese—is a victory for the underdogs: white men as white men. The scene is the deadly serious counterpart to the 1992 comic equivalent, *White Men Can't Jump*. In both films white men certainly *can* jump—reclaiming basketball dominance from the Black players who statistically rule the sport, thereby making basketball stand in for other areas of perceived to be threatened masculine "turf": access to jobs, education, women, and the streets.

The next three flashback scenes are more disturbing and less heroic: Derek proselytizes his racist message to his fellow skinheads and leads them in a vicious attack on an Asian-owned market; he argues with his sister, his mother, and her Jewish liberal date, Murray; and finally he murders the Black men who try to steal his truck, reprising the opening scene. In each of these flashbacks, Derek is afforded substantial screen time to argue for his racist views without any opposition that can compare to his articulate and forceful presentation. His mother offers some weak objections, Murray is easily cowed, and his sister Divina is brutally punished when she tries to counter him. In Danny's eyes (and hence the only perspective available to the audience), Derek is charismatic and persuasive and, the way the film has set it up, correct. Blacks *are* scary in this film, minorities *are* taking over, and only *weak* white people like the insipid Murray and Derek's mother are not willing to stand up for themselves and their browbeaten race.

As with Wright and *Romper Stomper*, director Kaye has been praised by some critics who consider it brave and daring to show what is so attractive about skinheads on the screen. As critic Ron Wells writes, Kaye "takes the risky move of demonstrating the lure of the racist propaganda and imagery. The glossy beauty of Norton, shaved, buffed and tattooed, is as seductive as his driven speeches, but nothing can hide the ugliness that always rises."[50] This is clearly Kaye's intention in any case. The web site for the film lists the various progressive social causes that Kaye supports (he is, by the way, Jewish).[51] The site features links to various antiracist groups, including the American Civil Liberties Union (ACLU), the Anti-Defamation League, Artists Against Racism, and Amnesty International. But while the violence ultimately is ugly—especially the raid on the grocery store and the gratuitous skull crushing of one of the men who tries to steal the truck—Derek is still the most beautiful and charismatic figure in the film when he is a skinhead. This problem is symptomatically revealed in the first version of the publicity poster for the film, which features a stylized image of the shirtless Derek, his hand tenderly touching the swastika on his chest (fig. 12). While perhaps Kaye meant this image to represent a moment of critical contemplation for the character, the image can easily be read as a tribute to the skinhead way. Indeed, not only does no one else in the film strike as elevated a pose as Derek in his prime but he is only a shell of his former self when he emerges from prison a transformed man. By so successfully portraying the power Derek garners through his racist response to minority threats, the film ultimately fails to be convincing in its antiracist message.[52]

The second major component of national psychobiography—the cure—is plagued by some of the same underlying problems as the diagnosis. Derek realizes that his racist dogma is empty first because the Aryan Brotherhood, which he joins on arriving at the prison, turns out to not really care very much about Nazi ideology: racial gangs are merely a survival strategy and are more about power than white blood. A disillusioned Derek begins to open up to the somewhat feminized Black laundry room supervisor with whom he works, leading to his snubbing the Aryan Brotherhood. This snub causes them to lose face, and so his racial "brothers" jump him in the shower and rape him. As he lies in the infirmary afterward, Derek breaks down in tears and asks Sweeney (his former English teacher and Danny's current principal, and a Black man) for help. It is a gesture that finally reintroduces emotional vulnerability to Derek's character, not seen since the "news footage" of his response to his father's death, the only other scene in which we see him cry. Unlike *Romper Stomper*, *American History X* is willing to show the "scared, small people" that skinheads really might be inside. But, like *Speak Up!* this move still requires that white men remain the center of everyone's attention and that this character's vulnerability provide the key point of identification for the audience. His cure/rehabilitation consists of remedying his pain by exchanging the invulnerability afforded him by racism for the invulnerability afforded him through the restoration of patriarchy. At the end of the film, he assumes the role of a father figure who has learned the hard way what is best for his family.

Sweeney shows Derek (and Danny) tremendous generosity, above and beyond the call of a school principal's duty. Derek's survival in prison once he forsakes the Aryan Brotherhood depends on the laundry room supervisor's intervention. The supervisor is also the only Black man who is not physically imposing in the film: he is small, comical, and manages to win Derek over by imitating a woman having sex. The film duplicates the political psychology of white men's psychical relationship to Black men already betrayed in *Pressure Point*, wherein their physical/sexual threat is neutralized by way of feminization. Derek's turnaround and his subsequent efforts to rescue his younger brother from the skinhead life are thus in large part a product of the efforts of the only two nonthreatening Black men in the film (Sweeney and the laundry room supervisor). What these men model for Derek is precisely the kind of liberal humanism that ostensibly says "all people are worthy of care and attention," when all too often what is really meant is that white men in particular must be coddled—indeed, rescued from themselves—so that the established social and gendered order of things can maintain its equilibrium.

The gender politics of the film pointedly illustrate who benefits from the care shown to Derek by his generous Black keepers. While still a skinhead, Derek apparently feels that he is the head of the household after his father's death. During the dinner table flashback in which he argues with his mother, Murray, and his sister, he is both utterly domineering (forcing food into his sister's mouth) and childish (accusing his mother of replacing his father too quickly). The mother screams "I'm ashamed you came out of my body!" but then explains ruefully, "He's just a boy without a father." At this point, the film draws a causal connection between male immaturity and domineering behavior (the classic profile of the fascist), which ultimately preserves a "good" version of mature patriarchal masculinity for democracy.

Indeed, by the time Derek is released he has apparently matured enough to legitimately assume the family's headship. In his absence, his family has suffered economic setbacks and his mother's health has deteriorated. Despite his previously brutal presence, the now converted Derek comes home to take charge and turn it all around. The sister who had such strong objections to his Nazi beliefs before he went to prison is now completely pliable. She offers to quit school to bring more money into the family (why she would not have done this before is unclear) and Derek says, in his newfound, benign-father fashion, that education is too important for her to quit. He orchestrates the care of the women (mother, sister, and younger sister), tucking his mother into bed several times. This is what he has apparently "earned" for his conversion from skinhead beliefs: paternal dominion over his female family members, who warmly accept their new leader. He is now ready to embark on his central mission; to rescue Danny from the skinhead life, though for this he is tragically too late.

If the diagnosis is that Derek's white supremacism is a reaction against a physical threat and an immature effort to assume the leadership of his fatherless family, the cure focuses on his realization that he is physically safer without his racism, which in turn results in his attainment of the maturity he needs to properly assume the leadership of his family. His identity is, after his conversion, once again aligned with normative patriarchal masculinity. Derek does not achieve any sense of a common social project with women and minorities as equals in a world of mutual respect. Never does he recognize the larger structural wrongs of racism—and certainly not of sexism—despite the fact that we are often reminded by various teachers how highly intelligent, and hence especially valuable, Derek and Danny are. In other words, the film's theory that skinheads are really scared underneath their tough veneer (a claim also made by Wright) does nothing to decenter the white man from his position as ideal citizen at the core of both fascist *and* democratic subjectivity.

Conclusion

Several variants of contemporary national psychobiography have at their core the skinhead, toward whom audiences are invited to be sympathetic. In *Speak Up!*, Søren is said to suffer from ordinary Oedipal fears. In *Romper Stomper*, racism is subsumed under struggles over love and friendship. And in *American History X* the skinhead life is an immature answer to the physical and emotional vulnerability of the white man. These narrative lines accomplish the major components needed to turn neo-Nazis into sympathetic characters in the political mainstream: white men become underdogs, they suffer ordinary human problems, and white privilege is virtually ignored. These films indulgently encourage the expression of white men's rage and legitimate their fears of being dislodged from a position of privilege, all the while reassuring them that not much really needs to change after all.[53]

Eve Sedgwick has pointed out that heterosexual male sentimentality and self-pity are accorded an extraordinarily high value in Western culture. She notes, "Its effects on our national politics, and international ideology and intervention, have been pervasive. . . . Poised between shame and shamelessness, this regime of heterosexual male self-pity has the projective potency of an open secret." In other words, men are considered to need special care and tending and are accorded an inordinate amount of space for the expression of their emotions because of a (false) cultural belief that men have difficulty expressing their feelings.[54] Thus, journalists and filmmakers who might otherwise not sympathize with the politics of the Far Right are often quick to grant some level of truth or validity to the emotions expressed by right-wing men. This creates a climate of sympathy for embattled white manhood that can extend even to skinheads and other neo-Nazis despite the fact that in their overt form their politics remain unacceptable to the mainstream concept of democracy.

Purveyors of political psychology in the World War II era believed in the liberal-humanist tradition, that the individual, if properly formed, could reasonably choose democracy (which honors the individual) over fascism (which subsumes the individual to the mass). Hence, popular theories as to the solution to skinhead violence continue to endorse a program whereby the patient is removed from the group (individualized) and then fortified in his or her individuality. This individualizing move is touted as a depoliticizing move. Skinheads are not *really* manifesting a belief in white supremacy; rather, they are suffering from personal, psychologically based inferiority. But of course in foregrounding "the individual" a new form of politicization has occurred; one in which white men who openly acknowledge that they are vulnerable still comprise the dominant subjects of a democracy wherein white privilege is preserved. Right-wing politics is thus but a symptom of failed masculine subjectivity to which normative patriarchal masculinity remains the solution. Political terrorists like McVeigh and his codefendant Terry Nichols are similarly profiled as losers in most things that accrue to conventional notions of masculine privilege (breadwinning, physical strength, social confidence, heterosexuality, and paternity) and are postulated to have turned to unacceptable political action as a result. As *Newsweek* put it, the path leads "from disappointment to delusion to fanaticism."[55] This sort of description prevents the politically wayward man from assuming a heroic stance, but it does so by naturalizing "healthy, democratic masculinity" expressed in terms of success in the realm of patriarchal norms of masculine privilege and authority.[56] While the perception of failed masculinity might very well influence the political subjectivity of men like McVeigh or Nichols—or skinheads—such an assertion typically avoids implicating patriarchy and racial superiority more generally (i.e., the expectation that white men should feel entitled to authority) and avoids the issue of ongoing white dominance.

The journalistic effort to cast members of the militia movement as "ordinary," discussed at the beginning of this chapter, similarly generates a space for sympathy and seems to appeal to a larger population that shares their fears about a loss of privilege if not a propensity for their deeds. Reporting on the militia movement almost always remarks on the unremarkableness of members, claiming that they are "drawn from the same status groups, same occupation groups . . . as we all are. . . . Their marriages are just as stable. They go to church. They are a little more pious than the average American."[57] The same issue of *Time* that reported McVeigh's profile generalizes even further:

> Experts in psychology and group behavior warn that anyone can fall prey to paranoia—given the right combination of peer pressure and repeated exposure to one viewpoint. By all accounts, the de-

scent into delusion is gradual. Everyone has experienced slights, insults or failures at one time or another, and most people find some way to cope. Or, if they don't a trusted friend or family member may persuade them to forget the past and get on with their lives. But if they cannot shake off the sense of humiliation, they may instead nourish their grudges and start a mental list of all the injustices in their lives. Rather than take a critical look at themselves, they blame their troubles on "the company," for example, or "the government" or "the system."[58]

Even reaching the end of a process with which "everyone" can relate remains within the confines of the normal; the article concludes that most people in these groups are just "ordinary people who take ordinary ideas to extremes."[59] What this *Time* reporter pointedly overlooks is that the vast majority of people who arrive at these extremes are white heterosexual men.

The strategy of subtly reinforcing the white man's central placement as the default model of the "ordinary" citizen actually exacerbates the problem. Indeed, Far Right extremism has begun to take a new form in the last few years. It is no longer about collective action in the traditional sense but about the "heroic" actions of self-chosen individuals. Operating within a concept of "leaderless resistance," this new Far Right eschews meetings and organizational structure for solo acts of terror still committed in the name of racist, antifeminist, homophobic, and/or antifederal causes. Men who commit these acts (abortion clinic and civil rights office bombings, bank robberies, and murders, for instance, including that committed by Buford Furrow) are conceived as part of a purely conceptual collective, the Phineas Priesthood, which glorifies their actions without the need for any contact between "members."[60] This clever strategy certainly makes law enforcement efforts difficult, but it also points to the bankruptcy of a liberal-humanist strategy that relies heavily on a belief in the fortified individual as a solution to Far Right extremism.

Profiling the Far Right in sympathetic terms—as on a continuum with normal or ordinary frustrations—of course serves the larger project of social conservatism, which is perhaps the real point of all these sympathetic profiles, rather than actually stemming the tide of violence. Sympathetic profiling hopes to ensure that the concerns of conservatives fall within the confines of legitimate, centrist, political debate. This is a narrative practice, I have argued, that betrays a common project with a white racist mentality, which Mike Hill describes as the effort "to remain 'undistinguished'—the struggle to be ordinary, to be as passive as omnipresent, as invisible as dominant, to be an essential feature of everyday life and yet unaccountable—[which] is something white folk are finding less and less winnable."[61] It is of course possible that casting these contradictory and undemocratic desires as "ordinary" exposes the fallacies of the social conservatism embedded in a liberal-humanist project. But for the most part the mainstream journalism surrounding the militia movement, like the films featuring skinheads, attempts to use politically wayward white men to assert the validity of the cultural dominance of white, heterosexual, Christian men, whose "ordinary" needs must be addressed, assuaged, and privileged in order to be remedied—or else risk the coherence of the nation.[62]

Michael Rogin writes, "An account of American political suppression must acknowledge the suppression of politics itself. It must notice the relations between politics and private life."[63] The "suppression of politics itself," I would argue, manifests in the way in which norms of masculine and white racial privilege are subtly reinforced, centered, and hence, "depoliticized" in the sense of being taken out of the realm of public criticism only to more profoundly base a larger national politics on this invisible center. It is an act of political suppression offered in place of a serious critical approach to changes in the global economy, which certainly have displaced many people—not just white men—and have amplified inequality along traditional axes of race/ethnicity and gender as well as socioeconomic class. It is a political suppression that negates the claims of feminist women, gay people, and ethnic minorities by reinforcing a white, patriarchal view of the world.

It would be naive to say that the fairly large-scale grievances of a subpopulation like the Far Right do not need to be addressed. But the reasons for these grievances should be weighed along with the proposed solutions. If the grievances are economic or political, they should be addressed as part of the larger structural systems of which they are a part. But if the grievances are about clinging to white privilege, or male privilege, or heterosexual privilege, then the rewards for relinquishing this privilege and participating in a truly egalitarian social system should be offered in their stead, not reassurance that white male heterosexuals do still occupy, if they'd only do it in a more benign form, democracy's fortified center and ought to be seen as its ideal citizenry.

In the final part of the book, I will consider the companion process to this reclamation of white men: the political demonization of women and queers. I'll do so, however, in a way that acknowledges that this struggle over a politicized private sphere—whether held up for critique (by feminists, for instance) or not (in family values rhetoric)—is an ever evolving and contentious process.

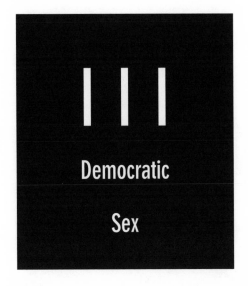

III

Democratic

Sex

7

The Iconology of the Sexy

Nazi Woman: Marlene Dietrich as

Political Palimpsest

∎

Women occupy a special place in the history of American demonology. Manifestly they have been made into victims whose persecution justifies revenge and into the guardians of civilized virtue who stand against aggression and anarchy. But women have also been cast, explicitly or implicitly, as the monsters. Countersubversion connects political to sexual anxiety by raising the specter of female power. —Michael Rogin, *Ronald Reagan, the Movie* (1987)[1]

. . . one of the girls in the evening gown says "I'm surprised that any American officer would care to listen to her. I don't see why the management keeps her on. It's a disgrace." "It is," one of the hosts agrees, "why they don't arrest that Nazi tramp or run her out of town beats me. But that's the way we run this war—like it was a soiree."—Ben Hecht, original treatment for *Notorious* (1945)[2]

In 1941, American editors translating sexologist Magnus Hirschfeld and his colleagues' 1930 study of World War I, *The Sexual History of the World War,* included a 1936 "Pulitzer Prize Winning Cartoon by C. D. Batchelor" as part of their effort to make the book appear relevant to the current conflict (fig. 13).[3] The cartoon features War (a seductively clad prostitute with a woman's body and a skull for a head) soliciting "Any European Youth" (a young man). The cartoon's caption reads War's words: "Come on in. I'll treat you right. I used to know your daddy." This coding of war as a woman, death as a woman, and ultimately

Fig. 13. Cartoon by C. D. Batchelor, 1936

fascism as a woman follows a trajectory of figurations of feminine evil extending from the nineteenth century. The concept, however, has been updated: in the background, a poster reading "Follies of 1936 starring Hitler, Mussolini . . . Now Playing" connects the concept of war with spectacle and entertainment and Hitler and Mussolini with the appeal of screen or stage stars. The conflations apparent in this cartoon center on the primary substitution of female sexuality for male aggression embodied in the suggestively clad woman we see and the figurative women Hitler and Mussolini become. It is the explicit and imaginary variant of the demonology Rogin defines in the epigraph above, where political subversion—whether from the Left or the Right—is rhetorically connected to female sexual power.

The conflict with fascism produced a number of images of female sexual danger, some of which are central to nationalist melodrama and national psychobiography. In nationalist melodrama, American and even German women functioned politically as emblems of democratic virtue and hence were in need of protection. What they were to be protected *from* is then embodied in the *Nazi* woman, with her promiscuity and perverse sexuality—the girls having extramarital sex in *Hitler's Children* (1942), for instance; the camp's matrons, who compel them to do it; or the domineering, seductive mother of the psychobiography genre, whose perverse desire for her son insures his fascism.

A second icon that combines the domineering and seductive characteristics of the Nazi woman is the mother's sexy counterpart, the femme fatale. This figure is pervasive in post–World War II film and literature, drawing of course on the longer history of images of feminine evil and the moral and sexual ambiguity she embodies. The specifics of the Nazi variant, however, most often figure her as a performer: a nightclub or cabaret singer, a political siren potentially dragging American men into her moral and political morass. Like the Nazi mom, she need not explicitly support Nazi politics; it is the spectacle of the singer—a replacement for the speeches of Hitler and Mussolini in the Batchelor cartoon—that stands in for the spectacular politics of fascism.

In Ben Hecht's original story treatment for what became Hitchcock's *Notorious* (1946), for instance, the female protagonist Alicia is written as a nightclub singer in a frame story, which was ultimately dropped from the script. Unlike the final film, which begins in an American courtroom where Alicia's father is being tried for treason, the treatment begins in a cafe in Cologne where American soldiers and German women gather. One of the officers wants to go inside and see the floor show, where the reputedly beautiful Alicia sings. This inspires the harsh comments in the epigraph from the women in shabby evening gowns: they snipe that she is not only notoriously beautiful but the widow of a notorious Nazi. The Nazi in question is Alex Sebastian, "the head Nazi brain in Brazil and head of the Gestapo underground in the U.S." Alicia sings, and her performance serves as a segue to Rio de Janeiro, one year earlier, where the bulk of the story takes place. This version of Alicia that never made it to the screen is another example of the deployment of a sexy "Nazi" woman as a central icon of the danger that fascism represented for democracy.

W. J. T. Mitchell notes that the history of Western thought reveals a profound distrust of images and a sense that they hold tremendous power, power that must either be contained (in the idol) or exploited (in the fetish).[4] Indeed, as Roland Barthes has noted, the image has a duplicitous relationship with meaning as either obvious or opaque. He writes, "Thus from both sides the image is felt to be weak in respect of meaning: there are those who think that the image is an extremely rudimentary system in comparison with language and those who think that signification cannot exhaust the image's ineffable richness."[5] The doubleness indeed provides a logic for the gendering of the image, as Mitchell, too, points out, where the fear of images and a sense of their uncontrollableness is coded as female in eighteenth-century aesthetic thought.[6]

The centrality of images and symbols to the Nazi regime contributed to what was to be feared about it. Hollywood depictions of Nazism indeed depend on these symbols, where uniforms, swastikas, and documentary footage of masses in geometric formations emblematize fascism when the domineering mother or femme fatale do not. This coding of fascism as representable through visual fetishism reveals the reason why these female icons so often serve as condensed signifiers of fascism in the anti-Nazi cinema. Unlike the male subjects of analysis in national psychobiographies, who were scripted to have been (almost) entirely explained, the femme fatale is sexy because she, like the image, is inexplicable or, as film theorist Mary Ann Doane has put it, "She harbors a threat which is not entirely legible, predictable, or manageable."[7]

The femme fatale is the epitome of what Teresa de Lauretis has identified more generally as "the position of woman in language and in cinema" in that "she finds herself only in a void of meaning, the empty space between the signs."[8] This function of cinematic images of women draws from nineteenth-century art and literature and their connection to the rhetoric of the nation. Bram Dijkstra, in his study of images of feminine evil, names the female narcissist as a prominent fin de siècle figure whose erotic self-sufficiency and egotism threatened the dominant image of female selfless virtue and whose self-enclosure was imaged as capable of destroying men frustrated by their lack of access. A second and related image he names is the sexually voracious woman. "Seen as jealous of man's exclusive capacity for spiritual transcendence, she was thought to be intent upon doing everything in her power to drag the male back into her erotic realm."[9]

The nineteenth-century project of aligning nationalism and middle-class respectability—George Mosse's thesis and the primary logic of nationalist melodrama—is embedded in these images of feminine evil. Mosse further suggests that the changing fate of the androgyne, a symbol of human unity for the Romantics and a monster for the Victorians, suggests how "strict gender division became central to national character."[10] Mosse notes that by the middle of the nineteenth-century the aggressive, gender transgressive femme fatale had become a common figure in popular literature in France, Germany, and England, where her "tough, domineering, and changeable" character came to stand for both sexual and moral ambiguity.[11]

One trajectory arising out of this coding of moral ambiguity is connected to anti-Semitism and indeed Nazi racial theory in general, as argued by Mosse, Dijkstra, and Klaus Theweleit's seminal study of writing by proto-Nazi men in Germany's post–World War I Freikorps.[12] But another trajectory is linked, by way of the persistence of images of feminine evil and gender transgression, to nationalism, to images *of* fascism as much as fascist images themselves. In the narrative logic that supplements the iconography of the Nazi femme fatale, indeed, the very thing that produces her iconology, she is associated with sadism, masochism, and, in more embedded fashion, lesbianism or bisexuality, much like the (male) fascist subject who preoccupied political psychologists of the wartime period. In this way, fascism fitted the femme fatale's already existing nationalist template and could thus be made to serve the anti-Nazi cause.[13]

The femme fatale houses deep ambivalence about her banishment from democracy's symbolic order. Indeed, her attractiveness itself is indulged and often either narratively or visually redeemed, for the rhetorically deployed alliance of fascism with sexual deviance not only figured fascism as abject but made it alluringly attractive. As Michel Foucault has said, "What makes power hold good, what makes it accepted, is simply the fact that it doesn't only weigh on us as a force that says no, but that it traverses and produces things, it induces pleasure, forms knowledge, produces discourse."[14] The alignment of fascism with sexual variation points to the proximity of the narrative formulas that produce pathologies and those that produce desire, a duality that creates the categories of appropriate "democratic sex" (sexuality and gender) while exposing the tenuousness of the containment these categories provide.

Indeed, in a very interesting way Hecht's original treatment, unlike the Hitchcock film, depicts the staging of this ambiguity through the nightclub singer icon, which serves not only as the epitome of Nazism's allure, as the singer appears in the opening scene quoted in the epigraph, but as democracy's hidden and misunderstood *hero*. In the treatment's flashback, Alicia is an American living in Brazil, the daughter of "one of the biggest importers" there, with an ex-airman boyfriend who now works for the State Department. He loves her, but, as the treatment puts it, "is a little irritated by her lack of politics." Her father, she soon finds out, is "chummy with the Nazis." She argues with her father, displaying her patriotism, and is convinced by a reporter who suspects her father is a traitor that she should contact U.S. intelligence. The treatment glosses over the specifics of how Alicia and Alex come to marry and how Alex and the boyfriend are both killed. Instead it returns quickly to the narrative frame and hook of the story. The captain, whose desire to hear the "Nazi tramp" sing was questioned by his likewise trampy companions, thanks Alicia for all that she has done and sympathizes with the fact that she cannot go public with her story. Alicia's efforts, it turns out, had helped disrupt the Nazi underground in the United States and hence *saved* democracy.

Thus, as the treatment puts it, "although the men for whom she worked are unable to speak out and tell her true story, . . . in their hearts she will always remain one of the heroes of the war." The final shot, then, is of Alicia being called, wearily, to the stage to sing; her song, the treatment says, "conceals the truth, the sadness of her misunderstood story." In the treatment, the doubleness of the icon of Nazi sex explains the captain's desire to hear her; he knows her to be not what she (politically) appears to be.

Hecht's story treatment is remarkable in its reworking of the icon even as she is still being built—a testament to his skills as a writer and to the icon's internal logics. Indeed, it seems as if Hecht might have been thinking of Alicia's role through the persona of an actress who would later get a chance to be Hitchcock's leading lady on another project: Marlene Dietrich. As it is Dietrich's persona more than any other that has contributed to the building of this political icon, it would only be right that she should be able to expose its doubleness, something she was able to do, though less directly, in Billy Wilder's *A Foreign Affair* in 1948. This chapter describes the creation of this politically specific variant of the Hollywood femme fatale both as an icon of fascism *and* an antidote to it. My analysis thereby interrogates the connection between gender, sexuality, and fascism in especially visual aspects of the cultural rhetoric of democracy.

Building a Political Icon: The Legacy of Lola Lola

The iconography of the "Nazi" nightclub singer can be traced rather directly to Lola Lola, the role Marlene Dietrich played in Josef von

Sternberg's 1930 *The Blue Angel,* although the rhetorical complexity this image assumes takes the years between her first appearance and the end of World War II to reach iconic maturity. Heinrich Mann's *Professor Unrat* (1904), the novel on which *The Blue Angel* is based, bears little resemblance to the film it inspired. Von Sternberg himself writes in his introduction to the English publication of the screenplay in 1968 that "None of the distinctive features that fill the film are indicated in the story by Mann."[15] Mann's novel is starkly critical of petit bourgeois society and the central character's malicious desire to vindicate his feelings of social and class inadequacy. Von Sternberg's Professor Rath, on the other hand, is on the whole sympathetic, a hopeless romantic who falls for a woman out of his sexual league.

In Mann's story, women are vital to building the illusions by means of which men can evade their failure to achieve the class status in which they are so invested. Rosa Frölich, the book's singer, is a star because enough people want to believe there is a star among them, especially Rath, who profits both financially and psychically from her success. Mann's title, translatable as "Professor Garbage" (a taunt his students use, playing on his name), reminds the reader that Rath is not all he believes himself to be. Von Sternberg's change of the title to *The Blue Angel* signals his shift in emphasis away from these self-delusional dynamics of the petit bourgeoisie to the erotics of the cabaret and, metonymically, the singer who performs there.

Von Sternberg describes Mann's story as being about "a teacher falling in love and marrying a cabaret singer by name of Rosa Frölich with child, resigning his position and then using his wife to obtain a footing which enabled him to make a gambling establishment that was to settle his score with society." He describes his transformation of the story via his changes to the female protagonist: "Rosa Frölich would be Lola-Lola, deprive her of her child, give the pupils intriguing photographs of her, make her heartless and immoral, invent details that are not in the book, and best of all change the role of the teacher to show the downfall of an enamored man."[16] What von Sternberg effectively did was excise the social criticism and substitute a tragic tale of an older man powerless in the face of an erotically powerful woman with a fickle heart: in short, a femme fatale. The consequences of this shift for the perception of the psychical construction of Nazism are enormous.

Von Sternberg's translation of Rosa into Lola Lola is based on an archetypal figure of dangerous female sexuality designed by nineteenth-century Belgian artist Félicien Rops (fig. 14). Von Sternberg has stated

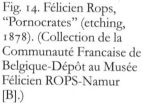

Fig. 14. Félicien Rops, "Pornocrates" (etching, 1878). (Collection de la Communauté Francaise de Belgique-Dépôt au Musée Félicien ROPS-Namur [B].)

that in casting the film he searched for an actress to fit this prototype, looking for "das Ewig-Weibliche" (the eternal feminine) that the part required, thereby colluding with the aggrandizement that Mann explicitly critiques. Rops's images epitomize a genre that saw women as vampires and animals, sexual creatures who aimed to destroy men.[17] On finding Marlene Dietrich, von Sternberg claims to have shaped her into the cinematic variant of this image, saying, "I am a teacher who took a beautiful woman, instructed her, presented her carefully, edited her charms, disguised her imperfections and led her to crystallize a pictorial aphrodisiac. She was a perfect medium, who with intelligence absorbed my direction, and despite her own misgivings responded to my conception of a female archetype."[18]

Von Sternberg's Lola Lola is also a verbal reference to Frank Wedekind's turn of the century "Lulu," whose extreme narcissism both drains the men around her of rational intelligence and inspires violence against her. Male characters exclaim, "I no longer know how or what I am thinking; when I listen to you I cease to think at all," but they also state that "beating and love-making, it's all one to a woman."[19] While Mann and Wedekind are contemporaries, their orientation toward their female characters reveals their vastly different theories on the origins of women's power over men. For Mann, the power is based on historical and class-specific mechanisms, while for Wedekind women's power over men is eternal.[20] Von Sternberg substituted Wedekind's logic for Mann's, a substitution legible not only in Lola Lola's name but in her words. In Wedekind's *Pandora Box,* Lulu's pimp, Schigolch, says of her "Die kann von der Liebe nicht leben, weil ihr Leben die Liebe ist" (She can't live off love because love is her life), while in von Sternberg's film Lola Lola sings "Ich bin von Kopf bis Fuss auf Liebe eingestellt, denn dass ist meine Welt und sonsst garnichts" (From head to toe, I am made for love, that is my world, there is nothing else).[21] Lola Lola is thus, as film scholar Judith Mayne puts it, "a pastiche, a collection of allusions," a set of signifying practices von Sternberg would continue to draw from in his later projects with Dietrich in Hollywood.[22]

Von Sternberg's self-conscious construction of the star makes explicit film scholar Richard Dyer's theory that a star's appearance in any one film includes the memory of all of his or her previous roles in addition to the offscreen and publicity persona the star has cultivated. Dyer also notes, however, how the resulting star image embodies contradictions that the star's multiple images manage, resolve, or—in "exceptional cases" like Dietrich's—embody an "alternative or oppositional position."[23] Such multiple possibilities for Dietrich's persona evolved in the course of the 1930s and 1940s, historically contemporaneous to the Nazi regime, though only retrospectively associated therewith.

On a practical level, Dietrich was contracted by Paramount (in a seven-picture exclusive deal with von Sternberg as director) so that the studio could compete with MGM's star Greta Garbo. As Dietrich's daughter, Maria Riva, put it in her biography of her mother, "every major studio was searching frantically for another such sublime creature—loaded with foreign mystery, European sophistication, hypnotic accented voice, and, if at all possible, high cheekbones and hooded eyes—with which to give the mighty MGM a run for the box-office revenues."[24] "Foreignness," taken in a variety of registers both national and sexual, indeed provided a dense site for the management (or not) of contradictions in Dietrich's early 1930s appeal. As film scholar Marcia Landy argues, "The question of national identity plays a central, though subtle, role among the many ways in which the Dietrich star persona was constructed. Dietrich's Germanness . . . is part of her star signature. She was German by origin but American by adoption, and she was outspoken in her criticism of the Nazis. . . . Yet prior to the war, the question of her nationality was more indeterminate . . . [so] Dietrich's connections to a specific nation become blurred, and her gender and sexual identity is generally indistinct."[25] In the pre–World War II period, then, Dietrich's Germanness, Landy argues, was diffused into the appeal of "foreignness" that she shared with Garbo; during and after the war, however, the specificity of Germanness came into sharper focus. This shift included the retroactive concatenation of her 1930s roles (especially in the films she made with von Sternberg), with particular prominence given to the Lola Lola character she played in *The Blue Angel*, the only film in which she portrays a German. While her characters in the other von Sternberg films might be Russian, French, Spanish, or vaguely "oriental," the indeterminacy of gender and sexuality is, as Dietrich's signature, an emblem of "Weimarness" as it becomes melded with "Naziness" by the end of the war.

Dietrich's much discussed penchant for menswear—featured in several of her film appearances as a nightclub performer and in her off-camera persona—is related both to the wider prevalence of cross-dressing roles in Hollywood in the 1930s, and to Dietrich's specifically Weimar appeal.[26] Dietrich's Hollywood production with von Sternberg, *Morocco*, was released in the United States a month prior to *The Blue Angel* (a German production) so that she could appear as an American star first and a German star second: in the former film, she appears in white top hat and tails, in the latter in the famous black top hat and garters (fig. 15). After both films were released, however, a fan card bearing the *Blue Angel* image was distributed in the United States to characterize the star.[27]

The timing of Dietrich's arrival also helps explain the suggested shift from a Weimar-inflected "foreignness," which was successful at the box office in the early to mid-1930s but then became unsuccessful in the late 1930s, to a complicated, more specific "Germanness" in the course of the war. Dietrich's arrival in 1930 corresponds, as Landy puts it, with the "lavish years" of Hollywood.[28] Dietrich's early von Sternberg films, including *The Blue Angel*, were released under the less strictly enforced Production Code of 1930. As film historian Gregory Black puts it, in the first three years of the 1930s, "a proliferation of films dealing with divorce, adultery, prostitution, and promiscuous behavior" presented a window of opportunity for stars like Dietrich and fellow Paramount

Fig. 15. Lola Lola, arms akimbo, in *The Blue Angel* (Josef von Sternberg, 1930). (Museum of Modern Art, Film Stills Archive.)

property Mae West.[29] Black sees some of this raciness and flouting of the tenuous Production Code as an effort to combat the lagging box office returns that resulted from the Depression. But this strategy exacerbated the conflict with the Legion of Decency and other parties that were pushing for national censorship, which further threatened the studios, so that, as Landy puts it, "within a few years—and for a number of reasons—a different version of national iconography would come to prevail that would make certain femmes fatales box office poison."[30]

Indeed, when *The Blue Angel* was presented to Jason Joy of the earlier less strict Hays Office, he wrote that the film "has many things in it which could not be undertaken successfully by us in this country, although on the whole it is not as bad as these offensive shots would at first make it appear to be."[31] By 1935, however, when Paramount applied for a re-release of the film, the PCA had been fortified under the direction of Joseph Breen, who replied, "I suggest that you withdraw this picture. It is a sordid story based on an illicit sex relationship between the two leading characters, and contains a great deal of offensive suggestiveness in its portrayal throughout."[32] Certainly the rise of fascism further tarnished the charm of European appeal: Dietrich's career began to falter.

During the window of opportunity, when the fashion was European stars and racy, lavish films, however, Dietrich's persona took shape. Film scholar Gaylyn Studlar has suggested that von Sternberg's idiosyncratic vision, expressed in these films of the early 1930s, speaks to a "masochistic aesthetic," where "the sexual repression and strict gender boundaries imposed by the patriarchal superego are rejected, and the erotic display of the androgyne is offered."[33] Part of this, Studlar asserts, has to do with the iconic textuality of von Sternberg's films. Von Sternberg's cinema, in film theorist Peter Wollen's account, sought to sever the existential bond between the natural world and the film image, to emphasize the iconic aspect of the sign "detached from the indexical in order to conjure up a world, comprehensible by virtue of resemblances to the natural world, yet other than it, a kind of dream world, a heterocosm."[34]

Both of these elements (iconic textuality and its related role in a masochistic scenario) began to fit, in the socially conservative rhetoric of wartime anti-Nazism, into a template of which the "Nazi" nightclub or cabaret singer was becoming a part: as an iconic/spectacular metaphor for the lure of Nazism and its hypothesized psychosexual underpinnings. Lola Lola is finally explicitly named as an icon of Nazism by Siegfried Kracauer in his 1947 study *From Caligari to Hitler,* which, as its title suggests, draws a fairly direct line between the cinema of Weimar Germany and the rise of the Nazi leader. Kracauer's "psychological history" casts Lola Lola as the film's narrative and erotic core, as he writes,

> The film's international success . . . can be traced to two major reasons, the first of which was decidedly Marlene Dietrich. Her Lola Lola . . . showed an impassivity which incited one to grope for the secret behind her callous egoism and cool insolence. That such a secret existed was also intimated by her veiled voice which, when she sang about her interest in love-making and nothing else, vibrated with nostalgic reminiscences and smoldering hopes. . . . The other reason for the film's success was its outright sadism. The masses are irresistibly attracted by the spectacle of torture and humiliation, and Sternberg deepened this sadistic tendency by making Lola Lola destroy not only [actor Emil] Jannings himself but his entire environment.[35]

In being destroyed by Lola Lola, Kracauer sees Professor Rath, the character Jannings plays, as a prototype for the future Nazi, as are his students, whose "sadistic cruelty results from the very immaturity which forces their victim into submission." "It is as if the film implied a warning," he continues, "for these screen figures anticipate what will happen in real life a few years later."[36] As both Rath and his students fall for Lola Lola's song, so, too, will they fall, in Kracauer's logic, for the fiery oratory of the Führer.

Kracauer's study, pessimistic as 1947 psychological analyses go but nonetheless influential in film studies, reflects the wartime practices of political psychologists and psychiatrists who analyzed the Nazi phenomenon. He echoes their socially conservative connection between deviant sexuality (here associated with Weimar) and Nazism, suggesting a continuity between the periods that virtually ignores the Nazis' rejection of all the cultural and sexual freedom for which Weimar stood.[37] The contours of this perception of continuity between Weimar and Nazi Germany is further shaped by antifeminist tendencies within the psychosexual trend in political psychology.

Film historian Patrice Petro has noted that popular characterizations of Weimar pull forward the image of Dietrich (and Louise Brooks from G. W. Pabst's *Pandora's Box*) rather than of stars like Asta Nielsen and Henny Porten, who made many more films in the Weimar period and whose star personas more accurately reflected the image of the independent "New Woman." As Petro writes: "Without a doubt, Dietrich and Brooks remain convenient figures upon which to project a reading of male subjectivity in crisis; as figures of female eroticism, they were typically featured in films where male characters are brought to their doom as a result of their uncompromising devotion to a feminine ideal. Given that Dietrich and Brooks only began their screen careers in the final years of the Weimar Republic, however, this kind of retrospective reading would seem to reveal as much about a fascination exerted by a certain type of woman in contemporary scholarship as it does about the figure of woman in the late Weimar period."[38] The fascination with a "certain type of woman," I would argue, is exercised with a particular political focus. The retroactive casting of Dietrich's late Weimar icon can be seen not as simply indicative of the legacy of female archetypes, nor as an erasure of the complex history of feminism and the changing role of women in Weimar society that Petro emphasizes, but as an emblem of the later theorized mind-set of German society at the dawn of the Nazi period.

Stanley Hochman writes in his introduction to the 1979 edition of *The Blue Angel* (novel and screenplay) that Mann's Professor Rath, in his vindictive and vengeful fantasies of getting his just desserts from a society that has wronged him, presents a portrait that "foreshadows that of a petty bourgeois type who was to swell the ranks of the Nazi party, and whose unleashed hatred was to convulse first Germany and then the world." Hochman reaches this conclusion despite the fact that the novel was published nearly twenty years prior to the Nazis' rise to power.[39] He reads von Sternberg's Rath, on the other hand, as a "prudish but loving man" whose "late awakening of both heart and flesh overwhelms prudence and brings about his subsequent degradation." He goes on to claim that "we" tend to "celebrate when Professor Rath is brought low by the fury of the townspeople" in the Mann novel, while in the Sternberg film "we" are "horror-stricken by the vision of an essentially honorable man destroyed by desire."[40] Ironically, Hochman's reading of Mann's Rath as proto-Nazi echoes Kracauer's reading of von Sternberg's Rath as proto-Nazi, a shift that, when it is unpacked, reveals something of the mechanism of the "contemporary fascination" that Petro intimates.

For Kracauer, the weak and masochistic Rath in von Sternberg's version points to a regressive susceptibility to authoritarianism, making Lola Lola fascism's ultimate icon. For Hochman, the shift to Mann's vindictive and petty Rath might indicate an embrace of Mann's more astute political analysis, but this is undermined by Hochman's marked sympathy for von Sternberg's Rath. In both cases, it is still Lola Lola who is bound together with political evil—either explicitly in Kracauer or implicitly in Hochman. Kracauer's quote continues: "A running motif in the film is the old church-clock which chimes a popular German tune devoted to the praise of loyalty and honesty . . .—a tune expressive of Jannings' inherited beliefs. In the concluding passage, immediately after Lola Lola's song has faded away, this tune is heard for the last time as the camera shows the dead Jannings. Lola Lola has killed him, and in addition her song has defeated the chimes."[41] By consolidating the sadism he reads in the film in the image of Lola Lola singing, Kracauer enacts the process by means of which images of women in classical film are fetishized, elevating her, however, to the status of a political fetish.[42] Hochman's sympathy for Rath, then, rescues him from political blame by intensifying the focus on the heartless cruelty of the dictator Lola Lola.

As Mayne remarks, there is a pattern of description in the various critiques of *The Blue Angel* by film scholars like John Baxter, Alexander Walker, and Donald Spoto, which leads her to conclude that "What is assumed, then, about *The Blue Angel* is that however complex or ambiguous the film may be in other ways, it tells nonetheless a straightforward story of a man who is humiliated by a woman."[43] It is, I would argue, not only this psychosexual model that makes Lola Lola stand in for fascism. Indeed, a second prominent, socially conservative mechanism sees her *ambiguity itself* as a sign of fascism.

Most historians of the role of women in Nazi Germany agree that the concept of separate spheres (men in the state, women in the home) most centrally characterized Nazi gender ideology, the Nazis' answer to Weimar's feminism and sexual liberalism, which were seen to have blurred the boundaries between men and women and hence to have weakened the German nation. In response to charges from outside Germany that the Nazis oppressed women through their ideology of separation, Nazi officials reiterated that they did indeed think men and women were not equal (as in "not the same"). In fact, they were radically different and hence had different duties and responsibilities, all of which were valued in the Nazi state.[44] Socially conservative journalists in the United States and Great Britain were at pains—as with other antifeminist policies—to distinguish between the Nazis' oft-propagated notion of separate spheres and radical difference between genders (a notion they, too, supported) and Nazism more generally (which they opposed). The prominent American journalist Dorothy Thompson, for instance, in a wartime article in *Ladies' Home Journal* claimed that the separation of men's and women's roles was necessary for the establishment of a balanced society, but she feared that the Nazis might use this theory to justify their extreme racial policies.[45]

A more radical attempt to disassociate the Nazis from their antifeminist policies of separate spheres led some wartime anti-Nazi journalists to claim just the opposite: that Nazi Germany *blurred* the boundaries between genders. Journalist F. Winder, for instance, wrote a vignette that featured this surprise:

> Over the freshly-tarred road which cuts straight across the fertile meadows of Holstein a strange-looking group on horseback was cantering along, looking somewhat out of place in these surroundings. All were wearing the khaki-colored uniforms of the former German colonial troops. Rifles slung across their shoulders swayed up and down in the rhythm of the canter. A revolver belt and two cartridge pouches supplemented this warlike equipment.
>
> As they jumped a ditch one of the riders lost his cap, and suddenly a blonde girl's head shone brightly in the sun. The others

turned around and all these booted, martial figures were revealed as young women between eighteen and twenty-two.[46]

While different in content, these efforts to characterize Nazi Germany as encouraging the blurring of gender boundaries share the logic that allows Kracauer to see Dietrich's Lola Lola as a proto-Hitler: Lola Lola the androgynous Weimar siren becomes Lola Lola the emblem of Nazism.

In her study of the "queer career" of character actor Agnes Moorehead, film scholar Patricia White asserts that the concatenation of characters Moorehead has played "attests to the ideological, narratological, and iconographic congruence among old maid, witch, and lesbian."[47] Dietrich's emblematic nature likewise attests to such a congruence between nightclub singer, androgyne, and Nazi. Cultural theorist Marjorie Garber notes that transvestism—which was closely associated with the Weimar/Nazi cabaret locale—signals a "category crisis" or "failure of definitional distinction, a borderline that becomes permeable, that permits of border crossings from one (apparently distinct) category to another." The blurring of the male-female boundary functions as "a sign of overdetermination—a mechanism of displacement from one blurred boundary to another . . . indicating the likelihood of a crisis somewhere, elsewhere."[48]

Earlier in the same passage, Garber remarks rather cursorily that the 1972 *Cabaret* is "a film which uses cross-dressing throughout as both a historically accurate and theatrically effective sign of German prewar decadence and the ambivalence of Nazi power."[49] It is this latter ambivalence, however, not only within the logic of fascism but within the logic of *antifascism* I would argue, that can be consolidated by the male transvestite and the female cabaret performer. In *Cabaret,* Dietrich's Lola Lola converges with her iconographical sister, Sally Bowles, and their subsequent versioning by female impersonators. Again, this convergence can be usefully traced through its development from the 1930s onward.

The 1930 image of Dietrich in her "proto-Nazi" Lola Lola role, onstage in garters, corset, and top hat, was reinforced and complicated by the published appearance of Christopher Isherwood's character, Sally Bowles. In this collection of short stories written in 1937 about the Berlin of the early 1930s, Isherwood's character came to cement the nightclub singer as a proto-Nazi emblem, even as his character herself is far more vulnerable and sympathetic than Lola Lola. In the postwar period, the popularity of the Sally Bowles figure, embodying Weimar sexual decadence, self-absorption, political apathy, and a certain naïveté, would go through numerous variations throughout the 1950s, 1960s, and 1970s. As film scholar Linda Mizejewski asserts in her study of these renditions, the postwar understanding of Germany in the 1930s ultimately "ends up being iconographic rather than analytical."[50] I would assert that the primary figure of that iconography is a *blend* of Dietrich's Lola Lola and Sally Bowles.

Mizejewski attributes much of Sally's performative character to the gay male subculture of which Isherwood was a part, the difference between Lola Lola and Sally being that Lola Lola is sexy in von Sternberg's archetypal way, while Isherwood's Sally is "sexy," making a show of female heterosexual spectacle.[51] From the concept of heterosexuality (in quotation marks), Mizejewski is able to posit that in the case of Sally Bowles Isherwood's ironic, campy distancing from the sexual woman permits a conflation with the text's other most significant distancing practices—of Isherwood's autobiographical stand-in character of Christopher from Nazism. Significant in this is that, despite the potential specificity of the camp practices for gay male cultural production, the conflation on the one hand colludes with the practices of marking fascism as a sexual Other, which had been going on in mainstream antifascist rhetoric as well, while on the other hand it heightens the ambivalence that both underpins socially conservative rhetorical practices and potentially undermines them.

Mizejewski theorizes the consolidation of images of proto-Nazi Germany around female nightclub singers to be due to a crisis in the reliability of the visual, inspired by the ethnic contiguity of Germans and white Americans/Britons, which required intensified encoding of Otherness in the images of Nazi Germany. The crisis is thus projected onto the cabaret singer as another version of the problem of what is or isn't visible, a problem consolidated around Dietrich's Lola Lola. Mizejewski writes, "This paradigm is reinforced by the reductive historical stereotype of Nazism itself as a sudden failure of vision, a vulnerability to spectacle, a fluke or aberration, rather than a phenomenon situated in mainstream European tradition. As referent for the image of the Weimar cabaret siren, Marlene Dietrich is herself part of the knowability crisis here—a 'good' German who comes to the United States but suspiciously retains her European accent, style, 'unknowability.'"[52] Mizejewski reads in this crisis that Dietrich embodies a key to the connections between the postwar fascination with Sally Bowles and the centrality of the question of how a "normal" person could become a

Nazi in which female (or transvestite) eroticism is aligned with fascism, political difference is inscribed as sexual difference, and "the grounds of the question become male intellect versus female materiality, a positioning of the 'innocent' British/American intellectual against the decadence of Weimar Berlin."[53] But the ambiguities between a star's life and the fictional characters she plays—especially those represented by Dietrich's wartime track record as a "good German"—also point to a second, less repressive series of cultural and political negotiations wherein Dietrich's sexy Nazi can come to *expand* notions of the sexual culture of democracy.

The possibilities for this latter function are indicated in the ambiguity that, for socially conservative rhetoricians, is disconcerting enough to warrant banishment from the democratic vocabulary. The very iconocity of von Sternberg's images of Dietrich in the 1930s, which, I have argued, help make her an emblem of Nazi spectacle, *also* help make her a potential emblem for precisely the opposite. As Studlar writes, "The iconic sign openly presents a lie: the illusion that it actually *is* the object rather than a false, recreative substitute. Simultaneously, it offers two germane truths, the truth of essential resemblance and the truth of its overt illusionism. Paradoxically, the overt illusionism of an iconic textuality allows von Sternberg's films to become anti-illusionary."[54]

Mayne, too, asserts this progressive possibility in that a "figure like Dietrich is both contained by patriarchal representation and resistant to it; this 'both/and,' rather than 'either/or,' constitutes the very possibility of a feminist reading of performance." Mayne goes on to assert that "If *The Blue Angel* has a special place in the mythology of Marlene Dietrich, it is in part because the film articulates a narrative and visual structure which would be associated with Dietrich for virtually all of her career."[55] But, I would add, it is a narrative and visual structure that, like the version of Alicia in the story treatment for *Notorious*, is only an emblem of Nazism for those who do not know better. For the enlightened, she is a potential champion of democracy.

Marlene Dietrich as Hollywood's Double Agent

In the postwar roles in which Dietrich makes explicit the iconic correspondence of her persona with Nazism, the rhetorical doubleness of the "Nazi" nightclub singer is crucial, especially in her two films with Billy Wilder, *A Foreign Affair* (1948) and *Witness for the Prosecution* (1957). Much of Dietrich's reemergence as a star after the war had to do with her wartime anti-Nazi activities. Like many members of the Hollywood film industry—especially those who were foreign born (whether Jewish or Gentile)—Dietrich proved her American patriotism by undertaking a variety of service activities for the war effort.[56]

Dietrich's ability to employ some of the specificity of her persona in her United Service Organization (USO) act illustrates the ways in which her association with illicit sexuality, Germany, cross-dressing, and spectacle could be just as well put to use *against* Nazism as coming to represent it. Biographer Steven Bach's account of her first USO show describes how actor Danny Thomas introduced her by announcing that she would not appear because "an American officer had pulled rank for her . . . *services*." The soldiers reportedly booed and catcalled (based more on the internal hierarchy of the military than their familiarity with Dietrich per se) until she called out from the auditorium "No, no, I'm here!" and walked onstage, cross-dressed in a U.S. Army officer's uniform. As Bach describes it, she then opened a small overnight case, withdrew evening slippers and one of her famous "sequins on nothing" evening gowns, and proceeded to change out of her uniform: "The guys went wild and at a key moment Thomas pulled her behind a screen and she emerged seconds later looking like the glamourous femme she was."[57] In this introduction to her act, Dietrich ingeniously deployed her two most famous styles: her penchant for menswear and fabulous evening gowns and her history as a Weimar era German performer.

A second remarkable deployment of her persona involves her inclusion of the German song "Lili Marlene" in her USO act.[58] The song was written in 1915 during World War I, but it got a new melody in the 1930s from Nazi composer Norbert Schultze. The song had been a favorite among German troops until its melancholy tone took on politically dangerous meanings after the Nazi defeat at Stalingrad, after which time Nazi propaganda minister Josef Goebbels banned it. As Bach puts it, " 'Lili Marlene' was a man's song, a soldier's song about his whore 'outside the barracks, by the corner light.' . . . it was a crossover song for a crossover soldier, and nothing more vividly demonstrated how Marlene's war transcended politics. She was an American, but she was German, too, and blood spilled was tragedy, no matter whose blood it was."[59] Significant in this, and not noted by Bach, is the contiguity of her screen persona and the sultry prostitute in "Lili Marlene." The figure illustrates the doubleness of the image of the "sexy Nazi" that she would come to embody.[60] Whatever anxieties might accrue to Dietrich's particular embodiment of androgyny—as a correlate to her Weimar legacy and hence her national ambiguity—are allayed in her USO performances. In the end it is the fabulous sequined gown that anchors her femininity, her obvious love for men that mitigates her occasional lesbian affairs, and her rousing American patriotism that dispels any negative aura around her German origins. This is not to say that she does not continue to function iconically as politically and sexually indeterminate, and hence potentially threatening, but rather that she is able, through her demonstrative femininity, heterosexuality, and patriotism, to make ambiguity "safe for democracy."

Having worked so hard to recast her persona as a woman working for American anti-Nazism, Dietrich is reported to have been reluctant to take the role of Erika von Schlütow in *A Foreign Affair* precisely because she didn't want to play the role of a Nazi.[61] What Wilder successfully banked on, however, was that the combination of her prewar screen personas and her wartime anti-Nazi credentials would make for the most acceptable and compelling embodiment of the sexual decadence of the sexy Nazi icon, in which American audiences could freely indulge since the actress herself was not a "real" Nazi. The management of these issues is apparent in the publicity journalism surrounding the film.

In the 9 June 1948 issue of *Life*, which features "Grandmother Dietrich" on the cover and promotion for *A Foreign Affair* inside, film critic Percy Knauth declares, "As a singer in the nightclub Marlene Dietrich enjoys a triumphant return to the same sexy role that made her famous 18 years ago in the German film *The Blue Angel*—the heartless siren who lures men to degradation and goes on singing."[62] The article is interspersed with images that both link Lola Lola and Erika von Schlütow, the Weimar cabaret singer and the Nazi singer, *and* treat them as simply part of a larger panoply of images that accrue to Dietrich as a star. On one page, there are a series of captioned stills from the film: Erika chatting with "Hitler"; Erika kicking off her shoe in fury; and finally Erika flirting with a colonel and an MP at the end of the film.[63] Another page features a photo spread titled "Marlene's legs span the era of talking films," which prominently includes three stills from *The Blue Angel* (Lola Lola sitting on the professor's lap, her famous barrel-sitting pose, and her famous hands on the hips pose; see fig. 15).[64]

In Knauth's article, Dietrich reportedly muses, "I sometimes wonder about this American morality," by way of commentary about having to reshoot one of her scenes because she showed too much leg. Knauth comments that forthrightness has been a characteristic of "Grandma Dietrich" ever since she arrived in the U.S., and recounts how she is amused by having inspired a fashion in stars with babies, after she was supposed to keep being a mother secret, but didn't. He continues: "It wasn't funny to the studio, though, and neither were some other things which this young actress from pre-Hitler Germany used to do, among them being her habit of wearing slacks, which caused a passionate commotion in Hollywood and in the nation's homes for years. Her stature in the film world was always strangely paradoxical: her pictures almost always caused outcries and controversies, and although the studios recognized her drawing power sufficiently to pay her, at one time, more than any other woman in the world, no one could say whether she was truly 'popular' or not." Immediately, Knauth mitigates this controversiality, deploying it in the service of the discussion of *A Foreign Affair* by adding, "It was not until World War II, in fact, that Marlene won a place of real fondness in the hearts of thousands of her countrymen. A citizen of the U.S. by then, she threw herself into the struggle against the land of her birth with an ardor and abandon unmatched by any big or little star of the screen or radio."[65]

Wilder, an Austrian émigré, had reportedly chosen Dietrich specifically as a pre-Hitler icon in order to inflect postwar Berlin with both the triumph over Nazism and sadness over the destruction of the city and its pre-Nazi life.[66] Direct references to *The Blue Angel*, many of which are mentioned in reviews of *A Foreign Affair*, include the appearance of Friedrich Holländer (who plays the piano and composed the songs just as in *The Blue Angel*) and a bass drum that advertises both the Hotel Eden (a popular Berlin club of the 1920s) and the Syncopators (a famous Berlin jazz band whose members were backup musicians on *The Blue Angel*). That Wilder would make this reprise of Lola Lola the former girlfriend of a high-ranking Nazi—*and* the most intriguing character in the film—speaks to his particular brand of astute cynicism.[67]

The film is set in Berlin's immediate postwar period and involves the shenanigans of Cap. Johnny Pringle (John Lund), who works for the De-Nazification Office and has fudged some signatures in order to prevent his ex-Nazi girlfriend Erika (Dietrich) from going to a labor camp for her political sins. Instead, she is a popular singer in a basement cabaret called the Lorelei, where she entertains Russian and American troops and the black market champagne flows freely. The name of the club pokes fun at Dietrich's role as a dangerous siren—her irresistibility occasioning the many gags aimed at the lack of willpower of the American military men, who cannot resist her.

The plot is set in motion by the arrival of Congresswoman Phoebe

Frost (Jean Arthur), a dry and efficient Republican from Iowa who is a member of a congressional committee sent to Berlin to report on the morale of the American occupation forces. Frost is the only woman on the committee and also the only one who interprets her job in terms of sexual morality, reminding her colleagues on the plane before they land that "12,000 of our boys are policing that pest hole down below and according to our reports they are being infected with a kind of moral malaria. It is our duty to their wives, their mothers, their sisters, to find the facts! And if these reports *are* true, to fumigate that place with all of the insecticides at our disposal." The inflammatory rhetoric of pestilence Frost uses is culled from the most extreme of the anti-Nazi rhetoric of wartime, but its power is undercut by the caricature of the moral crusader that Frost embodies. She wears her hair tightly braided on top of her head, no lipstick, speaks in cropped, officious tones, and moves in clipped, unsensual ways. She is immediately suspected, as her name confirms, of being frigid. The speech she makes on the plane interrupts a discussion among the male congressmen over what are clearly much more important matters such as what kind of material aid should be given to Germany, how its economy should be restructured, and the place of labor unions. The moral crusade is thus presented in the film as grounds ripe for comedy and ridicule, with Congresswoman Frost as the butt of its jokes.

In the article singing Dietrich's praises quoted above, Knauth de-scribes the film as a "good rousing comedy," noting that *A Foreign Affair*'s release coincided with another crisis (the Berlin Blockade) but that "With bland cockiness it portrays an uproarious Berlin where abso-lutely nothing is to be taken seriously," which is obviously meant as a selling point.[68] But as this lack of seriousness is mainly directed at the moralism of Frost, a member of Congress and the Defense Depart-ment's de-Nazification program, the film is nonetheless a political satire. Hence, it incurred extensive objections on the part of the Production Code Administration.[69]

In one sense, comedy has always been a controversial way to handle the Nazis: controversies also surrounded Charlie Chaplin's *The Great Dictator* (1940) and Ernst Lubitsch's *To Be or Not to Be* (1942), both of which addressed Nazi anti-Semitism when few other Hollywood films did. Lubitsch, a German Jew, defended his film, saying, "What I have satirized in this picture are the Nazis and their ridiculous ideology."[70] Of course, these films were also made before the end of the war, after which the extent of Nazi horrors became more widely known. Wilder does not address Nazi anti-Semitism or the Holocaust in *A Foreign Affair*. But while the Chaplin and Lubitsch films were criticized for inappropriate humor in a very unfunny world, Wilder's film was accused by the PCA of finding an inappropriate target: not the Nazis but the occupation forces, not the Nazi chanteuse but her moralizing, corn-fed, American counterpart. This was not a comedy ridiculing the Nazis, as the earlier films had been, but even at this early date a comedy about the ways in which anti-Nazism was already serving as a political rhetoric for other political agendas.

Wilder takes the complexities of the sexy Nazi icon as his playground by setting her up against a moralist who espouses the Nazi ideals of health and purity much more closely than Erika/Dietrich's persona does. In an earlier treatment of the film (before Dietrich was cast), Erika is described as "a big, handsome, beautifully molded woman—a Rhine maiden, a Valkyrie—but a Rhine maiden who had gone off the deep end, and a Valkyrie who had ridden the wrong way."[71] Clearly in this earlier conception of the story, Erika is meant to be the butt of some of the film's jokes: in the revision process, writers Wilder, Charles Brackett and Richard Breen shifted the burden of this variant of the Nazi ideal onto Frost and by extension the soldiers' wives, mothers, and sisters whose interests Frost protects. To cement this role, she arrives bearing a birthday cake for Johnny Pringle from Dusty, a long-forgotten Iowa girlfriend he hasn't seen in four years and to whom he clearly has no intention of returning. Like Frost's name, Dusty is clearly an appropriate nickname for a girl cast aside, pathetic in her clinging to a man who cares so little for her gestures of affection, as Johnny immediately barters the cake on the black market for a mattress to give to his sexy German girlfriend, Erika. The battle lines are thus drawn between the homey wholesomeness of American women and the erotic and explicitly sexual allure of German women, who, besides the lushly sensual Erika, are pictured as universally promiscuous, giggling airheads willing to do just about anything for a pack of cigarettes or a candy bar.

American men, of course, are placed in the middle of this battle, and ultimately it will be a story of the transfer of Johnny's affections from Erika von Schlütow to Phoebe Frost, who in the course of the film thaws considerably (fig. 16). But the comic motor of the first three-quarters of the film relies on Frost's having enlisted Johnny as an ally in her moral crusade (since they are both from Iowa) while he continually tries to throw her off the track of the Nazi past of his girlfriend, with whom he is not supposed to be fraternizing in the first place. Due to

Fig. 16. Johnny Pringle between Phoebe Frost and Erika von Schlütow in *A Foreign Affair* (Billy Wilder, 1948). (Museum of Modern Art, Film Stills Archive.)

Frost's characteristic tenacity as a moral pit bull, Johnny eventually resorts to seducing her in order to distract her, and in the flush of foolish love she engages in the sensual pleasures of Berlin and all but forgets about her mission. Erika meanwhile has played along to protect herself from discovery, but she gets increasingly jealous, engaging in extremely catty exchanges with Frost that emphasize their contrast as sexy and unsexy blonds.

When Frost and Johnny confront Erika as to who is protecting her, Erika deflects Frost's questions via insults to her appearance, playing to her lover Johnny all the while:

> *Erika*: You are an American woman?
>
> *Johnny*: (forced) We'll ask the questions here.
>
> *Frost*: What is the name of the man?
>
> *Erika*: Johnny. I see you don't believe in lipstick. And what a curious way to do your hair—or rather not to do it.
>
> *Johnny* (nervous): Do you know who you're talking to?

Erika: An American woman. And I'm a little disappointed to tell you the truth. We apparently have a false idea about the chic American woman. I guess that's just publicity from Hollywood.

This interchange illustrates the manner in which the Iowa congresswoman with her freshly scrubbed face and tight braids has in fact been substituted for the historical *Nazi* woman, with Wilder poking fun at Hollywood as an inverse of Nazi propaganda. In this way, Wilder's film praises the decadent and excessive Erika as the obviously more desirable alternative for an American man.[72]

Frost's ability to pass for a young German/Nazi woman is in fact crucial to the plot in that her initial access to Erika's performance and hence to the rumor that she was once the girlfriend of a powerful Nazi officer is obtained when she goes "under cover" as a giggling German fraulein who can only say "jawohl" and "Gesundheit," collecting evidence of fraternizing as she is easily picked up by two rather bumbling GIS. The second instance of her passing for German stresses the alliance of her look with the Nazi ideal even further in that Erika is able to pull strings with the police when they are both picked up during a raid on the Lorelei by claiming that the dumpy Frost is her country cousin—a further jab at Frost's homespun appearance.

Ultimately, the film does rectify this politically impolitic situation by having Frost soften her look as she falls in love with Johnny, bartering a typewriter for an evening gown, lipstick, and an eyebrow pencil. In a play on gender inversion typical of Wilder's humor, Frost of course requires Johnny's help to put these items on properly.[73] With her new look in place, Frost also softens her attitude toward sensual pleasure and sexual desire. As her transformation to a sexual woman parallels Erika's further implication as a Nazi, Johnny shifts his affections away from Erika and toward Frost. The original comic opposition between the sexy Nazi and the homely Iowan, which favored the former as an erotic icon, is thus somewhat neutralized—at least enough to satisfy the PCA—in the romantic resolution of the film.

This shift marks the manner in which Wilder's characterization of Erika not *only* undermines excessive moralism but helps make literal the Dietrich icon's association with Nazism in a more socially conservative vein. Although she is valorized throughout as universally appealing (virtually all GIS fall for her, with the exception of Colonel Plummer), she must ultimately be thrown over for Frost because of her dangerous lack of acceptable political ideals. Tellingly, the first indication that Erika is not politically clean comes obliquely via her sadomasochistic sexual dynamics with Johnny—the sexual perversity that extends beyond the implied variant of these dynamics of her cabaret singer persona to doom their romance by the film's end.

In the scene that raised the most controversy (but nonetheless stayed in the film), Erika spits toothpaste water into Johnny's face when he won't leave her alone as she brushes her teeth. Johnny then waits for her to emerge from the bathroom and grabs a hank of her hair, pulling her to him and wiping his face with it. Erika cries out in pain and whines "You have to be gentle! You're always hurting—you're always so mean to me!" As the scene goes on, it becomes clear that Erika and Johnny's erotic relationship relies on his punishing her for her political improprieties, forming the inverse or counterweight to the public perception of Erika as a sadist (via her nightclub act) and Johnny as the masochistic dupe.[74] As Erika needles him about giving her the mattress, she complains that Germans haven't slept in fifteen years, what with Hitler screaming on the radio and then the war. Johnny replies,

Johnny: No mattress will help you sleep. What you Germans need is a better conscience.
Erika: I have a good conscience. I have a new Führer now—you.
[She approaches him seductively, raising her arm.]
Erika (cont.): Heil Johnny.
[Her heiling hand comes to rest on his shoulder, leaving them in a lover's embrace.]
Johnny: You heil me again and I'll knock your teeth in.
Erika: You'll bruise your lips.
Johnny: How about I choke you a little . . .
[He puts his hands around her throat, still about to kiss her.]
Johnny (cont.): . . . break you in two. Build a fire under you, you blond witch.
[They almost kiss but are interrupted by the two MPs who knock at the door.][75]

Like this one, their other erotic encounters always involve his political recriminations against her until they become increasingly less erotic and finally serve as the grounds for his dumping her for Frost. Johnny and Erika actually kiss only once in the film (and this as part of a show Johnny must put on in front of Frost), an erotic logic that implies that these tense, accusatory interchanges signal a sexual scene not picturable on screen, a dynamic in which he makes her wait for acts beyond the limits of the Production Code and not containable in its acceptable onscreen kiss. By contrast, Johnny and Phoebe kiss numerous times, implying that there is nothing going on beyond them. In other words, the normative sexuality of the Hollywood screen kiss is reserved for his ultimately wholesome relationship with Frost, while the sex-tinged roughness of Johnny's prekiss conversations with Erika are decidedly perverse.[76]

Ultimately, Erika's association with Nazism is confirmed in the film's narrative not just by her iconic appearance and perversity but by means of visual proof, which literalizes her spectacular substitution for Nazi spectacle. Despite Johnny's attempts to dissuade her, Frost manages to get hold of a newsreel in which Erika appears. It begins with the familiar documentary footage of a Nazi rally and images of Goebbels giving an impassioned speech, facts that Johnny specifies for Frost even as these images would have been familiar to any American wartime audience. But the next scene is a fictional piece about an opera opening with Erika/Dietrich in a stunning gown and furs sitting next to the fictitious Hans Otto Birgel, leader of the Gestapo, in a snappy ss uniform. Johnny continues to try and cover for her, but he is clearly taken aback himself when in the next shot "Hitler" himself enters and kisses Erika's hand. As they whisper in each other's ears and laugh, Erika's ultimate cementing as a female version of a high-ranking Nazi is complete. In this way, two prominent cinematic images of the Nazi regime are brought together as documentary fact: (1) the mass rallies à la *Triumph of the Will*, which were ubiquitous in American wartime and postwar films about Nazism; and (2) Dietrich in furs (à la *Venus in Furs*), an entirely fictional image from the cultural imaginary around the sexuality of fascism.[77] The latter, then, becomes a cinematic substitution for the former.

Bosley Crowther, film critic for the *New York Times*, wrote extensively about Dietrich's reprise of her *Blue Angel* role in *A Foreign Affair*, stating that her performance is of interest "not only because it is brilliant but because it ties in so aptly with the past." Crowther revels in nostalgic delight, which "comes from our wistful discovery in Miss Dietrich's current role of the girl, now grown older and wiser, whom she played in 'The Blue Angel' years ago." He asserts that

> it doesn't take much imagination to see in Miss Dietrich's current role the still fascinating night-club charmer whom we saw in that other film—the same indestructible female who presumably rode the Nazi wave, slipped out the side door when it was crashing and is now back in business again. And somehow this fancied projec-

tion of that character into today enhances appreciation of the tacit ironies in this film. Think, when you're seeing this picture—and when you're hearing Miss Dietrich sing her cynical songs, 'Black Market' and 'Illusions,' especially—of that sensual and arrogant creature who lured the pompous Jannings to his doom when the Nazis were starting their big putsch and see if it doesn't do something to you.[78]

But what *kind* of something does this "sensual and arrogant creature" do? For Crowther, the answer seems to coincide with Wilder's own double-edged nostalgia for pre-Hitler Berlin and his blend of sorrow for the city's ruin and triumph in the Nazis' demise. But, as my analysis of the film has shown, the question of why Dietrich's Lola Lola would have a projected biography where she fraternized with Nazis and just as easily now takes up with American occupation forces is not entirely contained within this "wistful nostalgia." Instead, it stems from prominent and contradictory strains in wartime cultural rhetorics of democracy.

Erika's political fickleness is finally a marker of her indestructibility in this fictional biography and part of her erotic appeal. But the doubleness of this (her sexuality as politically dangerous yet acknowledged as appealing) on the one hand masks the real life consequences that such a popular association was in the process of producing as the Cold War was picking up speed (i.e., the persecution of homosexuals and the containment of women). On the other hand, however, the figure's doubleness suggests the association of the pleasures she embodies with political freedoms of the kind in which Frost, and indeed Crowther, are finally able to indulge: indeed, the dresses that Dietrich wears during her performances in *A Foreign Affair* are not reminiscent of the garters and top hat getup she wore in *Blue Angel*, nor are they representative of anything worn by Nazi stars. Rather, they are replicas of the gowns she wore on her anti-Nazi USO tours.

Thus, Dietrich's performance, which on one level is meant to emblematize "Nazi" allure, also quite explicitly quotes the actress's anti-Nazi activism. The entertainment industry went on to engage this wide range of versions of Dietrich's character in the 1950s, an examination of which will illuminate the double rhetorical function she continued to play for the rest of her career.

Lola Lola Fights (or Ignores) the Cold War

Cold War government policies against homosexuals clearly exemplify the material consequences an association of illicit sexuality and a perceived lack of political loyalty could have on people outside of the fantasies of Hollywood. As historian Jennifer Terry points out, a significant shift from understanding gay government employees as security risks to thinking of them as inherently disloyal is reflected in the change of focus from the executive order issued by President Truman in 1946 to President Eisenhower's executive orders between 1953 and 1954. The initial order considered homosexuals in the military to be susceptible to blackmail by Soviet espionage agents, while the latter presumed them to be *inherently* opposed to the American system of life and government.[79]

While lesbians were seldom explicitly mentioned in the congressional loyalty and security hearings of the 1950s, the seductress working for the Soviets and using her sexual skills to extract secrets from unwitting and gullible American men is, as is the adulteress whose excessive desires compromise the security of the home and hence the nation. What they have in common, rather obviously, is their threats to the sexual supremacy of men. Thus, while Lola Lola/Erika may represent an opportunity for "wistful nostalgia" for film viewers, the specter of the sexually untrustworthy woman was indeed contributing to government deployment of illicit sexuality in policy decisions that negatively affected people's lives.

Part of this sexually repressive political climate relied on the notion of psychical maturity political psychologists had made central to the dominant understanding of good health and citizenship—a notion defined in both gendered and sexual terms. In psychiatrist Edmund Strecker's work, for instance, psychical maturity for women included respect for male authority. Hence, his book *Their Mothers' Daughters* includes a gender-based distinction wherein, as Terry describes it, "independence was a necessary asset for male citizens, while for female citizens wifely dependence and maternal attentiveness were key." Strecker's chapter entitled "Feminism: the Biological Rejection" is followed by "Lesbianism: the Biological and Psychological Treason." Both consider feminism and lesbianism to be pathological interruptions of the normal orientation of women toward motherhood and hence treason against the nation.[80]

The Left is also not entirely free of these associations, as in the embedded biases revealed in the Frankfurt School's study of American prejudice, *The Authoritarian Personality* (1950). The authors of this study see promiscuity and homosexuality as psychically immature and hence related to the psychical immaturity they postulated was at the core of the prejudiced personality.[81] For the authors of *The Authoritarian Personality*, the judgment that homosexuality and promiscuity are pathological is considered to be a scientific, not a moral, judgment. The assumptions of the study with respect to homosexuality become even more acute with the lack of adequate consideration of the impact of gender on their profiles of prejudiced personalities. *The Authoritarian Personality* does not give equal consideration to its findings about women, although an effort is made to include a roughly equal amount of male and female interview subjects.[82]

The authors assert that prejudiced subjects tend to both aggrandize their parents and claim to have been victimized by them without considering that there might be a difference in the psychical structure of male and female grounds for feeling victimized. One female prejudiced subject whose response is quoted at length, for instance, states that her father is a "grand person" but that she is resentful about feeling neglected in comparison with her brothers, a response thought to be typical of prejudiced women. The likely reality of this neglect due to familial sexism is not considered by the interviewer. Instead, the conclusion is drawn that "Some of the other high-scoring women are resentful against their parents because of a feeling that their brothers were preferred by virtue of their being boys." The study concludes that these feelings of injustice lead to an unhealthy envy and resentment, which serves as a marker of the women's prejudice elsewhere instead of being noted as a legitimate gripe based on the likely material differences in the treatment of daughters that may or may not be connected to prejudice toward others.[83]

Unprejudiced women are indeed admitted to "sometimes develop a conflict between the satisfactions derived from emotional dependence on the man and a striving for independence that leads to competition with men," with the rebuttal that "in spite of these conflicts, retardations, and ambivalences, there seems to be more actual or potential heterosexuality" in unprejudiced women.[84] Although the study itself is not explicitly antifeminist, its primary faults emerge in the collusion of these findings with a context of broader beliefs in the antidemocratic nature of both homosexuality and feminism.[85] Dietrich's ongoing public presence as a sexual iconoclast does not reflect the sorts of consequential theories that were influencing policy, however, for her persona as a sexual adventuress *both* literalizes and undermines these characterizations.

The cover of the July 1955 issue of the Hollywood gossip magazine *Confidential*, whose subtitle, "Tells the Facts and Names the Names," plays ironically and perversely on the activities of the House Un-American Activities Committee, promises to tell "The Untold Story of Marlene Dietrich" with a cover photo of the actress dressed in a man's suit. Inside, the caption beneath another full-length photo of Dietrich in a suit, trenchcoat, and cane reads, "Her very first success on the stage was singing a strange love song—from one girl to another. But her boy friends really flipped when she actually started living up to the lyrics!"[86] While this article is clearly sensationalist tabloid material, the uncomfortable truth of the connection between "naming names" and outing Dietrich as a sometime lesbian is part of the ultimately rather interesting subversive logic of the publication.

In the article, the legacy of Dietrich's behavior is explicitly traced back to the sexual decadence of Weimar, where "Deviates singing of their strange love in public was the kind of thing that could only happen in Berlin after World War I. All through the roaring twenties, the German capital was a global headquarters for the most shameless perversions."[87] The article describes Dietrich's many affairs with both men and women, despite her being married, as she "played both sides of the street" as a "double-standard dolly." The article especially highlights her lesbian liaisons: with Claire Waldoff, a woman "old enough to be Dietrich's mother," whom the article claims she was dating at the time she met Josef von Sternberg; Mercedes d'Acosta, a Hollywood writer "who favored clothes that seemed to be tailored by Brooks Brothers"; Frede, the "queen of Paris' Lesbians," who ran a nightclub and marked the first girl *younger* than Dietrich, which the article assumes made her the aggressor; and Jo Carstairs, a multimillionaire "baritone babe" on whose yacht Dietrich was purported to have spent many a weekend on the French Riviera before the outbreak of World War II.

The interesting lack of information in the intervening fifteen years between the end of the relationship time line the article traces and its publication seems to explicitly *avoid* associating Dietrich or her proclivities with Nazism or Cold War politics, something that would probably be impossible anyway given her much publicized honorable war record. Instead, what emerges under the guise of "shock" at this sort of deviance is that Dietrich continues to come out looking sexy, cruising around Europe among the most wealthy and the most glamorous elites. Thus, while the common everyday lesbian or gay man was suffering from regular harassment by police in bar raids and psychiatrists everywhere else, a fan magazine like this one betrayed a running fascination with Dietrich's bisexuality as part of her allure as a star.

Elsewhere, however, Dietrich offered somewhat outrageous but still socially conservative advice to women on how to maintain a happy marriage. As historian Joanne Meyerowitz recounts, " 'To be completely a woman,' she wrote, 'you need a master.' She advised women to plan their clothes, their conversation, and their meals to please their husbands. After washing their dishes, 'like Phoenix out of the ashes,' women should emerge 'utterly desirable.' And they should not grumble. 'Some women,' Dietrich proclaimed, 'could do with a bit of spanking to answer their complaining.' "[88] Meyerowitz goes on to note that the article provoked indignation in many readers, who saw the star as out of touch with the realities of modern relationships.

In this eclectic climate, Dietrich once again appeared as a cabaret performer with a questionable political past in another Wilder film, *Witness for the Prosecution*, which was based on Agatha Christie's 1954 play of the same title.[89] Among the changes the film version makes are that Christine Vole (Dietrich) is not just a German actress, as in the play, but is, of course, a nightclub singer whom the male protagonist, Leonard Vole (Tyrone Power), met while he was stationed in Germany at the end of the war. The film invokes *The Blue Angel* in a flashback not in the original play, where, as Judith Mayne has pointed out, "Christine worked in a nightclub called 'The Blue Lantern,' and a poster outside the club is virtually identical to the one seen in *The Blue Angel*. The spectacle inside the club is a quotation of the earlier film, but with some significant changes. Christine stands on a small stage, singing, playing her accordion(!), and wearing a man's jacket and pants (thus evoking many other Dietrich films in which she is dressed in male attire)."[90] The film rather cleverly relies on Dietrich's image not only in *The Blue Angel*, as Mayne suggests, but in *A Foreign Affair* in that Christine is a suspicious character because of her Germanness and the implication that she bartered sexual favors for scarce goods in the postwar occupation years. Indeed, as biographer Bach notes, "Wilder and Kurnitz concocted a flashback . . . [that] became a self-homage to *A Foreign Affair*. Christine is another version of Erika von Schlütow, singing in an off-limits dive that was as nearly a replica of the earlier picture's Lorelei club as art director Alexander Trauner could make it."[91]

Christine's performance, playing an accordion in what resembles a sailor's uniform (the flashback taking place in the port city of Hamburg), evokes not only her other films, where she dresses in male attire as Mayne suggests, but also both her offscreen persona and her USO tour, where her playing of a musical saw was regularly among the memorable acts she performed. The denseness of these quotes to Dietrich's persona in this flashback all come to bear then on the plot, which, like the original story treatment of *Notorious* with which I began this chapter, first relies on the association of this image with both political and sexual untrustworthiness and then reveals the "sexy Nazi singer" to be in fact just the opposite. As Mayne writes, "Christine and Leonard are both playing parts, but unexpected parts: Leonard's façade of innocence and naivete conceals a heartless, selfish murderer, whereas Christine's cool, icy exterior conceals a woman who is desperately in love with her husband and wants to save him at any costs, even though she knows he is guilty."[92] The film is thus reflexive about its deployment of the "Dietrich as sexy Nazi" persona, even more explicitly undermining her condemnation than in *A Foreign Affair*.

Dietrich's persona indeed evolved in the Cold War period to represent a kind of misunderstood, ambivalently sympathetic, political character whose self-quotation became ever more dense. Stanley Kramer's 1962 *Judgment at Nuremberg*, for instance, casts Dietrich as the wife of a German general who lends a human face to the proceedings. As she walks with one of the American judges (Spencer Tracy), "Lili Marlene" plays in the background, again invoking Dietrich's national-boundary-transcending performances with the USO as well as her by then more prominent career as a stage performer in Las Vegas.[93] Her stage performances, beginning in 1953, consisted entirely of self-quotation, including songs sung in both extravagant evening gowns and men's formal attire.[94] "Lili Marlene" continued to be one of her trademark songs. By the time of her appearance in *Judgment at Nuremberg*, she had become an extremely dense cultural icon; embodying the history of associations of illicit sexuality and a fantasy of the femme fatale as an emblem of Nazism's seductive power and at the same time embodying the ongoing appeal that her self-reflexive persona enacted in the entertainment world.

It is indeed this self-reflexive *Marlene* who was lionized in the short-lived stage production that bore her name in 1999, which was, appropriately, a one-show woman.[95] Even after her death, Dietrich's memorialization in Germany has continued to reflect the political complexities of her character: her burial in Berlin in 1992 and efforts to name a street after her in the Schöneberg district where she was born have been met with support (by those who embrace her as an admirable German icon) and resistance (by those who see her as a traitor to Germany).[96] There are indeed many ways in which her legacy lives on.

Conclusion

Even as Dietrich could not appear as anything but Dietrich by this time in her long career, with all the complications to political rhetoric that her iconic status entailed, her Lola Lola character would soon come to have her own life well beyond the one Dietrich occupied. In 1959, *The Blue Angel* was remade, directed by Edward Dmytryk and released through 20th Century-Fox. The film by all accounts was a miserable flop. But in 1969 Italian director Luchino Visconti released *The Damned*, wherein Martin, the Oedipally unresolved son of an industrialist family, performs Dietrich's Lola Lola role in drag, singing one of her songs from *The Blue Angel* for his assembled family and guests while the Reichstag burns outside. The performance sparked an extended genre of films in the 1970s that invoked the Dietrich icon without Dietrich and used the Weimar cabaret as a site of both sexual and political ambiguity for their contemporary contexts.

With the reintroduction of fascism as a rhetorical counterpoint to the politics of the New Left, new uses of the Lola Lola figure, like the old ones, have both reinforced conservative ideologies of the relationship between sexuality, gender, and politics and significantly complicated them. Much has been written about the renewed "fascination" with fascism, to use Susan Sontag's term, that the many Dietrich citations signal, most of which concludes, as film historian Eric Rentschler does, that "the incessant recycling of Nazi sights and sounds surely represents a crucial measure of today's postmodernism."[97]

In his introduction to *The Use of Pleasure*, Foucault describes his project as "a history of ethical problematizations based on practices of the self." I would argue that the explosion of uses of the Dietrich icon, and indeed of fascist sexual scenarios of various tones and types, reflect a period of intense "ethical problematization" of this sort, resulting from a renegotiation of the politics of sexuality and hence of democratic subjectivity.[98] The many permutations of Lola Lola present a more directly sexual bent to the postmodern fascination Rentschler names and a more directly political one as well. Like the icon Dietrich herself embodied, the character to whom she lent textual complexity continues to give expression to a variety of political negotiations of the political place of sexuality. Then, as now, as the next chapter will go on to elaborate, the icon's density does not easily conform to any one particular rhetorical function.

8

Sexualized Nazis

and Contemporary Popular

Political Culture

■

She was the most dreaded Nazi of them all. With her 'Black Widows' she committed crimes so terrible—even the SS feared her. Until an American POW uses his sexual prowess to combat her insatiable appetite and bring her to her knees.—Jacket cover for *Ilsa, She Wolf of the SS* (1974)

Historian Claudia Koonz notes that despite the massive amount of scholarly attention paid to Nazi Germany, women supporters of the regime are rarely the object of study. She writes, "Women do not appear as historical actors. If we think of women at all, we imagine masses of plain Eva Brauns with a Leni Riefenstahl here and there, or perhaps an Irma Griese (the infamous 'bitch of Auschwitz') in riding boots and SS uniform."[1] These three images of "Nazi women" each serve a function in anti-Nazi rhetoric, often resulting in an understanding of women's political subjectivity that codes women's political power exclusively through sexuality.

The soft porn exploitation film *Ilsa, She Wolf of the SS*, for instance, draws from the last image that Koonz names. Pulling through the thinnest of historical threads, the film turns the horror of Griese into an occasion for a story of American sexual conquest of this "most dreaded Nazi," crafting an absurdly antifeminist tale.[2] The cover art on the video jacket of the film features Ilsa in an iconic Lola Lola pose: feet planted firmly apart and arms akimbo (figs. 15 and 17). In subsequent films in

Fig. 17. Publicity image of Ilsa, arms akimbo, in *Ilsa, She Wolf of the SS* (Don Edmunds, 1974). Her stance exactly mirrors that of Lola Lola, pictured in figure 15, capitalizing on the iconicity of the Lola Lola image.

the series, Ilsa (always played by Dyanne Thorne) follows up her concentration camp doctor role with a series of other authoritarian figures: *Ilsa, Harem Keeper of the Oil Sheiks* (Don Edmunds, 1976), *Ilsa, the Wicked Warden* (Jess Franco, 1978), and *Ilsa, Tigress of Siberia* (Jean LaFleur, 1979). Each time Ilsa is imaged in the same iconic pose—only her costume and accessories have changed.

While surely the plot is not the "point" of such productions, the rhetorical function of the sexy authoritarian woman still illuminates the broader cultural role such figures can play. Each of these roles is part of an erotic vocabulary that posits women's sexual authority in place of political authority, illustrating in exaggerated form the interchangeableness of each setting. That the series begins with Ilsa as a Nazi speaks to the ways in which the Nazi scenario serves as the prototype for the

Sexualized Nazis and Culture   249

subsequent variations. The Ilsa series in this way reflects a postmodern textual practice that disregards contextual specificity and drains signifiers of content; but the Ilsa series also marks a new moment in the ongoing history of rhetorical practices that have linked sexuality and politics in the wake of World War II.

As an extreme representation of what a Nazi woman is and what her image means, Ilsa serves as an excessive version of the sexy Nazi icon embodied in Marlene Dietrich. Indeed, Ilsa's image makes overt the more embedded associations that produced the icon of Lola Lola as she became emblematic of the psychosexual dynamics of fascism. Unlike the Dietrich image, however, Ilsa does not embody the doubleness (as fascist and as champion of democracy) that troubles the direct links she forges between politics and sexuality. Instead, the film itself maneuvers a different doubleness through the exploitation genre. Ilsa takes the one side of Lola Lola's iconic qualities (the woman as fascist) to such an extreme that her excessiveness as sexual/political evil is instanciated as camp. The socially conservative content of her image is not thereby dispelled; rather, it is recontextualized *as* an icon available for (albeit tasteless) textual play. *Ilsa, She Wolf of the SS* is thus a film that reveals two levels of post-1960s uses of sexualized Nazism: (1) as a conservative rhetoric that continues to demonize all but highly traditional sexual relations and (2) as a marker of the freedoms of expression upon which such pornographic texts rely.

First, let us address the content. The plot of *Ilsa, She Wolf of the SS* turns in two directions: The first involves the German-American prisoner of war (whose name is Wolf) mentioned on the jacket of the video, who escapes Ilsa's usual practice of castrating the male inmates she sleeps with due to his remarkable staying power. The rather obvious equation of her sexual insatiability with fascist power lust and imperialism is countermanded by Wolf's sexual prowess as a parallel to American national invincibility. The film expresses this plainly in the use of audio, ostensibly coming from a nearby radio, announcing that "enemy aircraft" (the Allied forces) are approaching, just as Wolf promises to satisfy Ilsa, saying, "you'll beg me to stop." The second plotline parallels the first, as Ilsa subjects a particularly willful female inmate to a series of sexual tortures in the service of her "feminist" experiments. Through these experiments, Ilsa hopes to prove that women have a higher pain threshold and should be granted more power in the Nazi hierarchy. Here it is the inmate, Anna, who refuses to beg Ilsa to stop—ironically thereby serving Ilsa's aims.

The film's antifeminism is thus also twofold: Ilsa (the "she wolf") must be made into a sexual submissive to Wolf in order to be vanquished, and her sadistic cruelty is linked to her intertwined fascist-feminist project. In this sense, it is feminism that must be vanquished in order to ensure democracy, making Ilsa a prescient prototype for the feminazi of the contemporary American right-wing imagination.[3] As in contemporary uses of the feminazi, antigay rhetoric is also deployed in the service of the film's political battle, as Ilsa's "experiments" are coded as lesbian sex wherein Ilsa roughly inserts objects into Anna's (off-screen) vagina while leering into her eyes.[4] The parallel plot structure is decidedly sexist, too, as the male protagonist is active and the female passive: Wolf neutralizes Ilsa through sexual dominance, while Anna can only resist Ilsa's sexual sadism and finally dies before exacting revenge.

Now, to the form. Clearly *Ilsa, She Wolf of the SS* is part of the ground-swell of pornographic depictions of Nazism that were all the rage in the early 1970s, and so the rather campy extremes depicted in this film need to be taken into account even as they reflect a broad range of conservative political discourses that, in their less exploitation-oriented forms, have served central rhetorical functions in defining political issues in the last three decades. Because of the obvious lasciviousness of the genre and its spirit of sexual libertarianism, *perhaps* this rhetoric is ultimately undermined. It is thus not the vaguely Lola Lola–like figure embodied in Ilsa who expresses doubleness here; instead, it is the entire practice of sexualizing the Nazi scenario.

Many cultural theorists who have examined the resurgence of images of Nazism in the 1970s assert that fascism thematizes a burgeoning postmodern sensibility, foregrounding spectacle over substance and circulating signs without the burden of history. This use of Nazism has not, as these critics would agree, entirely drained the phenomenon of political content. Whether as acts of "political bad faith," or reflecting a "simultaneous desire for absolute submission and total freedom," critics have most often looked, however, at the *overall* appeal of images of fascism rather than at the *specific* ways in which they might be deployed for a political rhetoric *about* sexuality.[5] I argue that both general and specific analyses are necessary.

Susan Sontag links the sexualization of Nazism with spectacle, claiming that "between sadomasochism and fascism there is a natural link. 'Fascism is theater,' as Genet said, as is sadomasochistic sexuality: to be involved in sadomasochism is to take part in a sexual theater, a staging of sexuality."[6] The psychosexual theories of fascism that linked it to sado-masochism in the course of the 1930s and 1940s are here deployed as evidence of a theatricality that resonates with the postmodern present. When Sontag asks, "Why has Nazi Germany, which was a sexually repressive society, become erotic?" it is a question that rightly identifies a renewed and highly sexual interest in the phenomenon. But it is also a question that neglects the longer rhetorical history behind it. Sontag writes, "If the message of fascism has been neutralized by an aesthetic view of life, its trappings have been sexualized," wherein she assumes that the sexualization of Nazism *follows* a process by which the political specificity of its politics is drained.[7] While on some level this assessment holds true as the uses of Nazism as a rhetorical rather than strictly historical phenomenon proliferate, this profligacy also speaks to the ways in which Nazi—and anti-Nazi—politics have sexualized politics all along. The dramatic increase in the invocation of Nazism as a sexual scenario is connected not only with sexual libertarianism, "an oppressive freedom of choice in sex," as Sontag puts it, but also with the complex ways these scenarios connect with feminism and antifeminism and gay rights and the persecution of homosexuals, in short, with the history of sexual politics and the sexual rendering of politics, which do indeed retain a prurient and exploitable interest in detailing sexual/political offenses but also continue to serve a central function in American political culture.

A completely different example of the use of World War II as a scenario for sexual politics, for instance, is *The Desert Peach*, a comic book series by Donna Barr. The series revolves around an imagined pacifist gay brother of German General Erwin Rommel, the Desert Fox. Pfirsich (peach) is a kind, gentle, and effeminate man who comes out while serving as an officer in Africa. According to Barr, *Comics Journal* gave the series a positive review in 1991, hailing "the Peach [as] 'a truly wonderful gay role model,' [sic] and the book itself as a work of 'confident, audacious, and utterly singular humanity.'"[8] Fans of the comic have sent in drawings featuring Pfirsich as a member of a gay nuclear family (fig. 18) or as a catalyst in antiwar activism (fig. 19).[9] Coming much later in the legacy of post-1960s uses of Nazism in sexual politics, this comic presents an opposite pole of rhetorical uses of the common association of Nazism with homosexuality—where the gay German officer is not a Nazi at all (building on the historical distinction between the army and the SS) and is indeed the hero of the comic's largely pacifist message.[10] Clearly, between Ilsa and Pfirsich a great range of political rhetorics can

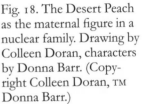

Fig. 18. The Desert Peach as the maternal figure in a nuclear family. Drawing by Colleen Doran, characters by Donna Barr. (Copyright Colleen Doran, TM Donna Barr.)

be invoked through even campy images of sexualized Nazis: from the dominant depictions that ally Nazism with sexual deviance to those that invert even this. None of these texts endorses fascism; all of them, however, use sexuality to different political ends.

As in 1948, when Billy Wilder's film *A Foreign Affair* and Siegfried Kracauer's book *From Caligari to Hitler* presented very different visions of the political function of the Lola Lola icon, so the various texts that deploy this icon (or Nazism more broadly) in the new proliferation of "sexy Nazi" images of the 1970s also put her to a variety of rhetorical uses. Indeed, the two films that Sontag mentions as enacting a "solemn eroticizing of fascism," Luchino Visconti's *The Damned* (1969) and Liliana Cavani's *The Night Porter* (1974), invoke the Dietrich/Lola Lola icon to different ends.[11] In *The Damned*, she appears as part of a drag performance by the film's central character, reflecting both his decadence (transgressing the boundaries of gender) and his Oedipal irresolution (signaling perversion), which serve as part of the film's explanation for his becoming a fascist. In *The Night Porter*, she appears as a cabaret

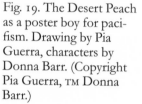

Fig. 19. The Desert Peach as a poster boy for pacifism. Drawing by Pia Guerra, characters by Donna Barr. (Copyright Pia Guerra, TM Donna Barr.)

performer in a concentration camp, muddying the boundaries between victims and perpetrators of Nazi political crimes. Critics have either panned or praised these films, depending on what sort of political project they imagine them to be staging.

Boundary blurring is often the characteristic of the Dietrich/Lola Lola icon that marks her as politically troubling. But, depending on the aims of the text in which she appears (or the aims of the critic interpreting the text), this blurring may or may not be seen as liberating in the postmodern sense. There are two major trajectories that the icon (and hence this chapter) follows, which characterize political sexuality in the postmodern moment. One focuses on the Oedipal underpinnings of the figure, and the other focuses on boundary transgression, especially with respect to gender. In the former, there are multiple narratives spun out of either psychical or actual acts of incest, which reflect larger cultural negotiations about the status of the "democratic" family. In the latter, there are multiple narratives spun out of either liberatory rhetorics of transgression as a positive act or conservative rhetorics insisting on boundary fortification.

While perhaps neutralizing Nazism's specific politics, these films (including even *Ilsa*) narrate and visualize larger trends in the rhetorical function of political sexuality in Western democratic culture. The postmodern sensibility of these representations does not drain politics; rather, it gives it form. This chapter aims to catalog the broad strains in these myriad uses and so point to the ways in which, as the centrality of sexuality to political rhetoric has become more overt, fascism has continued to be rhetorically central to the ongoing process of defining democracy over the last thirty years.

The Proliferation of Sexualized Nazis: Lola Lola after the 1960s

The political uses of the Lola Lola icon since the late 1960s bring together several threads of argument examined in the course of this book. Following on the logic of nationalist melodrama, the icon has sometimes served as an emblem of that which threatens the family or, following the logic of national psychobiography, she has served as a marker of Oedipal trouble, gender ambiguity, and the assorted perversions that stand against "healthy" democratic political subjectivity. In her more recent incarnations, she has also come to embody renewed negotiations of both of these trajectories over a postmodern terrain that often valorizes these previously demonized transgressions. Postmodernism, with its celebration of the inefficacy of boundaries and binaries and its purported de-Oedipalization of families, may have provided the conditions for the icon's resurgence. As a political icon, then, she can be deployed either in the service of this celebration or as a cause for heightened anxieties and hence the fortification of boundaries, binaries, and the Oedipal family. The films that deploy the Dietrich/Lola Lola icon are often caught between celebration and anxiety, mapping the terrain of political sexuality that she inhabits.

From the conservative side, concerns about the erosion of boundaries derive from the history of national discourse, which stakes much national imagery on a logic of difference and exclusion: "Othering" in Homi Bhabha's formulation.[12] By preserving these boundaries, the nation is then understood to be well ordered (an association of national order with strict gender dimorphism and the regulation of sexual contact, for instance). Hence, in building the binary of fascism/democracy, wartime and immediate postwar anti-Nazi films often characterized Nazism as having violated gender boundaries, despite the fact that Nazism extolled gender difference to an extreme. That Lola Lola's first screen reappearance without Dietrich should be a drag performance speaks to this legacy of associating fascism with gender inversion and homosexuality as well as to the history of Lola Lola specifically.

Following the logic of abjection as defined by psychoanalytic theorist Julia Kristeva, violence and sex both share symbolic power due to their dissolution of boundaries between bodies and between control and the loss thereof.[13] Abjection is the visceral rejection of those traces of this dissolution, either in the form of bodily fluids or with respect to the *social* body and hence the rejection of women, cross-dressing, homosexuality, and miscegenation. Kristeva argues that eroticism stands at the opposite pole from abjection and is hence closely tied thereto. The dual nature of images of sexualized Nazis, as erotic or as abject, is thus linked to the anti-Nazi displacement or merger of Nazism's violence with sex.

Klaus Theweleit has suggested that fascism itself functions by way of abjection, as he reads a rejection of sex and an embrace of purity and death in the writings of proto-Nazi Freikorps members.[14] *The Damned* stages its fascist character Martin's development into a full-blown Nazi by way of Theweleit's portrait. While the Lola Lola performance introduces the audience to Martin, this scene also serves as a bookend with the last shots of the film, wherein Martin, after having consummated his always too close relationship with his seductive mother and given her no choice but to commit suicide, is finally pictured in uniform giving a Nazi salute. In Theweleit's theory, sex would not be the operative desire here but rather Martin's desire to eradicate that which causes him anxiety: violence rather than sex.[15] In Visconti's film, the drag performance sets the stage for Martin's transformation and indicates his immaturity and perversion, but he is not fully converted to Nazism until he has completed this substitution.

Film historian Annette Insdorf writes that "Despite *The Damned*'s numerous scenes of murder and sexual perversion (rape, incest, pedophilia, transvestism), it constitutes a historically faithful tapestry of the rise of Nazism." It is, however, the inclusion of the former that marks this film's engagement with psychosexual theories of Nazism, toward which, as Insdorf also notes, filmmaker Visconti feels some ambivalence.[16] The scene in which Martin "cavorts in Dietrich drag while singing one of her numbers from *The Blue Angel*" marks a reinforcement of the connection of decadence and fascism, but it also presents the spectacle of the drag performance not merely for abjection but also for fascination.[17] Lola Lola thus inhabits a region between desire and abjection in this anti-Nazi film, establishing the general problematic of the 1970s cycle of Lola Lola incarnations.

The Damned's location of Lola Lola/Martin as ensconced in a family dynamic is also a new placement for the icon. In Dietrich's embodiment, Lola Lola mostly functions as a consolidation of fascism's seductiveness. In Martin, she appears as a symptom of Oedipal fallout. The Italian cycle of films, including *The Night Porter* and Bernardo Bertolucci's *The Conformist* (1971), all claim to address present-day fears of a rightist resurgence but do so through highly sexualized scenarios.[18] In this choice, all appear to be influenced by leftist theories of fascism, which see it as a "postpatriarchal" movement in which the state has replaced the father's traditional role, preventing the formation of an ego-fortified subjectivity from which political critique can arise. This fascist subject is coded as either latent or overtly homosexual or grasping to stage an Oedipal drama that did not adequately transpire within the family itself.

In the U.S., films using Nazism as a sexual scenario often engaged variants of these ideas as well, although here they were generally not addressed to fears of a rightist resurgence per se. Instead, American films thematized contemporary political crises as reflected in a culture of self-involvement, lack of political commitment, and sexual upheaval (including anxieties about a rising divorce rate, feminism, gay liberation, and sexual experimentation). Films like *The Formula* (John Avildsen, 1980) explicitly narrate a link between the 1970s and Nazi Germany, while films like *Just a Gigolo* (David Hemmings, 1979) present these links in terms of the era's parallel components: political turmoil, sexual decadence, and a lack of direction for men returning from war. Both films feature references to the Weimar cabaret as a site of political contention. In *The Formula*, images of Nazi atrocities are projected on the wall behind slinky dancers in a 1970s Berlin bar, while in *Just a Gigolo* Dietrich herself makes a cameo appearance as the madam for whom the protagonist (David Bowie) peddles his sexual wares.[19]

In the latter film, the protagonist is not a Nazi or proto-Nazi, as in the Italian films, but is apolitical. He returns from World War I only to find that his family home has become a brothel. As his father is suffering from hysterical paralysis contracted when he heard of Germany's defeat, his only option for making money is prostituting himself to either wealthy middle-aged divorcees or homosexual Nazis. The family has thus been corrupted by decadence, the father rendered impotent by defeat, and the war veteran reduced to prostitution: economic and political crises are primarily coded in sexual terms. Bowie's character shows no sign of interest in either Nazi ideology or its communist alternative, as these two factions engage in peripheral street fighting, yet he is nonetheless claimed as a martyr by the Nazis after his entirely accidental death. It is an ending through which the film seems to suggest that the hapless participants in this sexual/political madness are connected to the rise of fascism as much as those who have political opinions.

This type of character at the center of a story about Weimar sexual decadence is the culmination of a series of characters who are all, in one fashion or another, derivative of Christopher Isherwood's Sally Bowles, who represents the problem of political naïveté.[20] The primary Sally Bowles character of the 1970s is of course her most direct rendering in Bob Fosse's film version of *Cabaret* (1972), but she is also to be found in more coded form in *The Serpent's Egg* (Ingmar Bergman, 1978) and *Lili Marleen* (Rainer Werner Fassbinder, 1981).[21] Indeed, the lead character in *Lili Marleen* is a hybrid of the Lola Lola and Sally icons, as she becomes a celebrity among Nazis but claims "I'm only singing a song." She does not see a contradiction between her desire to help her Jewish boyfriend and his resistance organization and her status as an icon for the Nazis.

Willie, the Lola Lola/Sally character in *Lili Marleen* (Hanna Schygulla), takes the doubleness that Dietrich's real anti-Nazism lent to the Lola Lola icon to a more direct level: Dietrich, after all, never worked for the Nazis and only played a Nazi icon in Hollywood. Although both the fictional Willie and the real Dietrich sing "Lili Marleen," they do so from opposite sides of the conflict. This move drew fire from some critics, who consequently saw Fassbinder's film as making excuses for non-Nazi Germans who collaborated with the Nazis.[22] It is the inverse of the criticism leveled at *The Night Porter*, where once again the cabaret singer appears but this time singing a song for her captors. Her song, "Wenn ich mir was Wünschen Dürfte" (If I Could Wish for Something), is again a song that Dietrich recorded—in 1930, before the Nazis came to power—as written by Friedrich Holländer, composer for *The Blue Angel*. *The Night Porter* invokes the Dietrich icon to characterize moral ambiguity, a common practice, but as the reference seems to implicate a victim of the Nazis, the invocation parallels the equally unconscionable gesture of exonerating a Nazi collaborator in *Lili Marleen*.

Indeed, *The Night Porter* drew harsh criticism for crossing an already tenuous line in the use of Nazism as a sexual scenario, a line from which the other films had, at least on this count, steered clear. While many of these films share an ongoing engagement with the psychosexual reading of fascism that grew out of wartime political psychology, criticism was most harsh when films shifted too far from smearing the Nazis. This line drawing can be seen in a comparison of the critical reception of *Cabaret* and *The Night Porter*.

Most reviews of *Cabaret* praised the film's political project, if not everything about the production, with many commenting on the possible political warning the film issued in its forging of parallels between contemporary U.S. culture and the Germany of the early 1930s. A review that appeared in *Variety*, for instance, saw the film as "depicting disillusion and despair, a retreat from reality, a political unawareness and naivete, and all the other manifestations of a population ripe for radicalization from either pole," while Judith Crist of *New York* magazine described it as "a compassionate story of people trapped by their own indifference and slowly contaminated by their lack of involvement."[23] *The Night Porter*, on the other hand, was not initially thought by American reviewers to reflect any such contemporary criticism, despite Cavani's track record as a leftist documentarian. Instead, critics called the film a "piece of junk" (Vincent Canby), complained that its "porno-profundity is humanly and aesthetically offensive" (Pauline Kael), and described it as "eerily frivolous" (Geoffrey Minnish). Film scholar Henry Giroux dismissed it as "a thinly-disguised fascist propaganda film that glorifies sadism, brutality and exaggerated machismo."[24] Most reviews were more dismissive than alarmist, as evidenced in Stanley Kauffmann's comment that Cavani is "apparently humorless and, in a basic sense, stupid. Only a humorless person could so often cross over into the ridiculous; only a stupid one could believe that all this sexual-homicidal blatancy was symbolically illuminating."[25] Charles Champlin, writing for the *Los Angeles Times*, compared *The Night Porter* with *Cabaret* as follows: "*Cabaret* dealt with a decadent and poisonous time and place, but it kept its own perspective and became a strong, implicit comment on its own material. *The Night Porter*, which in a sense updates the same strain of decadence, is by contrast a sweaty, kinky undertaking which merely exploits its subject matter and defies belief right from the beginning."[26]

Minority opinions on the relative merits of these two films, however, immediately began to invert their political value, signaling thereby the development of a new, perhaps postmodern, sensibility about sexual imagery and images of Nazism. Stephen Farber, writing for the *New York Times*, writes that audiences watching *Cabaret* are "probably quite willing to accept the neat, unexamined parallels between sexual dissipation and Nazi brutality, parallels that seem equally dubious in *The Damned*." Farber sees *Cabaret*'s efforts to be read as "a cautionary tale for today, a warning that contemporary America, because of its new sexual freedom, is a sick society, comparable to Weimar Germany" as an ideology born of the minds of moralist hypocrites.[27] Farber's review was exceptional in its criticism of *Cabaret*'s sexual politics at the time the film was released, but he was joined two years later by Andrew Sarris, who voiced an inverse comparison similar to Champlin's when he wrote that "*The Damned* and *Cabaret* demonstrated to the film industry how audiences could be made to wallow in decadence in the name of social consciousness." Sarris goes on to offer a tempered but positive review of *The Night Porter* as a film that does not attempt realism since both of the lead actors (Charlotte Rampling and Dirk Bogarde) "have consolidated their iconographical identities within the past decade" and hence tend to evoke "the absurdist disorder of the 60s and 70s rather than the existential disorder of the 40s and 50s."[28] As minority opinions in the critical landscape, the views of Farber and Sarris helped define a new approach to the politics of this burgeoning genre of sexualized Nazis. They drew attention to the persistence of the use of sexual decadence as a means of building an opposition between fascism and democracy and also pointed to a different sensibility that a film like *The Night Porter* might express: as a film that bears a closer relation to the more recent history of rhetorical practices than to the historical phenomenon of Nazism.

Another line of debate surrounding these films has been the place of family dramas in sexualized political scenarios. It is a line of debate that continues to see family as central to democracy in various ways. In contrast to its central feature of spectacular and performative marginal sexualities, *Cabaret* posits a psychosexual diagnosis of Sally (Liza Minnelli) as driven by unresolved Oedipal attachments and presents these aspects entirely unspectacularly and unreflexively. Sally's fixation on her negligent father is offered as an explanation for her promiscuity and her eternal search for a rich man who will support her. Her Oedipal immaturity is indirectly connected to her lack of political awareness, but it is not, as in the case of films that revolve around Nazi characters, ultimately a reason to condemn her. Instead, her immaturity is also reflected in Natalia (Marisa Berenson), the film's Jewish supporting character, who likewise needs the approval of her parents for everything she does. Even though the film presents its cabaret scenes as sexual commentaries on political events, it offers no performative criticism of women's troubled relationships with paternal authority. It instead reinforces the alliance of female immaturity with the political norm.

Contrary to commentary on the role of sexual decadence in the film, many critics did see Fosse's addition of an Oedipal motivation for Sally's behavior as a flaw. Kauffmann, for instance, writes condescendingly that "she sleeps around like mad because she's in love with her diplomat father who rejects her. When she became American, she had to be 'explained,' and the explanation had to be Freudian."[29] Farber, the progressive iconoclast, takes this criticism further, complaining that the film " 'explains' Sally with that all-purpose character—an unloving father—and turns Isherwood's tribute to a resilient, amoral girl into a routine love story with a moralistic conclusion."[30] Farber's feminist criticism, which perhaps ignores the upbeat nature of the film's title song, contrasts strongly with nonfeminist critics like Roger Greenspun, who aside from praising Minelli's body notes that "Brian's bisexuality now has as much as Sally's accidental pregnancy to do with moving the plot, and it connects as well with a general theme of sick sexual ambiguity that runs through the film as a kind of working motif."[31] Greenspun represents the conservative voice wherein women's sexual and political subjectivity is less relevant than her legs while willfully ejecting sexual alternatives from the realm of acceptable behaviors. Indeed, Greenspun ignores the film's more socially progressive elements on this count; for instance, that Brian's newly overt bisexuality (his character is asexual in the story) is sympathetically handled.

Indeed, in the film's most dramatic departure from its usual cabaret format for musical numbers, the Chris character, Brian (Michael York), and Max (Helmut Griem), the pinnacle of a ménage à trois with Sally, are seated in a beer garden discussing politics. Brian voices concern that moderate Germans like Max will not be able to control the Nazis much longer. An androgynous young boy stands and begins singing what turns out to be a Nazi anthem, "Tomorrow Belongs to Me." He is joined by one after another traditionally dressed German extras. At the end of this scene, Brian asks, "Do you still think you'll be able to control them?" This afternoon turns out to be a prelude to Brian and Max having sex, as he later tells Sally, but his sexuality is linked not with fascism but (if anything) with antifascism. Brian becomes increasingly outspoken in his anti-Nazism as the film progresses. The garishly clad transvestites of the cabaret may also potentially offer criticism of the political events occurring outside the club, but the film is not entirely clear about this since Nazis are regularly seen among the members of the audience. It has thus been possible for critics and scholars to interpret the film in a variety of ways: as socially conservative (aligning fascism with decadence) or socially progressive (aligning sexual freedom with anti-Nazism).

The Night Porter goes further in its refusal to preserve the traditional conservative political relationship between family and sexuality. The film acknowledges a relationship between patriarchal female sexual subjectivity and authoritarianism (denied in *Cabaret*) by way of the sexual psychology of victims. Cavani's central female character, Lucia (Charlotte Rampling), clearly suffers from an unresolved Oedipus complex, but as she is a prisoner and not a Nazi the link between family dramas and politics troubled critics. Cavani evades the question of Lucia's ethnicity/religion—explaining her presence in the camp through her being the daughter of a socialist—a move that many critics who were deeply offended by the film overlooked, almost invariably assuming that she is Jewish. The purpose of this move, however, is to shift the terrain entirely over to issues of gender and so to mobilize popularly held beliefs in the fundamental masochism of the female sexual psyche, brought out in overt and performative form. Unlike *Cabaret*, which reserves the authority-dependence of its female characters for uncriticized moments of truth, *The Night Porter* eliminates any point of origin, making both the "original" interactions in the flashback concentration camp and the "re-created" sexual scenarios in the present equally theatrical.[32]

It is this shift that feminist film theorist Teresa de Lauretis championed in her praise of *The Night Porter* in *Film Quarterly* in 1976. De Lauretis sees Cavani as having invoked Nazism as a metaphor for patriarchy and the warping of female subjectivity that can occur under so oppressive a sexual system. In this sense, she extends the already prominent feminist rhetorical practice of invoking Nazism as a parallel to then-contemporary sexism, seeing the generalizability of the Nazi ideal of "Kinder, Küche, Kirche" (children, kitchen, church) in patriarchal cultures as the only realms legitimately open to women.[33] De Lauretis argues that "it is not Lucia's experience (her victimization, initiation, and subsequent unbreakable bondage to her oppressor-Father-lover) that serves as a metaphor for the infamy perpetrated by the Nazis on humanity, but Nazism and the atrocities committed in the camps that are the allegorical framework chosen by Cavani to investigate the dialectics of the male-female relationship in our contemporary, post-Nazi, society."[34] In this way, de Lauretis is able to suggest that the film's pairing of Max (Dirk Bogarde) as the Nazi/father and Lucia as the inmate/ daughter indeed privileges the second term. She writes, "The way in which Lucia is victimized, the truth she discovers in herself and lives out, the imagery of her bondage to the Father . . . are a true metaphor, however magnified, of the female condition. That the same ambivalence exists in the Father, who is nonetheless, objectively, the oppressor, only makes the metaphor complete."[35] In other words, de Lauretis argues that the film has not drained the politics out of Nazism but is about a different type of politics, feminist politics, where it is precisely sexuality ("the personal") that is political.

A second strain of film criticism, which also tried to retrieve the film from its detractors, pursued the erotic potency of the film (which de Lauretis's reading largely denies). Beverle Houston and Marsha Kinder for instance, writing in 1975, based their reclamation strategy on an insistence that the film is primarily about sex and secondarily about Nazis: "It's as if Cavani begins with the desire to create a powerful sado/masochistic story and then draws from the past the most extreme setting possible—the Nazi concentration camp—in order to enhance its imaginative power. This is quite different from setting out to make a film about the historical reality of Nazi brutality and then reducing it to a ro- mantic love story, which would be grotesquely immoral and obscene."[36] Houston and Kinder generalize the appeal of Lucia's regression to Max's "little girl," asking, "Who among the audience has not wanted to ease back into utter dependence, to be totally cared for by another? Thus, as Lucia stands quietly, arms upraised, waiting for Max to slip on her Sunday dress, she evokes identification even among those who must reject other aspects of the sado/masochism."[37] Between de Lauretis's and Houston and Kinder's readings lies a central debate of cultural feminism, the practitioners of which have variously insisted on sexuality as a political terrain.[38]

Michel Foucault was among those who categorically criticized *The Night Porter*, but his comments on the larger phenomenon of sexualized Nazis help to situate the debates more generally. He wrote that "No- body loves power anymore," at least in the form of fetishizing leaders, and so the Nazi fad in the 1970s was a symptom of "the beginnings of a re-eroticization of power, taken to a pathetic, ridiculous extreme."[39] This "re-eroticization of power" appears in a variety of both long- standing and contemporary forms in *The Night Porter*'s final sequence, wherein Max dresses in his well-preserved ss uniform and Lucia wears not her cabaret outfit nor an inmate's garb but the little girl's dress, which has appeared recursively throughout. As they finally leave the apartment and invite their execution, Lucia/Dietrich's cabaret song is reprised on the soundtrack. The mixing of two versions of role inequity underscores the plurality of systems of power on which the film's erotics work, while the cabaret once again stands for the ambiguity on which these erotics rely. *The Night Porter*, indeed, specifically eroticizes public scrutiny of private relationships, drawing on the Lola Lola trope as a marker of public/private boundary violations. Two trajectories leading out of the debates about *The Night Porter* follow from the dense re-eroticization of power performed in this final sequence: Nazism as a continued parallel, in various forms, to family dynamics; and Nazism as part of a theatrical sensibility that challenges the dominant system of surveillance, which hopes to limit the range of sexual expression in a democratic society.

In the rest of this chapter, I will pursue three ongoing strains of the uses of Nazism that give form to these trajectories: (1) as central to discussions of child abuse and the political symbology of family; (2) as central to assertions of sexual/political freedom; and (3) as central to an antifeminist, antiqueer counter-rhetoric arguing for the fundamental political need for difference between the sexes and the banishment of "perversions."

Child Abuse and the Nazi Scenario

> Every woman adores a Fascist,
> The boot in the face, the brute
> Brute heart of a brute like you.
>
> You stand at the blackboard, daddy,
> In the picture I have of you,
> A cleft in your chin instead of your foot
> But no less a devil for that, no not
> Any less the black man who
>
> Bit my pretty red heart in two.
> —Sylvia Plath, "Daddy" (1962)[40]

Sylvia Plath's poem reflects the most straightforward feminist use of Nazism as political rhetoric, wherein, as in de Lauretis's reading of *The Night Porter*, Nazism serves as a metaphor for patriarchy. This image of the father as Nazi extends to narratives not only of familial sexism but of child abuse, wherein intrafamilial abuse—especially incest—is frequently spoken of as a "private holocaust."

The feminist approach to incest and family violence counters the dominant discourse, which sees it as an aberration, instead asserting that violence is endemic to the social order and signals a struggle to maintain it.[41] This is in itself a political stance, of course, deriving from the central feminist tenet that "the personal is political." But the extension of the rhetorical use of Nazism to discussions of child abuse and incest more generally also highlights the centrality of narratives of dysfunctional families to contemporary political debate, often without an accompanying critique of patriarchy. In these latter narratives, children populate the national imaginary and perform a central role in narrating the nation and, indeed, democracy. Contemporary rhetorical uses of Nazism to characterize the dysfunctional family, in both feminist and patriarchy-supporting forms, continue some of the themes of nationalist melodrama transferred to the domestic scene. But these uses of Nazism also reflect a national subjectivity that is (1) highly privatized and (2) scripted through political/sexual trauma.

Psychologist Janice Haaken notes that "Increasingly, trauma stories have taken on a mythic tone in casting the survivor in dramatic combat with an archetypal personification of evil."[42] The stark oppositions of good and evil in these narratives easily lend themselves to Nazi metaphors, a phenomenon that Haaken critiques by warning that "While the Holocaust is often invoked to dramatize the private, unacknowledged pain of survivors, it also trivializes the vast distinctions in the magnitude and nature of trauma suffered by various oppressed groups."[43] Haaken sees the collapse of different experiences under the metaphor of Nazism as a corollary to the "adult child" movement, which sees the American middle-class family as deeply dysfunctional. As she notes, the public interest in missing and abused children and the adult child movement, though perhaps growing out of the feminist movement's influences, more commonly maintain an idealized notion of family life. They make the family both the seat of all sorts of larger social and personal problems and the cure. By scripting child abuse as a national crisis, these narratives are political in another sense; for they hope to recenter a normative notion of family life through a rhetorically politicized foregrounding of sexuality.[44]

The emergence of the adult child movement and "child within" therapies has coincided with the growth of both medical and public interest in child abuse. This interest, however, took a decided shift toward sexual rather than physical abuse in the course of the 1970s. Historian Ian Hacking notes that child abuse and incest were not commonly connected until 1975, after which time abuse by strangers steadily declined as a central interest of the child abuse movement.[45] The contemporaneous upsurge of images of sexualized Nazis is clearly connected to their use in this likewise now sexualized context. This is not to say that incest has not always been a dark component of some family's lives, but rather that a nearly exclusive focus on sexual abuse signals another side of the increasing centrality of sexuality to political rhetoric in the later twentieth century, with fascism once again serving as a conduit for the increase.

Feminist scholar Elizabeth Wilson warns that the heightened focus on incest narratives might reflect a bias whereby "the middle class has historically exhibited a lack of concern for the possible ill-effects of physical or psychological abuse as compared with sexual abuse," a bias that can be linked to the equation of the liberal-democratic nation with "respectability" and sexual propriety historically associated with the middle class.[46] Hacking, too, notes that the rise of the child abuse movement in the course of the 1980s concealed the material decline in social support of especially poor children during the Reagan and Bush presidencies. Anthropologist Marilyn Ivy suggests that in this era the abused child came "to bear a symbolic burden dependent on the fluidities of advanced capitalist social formations and identities," wherein the child is the ideal national subject because he or she is not seen as a political being, and so "privatization, familialization, and infantilization of these therapies have accorded well with the dominant American political climate, where the private sector, the individual, and the family are supposed to assume the burdens of the social."[47] Holocaust metaphors used in child abuse narratives assist not only in dramatizing the horror they describe but in replacing large-scale public forms of understanding political activity with small-scale, formerly "private," and certainly personal ones. Unlike the feminist project, which seeks to politicize our understanding of the personal, these narratives hope to personalize the political, thereby limiting the public sphere further by substituting nonpolitical actors (children) for the political agency of adults or else asserting a conservative notion of parental authority over a nation of children in the guise of "family values."

I will analyze two very different media texts in order to illustrate the range of issues involved in the process of personalizing the political: underground filmmaker Beth B and painter Ida Applebroog's experimental video *Belladonna* (1989) and Steven Spielberg's blockbuster film *Schindler's List* (1993).[48] Each of these texts deals with a parallel between Nazism and family dynamics, in a blend of victims and perpetrators in the former and in the substitution of the "good Nazi/father" for the bad in the latter. *Belladonna* very compellingly illustrates the manner in which different sorts of experiences become rhetorically fused under a banner of sexual/political victimization, while *Schindler's List* illustrates the ways in which paternal authority and social normativity continue to characterize the Hollywood hero as a corollary to antifascist political intervention.

Belladonna cuts together three versions of sexuality and violence that produce an unsettling mixture of psychosexual confession, Nazi brutality, and modern-day child abuse. The tape consists of a series of people repeatedly speaking fragments of the following texts: Freud's 1919 case history "A Child Is Being Beaten" (Freud's treatise on masochism), testimony from the posthumous trial of Nazi doctor Josef Mengele (1985), and testimony from the trial of Joel Steinberg for the abuse and murder of his young daughter (1988). Like *The Night Porter*, *Belladonna* levels private and public tribunals, as court and couch are made equivalent. As the catalog for a retrospective exhibition notes, Beth B's work displays "an attentiveness and a unique sensitivity to social and psychic history as recalled by participants/witnesses. In this respect, Beth B's ongoing artistic project is to investigate and reclaim the site where lyricism meets anguish, recollection exposes trauma and the act of speaking is valued as a therapeutic triumph."[49]

Most of B's installation and video work features the "talking heads" form of address, in which characters speak deeply traumatic or confessional monologues directly into the camera, the sources of which are often not revealed or not revealed until the end. Two of B's tapes, *Belladonna* and *Amnesia*, draw parallels between contemporary personal dramas and Nazism.[50] B's use of talking heads reflects television's organizing paradox, conveying intimacy through the public mediation of broadcast technology. Nazism, then, serves for B as the rhetorical link between the private and public arenas that the medium itself blurs. Art critic Joseph Di Mattia likens *Belladonna* to "a segment from 'Nightline' from an alternative universe where the guests can only speak the subtext of their most intimate thoughts," a subtext made primary, in which "childhood fears, sexual guilt and anxiety about physical punishment" are consequently no longer subtextual.[51] This seems a fitting strategy, perhaps *not* because it runs counter to current trends but rather because it duplicates and complicates them. *Belladonna* problematically enacts a merger between opposing tendencies: childhood-perverse sexuality (the male "child" who wants to be beaten as punishment for Oedipal desires in Freud's case history) and the physical abuse and consequent murder of a young girl.[52] The crimes of Mengele, reported with the same intimacy and emphasis on voyeuristic witnessing, also drift toward private, personal, and intimate realms that consequently replace, at least in form, more traditionally public tribunals and arenas for political debate.

Belladonna in this sense is a tape that uncomfortably oscillates between the two functions to which the Nazi trope is commonly put: as ultimate horror and erotic scenario. The two stories of childhood beatings, one wished for, the other not, are hard to distinguish from one another in the fragmented utterances of the tape's players. Freud's male patient, the only actual child who appears in the tape, says repeatedly, "I'm not a bad person," while his adult self details the contours of his guilty sexual fantasy. The defendant in the murder trial, the young girl's father, similarly claims his innocence and love for the girl he killed. The various accounts of Mengele's entirely disingenuous reassurances, also often told from a child's perspective, echo the murderous father Steinberg, but also the disavowals of the fantasizing adult child.

Of her choice not to reveal the sources of her testimonies until the end, B has said, "Maybe by not knowing who is speaking or where the source material comes from, the viewer can hear and understand what's being said more than they would if the identity of the speakers was known."[53] But the generalizable meaning of both the Freudian and, indeed, Nazi texts ensures that the information is always already filtered, already conflated. In this sense, the Steinberg story gets lost under Freud's recantation long ago, which erased the reality of child abuse and replaced it with a fantasy, while Nazi violence, stylized and theatrical, cannot escape the recognizability of Nazi eroticism/horror.[54] The cumulative effect of the Freudian and Nazi narratives is to obscure the victims (those killed by the Nazis and the daughter of the Steinberg couple) with the general diagnosis of a male sexual subject with a guilty conscience.[55]

The Nazi trope thus functions as an obscuring device because it is a readily available metaphor for *both* family violence and family erotics. However the fact that *Belladonna* does not document corporal punishment as an act, but rather documents testimony around it, speaks to the ways in which the tape is more about how these arenas *discursively* intertwine. As such, the tape portrays a deep cultural ambivalence about childhood sexuality, family violence, and a pervasive tendency to take a personal, therapeutic approach to political events, the consequence of which is the loss of distinction between rhetorically similar but materially very different historical experiences.

Given the dual rhetorical tendency by means of which Nazism (and especially the Holocaust) serves as a medium for transposing public, historical tragedies into intimate, familial realms, a companion rhetoric to the universal, dysfunctional family (and the subject it produces—the universal victim) tries to reverse the rhetorical flow, mending the family through the positing of a good father and mending the nation through the reinstatement of a benign patriarch. Rhetorics of the good father tend not to deny the status of the bad father as a villain; instead, the bad father is, in the dominant rhetoric, precisely the reason why the good father is needed. While Nazism does not figure as centrally as a rhetorical mediator in this process as it does in the creation of the father/villain, it does, as in *Belladonna*, function in his absolution (the repetition of "I'm not a bad person"). The rhetoric denies the feminist analysis, which would see paternalism as part of the problem, instead reinstating a buffed-up version of the tarnished father ideal.

The Promise Keepers movement is an example of this sort of rhetorical move, wherein men who have been less than ideal husbands and fathers join together in male-only, Christian, stadium events in order to procure the spiritual strength to go back to their families and resume their headship. Promise Keepers rhetoric claims that this is not a political but rather a "moral and spiritual" solution to what ails the nation, focusing on issues like unwed teenage motherhood, AIDS, and young male criminal behavior to which the movement sees itself as an answer, with antifeminism and homophobia corollary requirements. This is a strong example of Berlant's "nonpolitical political," wherein religious and other sentimental responses claim not to engage in the tainted political arena but actually do, of course, by redefining "what ails the nation" even as they claim to be doing so in nonpolitical terms.

Indeed, as the speaker who begins video artist Niklas Sven Vollmer's tape *Daddy Said So!* (1996), which is about a Promise Keepers event, recounts, the "messed up man" leads to not only a "messed up family" but a "messed up community," a "messed up country," and finally a "messed up world." Men, as fathers and husbands, are thus quite literally at the center of the Promise Keepers universe. Undergirding this endeavor is, as cultural critic Linda Kintz writes of Promise Keepers rhetorician Stu Weber, the strategic reconstruction of "the feminist critique of men's abdication of their responsibilities, even as he duplicitously begins to define feminism as a desire for male headship. . . . In setting out these absolute gender differences, he must criticize the tyrant in order to reestablish the legitimate male head."[56] It is this sort of logic, I would argue, that governs the story line of *Schindler's List*, wherein Schindler's heroic goodness is juxtaposed with the concentration camp director's badness and his redemption from indifferent Nazi to hero is in part achieved by way of shifting Schindler (Liam Neeson) from his indulgence in hedonistic pleasure to a sense of idealized paternal responsibility. This is, then, a second way in which Nazism has proven useful to contemporary social politics, providing a setting for the redemption of the wayward man.

To Spielberg's credit, the Schindler character is far more complex than most of his heroes, precisely because he isn't one at the start of the film. Schindler begins as a boozing, womanizing opportunist who appears not to have great moral trouble doing business with the Nazis (being a party member himself) and profiting from the war and the exploitation of Jewish labor. The fact that Oscar Schindler (the book and film are based on a true story) really did have a moral reckoning and came to protect the Jews in his employ is without question a positive change. But Thomas Keneally's book is far more complex in its portrait of this man and so maintains the enigma of Schindler throughout. Indeed, in the book the man's womanizing and appreciation for nice things is not diminished by his growing, passionate advocacy for the Jews in his employ.[57] Spielberg, by contrast, makes Schindler's change include a willingness to forsake material goods and a reawakened sexual propriety (he promises his wife fidelity) as a corollary to his admirable paternalism.

Early in the film, Schindler wins his first round of Nazi friends by throwing a raucous, drunken party with loose women and dancing girls in bowling derbies, tuxedo jackets, and hot pants, a *Cabaret*-like scene that is crosscut with images of countless Jews being herded and harassed. The crosscutting establishes the typical connection between Nazi decadence and brutality, self-indulgence and a lack of concern for the plight of others. Indeed, unlike *Cabaret*, Spielberg's images of decadence do not comment critically on the Nazi brutality with which they are juxtaposed; instead, a more direct connection is implied. This practice establishes Schindler at this point in the film as an unlikely savior to the Jewish victims of the men he wines and dines. A second crosscut sequence focuses on the plight of one particular Jewish woman, Helen Hirsch, Nazi labor camp commander Amon Goeth's hapless maid.

Spielberg's camera stays tight on Goeth's hands as he nearly caresses then strikes her, cutting to match the movement as an opulently clad nightclub singer seductively advances on Schindler. Again, Schindler's decadence marks his still too casual concern for the plight of Helen and by extension all Jews. Schindler's sexual escapades indeed express Goeth's repressed desires, as he substitutes violence for his sexual desire for the Jewish woman.

Yet this scene begins to mark Schindler's distinction from Goeth (Ralph Fiennes), in that the staging of the commander's advance on Helen parallels an earlier scene in the same basement, with the same lighting, wherein Schindler "reassures" her. Schindler clearly also instills sexual fear in the quivering young woman, but in what is supposed to be read as a gesture of magnanimity he instead offers her chocolate and kisses her on the forehead over her fearful protests, saying, "It's not that kind of kiss." With the megalomaniacal statement "I am Schindler," Spielberg's character is awash in a sea of sexual ambiguity; his creepy paternalism, however, is deployed as a sign of his later heroism. While Goeth substitutes violence for sex with Helen, Schindler substitutes fatherly affection, a gesture that will be inflated to a grand scale by the end of the film, as he ascends to the role of paternal savior to his hundreds of Jewish employees.[58]

The book opens with this scene, using it to initiate the story of Schindler's characterological enigma, the seeming aporia of why a Nazi guest of a brutal camp commander would go to the trouble of bringing chocolate to the mistreated Jewish maid.[59] Spielberg, however, by re-positioning the scene and contrasting it directly to Goeth, instead uses it to valorize the paternity Schindler so dramatically asserts. Indeed, the centrality of paternalism to the film's logic is emblematized in the poster used to publicize the film, which features an extreme close-up of an adult male hand clasping the hand of a child. By adding Schindler's entirely fabricated promise of fidelity to his wife, Spielberg greatly limits the complexity of the historical character Schindler was.

The compelling denseness of Keneally's Schindler perhaps signals that the paternal figure is being asked to serve an inordinate number of rhetorical functions in a cultural climate that both extols family values and focuses on the faults of men. Thus, Schindler's reaction to Helen, a young woman, is to turn her into a child rather than a fellow adult. But by aligning paternalism with sexual fidelity Spielberg makes Schindler's transformation akin to the Promise Keepers' project for the reclamation of wayward men. Spielberg's film thus makes overt the fact that such reclamation is a political activity, indeed, an anti-Nazi act. The Promise Keepers, meanwhile, mask the political nature of their project. What the Nazi setting does here is allow the direct expression of the political project that paternal reclamation represents. Whether as metaphor for family dysfunction, mediator between public and private traumas, or staging ground for political paternalism, the Nazi trope helps deliver the traditional family to a position of centrality in contemporary democratic political culture.

Sexual Libertarianism, Feminism, and the Nazi Trope

The second major trajectory that branches off from the debates over *The Night Porter* and the sexual use of Nazism moves in an opposite rhetorical direction, turning the conservative association of Nazism with perverse sexuality into an appropriable fantasy. Certain strains of feminist and queer discourse celebrate either the freedom to express an active and varied female sexuality or to valorize queer sexual practices as representationally sophisticated. These approaches turn the common association of Nazism with homosexuality and perversion back on itself. In so doing, they celebrate the textual freedoms brought by a postmodern sensibility and see sexual and representational freedom as fundamentally political freedoms.

In the course of the 1970s, feminists voiced diverging views of the place of pornography and sadomasochism in a feminist worldview, with some speaking out against both sexual practices and others insisting that sexual freedom is an important element of women's self-realization. The debate about feminist sadomasochism prominently invoked Nazi fetish play as a limiting case, with the anti-s/m side claiming that sexual play with Nazi items and scenarios reflects a duplication of the mind-set of historical Nazis and the pro-s/m side claiming that such play has little or nothing to do with historical Nazis.[60] As with criticism of the films that invoked Nazism as a sexual scenario, the political grounds for either argument relied on their different understanding of what was at stake, with both sides seeing themselves as furthering and protecting democracy. The argument sometimes centered on the classic nationalist associations of decadence with fascism and sexual propriety with democracy or on whether fantasy and material conditions could be separated.

Advocates of sexual freedom often countered conservative versions of the argument through recourse to an alternative strain of antifascist criticism different from that which ruled Cold War political psychology—one growing instead out of the work of Wilhelm Reich, for instance. Reich associated fascism with the repression of "natural sexuality" in his 1933 study *The Mass Psychology of Fascism* and saw the road to political utopia and peaceful living as a reconnection of the civilized self with the natural core. The German title of the book includes the subtitle "zur Sexualökonomie der politischen Reaktion und zur proletarischen Sexualpolitik" (Toward a Sexual Economy of Reactionary Politics and toward a Proletarian Sexual Politics), a title that includes both the terms of his analysis and his revolutionary plan for the future. In Reich's view, sexual suppression is deployed in the service of reactionary politics in that, unlike the suppression of material needs, which would lead eventually to revolution, the suppression of sexual needs "anchors itself as a moral defense," which then "prevents rebellion against both forms of suppression."[61]

Reich also thought that the Oedipus complex, from whence such sublimations issued, was not the cause of sexual restrictions but the result of them. The repression of other sexual outlets causes a fixation on the mother, which, due to an explicit taboo, leads to a displacement onto nationalism. Reich's theory is that the veneration of the mother in Oedipally fixated societies is a patriarchal denigration of matriarchy, a social system that would be more in tune with the natural sexual core. Reich thus advocated a more open sexual relationship to the world as an antidote to both Oedipus and nationalism, which he saw as mutually constitutive.

While he was not very influential at the time he was writing, Reich did ultimately influence the work of Frankfurt School political theorist Herbert Marcuse, who greatly influenced the student movements of the 1960s. Marcuse's *Eros and Civilization* (1955) asserted that aggression could be overcome through the nonrepressive re-eroticization of people's relations with each other and nature. This would require departure from an exclusive sexual focus on the genitals and a return to the "polymorphous perversity" of childhood sexuality—a re-eroticization of the entire body. In this way, according to Marcuse, alienated labor and the reification of the nongenital areas of the body that it relied on would be overcome, leading to a political utopia.[62] These ideas influenced the sexual liberation movements of the 1960s counterculture, which saw true political freedom to be attainable in part through bodily freedom. Avant-garde art practices of the 1960s also reflected this emphasis on breaking taboos, to the point where, as media theorist Patricia Mellencamp writes, "Because daily life and the sexual were founding terms, everyone could take action and be involved; the local and the global were elided; the personal *was* political."[63]

On the one hand, these ideas became more mainstream in the 1970s, becoming depoliticized and consumerist in nature as the form, but not the political spirit, of sexual liberty spread to the wider culture. On the other hand, feminism and the gay and lesbian rights movement continued to advocate sexuality as a politicized terrain. The conservative backlash against these new sexual/political values often collapsed these different approaches to sexual liberty, finally creating a flashpoint of political debate around the public funding of "obscene" art—often by feminist, gay, or lesbian artists—after Ronald Reagan became president in 1980.[64] As this timing ultimately coincided with the growing AIDS crisis, the gay community also became more thoroughly politicized, linking sexual puritanism with homophobia, public indifference to AIDS victims, and an unwillingness to provide sex education to help prevent the spread of the disease. By the late 1980s, sexual expression had once again become an issue of central political concern.

While images of Nazism no longer functioned as centrally as they did in the 1970s, one key player in the popular variation on this political debate did invoke these images: pop singer Madonna. Her 1990 music video for the song "Justify My Love," for instance, bills itself as an anticensorship statement, concluding with the line "poor is the man whose pleasures depend on the permission of others." The controversy around the video *Justify My Love* centered on whether MTV, the music video cable network, would broadcast it. The tape features a catalog of sexual alternatives, including threesomes, voyeurism, a much discussed lesbian kiss, and some glimpses of bondage and domination. Among these is an image lifted directly from *The Night Porter* of a bare-chested Charlotte Rampling look-alike in suspenders and something like an SS officer's cap, a third-generation Lola Lola icon. The textual invocation of *The Night Porter* recalls the controversy that that film originally inspired, which already centered on whether the erotic use of the Holocaust could be extricated from Nazi atrocities. Indeed, Madonna's use of this image is so decontextualized from the narrative of the original film that, in postmodern style, it becomes a tribute to the freedom of images more generally, not a statement intending to make any reference to Nazi history at all.

The rather short-lived flurry of "Madonna criticism," a blend of cultural studies and feminist studies, illuminates the ways in which this new variant of "Nazi" imagery was politically inscribed. These critics, too, claimed that Madonna's oblique references to Nazism were entirely severed from a historical reference to German fascism. Unlike the advocates for *The Night Porter* fifteen years earlier, the argument now was not that the Lola Lola image staged an equivalence between patriarchy and fascism or spoke to a universal urge to regress, but rather Madonna's advocates saw her as rewriting the terms of women's self-representation and championing the freedom to invoke whatever erotic scenario she liked. Feminist film scholar E. Ann Kaplan, for instance, claims that while Madonna's videos and performances, such as *Open Your Heart* (1986), *Express Yourself* (1989), and *Justify My Love*, drew on "the decadent Germany of the 1920s immediately preceding the Nazi era," the videos "rewrite such patriarchal narratives completely."[65] Professional iconoclast Camille Paglia likewise praises Madonna's performance in *Open Your Heart*, writing that she "plays Marlene Dietrich straddling a chair. Her eyes are cold, distant, all-seeing. . . . Playing with the outlaw personae of prostitute and dominatrix, Madonna has made a major contribution to the history of women."[66] Feminist scholar Cathy Schwichtenberg also writes in politically grand terms: "*Justify My Love* . . . opens up a Pandora's box of sexual prohibitions, which are judged as such through the maintenance of a single sexual standard. The kind of sexual morality, whether religious, political, or psychological, that legislates such a standard has, as [feminist theorist Gayle] Rubin notes, 'more in common with ideologies of racism than with true ethics.' "[67]

Madonna's history of playing with sexual images of women, from Marilyn Monroe to the Virgin Mary, surely helped insure that her invocation of Weimar and Nazi Germany would be read as an emblem of democratic sexual and representational freedom. Indeed, shortly after the release of *Justify My Love*, Madonna did a photo spread for *Rolling Stone* wherein she appears as a Jewess, a lesbian, a cross-dresser, a contortionist, and a patriot (all in 1930s-style sepia tones). The spread is emblematic of her refiguration of the functions these images have had in the history of eroticized Nazis, as she instead makes them markers of the new queer sexual politics of the early 1990s, which worked through a language of democracy. Thus, the images of Madonna kissing and lying about with women, standing in a suit among men in garter belts, and looking sultrily into the camera through a Star of David are culminated in the final photo of the spread, where she salutes the heavens as she lies half naked on a piano—wrapped in an American flag.[68]

Gender Dimorphism, Conservative Rhetoric, and the Feminazi

Queer political rhetoric valorizes both gender and sexual fluidity as freedom as well as seeing marginality (whether fluid or not) as a strong point of democratic pluralism.[69] Since images of fascism have been so central to the recent American history of sexual politics, these images form part of the textual play chest of postmodern queer strategies. The Christian Right's backlash against queer and feminist politics, then, willfully literalizes the use of Nazi images and indeed deploys rhetorical images of Nazism to opposite political ends.

Postmodernism figures negatively and prominently in the foundationalist visions of the various factions of the Christian Right. In often rather simplistic arguments that illustrate less than thorough readings of the available materials on postmodern theory, evangelists blame postmodernism for what they see as moral decay. Televangelist Pat Robertson, for instance, warns of "a virtual America—a poor imitation of a country—one obsessed with escaping into a false reality," which will replace the world of moral absolutes and foundational master narratives that he seeks to resuscitate.[70] "Gender feminism" (which includes queer theory) is named by Christian conservatives as one of the foremost culprits of postmodernism, sending the country down a path toward ultimate chaos and destruction.

Gene Veith, the Christian conservative author of *Postmodern Times*, appeared on Robertson's Christian Broadcasting Network program *Newswatch Today* and is quoted on the corresponding "fact sheet" put out by Robertson's 700 Club as saying, "postmodernism is dangerously similar to Hitler's Nazism and fascism." Veith bases his parallel on fascism's purported "irrationalism," which he extrapolates, warning that "examples of irrational postmodern influences can be found everywhere—in art, architecture, radical environmentalism, feminism, political correctness and science—they are most prevalent in television and movies."[71] Since feminism and environmentalism question the traditional master narratives of patriarchy and androcentrism, and hence deny the transcendent (and thus "rational") truths on which conservative Christians insist, they are "irrational" and, like the Nazis, bent on the destruction of the Christian definition of the nation and democracy.

The logic behind this parallel with Nazism pervades conservative Christian diatribes against gender feminism, which also includes gay rights activism. These diatribes alternately fixate on images of gender inversion (women who act like men and men who act like women) and on the eradication of gender difference (the elimination of the categories male and female). In order not to appear to be against women's rights, some rhetoricians of the Christian Right narrowly define true feminism (meaning pay equity, opposition to domestic violence, support for maternity leave), which they claim to support, while labeling as neofeminist any agenda that extends beyond these limited bounds. The conservative *Pro-Life Activist's Encyclopedia* describes the neofeminist as follows: "Anyone who personally knows a neofeminist realizes why she is so desperately unhappy and bitter. She is struggling pointlessly to become the very person she loathes so passionately: *A man.*"[72] Having established gender inversion as a strategy for discrediting feminists (i.e., they are not "real" women), the second tactic is deployed to discredit feminist claims to equity: "Neofeminists are trying to eliminate all distinctions between the genders. They are not seeking equality; they are striving for *identicality.*" Gender inversion and the eradication of gender differences both defy the strict division between men and women that undergirds the conservative Christian cosmology in which this rhetoric operates. Feminism and gay and lesbian rights threaten the Christian Right's vision of a gender-differentiated nation: hence, they can be seen as rhetorically "Nazi," and indeed the publication is full of references to parallels between feminism and Nazism.[73]

The dire images that a world without strict gender difference conjures for Christian conservatives can be found in a letter from evangelist James Dobson to his followers, wherein he describes the 1995 Beijing Conference on Women. Dobson explicitly links gender feminism and proponents of "homosexual and lesbian rights," claiming that they are hatching a conspiracy whereby "There will be absolutely no differences tolerated between the sexes. In short, the distinction between masculinity and femininity will utterly disappear from the culture of the world." Recalling the tactics used to defeat the Equal Rights Amendment in the 1970s and early 1980s, the outcome of the elimination of gender will be that "All household responsibilities will be divided 50/50 by governmental decree. Every business will be governed by strict 50/50 quotas. The military will also be apportioned equally between men and women, including ground combat assignments and any future selection of draftees." Images of government-enforced gender equity conjure the image of feminists as authoritarians, forcing their will upon the nation with the help of a liberal government. The pervasive association of Nazism with gender inversion helps to secure this image whereby gay men (whether in hypermasculine garb or in drag) and

Fig. 20. Advertisement for a T-shirt design featuring "Billary Clinrod," an amalgamation of President Bill Clinton and First Lady Hillary Rodham Clinton, meant to criticize the president by claiming he is ruled by his wife.

feminist women (often coded as lesbians and hence gender inverts as well) are the ringleaders of a modern day Nazism.[74]

A similar strategy is invoked in other conservative diatribes, which focus on first lady Hillary Clinton, often by picturing the president and his wife as gender inverts or as "Billary Clinton," an androgynous blend (figs. 20 and 21). The first Clinton administration was particularly beset by this sort of rhetoric from its arch-conservative opponents in ways that targeted many of Clinton's female appointees as well (the nickname of "Butch" Reno for Attorney General Janet Reno being the most obvious).[75] The neologism "feminazi" became a common conservative epithet used to address either feminist political agendas generally (especially abortion rights or dubious "political correctness," as discussed in chapter 3) or Hillary Clinton and Clinton appointees specifically. An extreme example of this sort of rhetoric can be found in Far Right extremist Texe Marrs's book *Big Sister Is Watching You!*, whose cover features an image of Hillary Clinton that is later compared to an image of Hitler in a similar pose.[76] The book goes on to attack the women in

Fig. 21. Advertisement for a comedy product catalog featuring President Bill Clinton and First Lady Hillary Rodham Clinton posed as the figures in the classic Grant Wood painting *American Gothic* (1930) with their gender roles inverted. The image is often captioned *American Pathetic*. (*Slick Times* magazine.)

Clinton's first administration, giving most of them male nicknames and implying that many are lesbians.[77]

While clearly this is an extreme example, the logic of these associations does echo widespread conservative antifeminist and antigay rhetoric, sounding what Kintz calls "structures of resonance" with more mainstream conservatism.[78] Indeed, even an ostensibly nonpolitical text like the 1990 made for TV movie *Hitler's Daughter* resonates with this logic. The plot of this film revolves around the need to locate the woman of the title who, due to her genetic heritage, is destined to want to replicate her father's regime. The investigators have identified three women who could potentially stand in positions of enough influence over American government to effect such a takeover: a newscaster who is having an affair with the vice president of the United States (who is running for president), the vice president's wife, and the other vice presidential candidate.[79] As they are women, their access to the presidency is indirect, so they need to manipulate the weak men with whom they are either sexually or professionally associated. Because of the genetic premise of the plot, the actions of all three women are suspected to be motivated by a devious desire to rule. The fact that logically two of these women are *not* Hitler's daughter but just ordinary career women means that viewers are encouraged to think that all ambitious women should be suspected of secretly being feminazis. While this is a truly frivolous film, the resonance with conservative antifeminism indicates that it presents a readily available cultural narrative.

By casting feminism as uniform rather than multifaceted and internally contentious, as it is, different sorts of anti-Nazi rhetoric can be compiled by antifeminists, which on the one hand associate feminism with institutional power (i.e., the tyranny of "political correctness") and at the same time associate it with moral degeneracy (i.e., support of abortion rights, gay and lesbian rights, and freedom of sexual expression). The image of Nazi decadence thus serves this double purpose of conservative rhetoric whereby family values are posited as the antifascist, democratic alternative.

Conclusion: New Political Directions for Images of Nazi Sexuality

Over the course of the last thirty years, the Nazi trope has been put to a wide array of uses in the rhetorical negotiation of the relative weight of public and private political concerns, in which sexuality plays a major role. "Nazi" sexuality has been championed as an arena of free sexual expression, held up as a dark mirror to patriarchy, and read as a sign of the moral bankruptcy of progressive politics. At the center of many of these rhetorical uses of Nazism stands the Dietrich/Lola Lola icon. Always complex and multiply understood even as she was being consolidated in the 1940s, the figure continues to serve as a sign of both fascism and deeper democracy. The vast majority of the current uses of sexualized Nazis reference the rhetorical history of this prominent mode of political representation in the United States and Europe rather than the material history of the Nazis' actual beliefs and deeds.

What often gets lost in these invocations of Nazism in contemporary political discourse is Nazi racism, which is typically displaced onto the history of ways in which the phenomenon has been used to address issues of gender and sexuality. There are, of course, other political arenas where Nazi racism continues to be central, but it is rare that issues of racism, sexuality, and gender are discussed together in the rhetorical examples described above. By way of a conclusion, then, I will analyze work by media artists Ellen Flanders (of Canada) and Rachel Schreiber (of the United States), each of whom have brought these three discourses together in order to point out new directions toward which the rhetorical uses of Nazism might be headed. Both of these artists complexly negotiate Jewishness, the postmemory of the Holocaust, sexuality, and gender in ways that build on the panoply of rhetorical uses to which the sexual imagery of Nazism has been put—including, once again, the Lola Lola icon.

Flanders's 1996 short film essay *Surviving Memory* takes as its central project the negotiation of queer and Jewish identity and political activism.[80] It features a series of encounters between Flanders (who is the speaking subject of the film) and various Jewish women, one of whom inhabits Israel as an allegorical figure of ethnicity and historical memory. The voice-over in the opening shot, which features Flanders and another woman kissing in a parking lot, says, "she complained that I only speak of my past lovers—I explained that without her I have no memory of anyone." The next shots serve to interpret this statement as melding lesbian desire with historical memory and ethnic identity: blue-toned images of sex (perhaps alluding to the blue-toned memory scenes in *The Night Porter*) are cut together with images from an unidentified contemporary political demonstration and an image of a tattooed arm reading "Yahweh" in Hebrew. The last of these images is particularly compelling in that it signals specifically Jewish transgressions and interpretive tensions. First, the tattoo oscillates between the edict against speaking or writing the name of God and recent reinterpretations thereof by cabalists, who have instead come to see the written word *Yahweh* as a sign of protection. Second, the tattoo invokes the Jewish prohibition against marking the body, making it both an invocation of Nazi tattooing practices in concentration camps (involuntary) and an invocation of the contemporary urban cultural trend in which (voluntary) tattooing is aligned with urban sexuality.

As a Jewish lesbian who will shortly be revealed to participate in the sexual play of urban s/m subculture, Flanders shifts the ground from a primary focus on sexual transgression, which characterizes the beginning of the tape, to one in which sexuality, religion, and ethnicity are entirely intertwined. Still photographs of concentration camp victims, Nazi banners, and a mug shot of a lesbian concentration camp inmate accompany the next voice-over progression: "At age six, I knew the Holocaust and died twice; at age 12, I tried Eichmann; and at age 19 I wore a pink triangle." The visual progression culminates in posters of neo-Nazi David Irving, which are plastered on the construction fences surrounding the rebuilding of fellow neo-Nazi Ernst Zundel's house in

Toronto after it was bombed by antiracist activists. As Flanders's personal chronology culminates in her coming out, signified by the wearing of the pink triangle, the film insists on maintaining the historical link between racism and homophobia that that symbol entails. The images of past and present Nazis here function to consolidate the political alliance of antiracist and antihomophobic agendas and between historical and contemporary political moments.

There are, however, two moments of ambivalence in the film that complicate these otherwise straightforward uses of Nazism and its symbols. The first one, occurring shortly after the above, features footage of a demonstration by the Aids Coalition to Unleash Power (ACT UP) and a voice-over lamenting, "For years I mourned my father's untimely death, but there was no commemoration ceremony. His cancer was not karposi sarcoma. His death had no meaning, I thought, as I traced my body in chalk on the street, climbed out of the mass grave, and put my friend James to rest." The "Silence = Death" slogan that characterizes the credo of AIDS activism visually coincides with the end of this monologue and signals a personal struggle with the practices of memorializing wherein her father's death, unconnected to prejudice, is difficult to script into a meaningful political narrative—either in terms of ethnicity/religion (of the Holocaust) or sexuality (the AIDS epidemic, which derives many of its symbols from drawing a parallel to the Holocaust).

The second moment of ambivalence occurs in the context of the next major segment of the film, wherein a series of negotiations illustrate the constructedness of gender as specifically related to Jewishness. Images of Flanders dressed in butch leather and a woman in a dress kissing at a bar are intercut with clips from the last Yiddish film made in Poland, *Yidl Mitn Fiddle* (1936), featuring a woman musician dressed as a man. The voice-over recounts, "She had a fetish for Jewish girls. 'I always hated that,' she confided in me. Dressed in leather, we went out that night—two Jewish girls: one boy, one woman." After another series of connections between past and present political action (featuring images of Jewish resistance fighters in World War II and ACT UP demonstrations), the scene is revisited, with Flanders this time accompanied by a man in a dress. Another clip from the Yiddish film shows the magical transformation of the woman into a wearer of men's clothing—a change her male lover rejects. The now modified voice-over explains, "He had a fetish for Jewish girls. We dressed in leather, and went out that night—two Jewish girls: one boy, one woman." Flanders continues to narrate their sexual encounter, during which the cross-dressed "woman" takes

Flanders's strapped on dildo into his mouth, exclaiming "I'm a little feygeleh" (the Yiddish word for "faggot"). Flanders then confesses, "I felt uneasy, my contradictions laid bare," as the Yiddish film shows the woman dressed as a boy being transformed again into a dress wearer.

This complex sequence again very specifically interconnects contemporary queer play involving gender and sexual categories and historical enactments of related gender dramas within Jewish culture. Instead of the more pervasive cultural association of gender transgression and boundary blurring with Nazism, Flanders connects them with Jewish negotiations of gender identity in the face of Nazi persecution. She describes her interest in Yiddish filmmaking in the 1930s as in part due to its dealing with how Jewish understandings of gender roles were different than those of the gentile world, and how in this historical moment Jewish film was trying to counter the anti-Semitic casting of Jewish men as effeminate by positing a difference between "old world" Jewish practices such as studying the Torah and new ones such as assimilation, reflecting more of the dominant notions of "manly" behavior.[81] Ultimately, Flanders valorizes gender transitivity, as both a Jew with a consciousness of history and a contemporary queer. Her ambivalence comes from the ways in which neither assimilation to norms nor resistance to them can guarantee political freedom. Flanders thus endorses, on the one hand, the postmodern political strategy of challenging essentialized, embodied identities but insists, on the other, on the historical constitution of specific gendered, sexual, and ethnic meanings. She proposes unqualified opposition to the politics of Nazism and other forms of racism and homophobia but also refuses the sort of rhetoric that would ally sexual "decadence" and gender inversion therewith.

Rachel Schreiber's 1996 video, *Please Kill Me; I'm a Faggot Nigger Jew*, approaches some of the same issues, taking as its overt subject the ways in which Nazism, and especially the Holocaust, have found their way into contemporary sexual practices. The tape begins with the typed solicitation that Schreiber (using the name Justine) has posted on an Internet listserv dedicated to s/m topics, saying that she wants to interview people who practice Nazi fetish s/m.[82] This source being established, the rest of the tape consists of an alternation between three elements: (1) voice-over readings of some of the replies she received to her online questionnaire, (2) typed text describing her childhood experiences with images of the Holocaust and her grandfather's photo album, and (3) the act of writing "Jude" (Jew) in Germanic script on her trimmed and shaved upper pubic region. All images are digitally mediated and appear as computer images. Schreiber thus interrogates the fantasy practices of her respondents by juxtaposing them with her own inescapable sense of history, in terms of both her childhood experiences and the way she experiences her body as Jewish.

The Internet responses range across a broad spectrum of sexual orientations and attitudes toward Nazi fetish s/m, beginning with the statement that also serves as the title of the piece, "Please kill me; I'm a faggot nigger Jew." This respondent is a submissive male, looking for "Aryan" women to dominate him as he plays a composite of the degraded categories he names. The next response is from a pair of women claiming to be Aryan lesbians, who see the accouterments of Nazi uniforms as sexy. Then there is a Jewish gay man who likes to use Nazi scenes to get him in the mood to submit to his dominator but doesn't see Nazis as sexy in themselves. There is a heterosexual woman who plays at scenes between ss and sa members or between Nazis and partisans but never Jews, and finally an Aryan male who defines himself as "homomasculine" and voices sadistic desires.[83]

This range of possible uses of Nazi fetishism raises issues about Internet personas as parallel to (or part of) the sort of sexual role-playing that is typical of s/m practice. Indeed, none of these identities is verifiable in the Internet environment. While Schreiber grants these written responses embodiment by recording them as voices (and thus provisionally anchoring at least the gender identity claimed in the response), she mostly chooses texts that either discuss posturing overtly or voice a self-conscious disassociation between the politics of the Nazis and the use of their political aura in sexual play. The paradox of granting embodied voices to the writings references the imagery over which they are read and with which they are intercut, all of which insist on Schreiber's own contrary movement toward more rather than less connection with the historical legacy of the Holocaust. It is this unresolvable tension that organizes the piece.

Schreiber's assumption of embodied Jewishness unfolds slowly in the course of the tape, as the activity of trimming pubic hair, shaving, and then inking the word *Jude* extends across its entire span. The typed text that narrates a series of coming of age experiences complicates the voice-over accounts from the respondents and lends intrigue to the obtuse activity of the naked lower torso. The first typed story describes how when she was a child watching a movie at synagogue the projector was turned off in the middle and the children told to leave the room. This practice is later revealed to have been an effort to shield them from the most gruesome images of the Holocaust—images also contained in a forbidden book at home, which Schreiber had already seen, unbeknownst to her parents. Images from the grandfather's photo album are not immediately contextualized but culminate in a typed account of finding the album when she was a young adult. She describes being especially struck by a photo of her grandfather on vacation at the World Exposition in Paris in 1937, standing in front of the Nazi pavilion, a swastika flag waving in the background. The type reads, "I was shocked when I realized that, while there was never a time in my life when I didn't know what that symbol meant, for him there had been a time when it meant nothing." These stories thus inscribe Schreiber into the history of the Holocaust, both in terms of her own introduction to the images most strongly associated with Nazism (death camps and swastikas) and her subsequent inability to remember a time when she didn't know what these images meant.

While the practitioners of Nazi fetish s/m on the soundtrack do not claim that these symbols of Nazism mean nothing—indeed, if they did, there would be no point in playing with them—the tension lies between Schreiber's deep sense of embodiment as a Jew raised with a strong sense of history and the kind of ungroundedness sexual play seems to enact. Schreiber does not condemn the virtual play she catalogs in the voices of the respondents per se but rather tries to situate herself within this cultural field. Indeed, one of the implications of the act of inking "Jude" on herself is to counter the respondents' tendency to script the role of the Jew as only that of victim, and not resister, to Nazi brutality. She thus inscribes her own body into history but also reclaims the act of marking a body's Jewishness for herself in a gesture that is in itself erotic.

The last segment of the tape, in which the washing and shaving are revealed as preparations for writing on her body, is accompanied, significantly, by a music track of the song "Wenn ich mir was Wünschen Dürfte" (If I could Wish for Something) as recorded by Marlene Dietrich in 1930. The lines of the song in German speak of ambivalence and a recognition that given the choice the singer would wish to be only somewhat happy so as not to lose the ability to feel sadness. Schreiber modifies this message, in the tape's final image, as the typed words "If I had one wish, I would wish for the sadness of the past" scroll by, followed by the computer command ">>Logoff." This modified lyric echoes the dominant sentiment of the tape, that the history of the Holocaust should not be lost in the free flow of wish-fulfilling fantasies. The final command further implies that the stories that have been typed in the course of the tape are in direct response to the statements of the online respondents to Schreiber's questionnaire.

The song itself, however, is densely referential not to the Holocaust itself but to the history of these sexual/representational practices, for it is the same song that Lucia sings in her controversial Lola Lola persona in one of the concentration camp flashbacks of *The Night Porter*. *The Night Porter*, as discussed in the course of this chapter, was a pivotal text in moving Nazi iconography away from history and making history into an image/toy of sexual rhetoric. This same image is referenced at another remove in Madonna's music video *Justify My Love*, which no longer references the Holocaust at all. Schreiber's tape, on the other hand, moves in the opposite direction—toward history rather than away from it. This sentiment is revealed in her choice of Dietrich's recording of the song instead of Rampling's. Dietrich, a highly complex icon of both "Nazi" sexuality and anti-Nazi activism, is the counterpart to Schreiber's critique of fetishized Jewish victims, as Dietrich, too, is at odds with the cultural currency of her image. Indeed, in 1930, when she recorded this song, the icon was under construction, as she had already shot *The Blue Angel* and given Lola Lola a screen presence that would never fade. She is once again accompanied by composer Friedrich Holländer, as in both *The Blue Angel* and *A Foreign Affair*, but before any of Germany's dark future could be known. In this sense, Schreiber's use of Dietrich's version echoes her account of her own shock upon realizing that, on looking at her grandfather's vacation photos, there had been a time when the swastika didn't mean anything, for neither did Dietrich's song. For Schreiber, this is nearly inconceivable, but it resonates with the claims of some of the Nazi fetishists who speak in the tape. Schreiber does not judge their sexual practices but articulates her own inability not to see herself implicated in these never really empty symbols.

In this way, Schreiber's tape and Flanders's film point to a new kind of dense ambivalence toward the icons of sexualized Nazis. As a representative of the complexity of rhetoric surrounding these images, Lola Lola can be sexy and she can be politically appropriated but she cannot be entirely divorced from both the history of Nazism and the history of the rhetorical uses to which they have been put. This is perhaps the new doubleness that the always double icon of Lola Lola now embodies.

Epilogue

■

To study the nation through its narrative address does not merely draw attention to its language and rhetoric; it also attempts to alter the conceptual object itself.
—Homi Bhabha, "Narrating the Nation" (1990)[1]

Political theorist Chantal Mouffe asserts a radical notion of democracy which strives to reconcile the tensions between liberalism, with its individualistic, rights-based notions of citizenship, and civic republicanism, with its emphasis on communitarian political participation. She confronts the problem of how to conceive of political community in a way compatible with liberal pluralism so as to avoid the ways in which the "common good" can be used for totalitarian ends.[2] In these not easily reconciled aspects of democracy lies the vast terrain of political debate wherein images of Nazism play wide-ranging roles. These images sometimes serve as a counterpoint to democratic freedom (a rights-based view of democracy) and sometimes as a counterpoint to the community democracy imagines (a civic republican view of democracy)—whether this be pluralist and progressive, as Mouffe hopes, or defined by conservative foundations. As such, fascism operates as what film theorist Teresa de Lauretis calls a "public fantasy," a historically mutable variant of the psychoanalytic concept of "original fantasies," which function to multiply and fundamentally define a vision of the world, the self, and many levels of social interaction in between.[3]

Certainly, fascism was one of the twentieth-century's organizing concepts, developing first into the cataclysm that was World War II and functioning rhetorically thereafter. In the course of the Nazi figure's rhetorical history, however, the world has changed. Perhaps the ultranationalist concept of fascism speaks now to a bygone era when nation-states organized the world in relation to colonial power and the capitalist system it underwrote. On a grand scale, fascism, as both an imaginary and a historical concept, serves to mediate the multisided project political theorist Arjun Appadurai describes as part of the concept of the "postnational." While the prefix *post* suggests that a large-scale shift to a global order has supplanted the nation-state as the primary form of allegiance and identity, Appadurai stresses that the nation is by no means a bygone form of social organization. Instead, he stresses that as the nation can no longer contain the social and political diversity of its populations within its borders so other forms of allegiance and affiliation are emerging to take its place.[4] Fascism, as the height of nationalist movements, I suggest, serves to reference a unified notion of nation in the face of political debates that arise in a diverse democratic society.

The many uses of fascism in especially American political rhetoric might very well speak to efforts to comprehend new transnational affinities in national terms—be they racial, sexual, political, or more local. Hence, we find the broad range of parallels drawn, especially by right-wing rhetoricians, between new cultural and political movements (feminism, gay and lesbian rights, and environmentalism in particular) and fascism. These rhetoricians reassert the efficacy of the conflation of democracy with the family/nation forged in nationalist melodrama. Fascism in this sense operates not as a nationalist movement but as an imperialist movement, allowing the concept of the nation to stand as its counterpoint. When conservative political theorists William Lind and William Marshner, for instance, write that "traditional values are functional values. If we want a society where things work . . . we must, as a society, follow traditional Western values," they are positing challenges to tradition as challenges to the nation.[5] This consolidation of tradition includes a longing for a national/political identity like the one articulated in the battle against fascism in World War II.

It is significant, however, that while the major impetus for a global move to a postnational world is transnational economic interests, most of the rhetorical work done by images of fascism is in the realm of culture. While the rhetorical invocation of fascism commonly continues to address state authority—which may also speak to a nostalgic understanding of national power—there are also many instances when diverse individual and subcultural rather than state behaviors are what are coded as fascist. The association of cultural diversity with fascism charted over the course of this book was already being forged during the war, in line with the rhetorical practices for regulating gender behavior and sexuality, especially with regard to the family, as symbolic national issues. That these realms would take center stage in domestic politics just as the world economy was becoming increasingly transnational—and do so in part through a rhetoric of frightening versus comforting nationalisms—suggests that perhaps the concept of fascism is serving to either interpret the new situation in historically comprehensible terms or deflect concerns about global economic trends onto more local, domestic turf.

Cultural theorist Ellen Messer-Davidow marks a shift within American right-wing think tanks in the late 1980s from their original focus on military industries and economic conservatism to cultural conservatism, responding, as the conservative Free Congress Foundation asserts, to what they see as a "cultural drift . . . [a] gradual emptying of a nation's values of their content, not by some violent overturning, but by slow evaporation in which the form is left—in rhetoric and often in manners—but the substance disappears."[6] The concept of cultural drift targets symptoms of rising postnational identities and affiliations. Thus, the cultural constituencies and political movements targeted by this conservative critique are often the American variant of the postnational imaginary that Appadurai describes—either in terms of nonnational affiliations or in terms of a focus on the self and sexuality as quintessentially local and intimate rather than on global realms. In the former, the genuine democratic claims of sexual minorities and women have found articulation, while the latter may be a retreat from public political engagement in the face of not yet manageable change. Conservative efforts to squelch the former as symptoms of the latter ignore this crucial distinction. The refrain of this study has been the importance of preserving the distinction, seeing the former as an important way in which the personal is understood in political terms, while the latter (including the conservative focus thereon) is a move into privatized politics, which very likely masks a lack of accountability for corporate economics or, more generously, expresses an anxious inability to comprehend global cultural change.

Both versions of these cultural projects have used images of fascism to articulate their aims. For the Right, using fascism to characterize cultural change both thematizes cultural struggles as national ones and reasserts national identity in the face of global change. Even here, however, national struggles have begun to take on a transnational cast, as in the discussion of the multinational concern over the plight of the white man or the persecution of Christians. Progressives, meanwhile, have more commonly embraced postnational affinities (in international feminist and gay and lesbian organizing, for instance), either invoking fascism against the national authority that continues to exist or using images of fascism as pieces of a cultural/political play set to either further express these postnational affinities or participate—sometimes apolitically—in the representational practices of postmodernism that in part express national dissolution with indifference or glee.

Central to all of these uses is the question of history. At the end of the last chapter, my analysis of the work of artists Ellen Flanders and Rachel Schreiber points to ways in which a politically progressive understanding of sexuality as *connected* to history might be able to both celebrate the freedom of fantasy and maintain a material ground. Imagining political subjectivity along these lines offers an example of a postnational use of fascism that builds both on the rhetorical and material histories of the phenomenon. Schreiber's 1994 video *This Is Not Erotica* expresses another such alternative vision of overtly politicized desire: it is a multiple desire or, as she writes, "sexual desire, desire for resistance, desire for the past, desire to know, to change."[7] Schreiber's video is an assertion of a "resistant" sexuality born not out of sexualized Nazis but out of sexualizing the history of women in the Jewish resistance. In this move, she does not suggest that sexuality should be disassociated from historical tragedy but that it is both a part of that history and part of the fantasy vocabulary that a consciousness of history makes available. The tape asserts a historical and contemporary affiliation through a transnational Jewishness (something already available in Jewish culture) but uses sexuality to assert an alternative political formation through both historical antifascism and an understanding of sexuality as a central discourse in democratic debate. My analysis of this tape thus serves as an appropriate, albeit open-ended, conclusion to this book.

Growing out of Schreiber's interest in complicating what she calls a fetishization of Jewish victimhood, the tape is organized around a sexual encounter between the subject of the tape (the artist) and her likewise Jewish lover.[8] In voice-over, the artist speaks to the lover, telling him that he may tie her up, as he requested, but on the condition that he not speak. Instead, he will listen to her tell stories as he explores her entire body with his tongue before he will be permitted to enter her. Super-8 visuals feature close-ups of the man licking her feet and slowly progressing in the course of the tape to her mouth, her hands bound above her head. Intercut with these visuals are photographs from Schreiber's great-grandfather's photo albums and various poetic shots of candles, sand, dice being thrown, and a rugged coastline. According to the terms of the encounter, the voice-over proceeds to tell stories, alternating between short biographies of three women resistance fighters (their acts of heroism, their counterattack on the Nazis, their sacrifice or survival), accounts of the couple's mutual history growing up in the same community, and Schreiber's accounts of her own grappling with the history encoded in her great-grandfather's photographs.

The interconnection of these "stories" is both poetic and concrete. Schreiber says that her lover reminds her of the photographs taken by her great-grandfather, a portrait photographer in Odessa who by chance left before the war, making it possible for her to have these photographs (and implicitly her existence). They are photographs of people she never knew, but, as she later goes on to say, she often fantasizes about what these people would look like in present day clothing and imagines her lover (whom she addresses as "you" throughout) as one of these people. Intercut with this linking of the lover and the photographs are two of the three stories of women resistance fighters—Rosa Robota and Zivia Lubetkin. This third element comes together with the lover and the photographs through Schreiber's confession that she sometimes fantasizes that they are fighting together in the resistance or at other times that they are imprisoned. This is a significant move in the tape whereby Schreiber hopes to build a sexual scenario out of resistance to the Nazis, rather than out of Nazi domination, and do so without losing a connection to the significance of this history. The choice to address the lover, and hence put the viewer in the position of the lover, further suggests that viewers join in this historical/sexual fantasy in order to imagine, Schreiber hopes, a new political/sexual subjectivity.

The particulars of this move unfold in the next series of stories. After the biography of Nuita Teitelboim (a saboteur and assassin of numerous Gestapo officers), Schreiber recounts how the day after the couple had sex for the first time in her parents' basement they watched a film about the Holocaust. The familiar footage of bodies, "skeletal and abject," transports her to the night before. She says, "I know my body has the same bones. I know our bodies bear the same marks. I know why it is your body that I want." This realization explicitly connects the couple's sexual relationship, via their bodies, with remembering the Holocaust in

•

terms of recognizing the lineage that connects them to both the Nazis' persecution of Jews and the lineage of Jews who resisted them. It is also, however, a move that encourages viewers to see their own bodies as written into political history as sexual/political actors as well.

Schreiber has interrogated the victim status of Jews in the ongoing legacy of both Nazi fetishism and more general cultural remembrance of the Holocaust, and she wants to complicate the category. Her position in the tape is thus *both* as the one who is tied up *and* the one who controls the encounter. At the same time, the inclusion of the resistance fighters' stories particularizes the actions of historical individuals—this is both fantasy *and* history in a combination that turns many of the conventions of sexualized uses of Nazism on their heads. Schreiber quotes writer Jeannette Winterson at the beginning of her catalog text for the tape: "Written on the body is a secret code, only visible in certain light; the accumulations of a lifetime gather there. In places the palimpsest is so heavily worked that the letters feel like braille."[9] Schreiber thus asserts that while it is not *bound* to history (she does, after all, make the Holocaust the stuff of fantasy and the tape is sexually charged) the enactment of fantasy does not lose its historical legacy. Sexuality is political but not as an object of political/moral judgment. Rather, it is a language through which one can become inscribed in both historical and contemporary political debate.

The aporia of the title, *This Is Not Erotica*, speaks to the unresolvable paradox of the ongoing personal and public negotiations of political history. It is an aporia that characterizes the larger phenomenon that has been the subject of this book, where fascism has played a central role in the cultural rhetoric of democracy through its myriad associations with sexuality but also where the various political deployments fluctuate between the strongly negative resonances of the historical phenomenon of Nazism and the pervasive flexibility it achieved precisely through its rhetorical deployment. Certainly, fascism is no longer understood as an exclusively national phenomenon. Instead, the cultural work the concept navigates is mutable to national or postnational political imaginaries in the course of the ongoing negotiation that is democracy.

Notes

Introduction

1 Michel Foucault, "Power and Strategies," in *Power/Knowledge: Selected Interviews and Other Writings, 1972–77*, trans. and ed. Colin Gordon (New York: Pantheon, 1980), 139.

2 Slavoj Žižek, *The Sublime Object of Ideology* (London and New York: Verso, 1989), 99.

3 Jürgen Habermas, "Citizenship and National Identity," in *The Condition of Citizenship*, ed. Bart van Steenbergen (London: Sage, 1994), 21–22.

4 Benedict Anderson's delineation of the characteristics of modern nationhood apply here, as he asserts that the nation is "imagined" in that although most members will never meet they still have a communal image that produces a sense of horizontal unity regardless of hierarchical inequalities. *Nationalism* is a neutral term for Anderson. See his *Imagined Communities: Reflections on the Origin and Spread of Nationalism* (London: Verso, 1983). For an account of the specifically American variant of this imagined nationhood, see Donald Pease, "National Identities, Postmodern Artifacts, and Postnational Narratives," *boundary 2* 19.1 (1992): 5.

5 Raymond Williams, *Keywords: A Vocabulary of Culture and Society* (New York: Oxford University Press, 1976), 82–87.

6 See, for instance, Dorinda Outram, *The Body and the French Revolution: Sex, Class, and Political Culture* (New Haven and London: Yale University Press, 1989); and Andrew Parker et al., eds., *Nationalisms and Sexualities* (New York and London: Routledge, 1992).

7 The growing movement for the civil rights of African-Americans did mobilize this internal contradiction through a wartime Double V campaign, which suggested a link between the international struggle against fascism and the national struggle against racism. See Thomas Cripps, *Making Movies Black: The Hollywood Message*

Movie from World War II to the Civil Rights Era (New York: Oxford University Press, 1993), 36.

8   Arjun Appadurai, "Disjuncture and Difference in the Global Cultural Economy," in *Colonial Discourse and Post-colonial Theory: A Reader*, ed. Patrick Williams and Laura Chrisman (New York: Columbia University Press, 1994), 331.

9   Homi Bhabha, "DissemiNation: Time, Narrative, and the Margins of the Modern Nation," in *Nation and Narration*, ed. Homi Bhabha (London and New York: Routledge, 1990), 299, 300. Bhabha is specifically referring to "racist fantasies of purity and persecution that must always return from the Outside," a point I am modifying to include political, and especially sexual, projections as well (317). See also Homi Bhabha, "The Other Question: The Stereotype and Colonial Discourse," *Screen* 24.6 (1983): 18–36.

10 George L. Mosse, *Nationalism and Sexuality: Respectability and Abnormal Sexuality in Modern Europe* (New York: Fertig, 1985).

11 Michel Foucault, *The History of Sexuality*, vol. 2: *The Use of Pleasure*, trans. Robert Hurley (New York: Vintage, 1990), 10.

12 Michel Foucault, *The History of Sexuality*, vol. 1: *An Introduction*, trans. Robert Hurley (New York: Vintage, 1980), 105–6.

13 Fredric Jameson, *The Political Unconscious: Narrative as a Socially Symbolic Act* (Ithaca: Cornell University Press, 1981), 63.

14 Alexis de Tocqueville, *Democracy in America*, trans. George Lawrence, ed. J. P. Mayer and Max Lerner (New York: Harper and Row, 1966), 565. The first volume of this work was originally published in French in 1835 and translated into English in 1838. For a further discussion of the role of women in de Tocqueville's views, see Ursula Vogel, "Marriage and the Boundaries of Citizenship," in *The Condition of Citizenship*, ed. Bart van Steenbergen (London: Sage, 1994), 76–89.

15 For further discussion of this "not political" idea, see Eli Zaretsky, "Hannah Arendt and the Meaning of the Public/Private Distinction," in *Hannah Arendt and the Meaning of Politics*, ed. Craig Calhoun and John McGowan (Minneapolis: University of Minnesota Press, 1997), 212.

16 Hannah Arendt, *The Origins of Totalitarianism* (New York: Harcourt Brace Jovanovich, 1973), 474. See also Zaretsky, 215.

17 Lauren Berlant, *The Queen of America Goes to Washington City: Essays on Sex and Citizenship* (Durham and London: Duke University Press, 1997), 5.

18 Jürgen Habermas, *The Structural Transformation of the Public Sphere: An Inquiry into a Category of Bourgeois Society*, trans. Thomas Burger (Cambridge: MIT Press, 1996). The book was originally published in German in 1962.

19 Arendt, 336.

20 Stephanie Coontz, *The Way We Never Were: American Families and the Nostalgia Trap* (New York: Basic Books, 1992), 98.

21 Lauren Berlant, "Intimacy: A Special Issue," *Critical Inquiry* 24 (1998): 283.

22 Berlant, *The Queen of America*, 20.

23 See, for instance, Jennifer Terry, *An American Obsession: Science, Medicine, and the Place of Homosexuality in Modern Society* (Chicago: University of Chicago Press: 1999); Lisa Duggan, "The Trials of Alice Mitchell: Sensationalism, Sexology, and the Lesbian Subject in Turn-of-the-Century America," *Signs: Journal of Women in Culture and Society* 18.4 (1993): 791–814; and the exchange between Judith Walkowitz (a histo-

rian) and Myra Jehlen (a literary theorist) transcribed in "Patrolling the Borders: Feminist Historiography and the New Historicism," *Radical History Review* 43 (1989): 23–43.

24 Bhabha, *Nation and Narration*, 297.

25 Noël Carroll, "Film, Rhetoric, and Ideology," in *Explanation and Value*~~~~~~~~ ed. Salim Kemal and Ivan Gaskell (Cambridge: Cambridge University~~~~ 215–37.

26 A. J. Greimas, *Structural Semantics: An Attempt at a Method*, trans. Danie~~ Ronald Schleifer, and Alan Velie (Lincoln: University of Nebraska~~~ This book was originally published in French in 1966. See also Jam~

27 Dana Polan, *Power and Paranoia: History, Narrative, and the American* *1950* (New York: Columbia University Press, 1986), 18–19.

1 Nazi Nationalist Melodrama: Science, Myth, and Paternal Authority in *Die Goldene Stadt*

1 Homi Bhabha, *The Location of Culture* (London and New York: Routledge, 1994), 13.

2 Doris Summer, for instance, identifies romance as a prominent genre in Latin American nation-building novels of the nineteenth century, wherein the figure of egalitarian romance is useful for narratives of internal reconciliation, while novels featuring an external threat typically make the patriarchal family the foundation of national strength, with gender equity consequently cast as unpatriotic. See Doris Summer, "Irresistible Romance: The Foundational Fictions of Latin America," in *Nation and Narration*, ed. Homi Bhabha (London and New York: Routledge, 1990), 71–98.

3 Quoted in Claudia Koonz, *Mothers in the Fatherland: Women, the Family, and Nazi Politics* (New York: St. Martin's, 1987), 80–81.

4 For a history of the political function of the genre, see Thomas Elsaesser, "Tales of Sound and Fury: Observations on the Family Melodrama," in *Film Genre Reader*, ed. Barry Keith Grant (Austin: University of Texas Press, 1986), 281. See also Peter Brooks, *The Melodramatic Imagination: Balzac, Henry James, Melodrama, and the Mode of Excess* (New York: Columbia University Press, 1985); and Peter Brooks, "Melodrama, Body, Revolution," in *Melodrama: Stage Picture Screen*, ed. Jacky Bratton, Jim Cook, and Christine Gledhill (London: British Film Institute, 1994), 11–24.

5 See, for instance, Tom Nairn, *The Break-Up of Britain: Crisis and Neo-nationalism* (London: Verso, 1981), 348. See also Benedict Anderson, *Imagined Communities: Reflections on the Origin and Spread of Nationalism* (London: Verso, 1983).

6 Homi Bhabha, "Introduction: Narrating the Nation," in *Nation and Narration*, ed. Homi Bhabha (London and New York: Routledge, 1990), 2.

7 Donald Pease writes that in the American case "the negative class, race and gender categories of these subject peoples were not a historical aberration but a structural necessity for the construction of a national narrative whose coherence depended upon the internal opposition between Nature's Nation and peoples understood to be constructed of a 'different nature'" ("National Identities, Postmodern Artifacts, and Postnational Narratives," *boundary 2* 19.1 [1992]: 4).

8 Historian Leila Rupp notes that both German and American journalism addressed to women during the war stressed their political roles as wives and mothers (*Mobilizing Women for War: German and American Propaganda, 1939–1945* [Princeton: Princeton University Press, 1978]).

9 Eric Rentschler, *The Ministry of Illusion: Nazi Cinema and Its Afterlife* (Cambridge: Harvard University Press, 1996), 7.

10 Wilhelm Reich, *The Mass Psychology of Fascism*, trans. Vincent R. Carfagno (New York: Farrar, Straus and Giroux, 1970), 83. The study was originally published in German in 1933 and translated into English in 1946.

11 For a sophisticated analysis that utilizes this understanding of Nazism, see Linda Schulte-Sasse, "The Jew as Other under National Socialism: Veit Harlan's *Jud Süss*," *German Quarterly* (winter 1988): 22–49.

12 Siegfried Kracauer, "Die kleine Ladenmädchen gehen ins Kino," in *Das Ornament der Masse* (Frankfurt am Main: Suhrkamp, 1977), 279–94; Siegfried Kracauer, *From Caligari to Hitler: A Psychological History of the German Film* (Princeton: Princeton University Press, 1947); Lotte Eisner, *The Haunted Screen* (Berkeley and Los Angeles: University of California Press, 1969). The book was originally published in French in 1952. Film scholar Patrice Petro, too, notes the strong association of melodrama with both Weimar cinema and Nazi ideology (*Joyless Streets: Women and Melodramatic Representation in Weimar Germany* [Princeton: Princeton University Press, 1989], 26).

13 Lowry further points out that Walter Benjamin's notion of the aestheticization of politics was really only operating in the first years of the Nazi ascent to power. By 1935, spectacular politics was mostly replaced by a reprivatization of the everyday, in consumer and leisure culture, which basically consisted of the Nazi version of Protestant, middle-class enticements: promised economic improvement, private happiness, and upward mobility within the Nazi order. Once the fascists had come to power, a privatized, passive population was, Lowry suggests, much easier to manage than one that had been mobilized even through illusory political participation. Stephen Lowry, *Pathos und Politik: Ideologie in Spielfilmen des Nationalsozialismus* (Tubingen: Max Niemayer Verlag, 1991), 24–31.

14 Gisela Bock, "Racism and Sexism in Nazi Germany: Motherhood, Compulsory Sterilization, and the State," in *When Biology Became Destiny: Women in Weimar and Nazi Germany*, ed. Renate Bridenthal, Atina Grossman, and Marion Kaplan (New York: Monthly Review Press, 1984), 271–96. See also Koonz.

15 The time line of Nazi anti-Semitism surrounding the film's racism is as follows: Hitler speaks of the "final solution" in January 1939 for the first time in public (at a Reichstagsrede), and six months later (just after the start of the war) Jews are forced to wear Stars of David and eastward deportations and mass shootings of Polish Jews begin. In the same year, the first two anti-Semitic films appear: *Robert and Bertram* and *Leinen aus Irland*. In 1940 comes *die Rothschilds* and in 1941 *Jud Süss* (also directed by Veit Harlan).

16 For a more complete history of the Production Code, see Francis G. Couvares, *Movie Censorship and American Culture* (Washington, DC: Smithsonian Institution Press, 1996); and Gregory D. Black, *Hollywood Censored: Morality Codes, Catholics, and the Movies* (Cambridge and New York: Cambridge University Press, 1994).

17 Rentschler, 9.

18 Richard Billinger, *Der Gigant* (Berlin: Suhrkamp Verlag, 1942).

19 Friedemann Beyer, *Die UFA-Stars im Dritten Reich: Frauen für Deutschland* (Munich: Wilhelm Heyne Verlag, 1991), 225–26.

20 See Mary Ann Doane's analysis of the classical Hollywood love story in *The Desire to Desire: The Woman's Film of the 1940s* (Bloomington: Indiana University Press, 1987), 96–122. See also Lea Jacobs, *The Wages of Sin: Censorship and the Fallen Woman Film, 1928–1942* (Madison: University of Wisconsin Press, 1991).

21 Beyer, 196. Söderbaum only worked with her husband, a loyalty she maintained even after the war when Harlan was forbidden to make films until 1950. His 1950s films with Söderbaum were all failures, and after his death in 1964 she didn't work as an actress again except for small appearances, basically as herself.

22 For further discussion of cross-cultural codes of gender, see Sherry B. Ortner and Harriet Whitehead, *Sexual Meanings: The Cultural Construction of Gender and Sexuality* (Cambridge and New York: Cambridge University Press, 1981).

23 Herbert Marcuse, "The Struggle against Liberalism in the Totalitarian View of the State," in *Negations: Essays in Critical Theory*, trans. Jeremy J. Shapiro (London: Free Association Books, 1988), 4. The essay was originally published in German, 1934. For further examples of the Left's ongoing notion of fascist irrationalism, see Max Horkheimer, *Eclipse of Reason* (New York: Oxford University Press, 1947); Nikos Poulantzas, *Fascism and Dictatorship: The Third International and the Problem of Fascism*, trans. Judith White, ed. Jennifer O'Hagan and Timothy O'Hagan (London: NLB, 1974); and Jürgen Habermas, *The Theory of Communicative Action*, trans. Thomas McCarthy (Boston: Beacon, 1985), 519–20.

24 George W. Herald, "Sex Is a Nazi Weapon," *American Mercury* 54 (June 1942): 662–63. The *American Mercury*'s conservatism has an interesting history in that the magazine was founded in 1924 by social cynic H. L. Mencken and became progressively more conservative beginning in World War II. A mouthpiece for anticommunism in the 1950s, it was taken over by the Defenders of the Christian Faith in 1961, a group founded by George Winrod in 1925. The group had gained considerable influence in the mid-1930s until Winrod's pro-Nazi views finally caused him to be charged with sedition in 1942. After the war's end, Winrod and his group again turned to anticommunism, which is how the group came to control the magazine (Winrod died in 1957). From then on, the *American Mercury* was nothing but an extreme right-wing publication, covering just about every subject near and dear to the Far Right (e.g., gun control, abortion, Jewish conspiracy, feminism, and the United Nations). At the time the articles I examine in this book were written, however, the magazine was not yet this extreme.

25 One of the first actions taken by the Nazis, for instance, was the establishment of "marriage loans," by means of which a (racially sound) heterosexual couple could borrow a thousand Reichmarks to get married, with 25 percent of the loan canceled with the birth of each child. Other economic incentives included tax breaks and subsidies for large families (Koonz, 149).

26 Clifford Kirkpatrick, *Nazi Germany: Its Women and Family Life* (Indianapolis and New York: Bobbs-Merrill, 1938), 107.

27 Lowry's reading coincides with mine, although he suggests that this implies that "perhaps all women are dangerously at the mercy of their drives" (Lowry, 94, my translation). I would not deny this feminist reading, but I suggest that these drives

in their *mythic* capacity are in fact *not* uniformly deemed to be dangerous in this film.

28 Klaus Theweleit, *Male Fantasies*, trans. Stephen Conway with Erica Carter and Chris Turner, vols. 1–2 (Minneapolis: University of Minnesota Press, 1987–89).

29 Lowry, 103 (my translation). He quotes the press packet for *Die Goldene Stadt*.

30 I owe the methodology of following recursive figures to Alain J.-J. Cohen. See, for instance, his "La citation du *Mépris* dans *Casino* de Scorsese. Du détail iconophagique," *La Licorne* 6 (1999): 193–206.

31 Proctor cites this passage from a textbook written by Erwin Baur, Eugen Fischer, and Fritz Lenz in 1927, which was translated into English in 1931 as *Human Heredity*. The book was well received in the United States, where the *Journal of Heredity* described it as "the standard textbook of human genetics" (Robert Proctor, *Racial Hygiene: Medicine under the Nazis* [Cambridge and London: Harvard University Press, 1988], 58).

32 Ibid., 38. Nazi sterilization policies actually took their lead from American laws that allowed the sterilization of the mentally ill and the criminally insane, and so here, too, a strict opposition between fascist and "democratic" beliefs should not be falsely construed (Proctor, 97). American immigration policies and laws prohibiting intermarriage of white and Black Americans were also praised by the Nazis. See, for instance, *Germany Speaks*, by "21 Leading members of Party and State," with a preface by Joachim von Ribbentrop, Reich minister for foreign affairs (London: Thornton Butterworth, 1938).

33 Elsaesser, 291. See also Steve Neale's discussion of the "if only" structure of melodramatic narratives in "Melodrama and Tears," *Screen* 27.6 (1986): 6–22.

34 Lowry provides an excellent reading of these figures with respect to the paradox of Nazi "blood and soil" traditionalism and the need for industrial modernization. He associates Christian exclusively with the city, however, overlooking his unique status as one of but three characters (the other two being Anna and her mother) who actually appear in both spaces (110–14).

35 Linda Schulte-Sasse describes *Jud Süss* as a reworking of an eighteenth-century bourgeois tragedy wherein Nazi theories of Jewish conspiracy merge with Nazi scientific beliefs about racial contamination to infuse then contemporary political and biological beliefs into the genre (Schulte-Sasse, 24).

36 The Nuremberg Laws of 1935 focused blame for racial and sexual transgressions *on men*, who were either guilty of "treason" against their own blood if they were German or guilty of "attacking German blood" if they were Jewish. Women could not be punished for the violation of these laws because they were considered to be passive in the sphere of sexual relations (Proctor, 133).

37 For an American variant of this belief, see Henry Herbert Goddard, *The Kallikak Family: A Study in the Heredity of Feeble-Mindedness* (New York: Macmillan, 1912), and its discussion in Proctor, 99–100.

38 Laura Mulvey, "Notes on Sirk and Melodrama," in *Visual and Other Pleasures* (Bloomington and Indianapolis: Indiana University Press, 1989), 39. The article was originally published in 1977.

39 Jan-Christopher Horak, "Liebe, Pflicht und die Erotik des Todes," in *Preussen im Film*, ed. Axel Marquardt and Heinz Rathsack (Berlin: Rowohlt, 1981), 207; Tania

Modleski, *Loving with a Vengeance: Mass-Produced Fantasies for Women* (New York and London: Methuen, 1982), 18.

40 Homi Bhabha, "DissemiNation: Time, Narrative, and the Margins of the Modern Nation," in *Nation and Narration*, ed. Homi Bhabha (London and New York: Routledge, 1990), 297.

2 American Nationalist Melodrama: Tales of *Hitler's Children*

1 Johann Wolfgang von Goethe, *Faust* (1833), as quoted in the film *Hitler's Children* (Edward Dmytryk, 1942).

2 Lauren Berlant, *The Queen of America Goes to Washington City: Essays on Sex and Citizenship* (Durham and London: Duke University Press, 1997). For an earlier study of instances of sexual wartime propaganda, see Magnus Hirschfeld et al., *The Sexual History of the World War* (New York: Cadillac, 1941).

3 Thomas Mann, for instance, complained as early as 1930 that Nazism represented a radical inhumanity in which politics (instead of religion) became the "opium of the masses" ("An Appeal to Reason," in *Order of the Day: Political Essays and Speeches of Two Decades* [New York: Knopf, 1942]).

4 Dagmar Herzog notes that Allied occupation forces also gave churches a significant role in the moral reeducation of the German population after the war, which underscores my analysis of the perception of Nazism as anti-Christian. (" 'Pleasure, Sex, and Politics Belong Together': Post-Holocaust Memory and the Sexual Revolution in West Germany," *Critical Inquiry* 24 [1998]: 413).

5 British conservatives, for instance, often claimed that Hitler himself was essentially moderate and fully capable of controlling the more extreme elements in his party. French conservatives meanwhile deployed their culturally pervasive hatred of Germany, but they did so in the interest of fostering a natively French variant of authoritarianism. A very useful analysis of the various anti-Nazisms can be found in Pierre Ayçoberry, *The Nazi Question: An Essay on the Interpretations of National Socialism (1922–1975)*, trans. Robert Hurley (New York: Random House, 1981).

6 An English translation of an article from the ss publication *Schwarze Korps* presents a series of qualifiers to reproductive conduct: "No man shall be able under the cover of 'racial duty' to develop into a Don Juan and then say he did it 'for his people.' German women are not free game. Within the Elite Guard, care has been taken to see that respect for the German woman and mother remains the supreme law of a manly, chivalrous attitude toward life—if necessary by force." The publication of such an article in an English-language magazine might well be seen as a pro-Nazi rebuttal to the sorts of sexual characterizations that claimed rampant promiscuity. See "Germany Needs 'Boy Fathers,' " *Living Age* 358 (April 1941): 136–39.

7 The agency was established in 1936 by Heinrich Himmler, head of the police forces and the ss. In 1943, the Protection of Marriage, Family, and Motherhood Law called for the death penalty in "extreme cases." See Gisela Bock, "Racism and Sexism in Nazi Germany: Motherhood, Compulsory Sterilization, and the State," in *When Biology Became Destiny: Women in Weimar and Nazi Germany*, ed. Renate Bridenthal, Atina Grossman, and Marion Kaplan (New York: Monthly Review

Press, 1984), 276. See also Claudia Koonz, *Mothers in the Fatherland* (New York: St. Martin's, 1987).

8   For a full discussion of the Frankfurt School position, see Martin Jay, *The Dialectical Imagination: A History of the Frankfurt School and the Institute of Social Research, 1923–1950* (Boston: Little, Brown, 1973).

9   See Hannah Arendt, *The Origins of Totalitarianism* (New York: Harcourt Brace Jovanovich, 1973), 474.

10 Among those opposed were the members of the American Communist Party, who influenced the Popular Front rhetoric of the New Deal era. Among those supporting fascism were anticommunists, some of whom, like the conservative Catholic priest Charles Coughlin, combined their anticommunism with anti-Semitism. For a discussion of American Far Right politics, see David H. Bennett, *The Party of Fear: The American Far Right from Nativism to the Militia Movement*, 2d ed. (New York: Vintage, 1995).

11 Homi Bhabha, "DissemiNation: Time, Narrative, and the Margins of the Modern Nation," in *Nation and Narration*, ed. Homi Bhabha (London and New York: Routledge, 1990), 291–322.

12 Rodney Collin, "Sex and the New Germany," *Living Age* 346 (1934): 26.

13 Clifford Kirkpatrick, *Nazi Germany: Its Women and Family Life* (Indianapolis and New York: Bobbs-Merrill, 1938), 149.

14 Ibid., 151–52.

15 Ibid., 200.

16 Ibid., 36.

17 In a letter to the *American Mercury* in 1940, a reader writes, "When the State of New York supports five institutions for morons, idiots, and imbeciles, carefully protecting them from the natural diseases that might finish them off, while good children, mentally and physically, are allowed to grow up under insane conditions, it is time we looked to this sort of stupidity before getting hot and bothered about something the Germans are doing" (Belinda Jelliffe, *American Mercury* 48 [April 1940]: 252). For a full discussion of Nazi and American similarities with regard to eugenics, see Robert Proctor, *Racial Hygiene: Medicine under the Nazis* (Cambridge and London: Harvard University Press, 1988); and Stefan Kuhl, *The Nazi Connection: Eugenics, American Racism, and German National Socialism* (New York: Oxford University Press, 1994).

18 Albert O. Hirschman, *The Rhetoric of Reaction: Perversity, Futility, Jeopardy* (Cambridge and London: Belknap Press of Harvard University Press, 1991), 7.

19 The term reputedly comes from a speech given by "a Nazi speaker" at a rally at Insterburg six months before Hitler came to power, in which the following oft-quoted statement was made: "Women must cease to serve as pleasure fillies and again become breeding mares." See, for instance, S. L. Solon and Albert Brandt, "Sex under the Swastika," *American Mercury* 47 (August 1939): 426.

20 Toni Christen, "Women without Hope," *Nation*, 2 December 1939, 598.

21 "Nazi Breeders," *Newsweek*, 4 May 1942, 38.

22 See, for instance, Anne O'Hare McCormick, "Homemaking under Hitler," *Ladies' Home Journal*, October 1933, 73, quoted in Ramona M. Rose, *Position and Treatment of Women in Nazi Germany as Viewed from the Perspective of the English Language Press, 1933–1945* (Vancouver: Tantalus Research, 1984), 14; E. Sylvia Pankhurst, "Women

in Totalitaria," *Living Age* 354 (June 1939): 338; Alice Hamilton, "The Enslavement of Women," in *Nazism: An Assault on Civilization*, ed. Pierre van Paassen and James Waterman Wise (New York: Harrison Smith and Robert Haas, 1934), 82; and "The Nazis Are Kind to Women," *New Republic*, 19 August 1936, 39–41.

23   Quentin Reynolds, "Woman's Place," *Collier's*, 25 November 1933, 49.

24   Murray Constantine, *Swastika Night* (London: Victor Gollancz, 1940), 69. The book was reissued by the Feminist Press under Burdekin's name in 1985.

25   Progressive theologians like Martin Niemoller and Dietrich Bonhoeffer, who were leaders of the anti-Nazi Confessional Church from 1935 on, were not immediately opposed to the fascist state. In fact, progressive Protestant theologians initially continued to see the protection of the citizenry and the family as something that belonged under the authority of the state or the secular world. The Confessional Church ultimately denounced Nazism as a "new religion" and challenged both its racial doctrine and the "Führer Prinzip" (leader concept) whereby young people were replacing their parents with Hitler and thereby unsettling the formerly mutually supportive bonds of family and community (Ayçoberry, 29).

26   William Martin, *With God on Our Side: The Rise of the Religious Right in America* (New York: Broadway Books, 1996), 11.

27   Martin, 16.

28   The quotes are from Solon and Brandt, 426, 427; Christen, 599; and "Nazi Breeders," 38, respectively.

29   George W. Herald, "Sex Is a Nazi Weapon," *American Mercury* 54 (June 1942): 658.

30   Ibid., 663.

31   Ibid., 660.

32   Michel Foucault, *The History of Sexuality*, vol. 1: *An Introduction*, trans. Robert Hurley (New York: Vintage, 1980), 105–6.

33   For a history of the Production Code Administration, see Francis G. Couvares, *Movie Censorship and American Culture* (Washington, DC: Smithsonian Institution Press, 1996); and Gregory D. Black, *Hollywood Censored: Morality Codes, Catholics, and the Movies* (Cambridge and New York: Cambridge University Press, 1994).

34   Jan-Christopher Horak, *Anti-Nazi-Filme: der deutschsprichigen emmigration von Hollywood, 1939–1945* (Münster: Maks Publikationen, 1985), 214 (my translation).

35   Ibid., 369.

36   The *Motion Picture Herald* pointed this out in a rare review of the film (13 November 1943).

37   As film scholar Thomas Doherty notes, many members of the industry had a personal investment in the war, as various actors enlisted, studio executives had sons in the service, and many were Jews or others (such as communists) who decried Nazi racism or otherwise held strong political convictions (*Projections of War: Hollywood, American Culture, and World War II* [New York: Columbia University Press, 1993], 14).

38   Joseph Breen (head of the PCA) to Edward Golden (the film's producer), 13 October 1942, "Hitler's Children" file, Margaret Herrick Library, Academy of Motion Picture Arts and Sciences (AMPAS), Beverly Hills, California. Breen had sent a letter to Golden on 21 August 1942, as a followup to their meeting about the script, wherein he writes, "May I take this opportunity of expressing our appreciation of

the splendid way in which you have handled this difficult story, and to wish you all success in the production of an outstanding picture."

39 Miriam Tooley (secretary to Mrs. James F. Looram) to Joseph Breen. On the PCA form, German characters are listed as both sympathetic and unsympathetic, while all the American characters and the Catholic bishop are sympathetic. The letter is in the "Hitler's Children" file, Margaret Herrick Library, Academy of Motion Picture Arts and Sciences, Beverly Hills, California.

40 Horak, 343.

41 Ibid., 369 (my translation).

42 Gregor Ziemer, *Education for Death: The Making of the Nazi* (London and New York: Oxford University Press, 1941); "Education for Death," *Reader's Digest*, February 1942, 129–44. See also Ziemer's "How Hitler Builds His 'Super Race,' " *Maclean's*, 15 October 1941, 43.

43 Edward A. Golden to Geoffrey Shurlock (of the PCA), 28 May 1942, "Hitler's Children" file, Margaret Herrick Library, Academy of Motion Picture Arts and Sciences, Beverly Hills, California.

44 Edward Dmytryk, *Odd Man Out: A Memoir of the Hollywood Ten* (Carbondale, IL: Southern Illinois University Press, 1996), 17.

45 *Hitler's Children* was written by Emmet Lavery, as was *Behind the Rising Sun*. For a discussion of the latter, see Doherty, 31–33.

46 Ziemer, *Education for Death*, 51, 40.

47 This undecidability is perhaps underscored by the casting of Bonita Granville as Anna, in that Granville, primarily a supporting and B movie actress, often played roles in which her moral fortitude was questionable.

48 Bosley Crowther, " 'Hitler's Children,' Fictionized Version of 'Education for Death,' Makes Its Appearance at the Paramount Theatre," *New York Times*, 25 February 1943, 27.

49 Doherty, 302.

50 "Hitler's Children," *Variety*, 30 December 1942, 16.

51 Doherty has a chapter on the contribution of Leni Riefenstahl's *Triumph of the Will* to American movie imagery of the Nazis. While the film was never commercially released nor readily accessible in America during the 1930s, it was well known around Hollywood and elements of it were incorporated into many wartime films (Doherty, 20).

52 The actual Gettysburg Address reads: "It is for us the living, rather, to be dedicated here to the unfinished work which they who fought here have thus far so nobly advanced. It is rather for us to be here dedicated to the great task remaining before us—that from these honored dead we take increased devotion to that cause for which they gave the last full measure of devotion—that we here highly resolve that these dead shall not have died in vain—that this nation, under God, shall have a new birth of freedom—and that government of the people, by the people, for the people, shall not perish from the earth" (*The World Almanac and Book of Facts, 1998* [Mahwah, NJ: World Almanac Books, 1997], 523).

53 Black, 39.

54 Comedies were more likely than other genres to mention the Nazi persecution of Jews or even to take anti-Semitism as a primary issue in the story. Examples

include Charlie Chaplin's *The Great Dictator* (1940), Ernst Lubitsch's *To Be or Not to Be* (1942), and Leo McCarey's *Once Upon a Honeymoon* (1942).

55 The dramatic logic of Anna's contested citizenship echoes efforts to reassure the American public that Americans of German descent (the largest category of white ethnic heritage in the nation) were in fact loyal Americans. No similar efforts to dramatize loyalty were made for Japanese-Americans, who were presumed to be constitutionally predisposed to loyalty toward Japan. On the contrary, Japanese-Americans were detained in internment camps following a decree of 19 February 1942. Democratic pluralism was sometimes invoked against Nazi racism/homogeneity in anti-Nazi films—but with the various pitfalls that reveal and belie American prejudice. Alfred Hitchcock's *Lifeboat* (1944), for instance, both addresses the question of whether Germans are "like us" and can be trusted in a pinch (they can't) and includes a Black man in the limited cast (a subordinate, but there nonetheless).

56 This is also in Ziemer, *Education for Death*, 33.

57 In *Once Upon a Honeymoon*, director Leo McCarey quite literally stages the opposition between democracy and fascist sterilization practices in a sequence in which Ginger Rogers and Cary Grant mistakenly end up in a Jewish ghetto (Ginger, in her furs, says "we're really in a fix now"). They are called into an office and begin to enter a door marked for sterilizations (in German) until they are righted and sent to a door directly opposite, behind which the American ambassador sits, apologizing profusely for the "mixup."

58 For background on this broad appeal, see Diane B. Paul, *Controlling Human Heredity, 1865 to the Present* (Atlantic Highlands, NJ: Humanities Press, 1995); and Carole R. McCann, *Birth Control Politics in the United States, 1916–1945* (Ithaca and New York: Cornell University Press, 1994). For the exchange between U.S. eugenics advocates and Nazis, see Kuhl.

59 American eugenicists tried to distinguish between "sensible" practices such as sterilizing the poor, disabled, and mentally handicapped and "excessive" ones such as sterilization as a form of political punishment. See, for instance, Kirkpatrick, 182–83. Germany issued a collection of essays in English in which leading members of the party responded to foreign criticisms, including the rumors that Germany was having the "politically undesirable . . . hauled up for sterilization." The essay denies this but tellingly goes on to detail which ailments *are* subject to sterilization, a clear indication that sterilizing "defectives" was judged to be unobjectionable to English-speaking audiences. See Walter Gross, "National Socialist Racial Thought," in *Germany Speaks: 21 Leading Members of Party and State*, prefaced by Joachim von Ribbentrop, Reich minister for foreign affairs (London: Thornton Butterworth, 1938), 70–71.

60 Crowther, 27.

61 "Education for Death" was directed by Clyde Geronimi. See Dave Smith, *Disney A to Z: The Official Encyclopedia* (New York: Hyperion, 1996), 156. For a discussion of Hollywood cartoons as a genre, see Eric Smoodin, *Animating Culture: Hollywood Cartoons from the Sound Era* (New Brunswick, NJ: Rutgers University Press, 1993).

62 Dana Polan notes that "the notion that marriages are constructed on the basis of a certain forcing of events seems to run through many films of the period," thus revealing "the fictions of wartime unity." Polan singles out *The Miracle of Morgan's*

Creek as a film that suggests that "there is no necessary logic that can bring together the issues of sexuality and commitment" (*Power and Paranoia: History, Narrative, and the American Cinema, 1940–1950* [New York: Columbia University Press, 1986], 116).

63 Holland's film about a Jewish adolescent passing as "Aryan" is thematized by his various life or death efforts to avoid exposure of his circumcised penis, the only visible marker of his Jewishness. In the course of the film, the boy suffers an attempted molestation by a homosexual Wehrmacht soldier who turns out not to be an anti-Semite and protects him from persecution. His first sexual intercourse is with a middle-aged Nazi woman who is apparently so self-involved and voracious that she does not notice. Finally, he falls in love with a fanatical Aryan girl who wants to procreate posthaste, and it is only for fear of discovery that he must invoke traditional morality to dissuade her. The film thus revisits many familiar arenas of wartime nationalist melodrama, but it doesn't make the case that either conservative sexual morality or sexual freedom should characterize fascism or antifascism across the board.

3 "Family Values" and "Naziana" in Contemporary Right-Wing Media

1 Ed Gellespie and Bob Schellhas, eds., *Contract With America: The Bold Plan by Rep. Newt Gingrich, Rep. Dick Armey, and the House Republicans to Change the Nation* (New York: Random House, 1994), 84.

2 Ibid., 79. For a critical analysis of the proposed policies, see John J. DiIulio Jr. and Donald F. Kettl, *Fine Print: The Contract with America, Devolution, and the Administrative Realities of American Federalism* (Washington, DC: Brookings Institution, Center for Public Management, 1995).

3 Gellespie and Schellhas, 65, 79.

4 Although it was written before the impeachment trial began, see Laura Kipnis, "Adultery," *Critical Inquiry* 24 (1998): 289–327. Kipnis notes that in national politics the "character issue" requires that the public act as "social detectives," thus extending the marital panopticon to the nation.

5 Lauren Berlant, "Intimacy: A Special Issue," *Critical Inquiry* 24 (1998): 288.

6 Stephanie Coonz, *The Way We Never Were: American Families and the Nostalgia Trap* (New York: Basic Books, 1992), 97.

7 Linda Kintz, *Between Jesus and the Market: The Emotions That Matter in Right-Wing America* (Durham and London: Duke University Press, 1997), 97; George Gilder, *Men and Marriage* (Gretna, LA: Pelican, 1993), 112, quoted in Kintz, 152–53. Gilder's book was originally published in 1973 as *Sexual Suicide*. See also Linda Kintz and Julia Lesage, eds., *Media, Culture, and the Religious Right* (Minneapolis: University of Minnesota Press, 1998).

8 Other rhetorical tricks that make this possible include a brand of American anti-Semitism that casts communism as a Jewish conspiracy (all purges by Stalin aside) and thus throws into doubt the patriotism of outspoken Jewish opponents of fascism during World War II. This is equally true of other outspoken opponents of anti-Semitism and prejudice, especially if they are foreign born.

9 See Jennifer Terry, "'Momism' and the Making of Treasonous Homosexuals," in *"Bad" Mothers: The Politics of Blame in Twentieth-Century America*, ed. Molly Ladd-Taylor and Lauri Umansky (New York: New York University Press, 1998), 169–90; John D'Emilio, "The Homosexual Menace: The Politics of Sexuality in Cold War America," in *Making Trouble: Essays on Gay History, Politics, and the University* (New York: Routledge, 1992), 57–73; and Michael Rogin, "Kiss Me Deadly: Communism, Motherhood, and Cold War Movies," *Representations* 6 (1984): 1–36.

10 William Martin, *With God on Our Side: The Rise of the Religious Right in America* (New York: Broadway Books, 1996), 33–34.

11 Some of the more notorious Christian Nazi supporters include Charles Coughlin, Gerald Winrod, and Gerald L. K. Smith. All combined anti-Semitism with anti-communism.

12 See Gregory D. Black, *Hollywood Censored: Morality Codes, Catholics, and the Movies* (Cambridge and New York: Cambridge University Press, 1994).

13 See, for instance Martin, 107, for a discussion of the 1962 conflict over sex education in Anaheim, California.

14 Herbert Marcuse, *Eros and Civilization: A Philosophical Inquiry into Freud* (Boston: Beacon, 1974), 202–3. The book was originally published in 1955.

15 Quoted in Martin, 155.

16 The quotes are from Falwell and Robison, respectively, as quoted in ibid., 164–67.

17 Quoted in ibid., 179.

18 Ellen Messer-Davidow, "Manufacturing the Attack on Liberalized Higher Education," *Social Text* 36 (1993): 46.

19 Lauren Berlant, *The Queen of America Goes to Washington City: Essays on Sex and Citizenship* (Durham and London: Duke University Press, 1997), 178.

20 For a full articulation of this argument, see chapter 5 ("Anti-Life Groups: The Holocaust Enablers and Promoters") in Brian Clowes, *Pro-Life Activist's Encyclopedia* (Stafford, VA: American Life League, 1995).

21 See Nancy F. Cott, *The Grounding of Modern Feminism* (New Haven and London: Yale University Press, 1987), 13.

22 James Dobson, August 1995, available at the time on the Focus on the Family website: ⟨http://cs.albany.edu/~ault/fof/fofbegin.html⟩. The current Focus on the Family address is ⟨http://www.family.org⟩.

23 Beverly LaHaye, *Who but a Woman? Concerned Women Can Make a Difference* (Nashville: Thomas Nelson, 1984), 13–14. For a valuable discussion of LaHaye and this passage, see Kintz, 80.

24 Conflations between sadism, feminism, and lesbianism can be found as early as La Forest Potter's *Strange Loves: A Study in Sexual Abnormalities* (New York: Padell Book Co., 1933); and Maurice Chideckel's *Female Sex Perversion: The Sexually Aberrated Woman as She Is* (New York: Eugenics Publishing Co., 1935).

25 Kintz, 236.

26 Ibid., 255. For examples of "reconstruction of masculinity" rhetoric, see Robert Timberg, *The Nightingale's Song* (New York: Simon and Schuster, 1995); and James William Gibson, *Warrior Dreams: Paramilitary Culture in Post-Vietnam America* (New York: Hill and Wang, 1994).

27 "Newspeak: Language of Delusion," in Clowes, *Pro-Life Activist's Encyclopedia*.

28 Ibid.

29 These strategies are pervasive in the antiabortion movement. See, for instance, the afterword by then surgeon general C. Everett Koop, entitled "The Slide to Auschwitz," in Ronald Reagan, *Abortion and the Conscience of the Nation* (Nashville: T. Nelson, 1984).

30 Berlant, *The Queen of America*, 99–100.

31 Berlant mentions the starving child/Holocaust victim/abortion homology in the sequel to the famous antiabortion film *The Silent Scream* called (remarkably) *The Eclipse of Reason* (ibid., 120–21). A similar homology between lynching/Holocaust/abortion victims was part of an antiabortion display sponsored by the California-based Center for Bio-Ethical Reform's Genocide Awareness Project, which toured college campuses in 1998 (fig. 2).

32 Kintz, 265.

33 For a profile of D. James Kennedy, see Pat Jordan, "The Calling," *Los Angeles Times Magazine*, 28 July 1996, 16–18, 28, 30. Jordan described the church's ideology as "Man should be as concerned with his prosperity on earth as his salvation in heaven, which is why it's every Christian's duty to involve himself in all aspects of secular society" (18).

34 Cal Thomas has used more overt anti-Nazi rhetoric in his syndicated columns as well. After an acquittal of Dr. Jack Kevorkian, which overturned a state law banning assisted suicide, Thomas wrote, "If a constitutional 'right' to die is upheld, then how long will it be before the state (or one's heirs) decides to mandate death? For the most plausible reasons, of course, and for the benefit of all. No one's talking Nazi Germany here, or are they?" See Cal Thomas, "Culture of Death, Imposed on the Unborn, Targets the Elderly," *Los Angeles Times*, syndicated column, 13 March 1996.

35 See Faye Ginsburg, "The 'Word-Made' Flesh: The Disembodiment of Gender in the Abortion Debate," in *Uncertain Terms: Negotiating Gender in American Culture*, ed. Faye Ginsburg and Anna Lowenhaupt Tsing (Boston: Beacon, 1990).

36 Rush Limbaugh, *The Way Things Ought to Be* (New York: Pocket Star Books, 1992), 194.

37 Texe Marrs, *Big Sister Is Watching You! Hillary Clinton and the White House Feminists Who Now Control America—and Tell the President What to Do* (Austin, TX: Living Truth Publishers, 1994). For a discussion of Marrs, see Kintz, 257.

38 See many issues of the *American Spectator* (especially April-May 1994) and Gennifer Flowers, *Passion and Betrayal* (Del Mar, CA: Emery Dalton, 1992).

39 George L. Mosse, *Nationalism and Sexuality: Respectability and Abnormal Sexuality in Modern Europe* (New York: H. Fertig, 1985), 105.

40 Skipp Porteous, "Inside Glen Eyrie Castle: The Organized Assault on Gay Rights," *Freedom Writer*, August 1994. See also Mel White, *Stranger at the Gate: To Be Gay and Christian in America* (New York: Simon and Schuster, 1994).

41 Barry D. Adam, *The Rise of a Gay and Lesbian Movement* (Boston: Twayne, 1987), 104.

42 The first attempt by the OCA to launch a state ballot initiative to block anti-discrimination laws against gay people was defeated in 1992 (Measure 9). The measure was reintroduced and defeated again in 1994 (Measure 13). Thereafter, the OCA turned its attention to promoting local city and county ordinances, many of which passed.

43 "OCA's Rise Meteoric since Start-up in 1986," *Oregonian*, 21 June 1993, B1, 4. Other

active anti-gay-rights groups include the following attendees at the Colorado for Family Values antigay strategizing conference in 1994: Focus on the Family, Concerned Women for America, the Christian Coalition, the Family Research Council, the Traditional Values Coalition, the Eagle Forum, the American Family Association, and the National Legal Foundation.

44 The Antelope Valley Springs of Life Church, located in Lancaster, California, also produces *The Report*, a weekly cable TV show, and publishes the *Lambda Report on Homosexuality*. In a prime example of right-wing organizing, Bill Horn, the producer of *The Report*, did a segment called "Sexual Orientation or Sexual Deviation: You Decide," eight thousand copies of which were distributed in California in 1991 while gay rights Assembly bill 101 was being debated. After California governor Pete Wilson vetoed the bill, the protests were filmed and included in *The Gay Agenda*, which Horn produced. According to the church, twenty-five thousand copies of the tape had been shipped across the country by February 1993, with especially high numbers going to Oregon and Colorado, where state antigay initiatives were under way. I am indebted to the progressive lobbying group People for the American Way, based in Washington, DC, for this information.

45 Chris Bull, "Lunatic Fringe," *The Advocate*, 30 May 1995, 21.

46 See Kevin Abrams, "The Other Side of the Pink Triangle," *Lambda Report on Homosexuality* 11.4 (August 1994): 11.

47 Adam, 102.

48 Quoted in David Gates with Mark Miller, "Dr. Laura, Talk Radio Celebrity: She Apologizes after Antagonizing the Gay Community," *Newsweek*, 20 March 2000, 52.

49 The OCA pamphlet cites dubious sources for its claims that the Nazi movement was homosexual, including Robert Waite, *The Psychopathic God: Adolf Hitler* (New York: Basic Books, 1977); and William Stevenson, *A Man Called Intrepid: The Secret War* (New York: Harcourt, Brace, Jovanovich, 1976).

50 Kevin Abrams and Scott Lively, *The Pink Swastika: Homosexuality in the Nazi Party* (Amity, OR: Lively Communications, 1995).

51 Judith Reisman, who holds a PH.D. in communications, is another "Jewish scholar" (named as such) whose antigay scholarship is often cited by Christian fundamentalist homophobes who want to deny that their movement is exclusively Christian. Reisman's book, *Kinsey, Sex, and Fraud*, claims to debunk the claim that 10 percent of the population has had significant same sex experiences (among other things). She is invoked as an "expert" in the Coral Ridge tape discussed below. See Judith A. Reisman and Edward Eichel, *Kinsey, Sex, and Fraud* (Lafayette, LA: Huntington House, 1990).

52 Abrams, "The Other Side of the Pink Triangle," 11.

53 Christine L. Mueller is Professor of History and Humanities and a specialist in German history at Reed College. See her "The Other Side of the Pink Triangle . . . Still a Pink Triangle" (online), dated 24 October 1994. Available from World Wide Web: ⟨http://www.lavenderlinks.com/topics/ourstory.html⟩.

54 Kevin Abrams and Christine Mueller, "Pink Triangle . . . or Pink Swastika? The Debate over Homosexual Nazis," *Lambda Report on Homosexuality* 12.3 (April–June 1995): 4–5.

55 Ibid., 5.

56 See Hans Johnson, "Pink Swastika Strategy Becomes a Centerpiece," *Washington Blade*, 30 June 1995, 43. Johnson says, "As curious as the CFV [Colorado for Family Values] argument may sound, it is by no means an anomaly among religious right groups active in assailing Gay civil rights."

57 Mike Shaver, "Citizens Project," *Freedom Watch* 3.4 (July-August 1994). Shaver reported on the Colorado for Family Values' closed-door, invitation only conference for nearly forty national organizations committed to "rolling back the militant gay agenda." Part of the conference featured workshops about how to package the antigay message in ways palatable to the mainstream public.

58 For a further discussion of Christian antigay videos, see Ioannis Mookas, "Faultlines: Homophobic Innovation in *Gay Rights, Special Rights*," *Afterimage* 22.7–8 (1995): 14–18.

59 In the ongoing volley of accusations of Nazism across the gulf of various social issues, *Hate, Lies, and Videotape*, the video made in response to *The Gay Agenda* by the Gay and Lesbian Emergency Media Campaign (also offered to the Joint Chiefs of Staff), likens the antigay tape to Nazi propaganda films about Jews. See Laurie Goodstein, "Gay-Rights Group Reels Off a Reply to Critics: New Video Compares Widely Publicized Anti-homosexual Film to Nazi, Klan Propaganda," *Washington Post*, 18 February 1993, A6.

60 The appeal to this sort of invasion of the home/nation image is also reflected in Kennedy's fundraising literature, where he writes, "They've spread across the country and they've gone too far!" invoking the specters of "our children and grandchildren" being forced to attend "pro-sodomy seminars" in public schools; pastors being sued for hate crimes because they preach the "biblical truth about homosexuality"; churches, local schools, nursing homes, and area businesses forced to interview and hire homosexuals; and Christian landlords and people with rooms to let in their homes forced to accept homosexual tenants (D. James Kennedy, Coral Ridge Ministries fundraising letter, 6 February 1995).

61 *Washington Blade*, 3 January 1991, according to the OCA voter pamphlet. The unattributed quote also appears in "Gay Naziism Today," *Lambda Report on Homosexuality* 12.3 (April–June 1995): 5.

62 Berlant has similarly commented that *The Gay Agenda* expresses fears of "mobocracy," the exploitation of democratic privileges by those who would destroy the social order (*The Queen of America*, 189). For a discussion of the ways in which Riefenstahl's footage has been central to, as Doherty puts it, "American movie memory," see Thomas Doherty, *Projections of War: Hollywood, American Culture, and World War II* (New York: Columbia University Press, 1993), 24.

63 PFLAG, "Pat Robertson Doesn't Want You to Hear These Hateful Words on TV," paid advertisement, *USA Today*, 20 December 1995, A12.

64 I am mainly referring to the roughly 60 percent of militia groups that do not openly espouse Nazi beliefs. Oddly enough, even avowed Nazi groups like the Militia of Montana, which does have links to Aryan Nations, still accuses the federal government of Nazism in matters of gun control. The majority of militia groups do not claim these beliefs, however, and insist that they are composed of more fundamentalist Americans with a closer adherence to the tenets of the original Constitution, the Bill of Rights, and often the Bible.

65 See "The Gun Lobby: With Another Showdown Pending in Congress, NRA Hard-

liners Seem to Thrive under Siege," *U.S. News and World Report*, 22 May 1995, 37. The common use of this parallel by anti-gun-control organizations made headlines when former president George Bush withdrew his lifetime membership from the group when NRA vice president Wayne LaPierre referred to federal BATF agents as "jack-booted thugs" in a fundraising letter. See "Right in Disarray as Bush Quits Gun Lobby," *Guardian*, 12 May 1995, sec. 1, 16.

66 Serge F. Kovaleski, "Women in Militias Say Ranks Are Not Just for Angry White Males," *Washington Post*, 9 September 1995, A2–3.

67 See, for instance, "Equal Hostility: Women Are Angry at Government, Too," *Wall Street Journal*, 12 May 1995, A1.

68 Quoted in Lou Chibbaro Jr., "Some Militias Linked to Anti-gay Organizations," *Washington Blade*, 19 May 1995.

69 Bull, 21. The quote is taken from an interview Matousek gave to the *Detroit Metro Times*.

70 Derrick Z. Jackson, "True American Terror Is in Handguns, not AK–47s," *Boston Globe*, 5 May 1995.

71 See Richard Shumate, "How Anti-gay Is the Militant Right?" *Windy City Times*, 11 May 1995, 1, 10.

72 Producer Linda Thompson is an attorney who rose to prominence with the popularity of the two Waco tapes among members of the patriot movements. For a profile, see Robert W. Lee, "An Insurrectionist Messenger," *New American*, 19 September 1994, 29–32.

73 Conspiracy theories are full of claims that various federal agencies (especially the CIA) are run by former Nazis. See Alex Constantine, *Psychic Dictatorship in the USA* (Portland, OR: Feral House, 1995). For a critical analysis, see Mark Fenster, *Conspiracy Theories: Secrecy and Power in American Culture* (Minneapolis: University of Minnesota Press, 1999). The documentary film *Waco: The Rules of Engagement* (William Gazecki, 1997) is more convincing than Thompson's tapes due to a more focused argument, which is backed up by various forms of evidence. Gazecki argues less that there was deliberate conspiracy than that the siege was destined to end tragically due to the attitudes of the BATF agents and the recklessness and inflexibility of the tactics used. The film still neglects to draw a parallel with government persecution of leftist groups, however.

74 "Corrupt and Criminal: Linda Thompson's View of Our Government Leaders," *Rutherford* (August 1995): 17.

75 See Laura Flanders, "Far-Right Militias and Anti-abortion Violence: When Will Media See the Connection?" *Extra! The Magazine of Fairness and Accuracy in Reporting*, July-August 1995, 11–12.

76 The concept of international persecution of Christians has more recently been taken up by Gary Bauer, head of the Family Research Council. Conservative Catholic Nina Shea, religion expert at the human rights group Freedom House, goes so far as to claim that "On a demographic scale, Christians are the most persecuted religious group in the world today" (46). See also Jeffrey Goldberg, "Washington Discovers Christian Persecution," *New York Times Magazine*, 21 December 1997, 46–62.

77 Jordan, 28.

78 Berlant, "Intimacy," 286.

4 Nazism, Psychology, and the Making
of Democratic Subjects

1   George W. Herald, "Sex Is a Nazi Weapon," *American Mercury* 54 (June 1942): 658.

2   "The Plot," *Newsweek*, 8 May 1995, 30.

3   Max Thomas Mehr and Regine Sylvester, "The Stone-Thrower from Eisenhutten-stadt," *Granta* 42 (1992): 133–42.

4   Ben Hecht, treatment for *Notorious*, "Notorious" file, Margaret Herrick Library, Academy of Motion Picture Arts and Sciences, Beverly Hills, California. The treatment is discussed at greater length in chapter 7.

5   Ellen Herman, *The Romance of American Psychology: Political Culture in the Age of Experts* (Berkeley: University of California Press, 1995), 4.

6   Ibid., 5. Wartime psychological experts held a wide range of policy-oriented positions dealing with the conduct of psychological warfare, administering internment camps, keeping track of public opinion and morale, and safeguarding the well-being of soldiers.

7   That is, while military psychiatry began earlier and was linked to the progressive "mental hygiene" movement, World War II marked a dramatic expansion of the field. On this earlier history, see Walter Bromberg, *Psychiatry between the Wars, 1918–1945: A Recollection* (Westport, CT: Greenwood, 1982); Alan Berube, *Coming out under Fire: A History of Gay Men and Women in World War Two* (New York: Free Press, 1990); and Elizabeth Lunbeck, *The Psychiatric Persuasion: Knowledge, Gender, and Power in Modern America* (Princeton: Princeton University Press, 1994).

8   Max Weber, *The Protestant Ethic and the Spirit of Capitalism*, trans. Talcott Parsons (New York: Scribner, 1958). The book was originally published in 1904.

9   Sigmund Freud, *Group Psychology and the Analysis of the Ego*, trans. James Strachey (London: Hogarth, 1945); *Totem and Taboo: Some Points of Agreement between the Mental Lives of Savages and Neurotics*, trans. James Strachey (New York: Norton, 1952); *Civilization and Its Discontents*, trans. James Strachey (New York: Norton, 1961); *Moses and Monotheism*, trans. Katherine Jones (New York: Knopf, 1939).

10 Herman, 33. Influential people who were followers of Freud included psychologists Franz Alexander, Erich Fromm, Karen Horney, and Harry Stack Sullivan and cultural anthropologists Gregory Bateson, Ruth Benedict, Geoffrey Gorer, Margaret Mead, and Edward Sapir.

11 See, for instance, Harold P. Lasswell, "The Psychology of Hitlerism," *Political Quarterly* 4 (1933): 380, cited in Herman, 35.

12 Freud, *Civilization*, 57.

13 Ibid., 66.

14 Ibid., 68–69.

15 Erik H. Erikson, "Hitler's Imagery and German Youth," *Psychiatry* 5 (1942): 475–93. Most of this article ended up in the section of *Childhood and Society* dedicated to fascism. See Erik H. Erikson, *Childhood and Society* (New York: Norton, 1950).

16 Erik H. Erikson, "On Nazi Mentality," in *A Way of Looking at Things: Selected Papers from 1930 to 1980, Erik H. Erikson*, ed. Stephen Schlein (New York: Norton, 1987), 342.

17 Ernest Jones, "The Psychology of Quislingism," *International Journal of Psycho-*

Analysis 22.1 (January 1941): 1–6, cited in Peter Loewenberg, "Psychohistorical Perspectives on Modern German History," *Journal of Modern History* 47 (1975): 238.

18   See also Fritz Wittels, "Collective Defense Mechanisms against Homosexuality," *Psychoanalytic Review* 31 (1944): 19–33. For a more general overview of psychoanalytic theories of homosexuality, see Kenneth Lewes, *The Psychoanalytic Theory of Male Homosexuality* (New York: Simon and Schuster, 1988).

19   Rodney Collin, "Sex and the New Germany," *Living Age* 346 (March 1934): 24–26. The piece was originally published in the *Spectator*, a London conservative weekly.

20   Walter C. Langer, *The Mind of Adolf Hitler: The Secret Wartime Report* (New York: Basic Books, 1972). The book was declassified and published for popular consumption in 1972, giving rise to lots of debate and controversy (much of it condemning psychohistory). Its publication coincided with a groundswell of interest in all things Nazi, a cultural development I consider at greater length in chapter 8.

21   Ibid., 167–68.

22   Ibid., 170.

23   Molly Ladd-Taylor and Lauri Umansky, Introduction to *"Bad" Mothers: The Politics of Blame in Twentieth-Century America*, ed. Molly Ladd-Taylor and Lauri Umansky (New York: New York University Press, 1998), 7. For further information on this earlier history, see Linda Kerber, *Women of the Republic: Intellect and Ideology in Revolutionary America* (Chapel Hill: University of North Carolina Press, 1980); and Mary P. Ryan, *The Empire of the Mother: American Writing about Domesticity, 1830–1860* (New York: Haworth, 1982).

24   The class and race politics of these theories of the influence of motherhood on children are also revealing, for it was mainly white middle-class mothers who were addressed by them since they had produced the next generation of the dominant class. Mothers of "inferior" races and classes produced inferior offspring no matter what they did in a eugenically minded intellectual climate. Hence, middle-class women were required to stay at home with their children while lower class women were not. This sort of distinction is still evident in arguments about "welfare mothers" today.

25   Freud, *Civilization*, 76.

26   Ibid., 79.

27   Ibid., 89.

28   Members of the Institute for Social Research, under the direction of Max Horkheimer after 1930, took steps toward combining psychoanalysis with Marxist critical theory, a combination that had been anathema to the prior generation of members. For a complete history, see Martin Jay, *The Dialectical Imagination: A History of the Frankfurt School and the Institute of Social Research, 1923–1950* (Boston and Toronto: Little, Brown, 1973).

29   Erich Fromm, "Sozialpsychologisher Teil," in *Studien über Autorität und Familie*, ed. Institut für Sozialforschung (Paris: Félix Alcan, 1936); "Zum Gefühl der Ohnmacht," *Zeitschrift für Sozialforschung* 4.1 (1937): 95–118; *Escape from Freedom* (New York: Farrar and Rinehart, 1941).

30   Jay, 95.

31   Ibid., 104–5. The unpublished article by Adorno is entitled "Social Science and Sociological Tendencies in Psychoanalysis."

32 Herbert Marcuse, *Eros and Civilization: A Philosophical Inquiry into Freud* (Boston: Beacon Press, 1955).

33 Wilhelm Reich, *The Mass Psychology of Fascism*, trans. Vincent R. Carfagno (New York: Farrar, Straus and Giroux, 1970), 89.

34 Institut für Sozialforschung, *Studien über Autorität und Familie: Forschungsberichte aus dem Institut für Sozialforschung* (Paris: Félix Alcan, 1936). The study consisted of survey questionnaires given to German doctors, young people, and unemployed workers of different countries. The surveys were first conducted in 1930 with German male workers, a subsequent analysis of which (after the Nazis came to power) found 10 percent to be authoritarian (meaning that they exercised authority at home but submitted to it outside), 15 percent anti-authoritarian, and 75 percent ambivalent.

35 For further discussion of this study, see Jay and also Pierre Ayçoberry, *The Nazi Question: An Essay on the Interpretation of National Socialism (1922–1975)*, trans. Robert Hurley (New York: Random House, 1981).

36 Franz Neumann, in his *Behemoth: The Structure and Practice of National Socialism, 1933–1944* (New York: Oxford University Press, 1944), differed from the other Frankfurt School members in that he saw the authoritarian personality as a product created by the Nazis not as an antecedent.

37 T. W. Adorno, Else Frenkel-Brunswik, Daniel J. Levinson, and R. Nevitt Sanford, *The Authoritarian Personality* (New York: Harper and Brothers, 1950).

38 Andrew Hewitt, *Political Inversions: Homosexuality, Fascism, and the Modernist Imaginary* (Stanford: Stanford University Press, 1996), 43–44.

39 Elaine Tyler May, *Homeward Bound: American Families in the Cold War Era* (New York: Basic Books, 1988), 71.

40 Carroll Smith-Rosenberg, *Disorderly Conduct: Visions of Gender in Victorian America* (New York: Knopf, 1985), 90.

41 George Mosse, *Nationalism and Sexuality: Respectability and Abnormal Sexuality in Modern Europe* (New York: Howard Fertig, 1985), 9.

42 Michel Foucault, *The History of Sexuality*, vol. 1: *An Introduction*, trans. Robert Hurley (New York: Vintage, 1980), 103.

43 Siegfried Kracauer, *From Caligari to Hitler: A Psychological History of the German Film* (Princeton: Princeton University Press, 1947).

44 Ibid., v.

45 Robert J. Corber, *In the Name of National Security: Hitchcock, Homophobia, and the Political Construction of Gender in Postwar America* (Durham: Duke University Press, 1993). For a further discussion of Hitchcock's homophobia and queer subplots, see the various authors in "Dossier on Hitchcock," in Corey K. Creekmur and Alexander Doty, *Out in Culture: Gay, Lesbian, and Queer Essays on Popular Culture* (Durham: Duke University Press, 1995): 183–306.

46 Hitchcock's *Spellbound* (1945), for instance, deals explicitly with a psychiatrist's attempt to understand her patient, but legend has it that he remarked "It's only a movie" when one of his psychoanalytic advisers complained that his choices were violating the theory. The comment is reported in the documentary *Hitchcock, Selznick, and the End of Hollywood* (Michael Epstein, 1999).

47 Teresa de Lauretis, *The Practice of Love: Lesbian Sexuality and Perverse Desire* (Bloomington and Indianapolis: Indiana University Press, 1994). Psychoanalysis has, of

course, enjoyed a prominent place in film theory since the 1970s in ways that differ substantially from Kracauer's earlier efforts. Maureen Turim suggests that psychoanalytic film theory can unpack the ways in which overt psychoanalytic narratives do not always satisfy the range of issues they raise. See her "Psychological Melodrama in the 1940s: *The Locket,*" *boundary 2* (1983–84): 321–32.

48 South America has been a favorite locale for postwar films about Nazis since a fair number of ranking Nazis escaped there at the end of the war. For specifics on the role of South America in the war, see Conn Stetson and Byron Fairchild, *The Framework of Hemisphere Defense: The U.S. Army in World War II, the Western Hemisphere,* vol. I (Washington, DC: Office of Military History, Department of the Army, 1960); and R. A. Humphreys, *Latin American and the Second World War,* vols. 1–2 (Atlantic Highlands, NJ: Humanities Press, 1981–82).

49 Tania Modleski, *The Women Who Knew Too Much: Hitchcock and Feminist Theory* (New York: Methuen, 1988), 58.

50 Robinson's edited volume addresses the purported wartime increase in "juvenile delinquency, general sexual looseness and wartime crime" (Victor Robinson, ed., *Morals in Wartime* [New York: Publishers Foundation, 1943], vii). Robinson was Professor of the History of Medicine at the Temple University School of Medicine. See also Philip Wylie, *Generation of Vipers,* 20th ed. (New York: Farrar and Rinehart, 1955), discussed below.

51 In German-speaking former Axis countries, the Nazis were transformed into drug dealers. That this should make sense indicates that there is some degree of interchangeableness between the "decadence" of drug addiction—a tradition from late-nineteenth-century texts—and that of Nazism. Eve Sedgwick points out that drug addiction and homosexuality are conceptually interrelated in Western culture. See Eve Kosofsky Sedgwick, *Epistemology of the Closet* (Berkeley and Los Angeles: University of California Press, 1990), 173.

52 Corber, 203.

53 Wylie, 206. Wylie elaborates on the moral decay for which moms (and enfranchised women generally) can be blamed. He writes, "Mom's first gracious presence at the ballot-box was roughly concomitant with the start toward a new all-time low in political scurviness, hoodlumism, gangsterism, labor strife, monopolistic thuggery, moral degeneration, civic corruption, smuggling, bribery, theft, murder, homosexuality, drunkenness, financial depression, chaos and war" (206).

54 In the 1955 edition of *Generation of Vipers,* Wylie includes a new introduction in which he reports that thus far his book had sold more than 180,000 copies. His lengthy list of boasts includes the claims that the American Library Association selected his book in 1950 as one of the major nonfiction works of the first half of the century and that "it no longer seems possible for any author, lay or scientific, to discuss motherhood and mom without noting that the dark side of that estate was defined earlier by me" (xii).

55 Edward Strecker, *Their Mothers' Sons: The Psychiatrist Examines an American Problem* (Philadelphia and New York: Lippincott, 1946), 133–34. Strecker was chair of the Department of Psychiatry at the University of Pennsylvania Medical School, a former president of the American Psychological Association, and an initial appointee to the National Advisory Mental Health Council (NIMH). During the war, he was a consultant to the surgeons general of the army and navy and an adviser to

the secretary of war. For a discussion of Strecker, see Jennifer Terry, "'Momism' and the Making of Treasonous Homosexuals," in Ladd-Taylor and Umansky, *"Bad" Mothers*, 169–90.

56 Strecker writes, "The German 'children' felt inferior and belittled. The other children would not play with them; mocked and derided them. . . . 'Don't fret children, Mom Fuehrer will fix it'" (134–36). He goes on to discuss "Nipponese Momism" as well, citing the Japanese devotion to the "Emperor-Mom" (139).

57 Wylie also calls moms the "thundering third sex," borrowing the label from nineteenth-century sexologists such as Karl Ulrichs, Havelock Ellis, and Richard von Krafft-Ebing, who used it to argue that homosexuals were neither male nor female but of another gender category (204). As I will go on to elaborate in part three, the Nazi dominatrix is the sexy counterpart to the decidedly unsexy but sexually ominous Nazi mom. Both are products of the masculinization of women via access to power, a consistent characterization that often, whether explicitly or not, inflects her with lesbianism/bisexuality.

58 Another wartime Hitchcock film, *Saboteur* (1942), features a related example of the horror of inappropriate gender behavior when the hero takes a long car ride with a Nazi agent, who spontaneously muses about his son. The boy's mother, it seems, wanted a girl, and so she lets the young son's hair grow long and has him wear dresses. This statement causes an intense outburst on the part of our all-American hero, who reads the practice as the production of a future pervert/Nazi.

59 Corber, 204.

60 Modleski, 60.

61 Dana Polan, *Power and Paranoia: History, Narrative, and the American Cinema, 1940–1950* (New York: Columbia University Press, 1986); Modleski, 65–66.

62 Modleski, 131, n. 6; Virginia Wright Wexman, "The Critic as Consumer: Film Study in the University, *Vertigo*, and the Film Canon," *Film Quarterly* 39.3 (1986): 32–41.

63 Modleski, 131, n. 6.

5 The American Nazi: Cold War Social Problem Films and National Psychobiography

1 Thomas C. Cochran, *The Great Depression and World War II, 1929–1945* (Glenview, IL: Scott, Foresman, 1968), 95.

2 When President Roosevelt officially recognized the Soviet government in 1933 (the same year the Nazis came to power in Germany), some of his opponents linked New Deal redistribution programs with communism and the expansion of federal powers with fascism. Earlier Red Scares (in the 1920s and earlier) attacked labor unions, feminists, and anarchists but were not linked to the federal government.

3 Walter Lippmann, *The Good Society* (Boston: Little, Brown, 1936). For a discussion, see Lynn Boyd Hinds and Theodore Otto Windt Jr., *The Cold War as Rhetoric: The Beginnings, 1945–1950* (New York: Praeger, 1991), 50.

4 Hinds and Windt, 48.

5 "Man of the Year," *Time*, 1 January 1940, 15; "Man of the Year," *Time*, 1 January 1942, 13.

6 Talcott Parsons, *Essays in Sociological Theory, Pure and Applied* (Glencoe, IL: Free Press, 1949), 104.

7 See Ellen Herman's discussion of wartime concerns over American "morale" and the postwar management of democracy in *The Romance of American Psychology: Political Culture in the Age of Experts* (Berkeley: University of California Press, 1995).

8 William G. Nunn was a particular proponent of the term *Double V* in the *Pittsburgh Courier*. See Thomas Cripps, *Making Movies Black: The Hollywood Message Movie from World War II to the Civil Rights Era* (New York: Oxford University Press, 1993), 28.

9 Gunnar Myrdal, *An American Dilemma: The Negro Problem and Modern Democracy* (New York and London: Harper and Brothers, 1944).

10 William Menninger, as quoted in Herman, 63. The passage is from Menninger's, *Psychiatry in a Troubled World: Yesterday's War and Today's Challenge* (New York: Macmillan, 1948). Herman credits Menninger with effecting the psychoanalytic turn in the psychiatric practices of the Armed Services, as four out of five civilian psychiatrists advising in the European theater had psychoanalytic training.

11 Bruno Bettelheim and Morris Janowitz, *Dynamics of Prejudice: A Psychological and Sociological Study of Veterans* (New York: Harper, 1950); Erik Erikson, *Childhood and Society* (New York: Norton, 1950); T. W. Adorno et al., *The Authoritarian Personality* (New York: Harper and Brothers, 1950). See also Jean-Paul Sartre's *Anti-Semite and Jew*, trans. George J. Becker (New York: Schocken, 1948), which was originally published in 1946; Lillian Smith, *Killers of the Dream* (New York: Norton, 1949); Gordon Allport, *The Nature of Prejudice* (Cambridge, MA: Addison-Wesley, 1954); R. Christie and Marie Jahoda, eds., *Studies in the Scope and Method of "The Authoritarian Personality"* (Glencoe, IL: Free Press, 1954).

12 See also Arthur Schlesinger Jr., *The Vital Center: The Politics of Freedom* (Boston: Houghton Mifflin, 1949); Lionel Trilling, *The Liberal Imagination: Essays on Literature and Society* (New York: Viking, 1950); and Leslie Fiedler, *An End to Innocence: Essays on Culture and Politics* (Boston: Beacon, 1955). For a discussion of this strategy by Cold War liberals, see Robert Corber, *In the Name of National Security: Hitchcock, Homophobia, and the Political Construction of Gender in Postwar America* (Durham: Duke University Press, 1993).

13 Robert Lindner, *The Fifty-Minute Hour: a Collection of True Psychoanalytic Tales*, 20th ed. (New York, Toronto, and London: Bantam, 1966). The book, originally published in 1954, was reissued by the Other Press in 1999.

14 In the television version, the patient was played by Robert Duvall and the analyst by Alexander Scourby.

15 These included *Rebel without a Cause: the Hypnoanalysis of a Criminal Psychopath* (New York: Grune and Stratton, 1944); *Must You Conform?* (New York: Rinehart, 1956); *Prescription for Rebellion* (New York: Rinehart, 1952); and *Stone Walls and Men* (New York: Odyssey, 1946). Lindner was trained by Theodor Reik, a student of Freud's.

16 Nathan Hale Jr., *The Rise and Crisis of Psychoanalysis in the U.S.: Freud and the Americans, 1917–1985* (New York and Oxford: Oxford University Press, 1995), 76–77, 276. Benjamin Spock, whose 1946 book *Baby and Child Care* (New York: Hawthorn, 1968) virtually raised a generation of children, was also a popularizing force

(Spock attended a psychoanalytic institute in the 1930s). The book sold 19 million copies by 1965.

17 Max Lerner, Introduction to Lindner, *The Fifty-Minute Hour*, ix. Lerner had both an academic and journalistic career, which included his 1957 book *America as a Civilization* (New York: Simon and Schuster, 1957).

18 See Hale's chapter on popularized psychoanalytic accounts, especially page 280.

19 Lindner, *The Fifty-Minute Hour*, 78.

20 I have not been able to locate a tape of this broadcast, and so my references to the program refer to the script, entitled "Destiny's Tot" (like Lindner's case history), adapted for television by S. Lee Pogostin, with copyright held by the Stanley Kramer Corp. ("Pressure Point" file, University of California, Los Angeles, Department of Special Collections, University Research Library).

21 Kramer entered production through independent channels, with the financing for *Home of the Brave*, his first film, coming from a private investor (Cripps, 222).

22 Quoted in Lester J. Keyser and Andre H. Ruszkowski, *The Cinema of Sidney Poitier: The Black Man's Changing Role on the American Screen* (San Diego and New York: A. S. Barnes, 1980), 70–71.

23 Quoted in Edward Mapp, *Blacks in American Films: Today and Yesterday* (Metuchen, NJ: Scarecrow Press, 1972), 62.

24 In the 1930s, the most common response to agitation to change offensive roles for Blacks was to eliminate them entirely, resulting in even fewer roles for Black actors (Cripps, 28–29).

25 *The Life of Emil Zola* (1937), for instance, conveys the Dreyfus affair without ever uttering the word *Jew*. *The Mortal Storm* (1940)—a "prematurely antifascist" film—is still cautious on this count, referring to the population targeted by the Nazis not as Jews but as "non-Aryans." The American Jewish Committee (a relatively conservative entity) thought it unwise to focus solely on the Nazis' treatment of Jews, and so thought their barbarities should be portrayed as if they were directed at everyone (Cripps, 216–17).

26 The centrality of race relations and racial imagery to the American film industry spans the entire length of its history, prompting Michael Rogin to write "American literature . . . established its national identity in the struggle between Indians and whites. [But] American film was born from white depictions of Blacks" (*Blackface, White Noise* [Berkeley: University of California Press, 1996], 15). Postwar psychological studies of white/Black racism include William Lloyd Warner et al., *Color and Human Nature: Negro Personality Development in a Northern City* (Washington, DC: American Council on Education, 1947); Robert Lee Sutherland, *Color, Class and Personality* (Washington, DC: American Council on Education, 1952); and Bertram Karon, *The Negro Personality: A Rigorous Investigation of the Effects of Culture* (New York: Springer, 1958). The strong history of Jewish/Black alliance in the fight against racism also forms a part of the historical milieu.

27 Singer, actor, and outspoken leftist activist Paul Robeson was an important predecessor to Poitier. Working mostly in Britain, Robeson made numerous films addressing racism. Harry Belafonte, Poitier's contemporary, was more bohemian and harder edged and so was ultimately pushed out of Hollywood (see Cripps, 252).

28 Arthur Laurents, *Home of the Brave* (New York: Random House, 1946). See also

Michele Wallace, "Race, Gender, and Psychoanalysis in Forties Film: *Lost Boundaries, Home of the Brave*, and *The Quiet One*," in *Black American Cinema*, ed. Manthia Diawara (New York: Routledge, 1993), 257–71.

29 Franz Fanon, *Black Skins, White Masks*, trans. Charles Lam Markmann (New York: Grove, 1967), 159–60, 165. The book was originally published in French in 1952.

30 Ruth Feldstein, "Antiracism and Maternal Failure in the 1940s and 1950s," in *"Bad" Mothers: The Politics of Blame in Twentieth-Century America*, ed. Molly Ladd-Taylor and Lauri Umansky (New York and London: New York University Press, 1998), 145.

31 In a script marked "final draft" and dated 13 September 1961, the doctor is still Jewish. With the announcement in *Variety* two months later that Poitier had been cast in the role, a new series of significant revisions began, with a script close to the shooting script completed by 3 March 1962 (the film was released in September). The first version of the film script was written by S. Lee Pogostin, who also had adapted Lindner's case for television. Hubert Cornfield, the director of the film, took over the revisions after this first version ("Pressure Point" file, University of California, Los Angeles, Department of Special Collections, University Research Library).

32 For an extended discussion of the narrative nature of psychoanalysis, see Roy Schafer, "Narration in the Psychoanalytic Dialogue," in *On Narrative*, ed. W. J. T. Mitchell (Chicago: University of Chicago Press, 1981).

33 Sander L. Gilman, *The Jew's Body* (New York: Routledge, 1991); *Freud, Race, and Gender* (New York: Routledge, 1993). See also Daniel Boyarin, *Unheroic Conduct: The Rise of Heterosexuality and the Invention of the Jewish Man* (Berkeley: University of California Press, 1996).

34 Included in this shift is the fact that women came to signify castration and lack. As Ann Pellegrini notes in her discussion of this phenomenon in Freud's thinking, Jewish women are left out of the equation (*Performance Anxieties: Staging Psychoanalysis, Staging Race* [New York: Routledge, 1997], 4).

35 This is how the exchange appears in the first film script by S. Lee Pogostin, which is an accurate but more compact transcription of the exchange in Lindner (122). See "Pressure Point" file, University of California, Los Angeles, Department of Special Collections, University Research Library.

36 Lindner, *The Fifty-Minute Hour*, 147–48.

37 Ibid., 149.

38 Rogin, 69.

39 The relevance of racial differences between patient and analyst is explored by later clinical work examining the particular dynamics of analytic situations like the one dramatized in *Pressure Point*. See Schachter and Butts, "Transference and Countertransference in Inter-racial Analyses," *Journal of the American Psychoanalytic Association* 16 (1971): 796. For a discussion and criticism of this article, see Neil Altman, *The Analyst in the Inner City: Race, Class, and Culture through a Psychoanalytic Lens* (Hillsdale, NJ, and London: Analytic Press, 1995), 91.

40 To Kramer and Cornfield's credit, a new dimension is added to the patient-doctor conflict around the parole confrontation in that two new scenes, not present in any of the earlier versions, portray the Doctor in conflict with his professional peers, who do not heed his judgment.

41 As Rogin writes, "Racial subordination formed the American nation, giving racist

stereotypes an intractable material base resistant to the liberal wish for equality. Thus white predation was inverted and assigned to colored nature, most famously in the attributions to Indians of violence and lack of respect for the property of others, and in the assignment to Black men of laziness and sexual desire for white women" (25).

42 Sander L. Gilman, *Difference and Pathology: Stereotypes of Sexuality, Race, and Madness* (Ithaca: Cornell University Press, 1985). Gilman delineates the connection especially between Black hypersexuality and "deviant" female sexuality (lesbians and lower-class prostitutes) and cites the fixation of doctors and anthropologists on the supposedly "overdeveloped" genitalia of African women, lesbians, and prostitutes.

43 Rogin, 34. For a contrast to the tradition of African-American performance formed under slavery, see Saidiya Hartman, *Scenes of Subjection: Terror, Slavery, and Self-Making in Nineteenth-Century America* (New York: Oxford University Press, 1997).

44 Lindner, *The Fifty-Minute Hour*, 151.

45 Ibid., 154.

46 Some Black feminists have argued against psychoanalysis (and middle-class white feminism), claiming the family as a source of strength rather than oppression. See Lola Young, *Fear of the Dark: 'Race,' Gender, and Sexuality in the Cinema* (London and New York: Routledge, 1996), 14.

47 These differences include seeing bad white mothers as individual neurotics while Black mothers as a group comprise a "cultural pathology." See Regina Kunzel's essay on how this distinction plays out in the different characterizations of white and Black unwed mothers in "White Neurosis, Black Pathology: Constructing Out-of-Wedlock Pregnancy in the Wartime and Postwar United States," in *Not June Cleaver: Women and Gender in Postwar America, 1945–1960*, ed. Joanne Meyerowitz (Philadelphia: Temple University Press, 1994), 304–31.

48 See Herman, 184. Fanon's work is an exception to this formulation (though no less supportive of patriarchal family organization) in that he postulated that instead of the Black family producing the "neurotic" African-American adult it was only once a Black person was forced to confront his or her degradation by white culture's sense of its own superiority that he or she would be doomed to a split ego imposed by a self-hating idealization of the white Other (Fanon, 143).

49 Thomas F. Pettigrew, *A Profile of the Negro American* (Princeton, NJ: Van Nostrand, 1964), 20. These data are from Pettigrew's own study, "Father Absence and Negro Adult Personality: A Research Note," which he cites as an unpublished paper. See also E. Franklin Frazier, *The Negro Family in the United States* (Chicago: University of Chicago Press, 1939); Charles Johnson, *Growing up in the Black Belt: Negro Youth in the Rural South* (Washington, DC: American Council on Education, 1941); Horace Cayton and St. Clair Drake, *Black Metropolis: A Study of Negro Life in a Northern City* (New York: Harcourt, Brace, 1945); Abram Kardiner and Lionel Ovesey, *The Mark of Oppression: A Psychological Study of the American Negro* (New York: Norton, 1951); and Kenneth Clark, *Dark Ghetto: Dilemmas of Social Power* (New York: Harper and Row, 1965).

50 Daniel P. Moynihan, *The Negro Family: The Case for National Action* (Washington, DC: Office of Policy Planning and Research, Department of Labor, 1965). Her-

man points out that Moynihan actually attributes lower educational achievement, high crime rates, etc. more to class than race, even though this is not how the report was ultimately understood. The misreading is in part due to the fact that it was released just as the Watts riots broke out in Los Angeles (Herman, 205–6).

51 Angela Y. Davis, *Women, Race, and Class* (New York: Vintage, 1981), 14.

52 Hortense J. Spillers, "Mama's Baby, Papa's Maybe: An American Grammar Book," *diacritics* (summer 1987): 74.

53 There is both sexist bias and an obvious lack of understanding of cultural difference in these conclusions. Pettigrew marks gender inversion, for instance, in that Black men scored higher on the "femininity" scale of the Minnesota Multiphasic Inventory (MMPI) because they agreed more often than white men with such "feminine" choices as "I would like to be a singer" and "I think that I feel more intensely than most people do." Black women were thought to be "masculine" because "Negro girls revealed interests generally associated with males; compared with the white girls, they value theoretical and political concerns more and religious and esthetic concerns less" (Pettigrew, 18–19).

54 Indeed, "disturbed sexual identification" and political consciousness are often collapsed in the evidence presented to characterize both "prejudiced" white women and fatherless Black men, as in each case a sense of systemic injustices (stemming from sexism and racism) perpetrated against them are interpreted as symptoms of their *political* as well as sexual maladjustment.

55 Herman, 190.

56 See M. M. Grossack, "Group Belongingness and Authoritarianism in Southern Negroes: A Research Note," *Phylon* 18 (1957): 261–66; G. A. Steckler, "Authoritarian Ideology in Negro College Students," *Journal of Abnormal and Social Psychology* 54 (1957): 396–99; and an unpublished paper of his own that Pettigrew cites "Authoritarianism among Negro Americans," 36.

57 Fanon, 166.

58 An interesting fictional example of this forging of equivalencies of fears between Nazis and American cultural minorities is manifested in Sidney Lumet's 1965 film *The Pawnbroker*, in which the phenomenon is complicated by the fact that it is a Jewish Holocaust survivor who collapses these groups and Nazis. Much has lately been made of the apparent conflict and/or alliance between Jews and Blacks, where complex issues are at stake. See my "Pressure Points: Political Psychology, Screen adaptation, and the Management of Racism in the Case History Genre," *Camera Obscura* 45 (2000): 1–43; Cornell West, *Race Matters* (Boston: Beacon Press, 1993); Michael Lerner and Cornel West, *Jews and Blacks: Let the Healing Begin* (New York: Grosset/Putnam, 1995); Robert Reid-Pharr, "Speaking through Anti-Semitism: The Nation of Islam and the Poetics of Black (Counter)Modernity," *Social Text* 49 (1996): 133–47; and Andrew Hacker, "Jewish Racism, Black Anti-Semitism," *Reconstruction* 1.3 (1991): 14–17.

59 The association of homosexuality with a regressive psychical structure developed independently of the analysis of fascism, but they began to merge in the manner of the psychical template for deviation described above. Psychoanalysts who made the connection explicit included Abram Kardiner, in *Sex and Morality* (New York: Bobbs-Merrill, 1954), and Edmund Bergler, in *One Thousand Homosexuals: Conspiracy of Silence or Curing and Deglamorizing Homosexuals?* (Paterson, NJ: Pageant, 1959).

60 As clinical psychologist Kenneth Lewes writes, "It is a striking fact of our history that both the conviction that homosexual object choice was necessarily psychopathological and the extremity of negative characterizations of homosexual general functioning became prominent in the years following World War II. . . . It is remarkable how many times in the postwar period homosexuals were compared to Nazis" (*The Psychoanalytic Theory of Male Homosexuality* [New York: New American Library, 1988], 232).

61 Clifford Kirkpatrick, *Nazi Germany: Its Women and Family Life* (Indianapolis and New York: Bobbs-Merrill, 1938), 103.

62 For research on the actual treatment of homosexuals in Nazi Germany, see Burkhard Jellonnek, *Homosexuelle unter dem Hakenkreuz: die Verfolgung von Homosexuellen im Dritten Reich* (Paderborn: F. Schöningh, 1990); and Geoffrey J. Giles, "'The Most Unkindest Cut of All': Castration, Homosexuality and Nazi Justice," *Journal of Contemporary History* 27 (1992): 41–61. For postwar Germany, see Robert G. Moeller, "'The Homosexual Man Is a 'Man,' the Homosexual Woman Is a 'Woman'": Sex, Society, and the Law in Postwar West Germany," *Journal of the History of Sexuality* 4.3 (1994): 395–429.

63 Rodney Collin, "Sex and the New Germany," *Living Age* 346 (March 1934): 25. Andrew Hewitt, in his study of the leftist variant of the connection between homosexuality and fascism, argues that dialectical thought is heterosexually coded, hence homosexuality appears undialectical, antihistorical, and *theoretically* fascistic. See Andrew Hewitt, *Political Inversions: Homosexuality, Fascism, and the Modernist Imaginary* (Stanford, CA: Stanford University Press, 1996), 9.

64 Adorno et al., 315–16.

65 Ibid., 318.

66 Lindner, *The Fifty-Minute Hour*, 150.

67 The Doctor's voice-over very obliquely comments that he "acted out satisfactions that were not always proper yet sharply revealing."

68 Lindner also claims that it is the patient's sadistic bisexuality (which he describes as being "indiscriminate"), not just his homosexuality, that characterizes the patient's psychopathy (*The Fifty-Minute Hour*, 150). For an analysis of the rhetorical role of sexual psychopathy, see Estelle Freedman, "'Uncontrolled Desires': The Response to the Sexual Psychopath, 1920–1960," in *Passion and Power: Sexuality in History*, ed. Kathy Peiss and Christina Simmons (Philadelphia: Temple University Press, 1989), 199–225.

69 The "jilted lover" explanation for fascism appears in the wartime B movie *Enemy of Women*, in which Joseph Goebbels recognizes Hitler as his führer on the same night that he is rejected by the fictional Maria Brandt. His lifelong obsession with her parallels his political fanaticism, seen to be a compensation for what he is lacking as a man. See Jan-Christopher Horak, *Anti-Nazi-Filme: der deutschsprachigen Emigration von Hollywood, 1939–1945* (Münster: MAKS Publicationen, 1985), 214.

70 Lindner, *The Fifty-Minute Hour*, 151.

71 It is possible, if not likely, that the submersion of the association of homosexuality with fascism represents a growing awareness of the oppression of sexual minorities. Adrian Scott, the producer of *Crossfire* (1947), for instance, justified the change of the novel's focus on homophobia to the film's focus on anti-Semitism thus: "In the book [*The Brick Foxhole*, the soldier] murders a fairy. He could have

murdered a negro, a foreigner or a jew. It would have been the same thing" (quoted in Corber, 86). See also Richard Brooks, *The Brick Foxhole* (New York: Harper, 1945). This parallel was also tenuously supported academically, as Donald Webster Corey, for instance, modeled his 1951 study of homophobia after Myrdal's 1944 book on American racism. See Donald Webster Corey, *The Homosexual in America: A Subjective Approach* (New York: Greenberg, 1951). Unfortunately, Corey later repudiated his views.

72 Mengele served as chief medical officer at Auschwitz and supervised a horrendous series of experiments meant to further Nazi eugenic aims. After the war, he fled to Argentina, where he narrowly escaped capture by Israeli agents in 1960, fleeing to Paraguay, and finally to Brazil, where his remains were identified through genetic testing in 1985.

6 Skinheads, Militiamen, and the Legacies of Failed Masculinity

1 Andrew Macdonald, *The Turner Diaries* (Hillsboro, WV: National Vanguard Books, 1993). The book was originally published in 1978. Pierce is a longtime fixture on the neo-Nazi scene. He was leader of the American Nazi Party in the 1960s, and his National Alliance continues to publish and distribute white supremacist books and periodicals and sponsor Pierce's shortwave radio programs.

2 Ibid., 48–49.

3 Ibid., 73. For a fuller account of the activities of The Order, see David H. Bennett, *The Party of Fear: The American Far Right from Nativism to the Militia Movement*, 2d ed. (New York: Vintage, 1995), 348; and Stephen Singular, *Talked to Death: The Murder of Alan Berg* (New York: Beech Tree Books, 1987).

4 The 1991 documentary *Blood in the Face*, for instance, directed by Anne Bohlen, Kevin Rafferty, and James Ridgeway, concludes by reminding viewers of former Ku Klux Klan leader and 1988 presidential hopeful David Duke's political origins. The filmmakers thus reverse the strategy of disassociation that the Duke campaign tried to deploy. See also James Ridgeway, *Blood in the Face: The Ku Klux Klan, Aryan Nations, Nazi Skinheads, and the Rise of the New White Culture* (New York: Thunder's Mouth Press, 1990).

5 *Australia/Israel Review* 23.9 (1998) as referred to in *Daily Telegraph*, 9 July 1998, 1.

6 Emma-Kate Symons, "I Don't Want Racists in My One Nation," *Daily Telegraph*, 10 July 1998, 4. See also David Bernstein, "One Nation List Causes Red Faces on Both Sides," *Sydney Morning Herald*, 10 July 1998, 17; Keith Austin, "Blacklisted: The Publication of the List of 2,000 One Nation Members and Donors Has Sparked a Debate Wider Than the Fight against Racism," *Sydney Morning Herald*, 10 July 1998, 13.

7 In the film, Schindler's list contains the names of Jews *saved* by Oscar Schindler, making this a very convoluted headline.

8 Greg Roberts, "One Nation Alleges Theft of Names List," *Sydney Morning Herald*, 10 July 1998, 4.

9 Stanley Fish, "Reverse Racism, or, How the Pot Got to Call the Kettle Black," in

There's No Such Thing as Free Speech, and It's a Good Thing, Too (New York: Oxford University Press, 1994), 68–69.

10 Letter from Anthony Ranyard, *Daily Telegraph*, 10 July 1998, 12.

11 Andrew Macdonald, *Hunter* (Hillsboro, WV: National Vanguard Books, 1989), 169, 208.

12 Ibid., 223.

13 Loretta J. Ross and Mary Ann Mauney, "The Changing Faces of White Supremacy" (Atlanta Center for Democratic Renewal, 1996), reprinted in *Critical White Studies: Looking behind the Mirror*, ed. Richard Delgado and Jean Stefancic (Philadelphia: Temple University Press, 1997), 552, 556.

14 "Equal Hostility: Some Women Are Angry at Government, Too," *Wall Street Journal*, 12 May 1995, A7.

15 *Los Angeles Times*, 27 July 1998, A11. The ad was paid for by the Alliance for Traditional Marriage—Hawaii, the American Family Association, Americans for Truth about Homosexuality, the Center for Reclaiming America, the Christian Family Network, the Christian Coalition, Citizens for Community Values, Colorado for Family Values, Concerned Women for America, Coral Ridge Ministries, Family First, the Family Research Council, the Liberty Counsel, the National Legal Foundation, and Kerusso Ministries.

16 Macdonald, *The Turner Diaries*, 38.

17 McVeigh's choice of 19 April for the bombing reflects his preoccupation with the 1993 conclusion to the Waco standoff. On this day, the remaining members of the religious group calling itself the Branch Davidians, led by David Koresh, were killed in a fire of questionable origin. The siege of the group's compound by federal law enforcement agencies is widely considered to have been sorely mishandled.

18 Furrow is a white supremacist who killed a Filipino American postman and shot and wounded five people, including three children, at a Jewish community center on 10 August 1999. Smith, a member of the racist World Church of the Creator, went on a shooting spree on 4 July 1999, killing two and wounding eight others before taking his own life.

19 Closing arguments delivered on 29 May 1997, transcript of U.S. District Court for the District of Colorado, Criminal Action no. 96–CR–68 (*United States of America, Plaintiff, v. Timothy James McVeigh, Defendant*).

20 There is little consistency about how the book is described in the news media. In Cable News Network (CNN) reports on the McVeigh trial, descriptions of *The Turner Diaries* range from "an anti-government diatribe that describes an attack on a federal building" (no mention of racism) to "a racist novel that begins with the bombing of a federal building." "Arms Dealer: McVeigh Wanted Detonation Cord 'Bad'" ⟨http://www.cnn.com⟩, 1 May 1997. "Friends, Fellow Soldiers Describe McVeigh as a Man of Valor, Contradictions" ⟨http://www.cnn.com⟩, 9 June 1997. "White Supremacist Novel Key Evidence in McVeigh Trial" ⟨http://www.cnn.com⟩, 24 March 1997.

21 Patricia King, "'Vipers' in the 'Burbs,'" *Newsweek*, 15 July 1996, 21.

22 In a similar move, an extended profile of McVeigh found on the CNN web site put it thus: "During his time in the Army, he also read and recommended to others "The Turner Diaries,"—a racist, anti-Semitic novel about a soldier in an underground army. A former roommate said that McVeigh would panic at the prospect

of the government taking away peoples' guns, but that he was not a racist and was basically indifferent to racial matters." Profile of Timothy McVeigh from ⟨http://www.cnn.com⟩, 12 April 1999.

23   What has come to be called the New Right—generally understood as those conservative social movements spawned in response to the rise of the New Left in the 1960s and 1970s—is not entirely "new" in that most of the movements are connected to much longer standing traditions (both mainstream and fringe) that have experienced various waves of prominence in American political history. Most have little or no explicit connection to neo-Nazism. See Sara Diamond, *Roads to Dominion: Right-Wing Movements and Political Power in the United States* (New York: Guilford Press, 1995), 23; and Russ Bellant, *Old Nazis, the New Right, and the Republican Party* (Boston: South End Press, 1988).

24   Not all skinheads are neo-Nazis, and some are explicitly antiracist. For example, members of Skinheads against Racial Prejudice (SHARP) spend most of their time either street fighting with neo-Nazi skinheads or complaining about the fact that they are often mistaken for neo-Nazis by people who don't know the difference. There is also a zine called *The GSM* (for the Gay Skinhead Movement), a subgroup of SHARP, that features many articles and letters in which gay SHARPs complain of being mistaken for neo-Nazis. For an account of the origins of the skinhead style, see Dick Hebdige, *Subculture: The Meaning of Style* (London: Methuen, 1979), 117.

25   Ross and Mauney, 555.

26   Various neo-Nazi skinhead groups went on to commit more than twenty-five murders in the United States alone between 1992 and 1995, with most victims being African-American, Latino-American, Asian-American, gay, lesbian, or homeless (Bennett, 434). These are the statistics of the Anti-Defamation League.

27   Morris Dees of the Alabama-based Southern Poverty Law Center, along with the Anti-Defamation League, subsequently brought suit on behalf of Seraw to connect WAR and Metzger to the murder and shut down his operation. Metzger lost his final appeal in 1993.

28   Bruce LaBruce's satire *No Skin Off My Ass* (1991) is an experimental film about a gay punk hairdresser who becomes obsessed with a skinhead. This film is clearly camp and doesn't really fall into the larger genre. La Bruce's more recent film, *Skin Flick* (1999), a porn tape featuring skinheads, cannot be so easily classified as camp. For a thoughtful review of the film, see Michael Achtman, "Über Allies: Do Fascism and Porn Mix?" *Xtra! Toronto's Gay and Lesbian Biweekly*, 18 November 1999, 33.

29   German social theorist Hans Magnus Enzensberger comments sarcastically on the German government's sympathetic response to skinhead violence: "The politicians, meanwhile, have taken the stage in a new role: they've become social workers. There have been pleas for understanding the harsh reality of unemployment; we have been asked to view the killers as being 'culturally disorientated' or as 'poor swine' who must be treated with the utmost patience. After all, it is hardly possible to expect such underprivileged persons to realize that setting fire to children is, strictly speaking, not permissible. Attention must be drawn all the more urgently to the inadequate supply of leisure activities available to the arsonists" ("The Great Migration," trans. Martin Chalmers, *Granta* 42 [1992]: 50).

30   The skinhead movement in Sweden follows the pattern established in other coun-

tries, having extensive links to other skinhead and larger white supremacist groups, especially in Great Britain and the United States. Members of The Order are said to have been in correspondence with Swedish skinheads (from prison), influencing the establishment of Vitt Ariskt Motstand (VAM, White Aryan Resistance). Books like *The Turner Diaries* and printed materials from American Nazi Gary Lauck also circulate among Swedish skinheads. See Anti-Defamation League, *The Skinhead International: A Worldwide Survey of Neo-Nazi Skinheads* (New York: Anti-Defamation League, 1995). The Nizkor Project, Hebrew for "we will remember," is dedicated to the victims of the Nazis, makes resources available on the Holocaust (and its denial), and tracks neo-Nazi groups. See ⟨http://www.nizkor.org⟩.

31 See, for instance, Walter C. Langer, *The Mind of Adolf Hitler: The Secret Wartime Report* (New York: Basic Books, 1972); Erik H. Erikson, "On Nazi Mentality," in *A Way of Looking at Things: Selected Papers from 1930 to 1980*, ed. Stephen Schlein (New York: Norton, 1987); and Harold P. Lasswell, "The Psychology of Hitlerism," *Political Quarterly* 4 (July-September 1933): 380.

32 Tamara Jones, "Germany's Troubles," *Los Angeles Times Magazine*, 7 March 1993, 17–18.

33 Perhaps the most absurd variant of the viewpoint that skinheads are merely vying for parental attention is reflected in a "checklist for parents" that appeared in the German tabloid *Bild* the day after a skinhead murdered three Turkish women. The checklist includes such suggestions as getting your potentially neo-Nazi son a membership in a sports club and having his new friends over for dinner as possible deterrents. See "Has My Child Become a Neo-Nazi?" reprinted in *Granta* 42 (1992): 143.

34 Kathy Dobie, "Long Day's Journey into White," *Village Voice*, 28 April 1992, 25.

35 Mark S. Hamm, *American Skinheads: The Criminology and Control of Hate Crime* (Westport, CT: Praeger, 1993), 183.

36 Gideon McLean, the skinhead bandleader whose image caused such a stir in the One Nation Party membership list publication discussed above, performs a song called "White Working Class Woman," for instance, which concludes with the lines "For my white working class woman / the future of our nation's in her hand / White working class woman / she is the pride of every man." McLean is a member of Southern Cross Hammer Skins, which has branches in both Melbourne and Sydney. Its motto is "We must secure the existence of our people and a future for white children," a slogan first coined by David Lane, an American neo-Nazi.

37 Australian neo-Nazi skinheads have a similar record of violence and political affiliation with larger groups, both domestic and international. The Australian Nationalist Movement and Australian National Action, two Far Right groups, actively recruited skinheads in 1993 and 1994. See Anti-Defamation League, *The Skinhead International*.

38 *Romper Stomper* press materials, Academy Entertainment, 2.

39 See, for instance, Paul Willis, *Learning to Labor: How Working Class Kids Get Working Class Jobs* (New York: Columbia University Press, 1977); and Fred Pfeil, "Sympathy for the Devils: Notes on Some White Guys in the Ridiculous Class War," in *Whiteness: a Critical Reader*, ed. Mike Hill (New York and London: New York University Press, 1997), 21–34.

40 *Romper Stomper* press materials, 9.

41 Tom O'Regan, *Australian National Cinema* (London and New York: Routledge, 1996), 150–51.

42 Lauren Berlant, *The Queen of America Goes to Washington City: Essays on Sex and Citizenship* (Durham and London: Duke University Press, 1997), 178.

43 O'Regan, 151.

44 Smith, the twenty-one-year-old white supremacist who went on a 4 July 1999 shooting spree, grew up in a wealthy Chicago suburb. He father is a doctor, his mother a real-estate agent.

45 Ed Scheid, "Pariah," Boxoffice Online Movie Reviews, ⟨http://www.boxoff.com⟩.

46 Film critic David Sterritt presents another twist on this dynamic, as he does not seek to identify with the skinheads in *Romper Stomper* but rather wants to identify with their victims. The work he does to absolve the incestuous father, however (as an especially aggrieved victim), reveals a persistent desire to find a flawed white man with which to identify, avoiding identification with women and people of color and ensuring a continued place for dominant white patriarchal privilege. See David Sterritt, "Romper Stomper," *Christian Science Monitor*, 11 June 1993, 12. See also Stephen Holden, "Of Skinheads High on Hate and Violence," *New York Times*, 9 June 1993, C17.

47 Randolph D. Calverhall, *Serpent's Walk* (Hillsboro, WV: National Vanguard Books, 1991), 78–79.

48 Macdonald, *Hunter*, 53.

49 Quoted in the review of *American History X* from Hollywood Online, ⟨http://www.hollywood.com⟩, cited on 11 February 1999.

50 Ron Wells, "American History X," *Film Threat Weekly* ⟨http://www.filmthreat.com⟩, cited on 19 October 1998.

51 The New Line Cinema website for the film claims: "Attracted to *American History X* because of the relevant social issues the film addresses, Kaye has put his talent toward other thought-provoking societal concerns, such as Greenpeace, Drug-Free America, Romanian orphans, and a documentary he has been making for the last four years that explores the abortion debate in the United States." *American History X* official website, ⟨http://www.historyx.com⟩.

52 Kaye filed suit against New Line Pictures, alleging that because it allowed Edward Norton to decide some edits his artistic and political vision had been compromised. Indeed, Kaye had negotiated for extra time in which to provide a balancing Black voice-over with playwright Derek Walcott, but he did not complete the work before the film was released. While attending the Berlin Film Festival, he made a statement at the Brandenberg Gate wherein he said that Norton's edits had the effect of "increasing his role while decreasing the integrity of the film." He added that "the producers denied me the opportunity to present a black voice to provide depth and balance to the film" (press release, 6 February 1999, Tony Kaye [source]). The problems of the film are, however, far more endemic. See also Patrick Goldstein, "Courting Trouble: In *American History X*, the Biggest Turf Battles Have Happened Off-Screen," *Los Angeles Times*, 13 September 1998, Calendar, 5.

53 A version of this genre is frequently invoked on a larger scale by right-wing politicians such as Helen Chenoweth (a congresswoman from Idaho) and Pauline

Hanson (the leader of Australia's One Nation Party), who claim that in the current political climate white Anglo-Saxon men are the most persecuted. See Charles Sykes, *A Nation of Victims: The Decay of the American Character* (New York: St. Martin's, 1992).

54 Eve Kosofsky Sedgwick, *Epistemology of the Closet* (Berkeley and Los Angeles: University of California Press, 1990), 145.

55 "The Plot," *Newsweek*, 8 May 1995, 29–30. Other news sources reported that McVeigh "was also a loner who never seemed to have a girlfriend, never talked about his family, and kept to his barracks reading *Guns & Ammo* and watching TV," while Nichols is described as a "spastic, nerdy kind of guy" (Elizabeth Gleick, " 'Something Big Is Going to Happen,' " *Time*, 8 May 1995, 51; "The Plot," 31). See also Sara Rimer, "With Extremism and Explosives, a Drifting Life Found a Purpose," *New York Times*, 28 May 1995, A1, 12–13.

56 Overt efforts to prevent the association of normative, patriarchal masculinity with McVeigh's acts include the fact that some reports note that he gave a copy of *The Turner Diaries* to an army buddy in 1989, implying that his desire to join the army was itself compensation for his flawed masculinity, while the spokesperson for the army claimed that it must have been after he left the army (as a result of another disappointing failure to make the Special Forces unit) that he turned to unacceptable politics. McVeigh categorically repudiated each of these efforts to profile him in this way, claiming that neither his parents' divorce nor his failure to become a Green Beret had a profound effect on him ("The Plot," 30; Gleick, 51).

57 Mark Potok and Katy Kelly, "Militia Movement's Draw: A Shared Anger, Fear," *USA Today*, 16 May 1995, D6. For his part, McVeigh, too, tried to put his most "normal" face on for a public interview—a "normality" the *Newsweek* reporters who interviewed him were readily willing to grant, stating that ". . . he seemed a lot more like a typical Gen-Xer than a deranged loner, much less a terrorist. His handshake was firm, and he looked his visitors right in the eye. He appeared a little nervous, maybe, but good-humored and self-aware. Normal" (David H. Hackworth and Peter Annin, "The Suspect Speaks Out," *Newsweek*, 3 July 1995, 23).

58 "Pssst! Calling All Paranoids," *Time*, 8 May 1995, 69.

59 For a nearly identical view, see Michael Janofsky, "Demons and Conspiracies Haunt a 'Patriot' World," *New York Times*, 31 May 1995, A18.

60 See, for instance, Linda Pattillo, "Shadowy Threat of Extremist Hate Groups Quietly Growing" ⟨http://www.cnn.com⟩, 24 April 1998. See also Hanna Rosen, "L.A. Shooting May Have Been Initiation Rite," *Washington Post*, 12 August 1999, A1.

61 Mike Hill, "Vipers in Shangri-la: Whiteness, Writing, and Other Ordinary Terrors," in *Whiteness: A Critical Reader*, ed. Mike Hill (New York and London: New York University Press, 1997), 2.

62 Fred Pfeil, for instance, writes that "The men's movement and the militias can be seen as differential responses to a general cultural and political situation, characterized by both a widespread confusion as to what men—including and perhaps especially white men—are supposed to be, mean, and do and a related uncertainty about what this country—as a polity but even more as what Benedict Anderson terms an 'imagined community'—is supposed to be, including whether it even works as a country any more" (Pfeil, 22). The extension of the concerns of white

men to the concerns of the entire nation is precisely the rhetorical move I have been describing.

63 Michael Rogin, *Ronald Reagan, the Movie and Other Episodes in Political Demonology* (Berkeley: University of California Press, 1987), 44.

7 The Iconology of the Sexy Nazi Woman: Marlene Dietrich as Political Palimpsest

1 Michael Rogin, *Ronald Reagan, the Movie and Other Episodes in Political Demonology* (Berkeley: University of California Press, 1987), 290.

2 Ben Hecht, treatment for *Notorious,* "Notorious" file, Margaret Herrick Library, Academy of Motion Picture Arts and Sciences, Beverly Hills, California.

3 Magnus Hirschfeld et al., *The Sexual History of the World War* (New York: Cadillac Publishing, 1941), 23. The study is in part dedicated to an analysis of sexual propaganda. The cartoon that was added to the English-language edition was inserted unironically by the American editors.

4 W. J. T. Mitchell, *Iconology: Image, Text, Ideology* (Chicago: University of Chicago Press, 1986).

5 Roland Barthes, *Image, Music, Text,* trans. Stephen Heath (New York: Hill and Wang, 1977), 32.

6 William Blake put it most famously when he wrote "Time is a man, Space is a woman." Edmund Burke (1757) and Gotthold Lessing (1766) also associated poetry and time with the masculine and painting and space with the feminine. See Mitchell, 112–13.

7 Mary Ann Doane, *Femmes Fatales: Feminism, Film Theory, Psychoanalysis* (New York: Routledge, 1991), 1.

8 Teresa de Lauretis, *Alice Doesn't: Feminist, Semiotics, Cinema* (Bloomington: Indiana University Press, 1984), 7–8.

9 Bram Dijkstra, *Idols of Perversity: Fantasies of Feminine Evil in Fin-de-Siècle Culture* (New York and Oxford: Oxford University Press, 1986), 145, 221. Images of sirens as symbols of sexual voracity are particularly relevant to my study given their luring and deadly song (258).

10 George Mosse, *Nationalism and Sexuality: Respectability and Abnormal Sexuality in Modern Europe* (New York: Howard Fertig, 1985), 17.

11 Ibid., 103–4. Mosse notes how the late-nineteenth-century cultural fall of the androgyne coincided with new pathologizing attitudes toward lesbianism.

12 Klaus Theweleit, *Male Fantasies,* trans. Stephen Conway with Erica Carter and Chris Turner, vols. 1–2 (Minneapolis: University of Minnesota Press, 1987–89).

13 Mosse notes that the nineteenth-century androgyne is similarly identified with sexually marginal figure such as sadists, masochists, homosexuals, and lesbians. These associations predate the rise of fascism.

14 Michel Foucault, "Truth and Power," interview with Alessandro Fontana and Pasquale Pasquino, in *Power/Knowledge: Selected Interviews and Other Writings, 1972–1977,* ed. and trans. Colin Gordon (New York: Pantheon, 1980), 119. The interview was conducted in Italian in 1977.

15 Josef von Sternberg, "Introduction," in *The Blue Angel: The Novel by Heinrich Mann,*

The Film by Josef von Sternberg (New York: Frederick Ungar, 1979), 259. The Mann novel was translated into English in 1932 after the film had made the story popular.

16   Ibid.

17   Dijkstra writes of figure 14, Rops's "Pornokrates" (1878), that the blindfolded woman is guided by a hog because hogs symbolize Circe, the bestial representative of sexual evil (325).

18   Von Sternberg, 260.

19   Frank Wedekind, *The Lulu Plays and Other Sex Tragedies,* trans. Stephen Spender (London: John Calder, 1972), 78, 122. Published in bits and pieces between 1892 and 1913, *Erdgeist* was published in its entirety in 1905 and *Büchse der Pandora* in 1906.

20   Wedekind's portrayal of Lulu can also be seen as a critique of bourgeois morality. See Erhard Weidl, "Nachwort," in *Lulu: Erdgeist, Büchse der Pandora,* by Frank Wedekind (Stuttgart: Philipp Reclam, 1989), 203.

21   See Wedekind, 173, and the refrain from the German version of "Falling in Love Again," the most famous song from *The Blue Angel* (composed by Friedrich Holländer).

22   Judith Mayne, "Marlene Dietrich, *The Blue Angel,* and Female Performance," in *Seduction and Theory: Readings of Gender, Representation, and Rhetoric,* ed. Dianne Hunter (Urbana and Chicago: University of Illinois Press, 1989), 33.

23   Richard Dyer, *Stars* (London: British Film Institute, 1979), 38.

24   Maria Riva, *Marlene Dietrich* (London: Bloomsbury, 1992), 78.

25   Marcia Landy, *Cinematic Uses of the Past* (Minneapolis and London: University of Minnesota Press, 1996), 170.

26   Among the other stars of the 1930s who occasionally appeared in men's attire are Katharine Hepburn (*Sylvia Scarlett* [1936] and *Christopher Strong* [1933]) and Greta Garbo (*Queen Christina* [1933]). The multiplicity of these practices shows that they are not only associated with Weimar Germany.

27   See Riva, 96, for a photo of the fan card. Dietrich's association with gay men and her occasional sexual liaisons with women also contributed to this "Weimar" appeal, as I will discuss further. See Andrea Weiss, "A Queer Feeling When I Look at You," in *Stardom: Industry of Desire,* ed. Christine Gledhill (London and New York: Routledge, 1991), 291. Weiss connects Garbo and Dietrich's androgyny to the emerging gay subculture of the 1930s.

28   Landy, 164.

29   Gregory D. Black, *Hollywood Censored: Morality Codes, Catholics, and the Movies* (Cambridge: Cambridge University Press, 1994), 58.

30   Landy, 166.

31   Jason S. Joy to Maurice McKenzie, 23 July 1930, "The Blue Angel" file, Margaret Herrick Library, Academy of Motion Picture Arts and Sciences, Beverly Hills, California.

32   Joseph Breen to Paramount, 8 October 1935 (in reply to application for Certificates of Approval for reissue), "The Blue Angel" file, Margaret Herrick Library, Academy of Motion Picture Arts and Sciences, Beverly Hills, California.

33   Gaylyn Studlar, *In the Realm of Pleasure: Von Sternberg, Dietrich, and the Masochistic Aesthetic* (Urbana and Chicago: University of Illinois Press, 1988), 64.

34   Peter Wollen, *Signs and Meaning in the Cinema* (Bloomington: Indiana University Press, 1969), 140, quoted in Studlar, 85.

35   Siegfried Kracauer, *From Caligari to Hitler: A Psychological History of the German Film* (Princeton: Princeton University Press, 1947), 217.

36   Ibid., 218.

37   While they were less sexually expressive overall, the film stars of the Nazi era were similar to Hollywood stars in significant ways. Marlene Dietrich was in fact courted by Ufa to return to Germany, but she refused due to her anti-Nazi politics, after which she and her sexy style were vilified there. Screen star Zarah Leander is widely viewed as the "Dietrich replacement" the German film industry came up with, as she is also a singer with a deep and sultry voice. See Friedemann Beyer, *Die UFA-Stars im Dritten Reich: Frauen für Deutschland* (Munich: Wilhelm Heyne Verlag, 1991), 158; and Eric Rentschler, *The Ministry of Illusion: Nazi Cinema and Its Afterlife* (Cambridge: Harvard University Press, 1996), 135–36.

38   Patrice Petro, *Joyless Streets: Women and Melodramatic Representation in Weimar Germany* (Princeton: Princeton University Press, 1989), 159–60.

39   Stanley Hochman, foreword to *The Blue Angel: The Novel by Heinrich Mann, the Film by Josef von Sternberg* (New York: Frederick Ungar, 1979), 5.

40   Ibid., 7.

41   Kracauer, 217–18.

42   For the classic formulation of woman as fetish in film, see Laura Mulvey's 1975 article "Visual Pleasure and Narrative Cinema," reprinted in *Visual and Other Pleasures* (Bloomington and Indianapolis: Indiana University Press, 1989), 14–28. For a discussion of state fetishism, see Michael Taussig, *The Nervous System* (New York: Routledge, 1992), 129.

43   Mayne, 32. Mayne is referring to John Baxter, *The Cinema of Josef Von Sternberg* (New York: Barnes, 1971); Donald Spoto, *Falling in Love Again: Marlene Dietrich* (Boston: Little, Brown, 1985); and Alexander Walker, *Dietrich* (London: Thames and Hudson, 1984).

44   Historian Leila Rupp writes, "Since National Socialism rejected the principle of equality as the hallmark of a decadent democratic order, the main concern of writers on women was not the equality of women and men, but rather the corollary of polarity, the concept of the separate spheres and duties of the two sexes" (*Mobilizing Women for War: German and American Propaganda, 1939–1945* [Princeton: Princeton University Press, 1978], 31–32).

45   Thompson writes, "if women only knew it, if they only realized fully in their minds and hearts and nerves what their great social function is, they would know that they are both the creators and preservers of civilization" ("The Stake for Women," *Ladies Home Journal,* October 1942, 6). For further discussion of this sort of journalism, see Ramona M. Rose, *Position and Treatment of Women in Nazi Germany as viewed from the Perspective of the English Language Press, 1933–1945* (Vancouver: Tantalus Research, 1984), 31.

46   F. Winder, "Nazi Amazons," *Living Age* 353 (1938): 452. See also "Women in Uniform," *Living Age* 354 (1938): 258–60; and an interesting feminist example decrying boundary blurring, E. Sylvia Pankhurst, "Women in Totalitaria," *Living Age* 356 (1939): 366–69.

47   Patricia White, "Supporting Character: The Queer Career of Agnes Moorehead,"

in *Out in Culture: Gay, Lesbian, and Queer Essays on Popular Culture,* ed. Corey K. Creekmur and Alexander Doty (Durham and London: Duke University Press, 1995), 108.

48 Marjorie Garber, *Vested Interests: Cross-Dressing and Cultural Anxiety* (New York: Routledge, 1992), 16–17.

49 Garber, 14. I discuss *Cabaret* at greater length in chapter 8.

50 Linda Mizejewski, *Divine Decadence: Fascism, Female Spectacle, and the Makings of Sally Bowles* (Princeton: Princeton University Press, 1992), 19.

51 Ibid., 60.

52 Ibid., 19.

53 Ibid.

54 Studlar, 98.

55 Mayne, 41.

56 Thomas Doherty, *Projections of War: Hollywood, American Culture, and World War II* (New York: Columbia University Press, 1993), 44–45. Dietrich's daughter claims that her anti-Nazism was already active in the early 1930s, as she made her house in Versailles a refugee haven as soon as Hitler was elected chancellor in 1930 (Riva, 206). Steven Bach reports that Dietrich paid for plane tickets for many movie industry refugees (including Wilder, Ernst Lubitsch, and William Dieterle) and helped them get jobs in Hollywood. She not only performed for the USO and at stamp and bond rallies but did other jobs at these events (making coffee, pushing a broom, doing whatever was necessary). Steven Bach, *Marlene Dietrich: Life and Legend* (New York: William Morrow, 1992), 270, 286.

57 Bach, 290–91. Dietrich also cross-dressed in *Seven Sinners* (1940), in a naval officer's uniform, as she sang a Holländer-Loesser song, "The Man's in the Navy."

58 The song is variously titled "Lili Marlene," a nod to Dietrich, or "Lili Marleen."

59 Bach, 292.

60 At the end of the war, Dietrich was awarded the U.S. government's Medal of Freedom (the civilian equivalent of the Congressional Medal of Honor) for her wartime service. Dietrich was clearly deeply conflicted about her family members who remained in Germany, however. Her sister Elisabeth lived and worked in Belsen, where the concentration camp was located, and Dietrich (aided by some of her gullible biographers and media handlers) let people believe that the sister was an inmate there. For a more accurate account, see Bach, 302; and Riva, 578.

61 Homer Dickens, *The Films of Marlene Dietrich* (New York: Cadillac Publishing, 1968), 181. This objection is corroborated by Riva.

62 Percy Knauth, "Movie of the Week: Marlene Dietrich Steals the Show in an Uproarious Hollywood Version of Low Life in Postwar Berlin," *Life,* 9 June 1948, 59. Dietrich's daughter had a baby around the time the film was released. Thereafter, the young grandmother was often called "Grandmother Dietrich," "The Most Glamourous Grandmother," and even "Gorgeous Grandmarlene." This is one of the many other ways in which Dietrich's persona defied conventional images of women.

63 Ibid., 60.

64 Ibid., 63.

65 Ibid., 64.

66 Wilder had shot footage of a bombed Berlin at the end of the war when he was an

officer for the U.S. Army. His duties were to approve or deny the Allied performing licenses required for every German stage performance during the occupation. His duties are reflected in the plot of *A Foreign Affair,* which revolves around whether Erika should be allowed to continue to sing in the club.

67 As biographer Axel Madsen writes, "There has never been a shortage of descriptions of Wilder. He has been called a Rasputin on celluloid, a poor man's Rilke, the misanthrope who can only see the bad side and must make a sick joke of it, the mixer of acid and *l'eau de rose,* in short, a man hating people for fun and profit" (*Billy Wilder* [Bloomington and London: Indiana University Press, 1969], 20).

68 Knauth, 59.

69 In a letter from PCA representative Stephen S. Jackson to Luigi Luraschi of Paramount Pictures dated 2 December 1947, Jackson writes, "we believe this material presents a very serious problem of industry policy with regard to the characterization of the members of the Congressional Committee and of the members of the American Army of Occupation" as well as the "over-emphasis on illicit sex" that runs through the script. A long series of letters about specific changes to the script and song lyrics ensued. See "A Foreign Affair" file, Margaret Herrick Library, Academy of Motion Picture Arts and Sciences, Beverly Hills, California.

70 Quoted in Annette Insdorf, *Indelible Shadows: Film and the Holocaust* (Cambridge and New York: Cambridge University Press, 1983), 73.

71 Second script for *A Foreign Affair,* dated 31 May 1947, by Brackett, Wilder, and Harari ("A Foreign Affair" file, Margaret Herrick Library, Academy of Motion Picture Arts and Sciences, Beverly Hills, California). The Valkyrie image also frequently appeared in anti-Nazi journalism, as in Ernst Klein's comment that under the Nazis "the character of the woman reveals itself in a peculiar hardness and harshness. Whereas the goddesses of Olympus were lovely, easy-going creatures, the deities of Valhalla presented themselves as females who could fight, ride and drink as hard as any man. The Germans adored that broad hipped, muscular Valkyrie Brunhild who could throw the heaviest javelin farther than any masculine athlete and could defeat every male adversary in wrestling matches" ("Woman in National Socialism," *Fortnightly* 157 [April 1942]: 286).

72 Many English and American journalists bemoaned the loss of the fashionable Weimar woman. As one journalist wrote in 1934, "Rouge and other feminine wiles are not in evidence, and the general atmosphere is wholesome in everything that Queen Victoria might approve" (Roger Shaw, "Visiting the Third Reich," *Review of Reviews and World's Work* [January 1934]: 38). Katharine Thomas was critical of the Nazis' treatment of women more broadly, but one of her criticisms was that "the shiny nose, the uncorseted figure, [and] the low heel [had become] the surest passport for a true Nazi woman" (*Women in Nazi Germany* [London: Victor Golland, 1943], 73).

73 Wilder plays with male cross-dressing in *Stalag 17* (1953) and *Some Like It Hot* (1959), usually with burly, utterly heterosexually coded men, as here in *A Foreign Affair.*

74 Dietrich's first sultry song in the film is "Black Market," during the performance of which one overeager GI stands up to take her up on the "wares" the song offers. She puts her hand on his forehead and forces him to sit down. The song went through numerous revisions in order to pass the PCA censors.

75 This version of the scene appears on blue sheets (revisions after the "final script") dated 15 December 1947 ("A Foreign Affair" file, Margaret Herrick Library, Academy of Motion Picture Arts and Sciences, Beverly Hills, California).

76 In the Valkyrie script version (31 May 1947), the MPS come in and charge Erika, as in the film, and are deflected by Johnny, also as in the film. But in this version Johnny says, "How about a kiss now, you Beast of Belsen?" after they leave, a far more overt reference to Nazi horrors than the final film contained. This line might also have been objectionable to Dietrich, whose sister lived there (though not in the camp). See "A Foreign Affair" file, Margaret Herrick Library, Academy of Motion Picture Arts and Sciences, Beverly Hills, California.

77 This particular version of the Dietrich icon calls on the image of the dominatrix from Leopold von Sacher-Masoch, *Venus in Furs,* trans. Jean McNeil, reprinted in *Masochism: An Interpretation of Coldness and Cruelty,* by Gilles Deleuze (New York: George Braziller, 1971). *Venus in Furs* was originally published in German in 1870.

78 Bosley Crowther, "Remembrance of Things: 'A Foreign Affair' and 'Easter Parade' Stir Fond Memories," *New York Times,* 4 July 1948, B1.

79 Jennifer Terry, *An American Obsession: Science, Medicine, and Homosexuality in Modern Society* (Chicago: University of Chicago Press, 1999), 334–44.

80 Jennifer Terry, "'Momism' and the Making of Treasonous Homosexuals," in *"Bad" Mothers: The Politics of Blame in Twentieth-Century America,* ed. Molly Ladd-Taylor and Lauri Umansky (New York: New York University Press, 1998), 180–81. Other conservative thinkers in this vein include sociologist Ferdinand Lundberg and psychoanalyst Marynia Farnham, whose 1947 best-seller described feminism as a mental illness, aligning it with both fascism and communism. See Ferdinand Lundberg and Marynia Farnham, *Modern Woman: The Lost Sex* (New York: Harper, 1947).

81 T. W. Adorno, Else Frenkel-Brunswik, Daniel J. Levinson, and R. Nevitt Sanford, *The Authoritarian Personality* (New York: Harper and Brothers, 1950).

82 The summary of the findings lets it suffice to say that "Considerations analogous to those made in the preceding paragraphs were also applied to women" without a specific delineation of these analogs being deemed necessary at any point in the study (ibid., 316). In statistical analysis, the difference between highly prejudiced and unprejudiced women is almost always negligible and hence not particularly supportive of their "analogous" claims, but these disappointing results do not inspire the reformulation of questions specific to their female subjects.

83 Ibid., 347–48.

84 Ibid., 405.

85 Literary scholar Andrew Hewitt writes that "the authoritarian personality is consistently assumed to be masculine, despite the inclusion of women in the analysis. . . . the movement toward an analysis of effeminization in male respondents necessarily leads to a marginalization of actual female respondents, for whom the model of effeminations clearly cannot hold (unless the feminine psyche is assumed to be fascistic from the outset)." Hewitt unfortunately does not pursue his suggestion that perhaps "the feminine psyche is assumed to be fascistic from the outset," nor does he consider that there are more subtle variants of gender inversion at play with regard to women (*Political Inversions: Homosexuality, Fascism, and the Modernist Imaginary* [Stanford, CA: Stanford University Press, 1996], 51).

86 Kenneth C. McLain, "The Untold Story of Marlene Dietrich," *Confidential: Tells the Facts and Names the Names* 3.3 (July 1955): 22. While some of these exploits have been confirmed by Riva, this particular article is short on historical accuracy.

87 Ibid., 24.

88 Joanne Meyerowitz, "Beyond the Feminine Mystique: A Reassessment of Postwar Mass Culture, 1946–1958," in *Not June Cleaver: Women and Gender in Postwar America, 1945–1960,* ed. Joanne Meyerowitz (Philadelphia: Temple University Press, 1994), 245. See also Marlene Dietrich, "How to Be Loved," *Ladies' Home Journal,* January 1954, 37, 85, 87.

89 Agatha Christie, *Witness for the Prosecution* (London: Samuel French, 1954).

90 Mayne, 42.

91 Bach, 384.

92 Mayne, 43.

93 Film scholar Annette Insdorf writes of *Judgment at Nuremberg* that it relies on the casting of recognizable stars, saying that some were used "for their suggestion of integrity," while others, especially Dietrich, were used to "connote the dubious psychological or moral states of their own film personas: for example, when the song 'Lili Marleen' accompanies Haywood's walk with this German woman, her identity resonates beyond the frame" (9). Insdorf does not elaborate on this "dubiousness."

94 Riva, 640. Riva also recounts how Dietrich sang songs to women as a regular part of her show insofar as she refused to change pronouns in love songs.

95 Sian Phillips performed as the Dietrich icon in the musical play *Marlene,* which was written by Pam Gems and directed by Sean Mathias. The play takes place onstage and backstage at one of Dietrich's concerts in Paris in 1969. *Marlene* originated in London and played for only three weeks in New York, from 11 April to 2 May 1999.

96 Reuters News Service, "Berlin's Marlene Dietrich Street hits resistance," dated 30 October 1996.

97 Susan Sontag, "Fascinating Fascism," *New York Review of Books* 6 February 1975, reprinted in *Under the Sign of Saturn* (New York: Vintage, 1981), 72–105; Rentschler, 7.

98 Michel Foucault, *The History of Sexuality,* vol. 2: *The Use of Pleasure,* trans. Robert Hurley (New York: Vintage, 1990), 10, 13.

8 Sexualized Nazis and Contemporary Popular Political Culture

1 Claudia Koonz, *Mothers in the Fatherland: Women, the Family, and Nazi Politics* (New York: St. Martin's, 1987), 3. Koonz describes the Braun image as "passive-docile," Riefenstahl as "ambitious, determined, opportunistic," and Griese as "heartless, brutish" (12).

2 Koonz notes that the few women who did work as camp matrons or guards are often described by survivors as the "most vicious" of the guards. While not denying their sadism, she cautions that it might be precisely *because* they are women that they seem exceptional in a context in which the relative comparison of ex-

treme cruelties is a rather pointless distinction (ibid., 404). For a survivor's description of Griese, see Olga Lengyel, *Five Chimneys: The Story of Auschwitz*, trans. Paul P. Weiss (London: Mayflower, 1972).

3   Koonz concludes that under the Nazis "some compliant, ambitious, and non-Jewish women profited from a kind of 'tokenism,' while the oppression of most women became more pervasive" (84). The issue of "Nazi feminists"—in other words, women who were not only unopposed to the ideology of fascism but advocated for their more active and broader participation—is also taken up by Leila Rupp in *Mobilizing Women for War: German and American Propaganda, 1939–1945* (Princeton: Princeton University Press, 1978).

4   The guards in the film are divided into two groups: the female ss members who accompany Ilsa and the beer-guzzling and lascivious male guards who indulge in the gang rape of women prisoners for sport. Among the latter group resides the film's one definitive lesbian, who apparently sleeps in the men's barracks and chooses female inmates who have scorned her for the men to rape. The male guards' violence is thus figured as a relay for perverse lesbian sex.

5   Alvin Rosenfeld sees Nazism as having been "lifted from its historical base and transmuted into forms of entertainment and political bad faith" (*Imagining Hitler* [Bloomington: Indiana University Press, 1985], xiv). See also Saul Friedlander, *Reflections of Nazism: An Essay on Kitsch and Death*, trans. Thomas Weyr (New York: Harper and Row, 1984), 19.

6   Susan Sontag, "Fascinating Fascism," *New York Review of Books*, 6 February 1975, reprinted in *Under the Sign of Saturn* (New York: Vintage, 1981), 103.

7   Ibid., 100.

8   Donna Barr, "His Story," *The Desert Peach, #18* (Seattle: MU Press, 1992), 13–20. Barr describes the genesis of the character as stemming from a costume party she attended in a faux German Army uniform in 1972 while serving in the U.S. Army. After she performed the character at several science fiction and comics conventions, the first issue of *The Desert Peach* was published in November 1988.

9   Fellow comic book artist Colleen Doran drew the picture of Pfirsich and his main love interest, Rosen, with an infant, and fellow comic book artist Pia Guerra drew the dreamy-looking Pfirsich with the pacifist message (ibid., 22, 24). The latter image is an homage to a Mike Dringenberg pin-up.

10 Donna Barr, e-mail exchange with the author, January 2000. Barr is very intent on the historical accuracy of her story's context, especially with regard to the German military and its distinction from the Nazi Party and the ss.

11 Sontag, 100.

12 Homi Bhabha, "DissemiNation: Time, Narrative, and the Margins of the Modern Nation," in *Nation and Narration*, ed. Homi Bhabha (London and New York: Routledge, 1990), 299.

13 Julia Kristeva, *Powers of Horror: An Essay on Abjection*, trans. Leon S. Roudiez (New York: Columbia University Press, 1982).

14 Klaus Theweleit, *Male Fantasies*, trans. Stephen Conway with Erica Carter and Chris Turner, vols. 1–2 (Minneapolis: University of Minnesota Press, 1987–89).

15 Theweleit writes that incest is not at the core of the fascist psyche in the usual sense but that "They want a contact with the opposite sex—or perhaps simply access to

sexuality itself—which cannot be *named*, a contact in which they can dissolve themselves while forcibly dissolving the other sex" (ibid., vol. 1, 205).

16   Annette Insdorf, *Indelible Shadows: Film and the Holocaust* (Cambridge and New York: Cambridge University Press, 1983), 138–39.

17   Ibid., 140. Lina Wertmüller's *Seven Beauties* (1975) banks more directly on abjection. The reference to Dietrich/Lola Lola occurs in a labor camp, where the commandant, a large, unattractive woman, sits, Dietrich-like, astride a chair with her legs spread, Nazi boots on, and wearing ordinary, lumpy underwear, as the protagonist (an inmate) tries to seduce her.

18   Peter Bondanella argues that the central tension of *The Night Porter* is between the ideas that nothing changes (history repeats itself) and time heals all wounds (or things change after all). The oscillation between history and memory is meant to reflect on the part fascism might play in the 1970s Italian present (*Italian Cinema: From Neorealism to the Present* [New York: Ungar, 1983]).

19   This was Dietrich's final screen appearance, which her daughter claims she accepted for purely financial reasons (Maria Riva, *Marlene Dietrich* [London: Bloomsbury, 1992], 765). Dietrich refused to appear on camera in Maximilian Schell's 1984 documentary about the star.

20   Christopher Isherwood, *Goodbye to Berlin* (London: Triad/Panther Books, 1977).

21   In *The Serpent's Egg*, cabaret performers fall on both sides of the conflict with Nazism. The Sally character is a Jewish cabaret singer with not a lot of brains but a heart of gold, but when the cabaret is raided by the Nazis (a nod to the fact that they at least billed themselves as antidecadent) one of the other performers eagerly points to the Jewish proprietor and participates in his condemnation.

22   See, for instance, Insdorf, 126.

23   "Cabaret," *Variety*, 16 February 1972, 18. Judith Crist's review for *New York* was cited in ads for the film. See, for instance, *New York Times*, 20 February 1972, B7.

24   Vincent Canby, "'Porter' Is Romantic Pornography," *New York Times*, 13 October 1974, B1, 6; Pauline Kael, "Stuck in the Fun," originally published in the *New Yorker*, 7 October 1974, and reprinted in *Reeling* (Boston: Little, Brown, 1976), 342; Geoffrey Minish, "*The Night Porter*: Last Tango in Auschwitz," *Take One* 4.5 (1974): 39–40; Henry Giroux, "The Challenge of Neo-fascist Culture," *Cineaste* 1.4 (1975): 31.

25   Stanley Kauffmann, "Stanley Kauffmann on Films," *New Republic*, 5 October 1974, 33.

26   Charles Champlin, "Love at First Rite in 'Night Porter,'" *Los Angeles Times*, 30 October 1974, D13.

27   Stephen Farber, "'Cabaret' May Shock Kansas," *New York Times*, 20 February 1972, B14.

28   Andrew Sarris, "The Nasty Nazis: History or Mythology?" *Village Voice*, 17 October 1974, 78.

29   Stanley Kauffmann, "Stanley Kauffmann on Films," *New Republic*, 4 March 1972, 22.

30   Farber, 14.

31   Roger Greenspun, "Liza Minnelli Stirs a Lively 'Cabaret,'" *New York Times*, 14 February 1972, A22.

32   If the film is read to suggest that a relationship between Max and Lucia was truly

possible, then I would have to agree that the film is morally unconscionable. But since Cavani had made several documentaries for Italian television on the subject of survivors I am assuming, along with Teresa de Lauretis, that this film is decidedly unrealistic. Of course, by transferring the insights she garnered from actual survivors into the psychosexual realm, much of the particularity of their experience is lost. For the most part, I am interested in this film as a text that inspired debate rather than coming to a definitive conclusion about its moral choices. See Teresa de Lauretis, "Cavani's *Night Porter*: A Woman's Film?" *Film Quarterly* 30.2 (1976–77): 35–38.

33 See Betty Friedan, *The Feminine Mystique* (New York: Norton, 1963); and Naomi Weisstein, "'Kinder, Kuche [sic], Kirche' as Scientific Law: Psychology Constructs the Female," in *Sisterhood Is Powerful: An Anthology of Writings from the Women's Liberation Movement*, ed. Robin Morgan (New York: Vintage, 1970), 228–45.

34 De Lauretis, 35–36.

35 Ibid., 37. The Polish-German film *Angry Harvest* (Agnieszka Holland, 1985) is a more recent offering that more closely conforms to de Lauretis's argument than *The Night Porter* does, as it features a much less erotically stylized sadomasochistic dynamic between a Jewish woman and a German farmer in which the heterosexual dynamic of protector/protected (a paternal relation) slides into that of captor/captive (a patriarchal relation).

36 Beverle Houston and Marsha Kinder, "*The Night Porter* as Daydream," *Literature and Film Quarterly* 3.4 (1975): 366–67.

37 Ibid., 369.

38 Interest in masochism, linked to postmodern subjectivity, became especially prominent among some feminist critics in the 1980s. Tania Modleski, for instance, writes that female masochism "does not point to an 'acceptance of femininity' but rather is meant to expose the position of women in patriarchal society and express contempt for it." Meanwhile, film theorist Kaja Silverman saw *The Night Porter* as an illustrative example of Lacanian concepts of lack and desire—an anti-identitarian psychical longing fitting to a postmodern frame where the efficacy of identity categories is questioned. See Tania Modleski, *The Women Who Knew Too Much: Hitchcock and Feminist Theory* (New York: Methuen, 1988), 237; and Kaja Silverman, "Masochism and Subjectivity," *Framework: A Film Journal* 12 (1980): 2–9.

39 Michel Foucault, "Film and Popular Memory," in *Foucault Live: Interviews, 1966–1984*, trans. Martin Jordin, ed. Sylvere Lotringer (New York: Semiotext(e), 1989), 98.

40 Sylvia Plath, "Daddy," in *The Norton Anthology of Literature by Women: The Tradition in English*, ed. Sandra M. Gilbert and Susan Gubar (New York and London: Norton, 1985), 2208.

41 See Vikki Bell, *Interrogating Incest: Feminism, Foucault, and the Law* (New York: Routledge, 1993), 57.

42 Janice Haaken, "The Recovery of Memory, Fantasy, and Desire: Feminist Approaches to Sexual Abuse and Psychic Trauma," *Signs* (summer 1996): 1083.

43 Ibid., 1079, n. 9.

44 See Marilyn Ivy, "Have You Seen Me? Recovering the Inner Child in Late Twentieth-Century America," *Social Text* 37 (1993): 27–52; and Annette Michelson, "Lolita's Progeny," *October* 76 (1996): 3–14. "Inner child" therapies, an off-

shoot of psychoanalysis, date back to the publication of Hugh Missildine's *Your Inner Child of the Past* (New York: Simon and Schuster, 1963).

45 Ian Hacking, "The Making and Molding of Child Abuse," *Critical Inquiry* 17 (1991): 253–88.

46 Elizabeth Wilson, "Not in This House: Incest, Denial, and Doubt in the White Middle Class Family," *Yale Journal of Criticism* 8 (1995): 53.

47 Ivy, 44, 47.

48 For a discussion of Beth B's earlier film work, see Clarke Taylor, "Overview of Underground," *Los Angeles Times*, 24 April 1983, Calendar, 45.

49 *Santa Monica Museum of Art Newsletter*, 5.2 (spring 1994).

50 *Amnesia* features talking heads of various actors making xenophobic remarks about foreigners, which are later revealed to be derived from sources that range from 1860 to 1992, over images of Nazis marching in the background.

51 Joseph Di Mattia, "No More Happy Endings," *Montage* (August-September 1990): 9. This article consists mainly of an interview with Beth B.

52 In "A Child Is Being Beaten," Freud describes how being beaten by the father substitutes for the castration the male child fears as retaliation for his desire for the mother. This transforms into desire for the father and a projection of the punishing figure onto the mother to disguise the homosexual implications of the fantasy. The patient conveys these various shifts by describing a dream in which "a child is being beaten." The child is revealed to be a youngster the patient doesn't like and finally the patient himself. There are several layers of displacement at work in the case, and hence the various acts of witnessing brutality with which this case is blended in *Belladonna* might begin to sound like a projection as well. This aspect is deeply problematic.

53 Di Mattia, 8–9.

54 The issue of Jewishness is completely submerged and obscured in *Belladonna*, in which, as in *The Night Porter*, the word *Jew* is never uttered. The racial constitution of the concentration camp inmates and the Jewishness of the Steinbergs are not addressed.

55 Ironically, the persistence with which violence against women and children is figured ensures its sexualization precisely because it functions not on its own but in relation to the therapy of the perpetrator. The various ways in which the death of a female inmate is recounted highlights its perversion, in keeping with the theatricality common to the uses of the sexualized Nazi scenario since the 1970s, with a ring of witnesses and a guard who sometimes "whistles an aria from *Madame Butterfly*." Finally, this one repeatedly invoked victim comes to stand in for the Steinberg child, whose death is never explicitly mentioned and who thus remains the true subtext of the tape.

56 Linda Kintz, *Between Jesus and the Market: The Emotions That Matter in Right-Wing America* (Durham and London: Duke University Press, 1997), 126–27. See also Stu Weber's *Tender Warrior: God's Intention for a Man* (Sisters, OR: Multnomah, 1993); *Locking Arms: God's Design for Masculine Friendships* (Sisters, OR: Multnomah, 1995); and the anthology *Seven Promises of a Promise Keeper* (Colorado Springs: Focus on the Family, 1994).

57 Thomas Keneally, *Schindler's List* (New York: Simon and Schuster, 1982).

58 Film scholar Miriam Bratu Hansen, in her survey of criticism of the film, also notes

that Spielberg follows a classical narrative form, which hinges on "the restoration of familial forms of subjectivity (Schindler as a super father-figure who has to renounce his promiscuity and return to marriage in order to accomplish his historic mission, the rescue of Jewish families)" ("*Schindler's List* Is Not *Shoah:* The Second Commandment, Popular Modernism, and Public Memory," *Critical Inquiry* 22 [1996]: 298). See also Yosefa Loshitzky, ed., *Spielberg's Holocaust: Critical Perspectives on Schindler's List* (Bloomington: Indiana University Press, 1997).

59 Keneally, 27.

60 See, for instance, Susan Leigh Star, "Swastikas: The Street and the University," in *Against Sadomasochism: A Radical Feminist Analysis*, ed. Robin Ruth Linden, Darlene R. Pagano, Diana E. H. Russell, and Susan Leigh Star (East Palo Alto: Frog in the Well, 1982), 131–36; and SAMOIS, eds., *Coming to Power: Writings and Graphics on Lesbian S/M* (Palo Alto: Up Press, 1981).

61 Wilhelm Reich, *The Mass Psychology of Fascism*, trans. Vincent R. Carfagno (New York: Farrar, Straus and Giroux, 1970), xi. The quote is from the preface to the third edition, published in 1942. Reich originally belonged to the Communist Party and was a member of psychoanalytic circles, a very unpopular combination with both groups in the 1920s. By the mid-1930s, he had been excluded from both.

62 Herbert Marcuse, *Eros and Civilization: A Philosophical Inquiry into Freud* (Boston: Beacon, 1974), 197–203.

63 Patricia Mellencamp, *Indiscretions: Avant-Garde Film, Video, and Feminism* (Bloomington: Indiana University Press, 1990), 66–67.

64 For an account of how conservative critics of feminist art misread the way these artists used sexuality in their art, see Christine Tamblyn, "The River of Swill: Feminist Art, Sexual Codes, and Censorship," *Afterimage* (October 1990): 10–13.

65 E. Ann Kaplan, "Madonna Politics: Perversion, Repression, or Subversion? Or Masks and/as Master-y," in *The Madonna Connection: Representational Politics, Subcultural Identities, and Cultural Theory*, ed. Cathy Schwichtenberg (Boulder: Westview, 1992), 157.

66 Camille Paglia, "Madonna II: Venus of the Radio Waves," in *Sex, Art, and American Culture: Essays* (New York: Vintage, 1992), 10–11.

67 Cathy Schwichtenberg, "Madonna's Postmodern Feminism: Bringing the Margins to the Center," in Schwichtenberg, *The Madonna Connection*, 137. She quotes Gayle Rubin's "Thinking Sex: Notes for a Radical Theory of the Politics of Sexuality," in *Pleasure and Danger: Exploring Female Sexuality*, ed. Carole S. Vance (Boston: Routledge and Kegan Paul, 1984), 283.

68 See photographer Steven Meisel's "Flesh and Fantasy," *Rolling Stone*, 13 June 1991, 43–50. This new political climate could result in Cavani, too, getting a second look. See Chantal Nadeau, "Girls on a Wired Screen: Cavani's Cinema and Lesbian S/M," in *Sexy Bodies: The Strange Carnalities of Feminism*, ed. Elizabeth Grosz and Elspeth Probyn (London and New York: Routledge, 1995), 220.

69 For the various efforts to negotiate identities, both firm and fluid, see Kate Bornstein, *Gender Outlaw: On Men, Women, and the Rest of Us* (New York: Vintage, 1994); C. Jacob Hale, "Consuming the Living, Dis(re)membering the Dead in the Butch/FTM Borderlands," *GLQ* 4.2 (1998): 340; Judith Halberstam, "Transgender Butch: Butch/FTM Border Wars and the Masculine Continuum," *GLQ* 4.2 (1998): 287–310; and Judith Halberstam, "F2M: The Making of Female Mas-

culinity," in *The Lesbian Postmodern*, ed. Laura Doan (New York: Columbia University Press, 1994), 210–28.

70   700 Club fact sheet, "Postmodernism: Undermining America's Moral Conscience," Christian Broadcasting Network, *Newswatch Today*, 5 January 1996.

71   Ibid. See also Gene Edward Veith, *Postmodern Times: A Christian Guide to Contemporary Thought and Culture* (Wheaton, IL: Crossway Books, 1994); and *Modern Fascism: Liquidating the Judeo-Christian Worldview* (St. Louis: Concordia, 1993).

72   Brian Clowes, "Neofeminism: Religion of Despair," in *Pro-Life Activist's Encyclopedia* (Stafford, VA: American Life League, 1995). Available from the World Wide Web: ⟨http://www.all.org/plae/plae.htm.⟩. Cited on 12 February 1998. Since repetition is the name of the game in these documents, the inversion claim is repeated to include men a bit farther on: "It seems that much of the pointless and fruitless anger and unrest in this society is caused by women who want to be men (and, to be fair, men who want to be women)."

73   See my discussion of antigay and antiabortion rhetoric in this publication in chapter 3.

74   James Dobson, letter dated August 1995, available at the time on the Focus on the Family website.

75   Performance scholar Diana Taylor notes that during the Malvinas/Falkland Islands conflict in Argentina in 1983, British Prime Minister Margaret Thatcher was often pictured wearing a pirate's patch over one eye, and cartoons featuring her husband as henpecked abounded. The political use of gender inversion to characterize female political figures is thus not at all limited to the U.S. context. See Diana Taylor, *Disappearing Acts: Spectacles of Gender and Nationalism in Argentina's "Dirty War"* (Durham: Duke University Press, 1997), 87.

76   Texe Marrs, *Big Sister Is Watching You! Hillary Clinton and the White House Feminists Who Now Control America—and Tell the President What to Do* (Austin, TX: Living Truth Press, 1993). Marrs heads the Living Truth Ministry and publishing house.

77   Linda Kintz's analysis of this book concurs that the feminazi conspiracy that Marrs posits centrally revolves around a rhetoric of gender inversion. In the course of the book, Marrs is able to equate strong women, Jews, sexual freedom, and multiculturalism with Nazism, while white Christian male proponents of patriarchy represent an imperiled traditional American democracy (ibid., 23, as discussed in Kintz, 261).

78   Kintz, 257.

79   Party affiliation is not revealed, although some reference to the 1984 bid of Geraldine Ferraro as Walter Mondale's historically first female vice-presidential running mate is certain.

80   My interpretations of Flanders's film are informed by interviews I conducted with her by e-mail in the fall of 1998.

81   Again, these are explanations provided by Flanders in e-mail interviews with the author, fall 1998.

82   The listserv Schreiber used was gl-asb.alt.sex.bondage. My interpretation of Schreiber's work has benefited from an extended interview and discussion with her by e-mail in the fall and winter of 1998–1999.

83   Schreiber published a print version of this project wherein she interjects a childhood story in which a friend brings over a doll identical to one she has, one child

claiming the doll is Christian and the other Jewish, the point being that people who seem to be engaging in the same act may be experiencing it very differently. See Rachel Schreiber, "Please Kill Me; I'm a Faggot Nigger Jew," *Davka: Jewish Cultural Revolution* 1.3 (1997): 20–21.

Epilogue

1   Homi Bhabha, "Introduction: Narrating the Nation" in *Nation and Narration*, ed. Homi Bhabha (London and New York: Routledge, 1990), 3.

2   Chantal Mouffe, "Democratic Citizenship and the Political Community," in *Community at Loose Ends*, ed. Miami Theory Collective (Minneapolis: University of Minnesota Press, 1991), 72.

3   Teresa de Lauretis, *The Practice of Love: Lesbian Sexuality and Perverse Desire* (Bloomington and Indianapolis: Indiana University Press, 1994), xvi.

4   Arjun Appadurai, "Patriotism and Its Futures," *Public Culture* 5 (1993): 421.

5   William S. Lind and William H. Marshner, eds., *Cultural Conservatism: Theory and Practice* (Washington, DC: Free Congress Foundation, 1991), 1, quoted in Ellen Messer-Davidow, "Manufacturing the Attack on Liberalized Higher Education," *Social Text* 11.3 (1993): 46.

6   *Cultural Conservatism: Toward a New Agenda* (Washington, DC: Institute for Cultural Conservatism/Free Congress Research and Education Foundation, 1987), 5, quoted in Messer-Davidow, 53. As Messer-Davidow writes, symptoms of this "drift" are "conspicuous consumption, a 'me-first' ethic, demands to eliminate racism and homophobia, scientific proposals to achieve zero-population growth and eliminate male aggression as the source of war, decreased religious and parental influence, deterioration of school education, women's and critical legal studies, rock videos. Blame goes to 60s cultural radicals and a new cast of 80s characters: yuppies and welfare recipients (both, oddly enough, produced by liberal largesse)" (45).

7   Rachel Schreiber, text from the catalog of the exhibition "Strange Fruits," Los Angeles Center for Photographic Studies, October 1995.

8   In an e-mail exchange I conducted with Schreiber in the fall of 1998, she wrote, "While a lot of work has been done which investigates why our culture is fascinated with fascism, my particular interest is in how Jews continue to be represented as victims, and how this role of Jew as victim has become the object of fetishization."

9   Jeannette Winterson, *Written on the Body* (New York: Vintage, 1992), 89.

Bibliography

Abrams, Kevin. "The Other Side of the Pink Triangle." *Lambda Report on Homosexuality: Monitoring the Homosexual Agenda in American Politics and Culture* 11.4 (August 1994): 11.

Abrams, Kevin, and Scott Lively. *The Pink Swastika: Homosexuality in the Nazi Party*. Amity, OR: Lively Communications, 1995.

Abrams, Kevin, and Christine Mueller. "Pink Triangle . . . or Pink Swastika? The Debate over Homosexual Nazis." *Lambda Report on Homosexuality: Monitoring the Homosexual Agenda in American Politics* (April-June 1995): 4–5.

Achtman, Michael. "Über Allies: Do Fascism and Porn Mix?" *Xtra! Toronto's Gay and Lesbian Biweekly*, 18 November 1999, 33.

Adam, Barry D. *The Rise of a Gay and Lesbian Movement*. Boston: Twayne, 1987.

Adorno, T. W., Else Frenkel-Brunswik, Daniel J. Levinson, and R. Nevitt Sanford. *The Authoritarian Personality*. New York: Harper and Brothers, 1950.

Allport, Gordon. *The Nature of Prejudice*. Cambridge, MA: Addison-Wesley, 1954.

Altman, Neil. *The Analyst in the Inner City: Race, Class, and Culture through a Psychoanalytic Lens*. Hillsdale, NJ, and London: Analytic Press, 1995.

American History X official website, ⟨http://www.historyx.com⟩.

Anderson, Benedict. *Imagined Communities: Reflections on the Origin and Spread of Nationalism*. London: Verso, 1983.

Anti-Defamation League, *The Skinhead International: A Worldwide Survey of Neo-Nazi Skinheads*. New York: Anti-Defamation League, 1995.

Appadurai, Arjun. "Disjuncture and Difference in the Global Cultural Economy." In *Colonial Discourse and Post-Colonial Theory: A Reader*. Edited by Patrick Williams and Laura Chrisman. New York: Columbia University Press, 1994. 324–39.

——. "Patriotism and Its Futures." *Public Culture* 5 (1993): 411–29.

Arendt, Hannah. *The Origins of Totalitarianism*. New York: Harcourt Brace Jovanovich, 1973.

"Arms Dealer: McVeigh Wanted Detonation Cord 'Bad.'" ⟨http://www.cnn.com⟩, 1 May 1997.

Austin, Keith. "Blacklisted: The Publication of the List of 2,000 One Nation Members and Donors Has Sparked a Debate Wider Than the Fight against Racism." *Sydney Morning Herald*, 10 July 1998, 13.

Ayçoberry, Pierre. *The Nazi Question: An Essay on the Interpretations of National Socialism (1922–1975)*. Translated by Robert Hurley. New York: Random House, 1981.

Bach, Steven. *Marlene Dietrich: Life and Legend*. New York: William Morrow, 1992.

Barr, Donna. "His Story." In *The Desert Peach, #18*. Seattle: MU Press, 1992. 13–20.

Barthes, Roland. *Image, Music, Text*. Translated by Stephen Heath. New York: Hill and Wang, 1977.

Baxter, John. *The Cinema of Josef Von Sternberg*. New York: A. S. Barnes, 1971.

Bell, Vikki. *Interrogating Incest: Feminism, Foucault, and the Law*. New York: Routledge, 1993.

Bellant, Russ. *Old Nazis, the New Right, and the Republican Party*. Boston: South End Press, 1988.

Bennett, David H. *The Party of Fear: The American Far Right from Nativism to the Militia Movement*. 2d ed. New York: Vintage, 1995.

Bergler, Edmund. *One Thousand Homosexuals: Conspiracy of Silence or Curing and Deglamorizing Homosexuals?* Paterson, NJ: Pageant Books, 1959.

Berlant, Lauren. "Intimacy: A Special Issue." *Critical Inquiry* 24 (1998): 281–88.

——. *The Queen of America Goes to Washington City: Essays on Sex and Citizenship*. Durham and London: Duke University Press, 1997.

Bernstein, David. "One Nation List Causes Red Faces on Both Sides." *Sydney Morning Herald*, 10 July 1998, 17.

Berube, Alan. *Coming out under Fire: A History of Gay Men and Women in World War Two*. New York: Free Press, 1990.

Bettelheim, Bruno, and Morris Janowitz. *Dynamics of Prejudice: A Psychological and Sociological Study of Veterans*. New York: Harper, 1950.

Beyer, Friedemann. *Die UFA-Stars im Dritten Reich: Frauen für Deutschland*. Munich: Wilhelm Heyne Verlag, 1991.

Bhabha, Homi. "DissemiNation: Time, Narrative, and the Margins of the Modern Nation." In *Nation and Narration*. Edited by Homi Bhabha. London and New York: Routledge, 1990. 291–322.

——. "Introduction: Narrating the Nation." In *Nation and Narration*. Edited by Homi Bhabha. London and New York: Routledge, 1990. 1–7.

——. *The Location of Culture*. London and New York: Routledge, 1994.

——. "The Other Question: The Stereotype and Colonial Discourse." *Screen* 24.6 (1983): 18–36.

Billinger, Richard. *Der Gigant*. Berlin: Suhrkamp Verlag, 1942.

Black, Gregory D. *Hollywood Censored: Morality Codes, Catholics, and the Movies*. Cambridge and New York: Cambridge University Press, 1994.

Bock, Gisela. "Racism and Sexism in Nazi Germany: Motherhood, Compulsory Sterilization, and the State." In *When Biology Became Destiny: Women in Weimar and Nazi*

Germany. Edited by Renate Bridenthal, Atina Grossman, and Marion Kaplan. New York: Monthly Review Press, 1984. 271–96.

Bondanella, Peter. *Italian Cinema: From Neorealism to the Present*. New York: F. Ungar, 1983.

Bornstein, Kate. *Gender Outlaw: On Men, Women, and the Rest of Us*. New York: Vintage, 1994.

Boyarin, Daniel. *Unheroic Conduct: The Rise of Heterosexuality and the Invention of the Jewish Man*. Berkeley: University of California Press, 1996.

Bromberg, Walter. *Psychiatry between the Wars, 1918–1945: A Recollection*. Westport, CT: Greenwood, 1982.

Brooks, Peter. "Melodrama, Body, Revolution." In *Melodrama: Stage Picture Screen*. Edited by Jacky Bratton, Jim Cook, and Christine Gledhill. London: British Film Institute, 1994. 11–24.

——. *The Melodramatic Imagination: Balzac, Henry James, Melodrama, and the Mode of Excess*. New York: Columbia University Press, 1985.

Brooks, Richard. *The Brick Foxhole*. New York: Harper, 1945.

Bull, Chris. "Lunatic Fringe." *The Advocate*, 30 May 1995, 21.

Burdekin, Katharine. *Swastika Night*. Old Westbury, NY: Feminist Press, 1985.

"Cabaret." *Variety*, 16 February 1972, 18.

Calverhall, Randolph D. *Serpent's Walk*. Hillsboro, WV: National Vanguard Books, 1991.

Canby, Vincent. "'Porter' Is Romantic Pornography." *New York Times*, 13 October 1974, B1, 6.

Carroll, Noël. "Film, Rhetoric, and Ideology." In *Explanation and Value in the Arts*. Edited by Salim Kemal and Ivan Gaskell. Cambridge: Cambridge University Press, 1993. 215–37.

Cayton, Horace, and St. Clair Drake. *Black Metropolis: A Study of Negro Life in a Northern City*. New York: Harcourt, Brace, 1945.

Champlin, Charles. "Love at First Rite in 'Night Porter.'" *Los Angeles Times*, 30 October 1974, D13.

Chibbaro, Lou. "Some Militias Linked to Anti-gay Organizations." *Washington Blade*, 19 May 1995.

Chideckel, Maurice. *Female Sex Perversion: The Sexually Aberrated Woman as She Is*. New York: Eugenics Publishing, 1935.

Christen, Toni. "Women without Hope." *Nation*, 2 December 1939, 598.

Christie, Agatha. *Witness for the Prosecution*. London: Samuel French, 1954.

Christie, R., and Marie Jahoda, eds. *Studies in the Scope and Method of "The Authoritarian Personality."* Glencoe, IL: Free Press, 1954.

Clark, Kenneth. *Dark Ghetto: Dilemmas of Social Power*. New York: Harper and Row, 1965.

Clowes, Brian. *Pro-Life Activist's Encyclopedia*. Stafford, VA: American Life League, 1995.

Cochran, Thomas C. *The Great Depression and World War II, 1929–1945*. Glenview, IL: Scott, Foresman, 1968.

Cohen, Alain J.-J. "La citation du *Mépris* dans *Casino* de Scorsese: Du détail iconophagique." *La Licorne* 6 (1999): 193–206.

Collin, Rodney. "Sex and the New Germany." *Living Age* 346 (March 1934): 24–26.

Constantine, Alex. *Psychic Dictatorship in the USA*. Portland, OR: Feral House, 1995.

Constantine, Murray. *Swastika Night*. London: Victor Gollancz, 1940.

Coontz, Stephanie. *The Way We Never Were: American Families and the Nostalgia Trap*. New York: Basic Books, 1992.

Corber, Robert. *In the Name of National Security: Hitchcock, Homophobia, and the Political Construction of Gender in Postwar America*. Durham: Duke University Press, 1993.

Corey, Donald Webster. *The Homosexual in America: A Subjective Approach*. New York: Greenberg, 1951.

"Corrupt and Criminal: Linda Thompson's View of Our Government Leaders." *Rutherford* (August 1995): 14–17.

Cott, Nancy F. *The Grounding of Modern Feminism*. New Haven and London: Yale University Press, 1987.

Couvares, Francis G. *Movie Censorship and American Culture*. Washington, DC: Smithsonian Institution Press, 1996.

Creekmur, Corey K., and Alexander Doty. *Out in Culture: Gay, Lesbian, and Queer Essays on Popular Culture*. Durham: Duke University Press, 1995.

Cripps, Thomas. *Making Movies Black: The Hollywood Message Movie from World War II to the Civil Rights Era*. New York: Oxford University Press, 1993.

Crowther, Bosley. "'Hitler's Children,' Fictionized Version of 'Education for Death,' Makes Its Appearance at the Paramount Theatre." *New York Times*, 25 February 1943, A27.

——. "Remembrance of Things: 'A Foreign Affair' and 'Easter Parade' Stir Fond Memories." *New York Times*, 4 July 1948, B1.

Cultural Conservatism: Toward a New Agenda. Washington, DC: Institute for Cultural Conservatism/Free Congress Research and Education Foundation, 1987.

Davis, Angela Y. *Women, Race, and Class*. New York: Vintage, 1981.

De Lauretis, Teresa. *Alice Doesn't: Feminist, Semiotics, Cinema*. Bloomington: Indiana University Press, 1984.

——. "Cavani's Night Porter: A Woman's Film?" *Film Quarterly* 30.2 (1976–77): 35–38.

——. *The Practice of Love: Lesbian Sexuality and Perverse Desire*. Bloomington and Indianapolis: Indiana University Press, 1994.

D'Emilio, John. "The Homosexual Menace: The Politics of Sexuality in Cold War America." In his *Making Trouble: Essays on Gay History, Politics, and the University*. New York: Routledge, 1995. 57–73

Diamond, Sara. *Roads to Dominion: Right-Wing Movements and Political Power in the United States*. New York: Guilford Press, 1995.

Dickens, Homer. *The Films of Marlene Dietrich*. New York: Cadillac Publishing, 1968.

Dietrich, Marlene. "How to Be Loved." *Ladies' Home Journal*, January 1954, 37, 85, 87.

DiIulio, John J., and Donald F. Kettl. *Fine Print: The Contract with America, Devolution, and the Administrative Realities of American Federalism*. Washington, DC: Brookings Institution, Center for Public Management, 1995.

Dijkstra, Bram. *Idols of Perversity: Fantasies of Feminine Evil in Fin-de-Siècle Culture*. New York and Oxford: Oxford University Press, 1986.

Di Mattia, Joseph. "No More Happy Endings." *Montage* (August-September 1990): 9.

Doane, Mary Ann. *The Desire to Desire: The Woman's Film of the 1940s*. Bloomington: Indiana University Press, 1987.

——. *Femmes Fatales: Feminism, Film Theory, Psychoanalysis*. New York: Routledge, 1991.

Dobie, Kathy. "Long Day's Journey into White." *Village Voice*, 28 April 1992, 22–32.

Doherty, Thomas. *Projections of War: Hollywood, American Culture, and World War II*. New York: Columbia University Press, 1993.

Dmytryk, Edward. *Odd Man Out: A Memoir of the Hollywood Ten*. Carbondale: Southern Illinois University Press, 1996.

Duggan, Lisa. "The Trials of Alice Mitchell: Sensationalism, Sexology, and the Lesbian Subject in Turn-of-the-Century America." *Signs: Journal of Women in Culture and Society* 18.4 (1993): 791–814.

Dyer, Richard. *Stars*. London: British Film Institute, 1979.

Eisner, Lotte. *The Haunted Screen*. Berkeley and Los Angeles: University of California Press, 1969.

Elsaesser, Thomas. "Tales of Sound and Fury: Observations on the Family Melodrama." In *Film Genre Reader*. Edited by Barry Keith Grant. Austin: University of Texas Press, 1986. 278–308.

Enzensberger, Hans Magnus. "The Great Migration." Translated by Martin Chalmers. *Granta* 42 (1992): 15–51.

"Equal Hostility: Women Are Angry at Government, Too." *Wall Street Journal*, 12 May 1995, A1, 7.

Erikson, Erik H. *Childhood and Society*. New York: Norton, 1950.

——. "Hitler's Imagery and German Youth." *Psychiatry* 5 (1942): 475–93.

——. "On Nazi Mentality." In *A Way of Looking at Things: Selected Papers from 1930 to 1980, Erik H. Erikson*. Edited by Stephen Schlein. New York: Norton, 1987.

Fanon, Franz. *Black Skins, White Masks*. Translated by Charles Lam Markmann. New York: Grove, 1967.

Farber, Stephen. "'Cabaret' May Shock Kansas." *New York Times*, 20 February 1972, B1, 14.

Feldstein, Ruth. "Antiracism and Maternal Failure in the 1940s and 1950s." In *"Bad" Mothers: The Politics of Blame in Twentieth-Century America*. Edited by Molly Ladd-Taylor and Lauri Umansky. New York and London: New York University Press, 1998. 145–68.

Fenster, Mark. *Conspiracy Theories: Secrecy and Power in American Culture*. Minneapolis: University of Minnesota Press, 1999.

Fiedler, Leslie. *An End to Innocence: Essays on Culture and Politics*. Boston: Beacon Press, 1955.

Fish, Stanley. "Reverse Racism or How the Pot Got to Call the Kettle Black." In *There's No Such Thing as Free Speech, and It's a Good Thing, Too*. New York: Oxford University Press, 1994. 60–69.

Flanders, Laura. "Far-Right Militias and Anti-abortion Violence: When Will Media See the Connection?" *Extra! The Magazine of Fairness and Accuracy in Reporting* (July-August 1995): 11–12.

Flowers, Gennifer. *Passion and Betrayal*. Del Mar, CA: Emery Dalton Books, 1992.

Foucault, Michel. "Film and Popular Memory." In *Foucault Live: Interviews, 1966–1984*. Translated by Martin Jordin, edited by Sylvere Lotringer. New York: Semiotext(e), 1989. 89–106.

——. *The History of Sexuality*. Vol. 1: *An Introduction*. Translated by Robert Hurley. New York: Vintage, 1980.

——. *The History of Sexuality*. Vol. 2: *The Use of Pleasure*. Translated by Robert Hurley. New York: Vintage, 1990.

——. "Power and Strategies." In *Power/Knowledge: Selected Interviews and Other Writings, 1972–1977*. Translated and edited by Colin Gordon. New York: Pantheon, 1980. 134–45.

——. "Truth and Power." In *Power/Knowledge: Selected Interviews and Other Writings, 1972–1977*. Translated and edited by Colin Gordon. New York: Pantheon, 1980. 109–33.

Frazier, E. Franklin. *The Negro Family in the United States*. Chicago: University of Chicago Press, 1939.

Freedman, Estelle. "'Uncontrolled Desires': The Response to the Sexual Psychopath, 1920–1960." In *Passion and Power: Sexuality in History*. Edited by Kathy Peiss and Christina Simmons. Philadelphia: Temple University Press, 1989. 199–225.

Freud, Sigmund. *Civilization and Its Discontents*. Translated by James Strachey. New York: Norton, 1961.

——. *Group Psychology and the Analysis of the Ego*. Translated by James Strachey. London: Hogarth, 1945.

——. *Moses and Monotheism*. Translated by Katherine Jones. New York: Knopf, 1939.

——. *Totem and Taboo: Some Points of Agreement between the Mental Lives of Savages and Neurotics*. Translated by James Strachey. New York: Norton, 1952.

Friedan, Betty. *The Feminine Mystique*. New York: Norton, 1963.

Friedlander, Saul. *Reflections of Nazism: An Essay on Kitsch and Death*. Translated by Thomas Weyr. New York: Harper and Row, 1984.

"Friends, Fellow Soldiers Describe McVeigh as a Man of Valor, Contradictions." ⟨http://www.cnn.com⟩, 9 June 1997.

Fromm, Erich. *Escape from Freedom*. New York: Farrar and Rinehart, 1941.

——. "Sozialpsychologisher Teil." In *Studien über Autorität und Familie: Forschungsberichte aus dem Institut für Sozialforschung*. Edited by Institut für Sozialforschung. Paris: Félix Alcan, 1936.

——. "Zum Gefühl der Ohnmacht." *Zeitschrift für Sozialforschung* 4.1 (1937): 95–118.

Garber, Marjorie. *Vested Interests: Cross-Dressing and Cultural Anxiety*. New York: Routledge, 1992.

Gates, David, with Mark Miller. "Dr. Laura, Talk Radio Celebrity: She Apologizes after Antagonizing the Gay Community." *Newsweek*, 20 March 2000, 52.

"Gay Naziism Today." *Lambda Report on Homosexuality: Monitoring the Homosexual Agenda in American Politics* (April-June 1995): 5.

Gellespie, Ed, and Bob Schellhas, eds. *Contract with America: The Bold Plan by Rep. Newt Gingrich, Rep. Dick Armey, and the House Republicans to Change the Nation*. New York: Random House, 1994.

"Germany Needs 'Boy Fathers.'" *Living Age* 358 (1941): 136–39.

Germany Speaks: 21 Leading Members of Party and State. Preface by Joachim von Ribbentrop. London: Thornton Butterworth, 1938.

Gibson, James William. *Warrior Dreams: Paramilitary Culture in Post-Vietnam America*. New York: Hill and Wang, 1994.

Gilder, George. *Men and Marriage*. Gretna, LA: Pelican, 1993.

Giles, Geoffrey J. "'The Most Unkindest Cut of All': Castration, Homosexuality, and Nazi Justice." *Journal of Contemporary History* 27 (1992): 41–61.

Gilman, Sander L. *Difference and Pathology: Stereotypes of Sexuality, Race, and Madness*. Ithaca: Cornell University Press, 1985.

——. *Freud, Race, and Gender*. New York: Routledge, 1993.

——. *The Jew's Body*. New York: Routledge, 1991.

Ginsburg, Faye. "The 'Word-Made' Flesh: The Disembodiment of Gender in the Abortion Debate." In *Uncertain Terms: Negotiating Gender in American Culture*. Edited by Faye Ginsburg and Anna Lowenhaupt Tsing. Boston: Beacon, 1990.

Giroux, Henry. "The Challenge of Neo-fascist Culture." *Cineaste* 1.4 (1975): 31.

Gleick, Elizabeth. " 'Something Big Is Going to Happen.' " *Time*, 8 May 1995, 50–53.

Goddard, Henry Herbert. *The Kallikak Family: A Study in the Heredity of Feeble-Mindedness*. New York: Macmillan, 1912.

Goldberg, Jeffrey. "Washington Discovers Christian Persecution." *New York Times Magazine*, 21 December 1997, 46–62.

Goldstein, Patrick. "Courting Trouble: In *American History X*, the Biggest Turf Battles Have Happened Off-Screen." *Los Angeles Times*, 13 September 1998, Calendar, 5.

Goodstein, Laurie. "Gay-Rights Group Reels off a Reply to Critics: New Video Compares Widely Publicized Anti-homosexual Film to Nazi, Klan Propaganda." *Washington Post*, 18 February 1993, A6.

Greenspun, Roger. "Liza Minnelli Stirs a Lively 'Cabaret.' " *New York Times*, 14 February 1972, A22.

Greimas, A. J. *Structural Semantics: An Attempt at a Method*. Translated by Daniele McDowell, Ronald Schleifer, and Alan Velie. Lincoln: University of Nebraska Press, 1984.

Gross, Walter. "National Socialist Racial Thought." In *Germany Speaks: 21 Leading Members of Party and State*. Preface by Joachim von Ribbentrop. London: Thornton Butterworth, 1938. 64–75.

Grossack, M. M. "Group Belongingness and Authoritarianism in Southern Negroes: A Research Note." *Phylon* 18 (1957): 261–66.

"The Gun Lobby: With Another Showdown Pending in Congress, NRA Hard-Liners Seem to Thrive under Siege." *U.S. News and World Report*, 22 May 1995, 37.

Haaken, Janice. "The Recovery of Memory, Fantasy, and Desire: Feminist Approaches to Sexual Abuse and Psychic Trauma." *Signs* (summer 1996): 1069–94.

Habermas, Jürgen. "Citizenship and National Identity." In *The Condition of Citizenship*. Edited by Bart van Steenbergen. London: Sage, 1994. 20–35.

——. *The Structural Transformation of the Public Sphere: An Inquiry into a Category of Bourgeois Society*. Translated by Thomas Burger. Cambridge: MIT Press, 1996.

——. *The Theory of Communicative Action*. Translated by Thomas McCarthy. Boston: Beacon, 1985.

Hacker, Andrew. "Jewish Racism, Black Anti-Semitism." *Reconstruction* 1.3 (1991): 14–17.

Hacking, Ian. "The Making and Molding of Child Abuse." *Critical Inquiry* 17 (1991): 253–88.

Hackworth, David H., and Peter Annin. "The Suspect Speaks Out." *Newsweek*, 3 July 1995, 23–26.

Halberstam, Judith. "F2M: The Making of Female Masculinity." In *The Lesbian Postmodern*. Edited by Laura Doan. New York: Columbia University Press, 1994. 210–28.

——. "Transgender Butch: Butch/FTM Border Wars and the Masculine Continuum." *GLQ* 4.2 (1998): 287–310.

Hale, C. Jacob. "Consuming the Living, Dis(re)membering the Dead in the Butch/FTM Borderlands." *GLQ* 4.2 (1998): 311–48.

Hale, Nathan. *The Rise and Crisis of Psychoanalysis in the U.S.: Freud and the Americans, 1917–1985*. New York and Oxford: Oxford University Press, 1995.

Hamilton, Alice. "The Enslavement of Women." In *Nazism: An Assault on Civilization*. Edited by Pierre van Paassen and James Waterman Wise. New York: Harrison Smith and Robert Haas, 1934.

Hamm, Mark S. *American Skinheads: The Criminology and Control of Hate Crime*. Westport, CT: Praeger, 1993.

Hansen, Miriam Bratu. "*Schindler's List* Is Not *Shoah:* The Second Commandment, Popular Modernism, and Public Memory." *Critical Inquiry* 22 (1996): 292–312.

Hartman, Saidiya. *Scenes of Subjection: Terror, Slavery, and Self-Making in Nineteenth-Century America*. New York: Oxford University Press, 1997.

"Has My Child Become a Neo-Nazi?" Reprinted in *Granta* 42 (1992): 143.

Hebdige, Dick. *Subculture: The Meaning of Style*. London: Methuen, 1979.

Herald, George W. "Sex Is a Nazi Weapon." *American Mercury* 54 (June 1942): 662–63.

Herman, Ellen. *The Romance of American Psychology: Political Culture in the Age of Experts*. Berkeley: University of California Press, 1995.

Herzog, Dagmar. " 'Pleasure, Sex, and Politics Belong Together': Post-Holocaust Memory and the Sexual Revolution in West Germany." *Critical Inquiry* 24 (1998): 393–444.

Hewitt, Andrew. *Political Inversions: Homosexuality, Fascism, and the Modernist Imaginary*. Stanford: Stanford University Press, 1996.

Hill, Mike. "Introduction: Vipers in Shangri-la: Whiteness, Writing, and Other Ordinary Terrors." In *Whiteness: A Critical Reader*. Edited by Mike Hill. New York and London: New York University Press, 1997. 1–18.

Hinds, Lynn Boyd, and Theodore Otto Windt Jr. *The Cold War as Rhetoric: The Beginnings, 1945–1950*. New York: Praeger, 1991.

Hirschfeld, Magnus, et al. *The Sexual History of the World War*. New York: Cadillac Publishing, 1941.

Hirschman, Albert O. *The Rhetoric of Reaction: Perversity, Futility, Jeopardy*. Cambridge and London: Belknap Press of Harvard University Press, 1991.

"Hitler's Children." *Variety*, 30 December 1942, 16.

Hochman, Stanley. Foreword to *The Blue Angel: The Novel by Heinrich Mann, The Film by Josef von Sternberg*. New York: Ungar, 1979. 5–7.

Holden, Stephen. "Of Skinheads High on Hate and Violence." *New York Times*, 9 June 1993, C17.

Hollywood Online. "*American History X*." ⟨http://www.hollywood.com⟩, cited on 11 February 1999.

Horak, Jan-Christopher. *Anti-Nazi-Filme: der deutschsprichigen emmigration von Hollywood, 1939–1945*. Münster: Maks Publikationen, 1985.

——. "Liebe, Pflicht, und die Erotik des Todes." In *Preussen im Film*. Edited by Axel Marquardt and Heinz Rathsack. Berlin: Rowohlt, 1981. 205–18.

Horkheimer, Max. *Eclipse of Reason*. New York: Oxford University Press, 1947.

Houston, Beverle, and Marsha Kinder. "*The Night Porter* as Daydream." *Literature and Film Quarterly* 3.4 (1975): 366–67.

Humphreys, R. A. *Latin American and the Second World War*. Vols. 1–2. Atlantic Highlands, NJ: Humanities Press, 1981–82.

Insdorf, Annette. *Indelible Shadows: Film and the Holocaust*. Cambridge and New York: Cambridge University Press, 1983.

Institut für Sozialforschung. *Studien über Autorität und Familie: Forschungsberichte aus dem Institut für Sozialforschung*. Paris: Félix Alcan, 1936.

Isherwood, Christopher. *Goodbye to Berlin*. London: Triad/Panther Books, 1977.

Ivy, Marilyn. "Have You Seen Me? Recovering the Inner Child in Late Twentieth-Century America." *Social Text* 37 (1993): 27–52.

Jackson, Derrick Z. "True American Terror Is in Handguns, Not AK–47s." *Boston Globe*, 5 May 1995.

Jacobs, Lea. *The Wages of Sin: Censorship and the Fallen Woman Film, 1928–1942*. Madison: University of Wisconsin Press, 1991.

Jameson, Fredric. *The Political Unconscious: Narrative as a Socially Symbolic Act*. Ithaca: Cornell University Press, 1981.

Janofsky, Michael. "Demons and Conspiracies Haunt a 'Patriot' World." *New York Times*, 31 May 1995, A18.

Jay, Martin. *The Dialectical Imagination: A History of the Frankfurt School and the Institute of Social Research, 1923–1950*. Boston: Little, Brown, 1973.

Jelliffe, Belinda. Letter to the *American Mercury* 48 (April 1940): 252.

Jellonnek, Burkhard. *Homosexuelle unter dem Hakenkreuz: die Verfolgung von Homosexuellen im Dritten Reich*. Paderborn: Schöningh, 1990.

Johnson, Charles. *Growing up in the Black Belt: Negro Youth in the Rural South*. Washington, DC: American Council on Education, 1941.

Johnson, Hans. "Pink Swastika Strategy Becomes a Centerpiece." *Washington Blade*, 30 June 1995, 43.

Jones, Ernest. "The Psychology of Quislingism." *International Journal of Psycho-Analysis* 22.1 (January 1941): 1–6.

Jones, Tamara. "Germany's Troubles." *Los Angeles Times Magazine*, 7 March 1993, 14–20.

Jordan, Pat. "The Calling." *Los Angeles Times Magazine*, 28 July 1996, 16–18, 28, 30.

Kael, Pauline. "Stuck in the Fun." In *Reeling*. Boston: Little, Brown, 1976. 342.

Kaplan, E. Ann. "Madonna Politics: Perversion, Repression, or Subversion? Or Masks and/as Master-y." In *The Madonna Connection: Representational Politics, Subcultural Identities, and Cultural Theory*. Edited by Cathy Schwichtenberg. Boulder: Westview, 1992. 149–65.

Kardiner, Abram. *Sex and Morality*. New York: Bobbs-Merrill, 1954.

Kardiner, Abram, and Lionel Ovesey. *The Mark of Oppression: A Psychological Study of the American Negro*. New York: Norton, 1951.

Karon, Bertram. *The Negro Personality: A Rigorous Investigation of the Effects of Culture*. New York: Springer, 1958.

Kauffmann, Stanley. "Stanley Kauffmann on Films." *New Republic*, 4 March 1972, 22, 33.

——. "Stanley Kauffmann on Films." *New Republic*, 5 October 1974, 18, 33.

Keneally, Thomas. *Schindler's List*. New York: Simon and Schuster, 1982.

Kerber, Linda. *Women of the Republic: Intellect and Ideology in Revolutionary America*. Chapel Hill: University of North Carolina Press, 1980.

Keyser, Lester J., and Andre H. Ruszkowski. *The Cinema of Sidney Poitier: The Black Man's Changing Role on the American Screen*. San Diego and New York: A. S. Barnes, 1980.

King, Patricia. " 'Vipers' in the 'Burbs.' " *Newsweek*, 15 July 1996, 20–23.

Kintz, Linda. *Between Jesus and the Market: The Emotions That Matter in Right-Wing America*. Durham and London: Duke University Press, 1997.

Kintz, Linda, and Julia Lesage, eds. *Media, Culture, and the Religious Right*. Minneapolis: University of Minnesota Press, 1998.

Kipnis, Laura. "Adultery." *Critical Inquiry* 24 (1998): 289–327.

Kirkpatrick, Clifford. *Nazi Germany: Its Women and Family Life*. Indianapolis and New York: Bobbs-Merrill, 1938.

Klein, Ernst. "Woman in National Socialism." *Fortnightly* 157 (April 1942): 286.

Knauth, Percy. "Movie of the Week: Marlene Dietrich Steals the Show in an Uproarious Hollywood Version of Low Life in Postwar Berlin." *Life*, 9 June 1948, 59–64.

Koonz, Claudia. *Mothers in the Fatherland: Women, the Family, and Nazi Politics*. New York: St. Martin's, 1987.

Koop, C. Everett. "The Slide to Auschwitz." Afterword to *Abortion and the Conscience of the Nation*, by Ronald Reagan. Nashville: T. Nelson, 1984.

Kovaleski, Serge F. "Women in Militias Say Ranks Are Not Just for Angry White Males." *Washington Post*, 9 September 1995, A2–3.

Kracauer, Siegfried. "Die kleine Ladenmädchen gehen ins Kino." In *Das Ornament der Masse*. Frankfurt am Main: Suhrkamp, 1977. 279–94.

——. *From Caligari to Hitler: A Psychological History of the German Film*. Princeton: Princeton University Press, 1947.

Kristeva, Julia. *Powers of Horror: An Essay on Abjection*. Translated by Leon S. Roudiez. New York: Columbia University Press, 1982.

Kuhl, Stefan. *The Nazi Connection: Eugenics, American Racism, and German National Socialism*. New York: Oxford University Press, 1994.

Kunzel, Regina. "White Neurosis, Black Pathology: Constructing Out-of-Wedlock Pregnancy in the Wartime and Postwar United States." In *Not June Cleaver: Women and Gender in Postwar America, 1945–1960*. Edited by Joanne Meyerowitz. Philadelphia: Temple University Press, 1994. 304–31.

Ladd-Taylor, Molly, and Lauri Umansky, eds. "Introduction." In *"Bad" Mothers: The Politics of Blame in Twentieth-Century America*. New York: New York University Press, 1998.

LaHaye, Beverly. *Who but a Woman? Concerned Women Can Make a Difference*. Nashville: Thomas Nelson, 1984.

Landy, Marcia. *Cinematic Uses of the Past*. Minneapolis and London: University of Minnesota Press, 1996.

Langer, Walter C. *The Mind of Adolf Hitler: The Secret Wartime Report*. New York: Basic Books, 1972.

Lasswell, Harold P. "The Psychology of Hitlerism." *Political Quarterly* 4 (1933): 380.

Laurents, Arthur. *Home of the Brave*. New York: Random House, 1946.

Lee, Robert W. "An Insurrectionist Messenger." *New American*, 19 September 1994, 29–32.

Lengyel, Olga. *Five Chimneys: The Story of Auschwitz*. Translated by Paul P. Weiss. London: Mayflower, 1972.

Lerner, Max. *America as a Civilization*. New York: Simon and Schuster, 1957.

——. Introduction to *The Fifty-Minute Hour: A Collection of True Psychoanalytic Tales*, by Robert Lindner. New York: Bantam, 1966.

Lerner, Michael, and Cornel West. *Jews and Blacks: Let the Healing Begin*. New York: Grosset/Putnam, 1995.

Lewes, Kenneth. *The Psychoanalytic Theory of Male Homosexuality*. New York: New American Library, 1988.

Limbaugh, Rush. *The Way Things Ought to Be*. New York: Pocket Star Books, 1992.

Lind, William S., and William H. Marshner, eds. *Cultural Conservatism: Theory and Practice*. Washington, DC: Free Congress Foundation, 1991.

Lindner, Robert. *The Fifty-Minute Hour: A Collection of True Psychoanalytic Tales*. 20th ed. New York, Toronto, and London: Bantam, 1966.

——. *Must You Conform?* New York: Rinehart, 1956.

——. *Prescription for Rebellion*. New York: Rinehart, 1952.

——. *Rebel Without a Cause: The Hypnoanalysis of a Criminal Psychopath*. New York: Grune and Stratton, 1944.

——. *Stone Walls and Men*. New York: Odyssey, 1946.

Lippmann, Walter. *The Good Society*. Boston: Little, Brown, 1936.

Loewenberg, Peter. "Psychohistorical Perspectives on Modern German History." *Journal of Modern History* 47 (1975): 229–79.

Loshitzky, Yosefa, ed. *Spielberg's Holocaust: Critical Perspectives on Schindler's List*. Bloomington: Indiana University Press, 1997.

Lowry, Stephen. *Pathos und Politik: Ideologie in Spielfilmen des Nationalsozialismus*. Tübingen: Max Niemayer Verlag, 1991.

Lunbeck, Elizabeth. *The Psychiatric Persuasion: Knowledge, Gender, and Power in Modern America*. Princeton: Princeton University Press, 1994.

Lundberg, Ferdinand, and Marynia Farnham. *Modern Woman: The Lost Sex*. New York: Harper, 1947.

Macdonald, Andrew. *Hunter*. Hillsboro, WV: National Vanguard Books, 1989.

——. *The Turner Diaries*. Hillsboro, WV: National Vanguard Books, 1993.

Madsen, Axel. *Billy Wilder*. Bloominton and London: Indiana University Press, 1969.

"Man of the Year." *Time*, 1 January 1940, 14–17.

"Man of the Year." *Time*, 1 January 1942, 13–15.

Mann, Thomas. "An Appeal to Reason." In *Order of the Day: Political Essays and Speeches of Two Decades*. New York: Knopf, 1942.

Mapp, Edward. *Blacks in American Films: Today and Yesterday*. Metuchen, NJ: Scarecrow Press, 1972.

Marcuse, Herbert. *Eros and Civilization: A Philosophical Inquiry into Freud*. Boston: Beacon, 1974.

——. "The Struggle against Liberalism in the Totalitarian View of the State." In *Negations: Essays in Critical Theory*. Translated by Jeremy J. Shapiro. London: Free Association Books, 1988. 3–42.

Marrs, Texe. *Big Sister Is Watching You! Hillary Clinton and the White House Feminists Who Now Control America—and Tell the President What to Do*. Austin, TX: Living Truth Publishers, 1994.

Martin, William. *With God on Our Side: The Rise of the Religious Right in America*. New York: Broadway Books, 1996.

May, Elaine Tyler. *Homeward Bound: American Families in the Cold War Era*. New York: Basic Books, 1988.

Mayne, Judith. "Marlene Dietrich, *The Blue Angel*, and Female Performance." In *Seduction and Theory: Readings of Gender, Representation, and Rhetoric.* Edited by Dianne Hunter. Urbana and Chicago: University of Illinois Press, 1989. 28–46.

McCann, Carole R. *Birth Control Politics in the United States, 1916–1945.* Ithaca and New York: Cornell University Press, 1994.

McCormick, Anne O'Hare. "Homemaking under Hitler." *Ladies' Home Journal,* October 1933, 73–76.

McLain, Kenneth C. "The Untold Story of Marlene Dietrich." *Confidential: Tells the Facts and Names the Names* 3.3 (July 1955): 22–25, 56, 58.

Mehr, Max Thomas, and Regine Sylvester. "The Stone-Thrower from Eisenhuttenstadt." *Granta* 42 (1992): 133–42.

Mellencamp, Patricia. *Indiscretions: Avant-Garde Film, Video, and Feminism.* Bloomington: Indiana University Press, 1990.

Menninger, William. *Psychiatry in a Troubled World: Yesterday's War and Today's Challenge.* New York: Macmillan, 1948.

Messer-Davidow, Ellen. "Manufacturing the Attack on Liberalized Higher Education." *Social Text* 36 (1993): 40–80.

Meyerowitz, Joanne. "Beyond the Feminine Mystique: A Reassessment of Postwar Mass Culture, 1946–1958." In *Not June Cleaver: Women and Gender in Postwar America, 1945–1960.* Edited by Joanne Meyerowitz. Philadelphia: Temple University Press, 1994, 229–62.

Michelson, Annette. "Lolita's Progeny." *October* 76 (1996): 3–14.

Minish, Geoffrey. "*The Night Porter*: Last Tango in Auschwitz." *Take One* 4.5 (1974): 39–40.

Missildine, Hugh. *Your Inner Child of the Past.* New York: Simon and Schuster, 1963.

Mitchell, W. J. T. *Iconology: Image, Text, Ideology.* Chicago: University of Chicago Press, 1986.

Mizejewski, Linda. *Divine Decadence: Fascism, Female Spectacle, and the Makings of Sally Bowles.* Princeton: Princeton University Press, 1992.

Modleski, Tania. *Loving with a Vengeance: Mass-Produced Fantasies for Women.* New York and London: Methuen, 1982.

——. *The Women Who Knew Too Much: Hitchcock and Feminist Theory.* New York: Methuen, 1988.

Moeller, Robert G. " 'The Homosexual Man Is a 'Man,' the Homosexual Woman Is a 'Woman' ": Sex, Society, and the Law in Postwar West Germany." *Journal of the History of Sexuality* 4.3 (1994): 395–429.

Mookas, Ioannis. "Faultlines: Homophobic Innovation in *Gay Rights, Special Rights.*" *Afterimage* 22.7–8 (1995): 14–18.

Mosse, George L. *Nationalism and Sexuality: Respectability and Abnormal Sexuality in Modern Europe.* New York: Howard Fertig, 1985.

Mouffe, Chantal. "Democratic Citizenship and the Political Community." In *Community at Loose Ends.* Edited by the Miami Theory Collective. Minneapolis: University of Minnesota Press, 1991. 70–82.

Mueller, Christine L. "The Other Side of the Pink Triangle . . . Still a Pink Triangle." ⟨http://www.lavenderlinks.com⟩, 24 October 1994.

Mulvey, Laura. "Notes on Sirk and Melodrama." In *Visual and Other Pleasures.* Bloomington and Indianapolis: Indiana University Press, 1989. 39–48.

——. "Visual Pleasure and Narrative Cinema." In *Visual and Other Pleasures*. Bloomington and Indianapolis: Indiana University Press, 1989. 14–28.

Myrdal, Gunnar. *An American Dilemma: The Negro Problem and Modern Democracy*. New York and London: Harper and Brothers, 1944.

Nadeau, Chantal. "Girls on a Wired Screen: Cavani's Cinema and Lesbian S/M." In *Sexy Bodies: The Strange Carnalities of Feminism*. Edited by Elizabeth Grosz and Elspeth Probyn. London and New York: Routledge, 1995. 211–30.

Nairn, Tom. *The Break-up of Britain: Crisis and Neo-Nationalism*. London: Verso, 1981.

"The Nazis Are Kind to Women." *New Republic*, 19 August 1936, 39–41.

"Nazi Breeders." *Newsweek*, 4 May 1942, 38.

Neale, Steve. "Melodrama and Tears." *Screen* 27.6 (1986): 6–22.

Neumann, Franz. *Behemoth: The Structure and Practice of National Socialism, 1933–1944*. New York: Oxford University Press, 1944.

"OCA's Rise Meteoric since Start-up in 1986." *Oregonian*, 21 June 1993, B1, 4.

O'Regan, Tom. *Australian National Cinema*. London and New York: Routledge, 1996.

Ortner, Sherry B., and Harriet Whitehead. *Sexual Meanings: The Cultural Construction of Gender and Sexuality*. Cambridge and New York: Cambridge University Press, 1981.

Outram, Dorinda. *The Body and the French Revolution: Sex, Class, and Political Culture*. New Haven and London: Yale University Press, 1989.

Pankhurst, E. Sylvia. "Women in Totalitaria." *Living Age* 354 (June 1939): 366–69.

Paglia, Camille. "Madonna II: Venus of the Radio Waves." In *Sex, Art and American Culture: Essays*. New York: Vintage, 1992.

Parents, Friends, and Family of Lesbians and Gays (PFLAG). "Pat Robertson Doesn't Want You to Hear These Hateful Words on TV." Paid advertisement in *USA Today*, 20 December 1995, A12.

Parker, Andrew, Mary Russo, Doris Sommer, and Patricia Yaeger, eds. *Nationalisms and Sexualities*. New York and London: Routledge, 1992.

Parsons, Talcott. *Essays in Sociological Theory, Pure and Applied*. Glencoe, IL: Free Press, 1949.

Pattillo, Linda. "Shadowy Threat of Extremist Hate Groups Quietly Growing." ⟨http://www.cnn.com⟩, 24 April 1998.

Paul, Diane B. *Controlling Human Heredity, 1865 to the Present*. Atlantic Highlands, NJ: Humanities Press, 1995.

Pease, Donald. "National Identities, Postmodern Artifacts, and Postnational Narratives." *boundary 2* 19.1 (1992): 1–13.

Pellegrini, Ann. *Performance Anxieties: Staging Psychoanalysis, Staging Race*. New York: Routledge, 1997.

Petro, Patrice. *Joyless Streets: Women and Melodramatic Representation in Weimar Germany*. Princeton: Princeton University Press, 1989.

Pettigrew, Thomas F. *A Profile of the Negro American*. Princeton: Van Nostrand, 1964.

Pfeil, Fred. "Sympathy for the Devils: Notes on Some White Guys in the Ridiculous Class War." In *Whiteness: A Critical Reader*. Edited by Mike Hill. New York and London: New York University Press, 1997. 21–34.

Plath, Sylvia. "Daddy." In *The Norton Anthology of Literature by Women: The Tradition in English*. Edited by Sandra M. Gilbert and Susan Gubar. New York and London: Norton, 1985, 2208.

"The Plot," *Newsweek*, 8 May 1995, 28–34.

Polan, Dana. *Power and Paranoia: History, Narrative, and the American Cinema, 1940–1950.* New York: Columbia University Press, 1986.

Porteous, Skipp. "Inside Glen Eyrie Castle: The Organized Assault on Gay Rights." *Freedom Writer* (August 1994).

Potok, Mark, and Katy Kelly. "Militia Movement's Draw: A Shared Anger, Fear." *USA Today*, 16 May 1995, D6.

Potter, La Forest. *Strange Loves: A Study in Sexual Abnormalities.* New York: Padell, 1933.

Poulantzas, Nikos. *Fascism and Dictatorship: The Third International and the Problem of Fascism.* Translated by Judith White, edited by Jennifer and Timothy O'Hagan. London: NLB, 1974.

Proctor, Robert. *Racial Hygiene: Medicine under the Nazis.* Cambridge and London: Harvard University Press, 1988.

"Profile of Timothy McVeigh" (online). Dated 12 April 1999. Available on the World Wide Web: ⟨http://cnn.com/resources/newsmakers/usnewsmakers/mcveigh.html/⟩.

"Pssst! Calling All Paranoids." *Time*, 8 May 1995, 69.

Ranyard, Anthony. Letter to the *Daily Telegraph*, 10 July 1998, 12.

Reich, Wilhelm. *The Mass Psychology of Fascism.* Translated by Vincent R. Carfagno. New York: Farrar, Straus and Giroux, 1970.

Reid-Pharr, Robert. "Speaking through Anti-Semitism: The Nation of Islam and the Poetics of Black (Counter)Modernity." *Social Text* 49 (1996): 133–47.

Reisman, Judith A., and Edward Eichel. *Kinsey, Sex, and Fraud* (Lafayette, LA: Huntington House, 1990).

Rentschler, Eric. *The Ministry of Illusion: Nazi Cinema and Its Afterlife.* Cambridge: Harvard University Press, 1996.

Reuters News Service. "Berlin's Marlene Dietrich Street Hits Resistance" (online). Dated 30 October 1996. Available on the World Wide Web: ⟨http://www.elibrary.com/⟩.

Reynolds, Quentin. "Woman's Place." *Collier's*, 25 November 1933, 22, 48–49.

Ridgeway, James. *Blood in the Face: The Ku Klux Klan, Aryan Nations, Nazi Skinheads, and the Rise of the New White Culture.* New York: Thunder's Mouth Press, 1990.

"Right in Disarray as Bush Quits Gun Lobby." *Guardian*, 12 May 1995, A1, 16.

Rimer, Sara. "With Extremism and Explosives, a Drifting Life Found a Purpose." *New York Times*, 28 May 1995, A1, 12–13.

Riva, Maria. *Marlene Dietrich.* London: Bloomsbury, 1992.

Roberts, Greg. "One Nation Alleges Theft of Names List." *Sydney Morning Herald*, 10 July 1998, 4.

Robinson, Victor, ed. *Morals in Wartime.* New York: Publishers Foundation, 1943.

Rogin, Michael. *Blackface, White Noise.* Berkeley: University of California Press, 1996.

——. "Kiss Me Deadly: Communism, Motherhood, and Cold War Movies." *Representations* 6 (1984): 1–36.

——. *Ronald Reagan, the Movie and Other Episodes in Political Demonology.* Berkeley: University of California Press, 1987.

Rose, Ramona M. *Position and Treatment of Women in Nazi Germany as Viewed from the Perspective of the English Language Press, 1933–1945.* Vancouver: Tantalus Research, 1984.

Rosen, Hanna. "L.A. Shooting May Have Been Initiation Rite." *Washington Post*, 12 August 1999, A1.

Rosenfeld, Alvin H. *Imagining Hitler*. Bloomington: Indiana University Press, 1985.

Ross, Loretta J., and Mary Ann Mauney. "The Changing Faces of White Supremacy." In *Critical White Studies: Looking behind the Mirror*. Edited by Richard Delgado and Jean Stefancic. Philadelphia: Temple University Press, 1997. 552–60.

Rubin, Gayle. "Thinking Sex: Notes for a Radical Theory of the Politics of Sexuality." In *Pleasure and Danger: Exploring Female Sexuality*. Edited by Carole S. Vance. Boston: Routledge and Kegan Paul, 1984. 267–319.

Rupp, Leila. *Mobilizing Women for War: German and American Propaganda, 1939–1945*. Princeton: Princeton University Press, 1978.

Ryan, Mary P. *The Empire of the Mother: American Writing about Domesticity, 1830–1860*. New York: Haworth, 1982.

Sacher-Masoch, Leopold von. *Venus in Furs*. Translated by Jean McNeil. Reprinted in *Masochism: An Interpretation of Coldness and Cruelty*, by Gilles Deleuze. New York: George Braziller, 1971. 141–271.

SAMOIS, eds. *Coming to Power: Writings and Graphics on Lesbian S/M*. Palo Alto: Up Press, 1981.

Sarris, Andrew. "The Nasty Nazis: History or Mythology?" *Village Voice*, 17 October 1974, 77–78.

Sartre, Jean-Paul. *Anti-Semite and Jew*. Translated by George J. Becker. New York: Schocken, 1948.

Schachter, J., and H. Butts. "Transference and Countertransference in Inter-racial Analyses." *Journal of the American Psychoanalytic Association* 16 (1971): 792–808.

Schafer, Roy. "Narration in the Psychoanalytic Dialogue." In *On Narrative*. Edited by W. J. T. Mitchell. Chicago: University of Chicago Press, 1981. 25–49.

Scheid, Ed. "Pariah," Boxoffice Online Movie Reviews, ⟨http://www.boxoff.com⟩.

Schlesinger, Arthur. *The Vital Center: The Politics of Freedom*. Boston: Houghton Mifflin, 1949.

Schreiber, Rachel. "Please Kill Me; I'm a Faggot Nigger Jew." *Davka: Jewish Cultural Revolution* 1.3 (1997): 20–21.

Schulte-Sasse, Linda. "The Jew as Other under National Socialism: Veit Harlan's *Jud Süss*." *German Quarterly* (winter 1988): 22–49.

Schwichtenberg, Cathy. "Madonna's Postmodern Feminism: Bringing the Margins to the Center." In *The Madonna Connection: Representational Politics, Subcultural Identities, and Cultural Theory*. Edited by Cathy Schwichtenberg. Boulder: Westview, 1992. 129–45.

Sedgwick, Eve Kosofsky. *Epistemology of the Closet*. Berkeley and Los Angeles: University of California Press, 1990.

Seven Promises of a Promise Keeper. Colorado Springs: Focus on the Family, 1994.

Shaver, Mike. "Citizens Project." *Freedom Watch* 3.4 (July-August 1994). People for the American Way clippings archive. Washington, D.C.

Shaw, Roger. "Visiting the Third Reich." *Review of Reviews and World's Work* (January 1934): 38.

Shumate, Richard. "How Anti-gay is the Militant Right?" *Windy City Times*, 11 May 1995, 1, 10.

Silverman, Kaja. "Masochism and Subjectivity." *Framework: A Film Journal* 12 (1980): 2–9.

Singular, Stephen. *Talked to Death: The Murder of Alan Berg.* New York: Beech Tree Books, 1987.

Smith, Dave. *Disney A to Z: The Official Encyclopedia.* New York: Hyperion, 1996.

Smith, Lillian. *Killers of the Dream.* New York: Norton, 1949.

Smith-Rosenberg, Carroll. *Disorderly Conduct: Visions of Gender in Victorian America.* New York: Knopf, 1985.

Smoodin, Eric. *Animating Culture: Hollywood Cartoons from the Sound Era.* New Brunswick, NJ: Rutgers University Press, 1993.

Solon, S. L., and Albert Brandt. "Sex under the Swastika." *American Mercury* 47 (August 1939): 426.

Sontag, Susan. "Fascinating Fascism." In *Under the Sign of Saturn.* New York: Vintage, 1981. 72–105.

Spillers, Hortense J. "Mama's Baby, Papa's Maybe: An American Grammar Book." *diacritics* (summer 1987): 65–81.

Spock, Benjamin. *Baby and Child Care.* New York: Hawthorn, 1968.

Spoto, Donald. *Falling in Love Again: Marlene Dietrich.* Boston: Little, Brown, 1985.

Star, Susan Leigh. "Swastikas: The Street and the University." In *Against Sadomasochism: A Radical Feminist Analysis.* Edited by Robin Ruth Linden, Darlene R. Pagano, Diana E. H. Russell, and Susan Leigh Star. East Palo Alto: Frog in the Well, 1982. 131–36.

Steckler, G. A. "Authoritarian Ideology in Negro College Students." *Journal of Abnormal and Social Psychology* 54 (1957): 396–99.

Sterritt, David. "Romper Stomper." *Christian Science Monitor,* 11 June 1993, 12.

Stetson, Conn, and Byron Fairchild. *The Framework of Hemisphere Defense: The U.S. Army in World War II, the Western Hemisphere.* Vol. 1. Washington, DC: Office of Military History, Department of the Army, 1960.

Stevenson, William. *A Man Called Intrepid: The Secret War.* New York: Harcourt, Brace, Jovanovich, 1976.

Strecker, Edward. *Their Mothers' Sons: The Psychiatrist Examines an American Problem.* Philadelphia and New York: Lippincott, 1946.

Studlar, Gaylyn. *In the Realm of Pleasure: Von Sternberg, Dietrich, and the Masochistic Aesthetic.* Urbana and Chicago: University of Illinois Press, 1988.

Summer, Doris. "Irresistible Romance: The Foundational Fictions of Latin America." In *Nation and Narration.* Edited by Homi Bhabha. London and New York: Routledge, 1990. 71–98.

Sutherland, Robert Lee. *Color, Class, and Personality.* Washington, DC: American Council on Education, 1952.

Sykes, Charles. *A Nation of Victims: The Decay of the American Character.* New York: St. Martin's, 1992.

Symons, Emma-Kate. "I Don't Want Racists in My One Nation." *Daily Telegraph,* 10 July 1998, 4.

Tamblyn, Christine. "The River of Swill: Feminist Art, Sexual Codes, and Censorship." *Afterimage* (October 1990): 10–13.

Taussig, Michael. *The Nervous System.* New York: Routledge, 1992.

Taylor, Clarke. "Overview of Underground," *Los Angeles Times*, 24 April 1983, Calendar, 45.

Taylor, Diana. *Disappearing Acts: Spectacles of Gender and Nationalism in Argentina's 'Dirty War'*. Durham, NC: Duke University Press, 1997.

Terry, Jennifer. *An American Obsession: Science, Medicine, and the Place of Homosexuality in Modern Society*. Chicago: University of Chicago Press, 1999.

——. "'Momism' and the Making of Treasonous Homosexuals." In *"Bad" Mothers: The Politics of Blame in Twentieth-Century America*. Edited by Molly Ladd-Taylor and Lauri Umansky. New York: New York University Press, 1998. 169–90.

Theweleit, Klaus. *Male Fantasies*. Translated by Stephen Conway with Erica Carter and Chris Turner. Vols. 1–2. Minneapolis: University of Minnesota Press, 1987–89.

Thomas, Cal. "Culture of Death, Imposed on the Unborn, Targets the Elderly." *Los Angeles Times*, 13 March 1996.

Thomas, Katharine. *Women in Nazi Germany*. London: Victor Golland, 1943.

Thompson, Dorothy. "The Stake for Women." *Ladies' Home Journal*, October 1942, 6.

Timberg, Robert. *The Nightingale's Song*. New York: Simon and Schuster, 1995.

Tocqueville, Alexis de. *Democracy in America*. Translated by George Lawrence, edited by J. P. Mayer and Max Lerner. New York: Harper and Row, 1966.

Trilling, Lionel. *The Liberal Imagination: Essays on Literature and Society*. New York: Viking, 1950.

Turim, Maureen. "Psychological Melodrama in the 1940s: *The Locket*." *boundary 2* (1983– 84): 321–32.

Veith, Gene Edward. *Modern Fascism: Liquidating the Judeo-Christian Worldview*. St. Louis: Concordia, 1993.

——. *Postmodern Times: A Christian Guide to Contemporary Thought and Culture*. Wheaton, IL: Crossway Books, 1994.

Vogel, Ursula. "Marriage and the Boundaries of Citizenship." In *The Condition of Citizenship*. Edited by Bart van Steenbergen. London: Sage, 1994. 76–89.

Von Sternberg, Josef. "Introduction." In *The Blue Angel: The Novel by Heinrich Mann, the Film by Josef von Sternberg*. New York: Frederick Ungar, 1979. 257–63.

Waite, Robert. *The Psychopathic God: Adolf Hitler*. New York: Basic Books, 1977.

Walker, Alexander. *Dietrich*. London: Thames and Hudson, 1984.

Walkowitz, Judith, and Myra Jehlen. "Patrolling the Borders: Feminist Historiography and the New Historicism." *Radical History Review* 43 (1989): 23–43.

Wallace, Michele. "Race, Gender, and Psychoanalysis in Forties Film: *Lost Boundaries, Home of the Brave*, and *The Quiet One*." In *Black American Cinema*. Edited by Manthia Diawara. New York: Routledge, 1993. 257–71.

Warner, William Lloyd, et al. *Color and Human Nature: Negro Personality Development in a Northern City*. Washington, DC: American Council on Education, 1947.

Weber, Max. *The Protestant Ethic and the Spirit of Capitalism*. Translated by Talcott Parsons. New York: Scribner, 1958.

Weber, Stu. *Locking Arms: God's Design for Masculine Friendships*. Sisters, OR: Multnomah, 1995.

——. *Tender Warrior: God's Intention for a Man*. Sisters, OR: Multnomah, 1993.

Wedekind, Frank. *The Lulu Plays and Other Sex Tragedies*. Translated by Stephen Spender. London: John Calder, 1972.

Weidl, Erhard. "Nachwort." In *Lulu: Erdgeist, Büchse der Pandora* by Frank Wedekind. Stuttgart: Philipp Reclam, 1989. 183–206.

Weiss, Andrea. "A Queer Feeling When I Look at You." In *Stardom: Industry of Desire.* Edited by Christine Gledhill. London and New York: Routledge, 1991. 283–99.

Weisstein, Naomi. "'Kinder, Kuche [sic], Kirche' as Scientific Law: Psychology Constructs the Female." In *Sisterhood Is Powerful: An Anthology of Writings from the Women's Liberation Movement.* Edited by Robin Morgan. New York: Vintage, 1970. 228–45.

Wells, Ron. "American History X" (online). *Film Threat Weekly.* Dated 19 October 1998. Available on the World Wide Web: ⟨http://www.filmthreat.com⟩.

West, Cornell. *Race Matters.* Boston: Beacon, 1993.

Wexman, Virginia Wright. "The Critic as Consumer: Film Study in the University, *Vertigo*, and the Film Canon." *Film Quarterly* 39.3 (1986): 32–41.

White, Mel. *Stranger at the Gate: To Be Gay and Christian in America.* New York: Simon and Schuster, 1994.

White, Patricia. "Supporting Character: The Queer Career of Agnes Moorehead." In *Out in Culture: Gay, Lesbian, and Queer Essays on Popular Culture.* Edited by Corey K. Creekmur and Alexander Doty. Durham and London: Duke University Press, 1995. 91–114.

"White Supremacist Novel Key Evidence in McVeigh Trial." ⟨http://www.cnn.com⟩, 24 March 1997.

Williams, Raymond. *Keywords: A Vocabulary of Culture and Society.* New York: Oxford University Press, 1976.

Willis, Paul. *Learning to Labor: How Working Class Kids Get Working Class Jobs.* New York: Columbia University Press, 1977.

Wilson, Elizabeth. "Not in This House: Incest, Denial, and Doubt in the White Middle Class Family." *Yale Journal of Criticism* 8 (1995): 35–58.

Winder, F. "Nazi Amazons." *Living Age* 353 (1938): 452–53.

Winterson, Jeannette. *Written on the Body.* New York: Vintage International, 1992.

Wittels, Fritz. "Collective Defense Mechanisms against Homosexuality." *Psychoanalytic Review* 31 (1944): 19–33.

Wollen, Peter. *Signs and Meaning in the Cinema.* Bloomington: Indiana University Press, 1969.

"Women in Uniform," *Living Age* 354 (May 1938): 258–60.

The World Almanac and Book of Facts, 1998. Mahwah, NJ: World Almanac Books, 1997.

Wylie, Philip. *Generation of Vipers.* 20th ed. New York: Farrar and Rinehart, 1955.

Young, Lola. *Fear of the Dark: 'Race,' Gender, and Sexuality in the Cinema.* London and New York: Routledge, 1996.

Zaretsky, Eli. "Hannah Arendt and the Meaning of the Public/Private Distinction." In *Hannah Arendt and the Meaning of Politics.* Edited by Craig Calhoun and John McGowan. Minneapolis: University of Minnesota Press, 1997. 207–31.

Ziemer, Gregor. "Education for Death." *Reader's Digest* (February 1942): 129–44.

——. *Education for Death: The Making of the Nazi.* London and New York: Oxford University Press, 1941.

——. "How Hitler Builds His 'Super Race.'" *Maclean's*, 15 October 1941, 43.

Žižek, Slavoj. *The Sublime Object of Ideology.* London and New York: Verso, 1989.

Index

■

Anti-Semitism (*cont.*)
  160, 172–73, 176–77, 179–80, 182,
  191–95, 234–35, 283, 296 n.15, 298
  n.36, 300 n.10, 302 n.54, 304 n.8, 305
  n.11, 316 n.25, 320 n.71, 322 n.18, 339
  n.77. See also Pierce, Willam
Apathy: political, 257–60
Appadurai, Arjun, 6, 288–89
Arendt, Hannah, 10, 12
Authoritarian Personality, The. See Frankfurt
  School

B, Beth: *Amnesia,* 337 n.50; *Belladonna*
  (with Ida Applebroog), 266–69, 337
  nn.52, 54, 55
Barr, Donna: *Desert Peach, The,* 252–54,
  334 nn.8, 9, 10
Barthes, Roland, 215–16
Benjamin, Walter. *See* Frankfurt School
Berlant, Lauren, 11–13, 43, 72, 73–74,
  79–80, 83, 86, 104, 137, 269, 306 n.31,
  308 n.62
Bertolucci, Bernardo: *Conformist, The,*
  257
Bettleheim, Bruno, 143
Bhabha, Homi, 7–8, 15, 23, 25, 41, 47,
  87, 121, 255, 287, 294 n.9
Blackness: blackface, 163–64; images of
  men, 136, 138, 149–52, 155–69, 191,
  194, 202–5, 319 nn.53, 54; images of
  women, 160, 165–68; subjectivity, 318
  n.48, 319 n.53. *See also* Racial identity;
  Racism
Bisexuality. *See* Sexuality
Blue Angel, The, 19, 218–30, 232–33, 239–
  40, 244, 246–51, 253–58, 264, 286. *See
  also* Dietrich, Marlene; von Sternberg,
  Josef
Boys from Brazil, The, 174–75. *See also*
  Mengele, Josef
Brooks, Louise, 225. *See also* Wedekind,
  Frank
Bureau of Alcohol, Tobacco, and Fire-
  arms (BATF), 73, 98–102. *See also* Anti-
  federal government rhetoric; Ruby
  Ridge; Waco
Bush, George, 266

Cabaret, 228, 258–62, 270. *See also* Diet-
  rich, Marlene: as Sally Bowles; Isher-
  wood, Christopher
Camp: sensibility, 229, 250–51, 253, 323
  n.28
Capra, Frank: "Why We Fight," 141
Carter, Jimmy, 78–79
Cavani, Lilliana, 336 n.32, 338 n.68; *Night
  Porter, The,* 253–54, 257–64, 267, 272,
  274–75, 281, 286, 335 n.18, 337 n.54
Chaplin, Charlie: *Great Dictator, The,* 234–
  35, 303 n.54. *See also* Comedy
Child abuse, 267–69. *See also* Incest
Christianity: anti-Nazi, 3, 45, 50–54,
  71–105, 299 n.4, 301 n.25. *See also*
  Family values rhetoric; Nationalism:
  nationalist melodrama; Nazism; Social
  conservative organizations; Social
  conservatives
Civil rights movement, 77, 149, 169, 187,
  293 n.7; *See also* Blackness; Racism
Class. *See* Global economy
Clinton, Bill, 72, 88, 98, 100–102, 278–
  79; Health Security Plan, 73, 84–88;
  impeachment, 304 n.4. See also *Waco
  II: The Big Lie Continues; Who Lives?
  Who Dies? Who Cares?*
Clinton, Hillary, 87–88, 278–79
Cold War, 18, 123–24, 131, 138–75, 240–
  45. *See also* Nationalism: national psy-
  chobiography; *Pressure Point*
Comedy, 233–40, 302 n.54. *See also*
  Sturges, Preston; Wilder, Billy
Conspiracy theory, 309 n.73. *See also* Anti-
  federal government rhetoric
Cornfield, Hubert, 18, 144–45, 165, 171–
  72, 317 nn.31, 40. See also *Pressure
  Point*
Cross-dressing, 228, 230–31, 233, 243–
  45, 256, 261, 275, 282, 314 n.58, 328
  n.26, 330 n.57, 331 n.73. *See also* An-
  drogyny; Drag
Crossfire, 148, 320 n.71. *See also* Dmytryk,
  Edward; Nationalism: national
  psychobiography
Crowther, Bosley. *See* Journalism
Cultural rhetoric: as a concept, 13–17

Homosexuality. *See* Sexuality
Horkhiemer, Max. *See* Frankfurt School

Ilsa, She Wolf of the SS, 248–51, 255, 334
n.4. *See also* Exploitation films
Images: iconology, 215–47
Incest, 197–201, 254, 265–66. *See also*
Feminism; Psychoanalysis: Oedipus
complex
Internet, 283–85
Isherwood, Christopher, 228–30, 258,
261. See also *Cabaret*

Japan, 58, 314 n.56; and Japanese Americans, 303 n.55. *See also* Dmytryk, Edward; Racism
Jewishness, 281–84, 290–92, 337 n.54;
images of men, 138, 149–56, 159, 162,
164, 192–95, 203; images of women,
172–73, 260, 270–71, 275, 281–86,
290–92, 317 n.34; resistance fighters,
282, 290–92. *See also* B, Beth; Flanders,
Ellen; Freud, Sigmund; Holocaust;
Schreiber, Rachel
Journalism, 14, 23–24, 31, 47–54, 109–
12, 141, 178–81, 183–86, 195, 227–28,
243–44; Crowther, Bosley, 59, 64,
239–240; film reviews, 59, 64, 199,
207–8, 232–33, 239–40, 258–62;
Mencken, H. L., 297 n.24; Thompson,
Dorothy, 329 n.45
Judgment at Nuremberg, 147, 245, 333 n.93.
See also Dietrich, Marlene; Kramer,
Stanley
Jud Süss, 298 n.35. *See also* Harlan, Veit
Just a Gigolo, 257–58. *See also* Dietrich,
Marlene

Kaye, Tony, 325 nn.51, 52. See also *Amer-
ican History X*
Keneally, Thomas, 270–71. See also
Schindler's List
Kennedy, D. James. *See* Social
conservatives
Kennedy, John F., 77
Kirkpatrick, Clifford, 31–32, 48–49, 169
Kracauer, Siegfried, 26, 122–23, 224–26,

228, 253. *See also* Nationalism: national
psychobiography
Kramer, Stanley, 144–45, 147–51, 157,
160, 245, 316 n.21, 317 n.40. See also
*Defiant Ones, The; Home of the Brave;
Judgment at Nuremberg; Pressure Point*

LaBruce, Bruce: *No Skin Off My Ass* and
Skin Flick, 3232 n.28. *See also* Camp;
Skinheads
Lacan, Jacques, 7, 121, 336 n.38
Langer, Walter C., 116–17, 311 n.20. *See also*
Nationalism: national psychobiography
Leander, Zarah, 329 n.37
Lerner, Max, 145, 316 n.17
Lesbianism. *See* Sexuality
Liberalism, 45, 51, 73, 124, 129, 139, 146,
178; liberal humanism, 191–92, 195,
200, 204, 206–10. *See also* Democracy;
Nationalism: national psychobiogra-
phy; New Deal
Life is Beautiful, 69
Lili Marleen, 258; "Lili Marleen" (song),
333 n.93. *See also* Dietrich, Marlene
Linder, Robert, 138, 144–47, 149–56,
161, 163, 165, 170–74, 192, 315 n.15.
See also *Pressure Point*
Lola Lola. See *Blue Angel, The;* Dietrich,
Marlene
Lubitsch, Ernst: *To Be or Not to Be,* 234–
35, 303 n.54, 330 n.56. *See also* Comedy

Macdonald, Andrew. *See* Pierce, William
Madonna: *Justify My Love,* 274–75, 286;
Open Your Heart, 275
Mann, Heinrich, 219–21, 225–26. See
also *Blue Angel, The*
Mann, Thomas, 299 n.3
Marcuse, Herbert, 78, 119–21, 273
Masculinity. *See* Gender
Masochism. *See* Sadomasochism
McVeigh, Timothy, 109, 111, 178, 184–
85, 187, 207, 322 nn.17, 22, 326 nn.55,
56, 57; Oklahoma City bombing, 72,
178, 183–84. *See also* Anti-federal gov-
ernment rhetoric; Anti-gun control
rhetoric; Militia movement; Waco

fascism as, 213–47; and spectacle, 254, 260–64. *See also* Dietrich, Marlene

Pettigrew, Thomas, 166–68, 319 n.53. *See also* Frankfurt School: *Authoritarian Personality, The*; Nationalism: national psychobiography; Racism

Pierce, William, 176, 181; *Hunter,* 181–82, 200; *Turner Diaries, The,* 176–79, 184–85, 188, 321 n.1, 322 nn.20, 22, 324, n.30, 326 n.56

Pink swastika, 73, 92–94. *See also* Family values rhetoric

Pink triangle, 91–93, 281–82. *See also* Gay and lesbian rights

Poitier, Sidney, 138, 144, 147–52, 156–63, 171, 191, 316 n.27, 317 n.31. See also *Defiant Ones, The*; Kramer, Stanley; *Pressure Point*

Political correctness, 278, 280

Political psychology. *See* Psychology

Popular Front, 124. *See also* New Deal

Postcolonialism, 6–8, 169. *See also* Appadurai, Arjun; Bhabha, Homi; Fanon, Franz; Postnationalism

Postmodernism, 246, 250–52, 254–55, 259–60, 272, 274–76, 283, 290, 336 n.38

Postnationalism, 288–90, 292

Poverty. *See* Global economy

Pressure Point, 18, 138–40, 144–74, 191–92, 204, 317 nn.31, 39, 40. *See also* Kramer, Stanley; Lindner, Robert; Nationalism: national psychobiography; Poitier, Sidney

Private sphere. *See* Public sphere

Production Code Administration (PCA), 27, 55–57, 60, 148, 222–23, 234–35, 237–38, 331 nn.69, 74

Pro-life rhetoric. *See* Family values rhetoric

Promiscuity. *See* Sexuality

Psychoanalysis, 18, 114, 116–37, 143–74, 191–95, 313 n.47, 315 n.10, 317 n.39, 318 nn.46, 48, 319 n.59, 320 n.60, 332 n.80, 337 n.44, 338 n.61; abjection, 256–57; Oedipus complex, 114–22, 125–36, 146, 151–52, 154–57, 160,

162–68, 170, 173–75, 192–95, 246, 253–57, 260–64, 267–68, 273, 334 n.15, 337 n.52; popular, 144–75, 312 n.46, 315 n.16. *See also* Freud, Sigmund; Nationalism: national psychobiography

Psychobiography. *See* Nationalism

Psychology: adult child movement, 265–66; political, 109, 111, 114, 224–27, 241–43, 255–59, 272–73, 310 n.6, 313 n.50. *See also* Psychoanalysis

Public sphere: as replaced by or merged with private sphere, 9–13, 20, 43–44, 54, 66, 68, 72, 74–75, 79–80, 89–90, 104, 129, 134–37, 183, 187, 190, 197–98, 201, 207, 209–10, 264–72, 280, 292, 301 n.25

Queer sensibility, 113, 272, 276, 281–83. *See also* Gay and lesbian rights; Gender; Sexuality

Racial identity, 317 nn.31, 39, 319 n.58. *See also* Blackness; Jewishness; Whiteness

Racism, 5–7, 27, 29–40, 53, 60–61, 63, 65, 78, 100, 109–12, 120, 129, 139, 142–44, 147–69, 176–210, 227, 275, 280, 282–83, 293 n.7, 295 n.7, 298 n.36, 303 n.55, 304 n.8, 311 n.24, 316 n.24, 316 nn.26, 27, 317 n.40, 318 nn.41, 42, 48, 319 nn.50, 54, 320 n.71, 322 n.18, 337 n.50. *See also* Anti-Semitism; Neo-Nazi organizations; Pierce, William; Skinheads

Racist organizations: Ku Klux Klan, 183, 321 n.4; Phineas Priesthood, 208. *See also* Neo-Nazi organizations; Skinheads; White supremacism

Reagan, Ronald, 266, 274

Reich, Wilhelm, 26, 120, 273, 338 n.61

Reproduction. *See* Eugenics; Nationalism: nationalist melodrama

Republican Party. *See* Family values rhetoric

Riefenstahl, Leni, 19, 248, 333 n.1; *Triumph of the Will,* 19, 96, 239, 302 n.51, 308 n.62

Rightist organizations, 176–210; *See also* Racist organizations; Neo-Nazi organizations; Social conservative organizations

Robertson, Pat. *See* Social conservatives

Robeson, Paul, 149, 316 n.27

Rome: Open City. See Rossellini, Roberto

Romper Stomper, 189–90, 195–204, 206, 325 n.46. *See also* Skinheads

Rops, Félicien, 219–20, 328 n.17

Rossellini, Roberto: *Germany, Year Zero* and *Rome: Open City,* 123, 124

Ruby Ridge: siege on, 100. *See also* Anti-federal government rhetoric; Anti-gun control rhetoric; Bureau of Alcohol, Tobacco, and Firearms (BATF); White supremacism

Sadism. *See* Sadomasochism: sadism

Sadomasochism, 6, 9, 11, 115, 217, 224–26, 238, 251–52, 272, 274–75, 281, 283–85, 336 n.35; masochism, 118–19, 122, 262–63, 267–68, 290–92, 332 n.77, 336 n.38, 337 n.52; sadism, 120, 171, 250–51, 259, 305 n.24, 320 n.68, 333 n.2, 335 n.15. *See also* Sexuality

Schell, Maximilian: *Marlene,* 335 n.19. *See also* Dietrich, Marlene

Schindler's List, 180, 267, 270–72, 321 n.7, 338 n.58. *See also* Nationalism: nationalist melodrama

Schreiber, Rachel, 240 n.8; *Please Kill Me; I'm a Faggot Nigger Jew,* 280–81, 283–86, 290, 339 n.83; *This is Not Erotica,* 290–92

Serpent's Egg, The, 335 n.21

Sexism, 205, 319 nn.53, 54. *See also* Family values rhetoric; Feminism

Sexuality: bisexuality, 217, 232, 243–44, 261, 274, 314 n.57, 320 n.68; frigidity, 234–37; gay men, 83, 89–90, 93, 95–97, 194; heterosexuality, 116, 119, 124, 128, 136, 158, 162, 167, 169–74, 194–201, 206, 208–9, 229, 232–33, 235–40, 262–63, 284, 290–92, 320 n.63, 336 n.35; homosexuality, 6, 115–16, 119, 121–25, 131, 136, 152, 162, 169–74,

192, 242, 252, 256–57, 282–84, 313 nn.51, 53, 314 n.57, 319 n.59, 320 nn.60, 63; lesbianism, 82–83, 88–90, 96, 100, 217, 241, 243, 251, 275, 278–79, 281, 284, 305 n.24, 314 n.57, 318 n.42, 327 n.11, 333 n.94, 334 n.4; and national imagery, 7–9; promiscuity, 3, 6, 9–11, 19, 45, 50, 52, 55, 62–65, 126–28, 222, 235, 242, 250, 299 n.6, 338 n.58. *See also* Drag; Gay culture; Gender; Sadomasochism; Sexual freedom

Sexual freedom, 78, 240, 250, 252, 260–64, 272–76, 280, 339 n.77

Skinheads, 19, 109–11, 177, 180, 188–207, 209, 323 nn.24, 26, 28, 29; in Australia, 195–201, 324 nn.36, 37; in Germany, 109–11, 194, 324 n.33; in Sweden, 191–95, 323 n.30; in the United States, 201–7. See also *American History X;* Neo-Nazi organizations; Racism; Racist organizations; *Romper Stomper; Speak Up! It's So Dark*

Social conservative organizations, 178, 182, 184, 208, 250–51, 276–77; American Life League, 82–83; Antelope Valley Springs of Life Ministries, 73, 90, 95, 307 n.44; Colorado for Family Values, 308 nn.56, 57; Concerned Women for America, 82; Coral Ridge Ministries, 73, 77, 84–85, 91, 94–96; Defenders of the Christian Faith, 297 n.24; Focus on the Family, 81–82, 277; Heritage Foundation, 85; Moral Majority, 73, 84; National Right to Life, 86; Oregon Citizen's Alliance, 89–92, 97, 306 n.42, 307 n.49; Promise Keepers, 269–72. *See also* New Right

Social conservatives, 44–45, 51, 181; Abrams, Kevin, 93–94, 96; Dobson, James, 81–82, 277; Falwell, Jerry, 79, 97, 181; Graham, Billy, 76; Kennedy, D. James, 84–85, 94–97, 104, 306 n.33, 308 n.60; La Haye, Beverly; 82; Limbaugh, Rush, 87; Lively, Scott, 92; Reisman, Judith, 307 n.51; Robertson, Pat, 91, 97, 181, 276; Robison, James,

79; Schlessinger, "Dr. Laura," 91–92; Swaggert, Jimmy, 181. *See also* Family values rhetoric; Social conservative organizations

Social problem films, 138–74

Söderbaum, Kristina, 25, 30–31, 34, 297 n.21. *See also* *Goldene Stadt, Die*; Harlen, Veit

Sontag, Susan, 246, 251–52

Speak Up! It's So Dark, 189–97, 199, 202, 204, 206. *See also* Skinheads

Spielberg, Steven. See *Schindler's List*

Stalin, Joseph, 140–41, 304 n.8. *See also* Anti-communism; Totalitarianism

Sterilization. *See* Eugenics

Stone, Oliver: *Talk Radio,* 179–80

Strecker, Edward, 130–32, 135, 241, 313 n.55, 314 n.56. *See also* Psychology: political; Psychoanalysis

Sturges, Preston: *Miracle of Morgan's Creek,* 68–69, 303 n.62

Television, 144, 147–48; talk shows, 189. See also *Who Lives? Who Dies? Who Cares?*; *"Gay Rights": Private Lives and Public Policy*

Theweleit, Klaus, 33, 217, 256

Thompson, Linda, 73, 98, 101–2, 309 nn.72, 73. *See also Waco II: The Big Lie Continues*

Totalitarianism: concept of, 75–78, 102, 139–41. *See also* Anti-communism

Transgender. *See* Gender; Queer sensibility

Transvestitism. *See* Cross-dressing

Triumph of the Will. See Riefenstahl, Leni

Turner Diaries, The. See Pierce, William

United Service Organization (USO), 231, 240, 245, 330 n.56

Video. *See* B, Beth; *"Gay Rights": Private Lives and Public Policy*; Madonna; Schreiber, Rachel; Vollmer, Niklas; *Waco II: The Big Lie Continues; Who Lives? Who Dies? Who Cares?*

Visconti, Luchino. See *Damned, The*

Vollmer, Niklas: *Daddy Said So!,* 269

von Sternberg, Josef, 19, 218–26, 230; *Morocco,* 222. See also *Blue Angel, The*; Dietrich, Marlene

Waco (siege), 73, 98, 100–102, 322 n.17; *Waco: The Rules of Engagement,* 309 n.73. *See also* Anti-gun control rhetoric; Militia movement; *Waco II: The Big Lie Continues*

Waco II: The Big Lie Continues, 73, 98. 101–3. *See also* Thompson, Linda

Wedekind, Frank, 220–21, 328 n.20; *Pandora's Box,* 221, 225

Weimar republic, 122, 222, 224–33, 243, 257–62, 275, 328 nn.26, 27, 331 n.72. *See also* Dietrich, Marlene

Welles, Orson: *Stranger, The,* 68

Wertmüller, Lina: *Seven Beauties,* 335 n.17

West, Mae, 223

White Men Can't Jump, 202

White supremacism, 176, 180, 182–85, 188, 207, 322 n.18, 325 n.44. *See also* Neo-Nazi organizations; Racism; Racist organizations; Skinheads

Whiteness: male subjectivity, 138–75, 177–80, 185–210, 325 n.46, 326 nn.53, 62; women, 158–62, 198–201, 235–37, 319 n.54. See also Frankfurt School: *Authoritarian Personality, The*; Men; Racial identity; Racism; White supremacism; Women

Wilder, Billy, 19, 330 n.56, 331 nn.66, 67, 73; *Witness for the Prosecution,* 230, 244–45. See also *Foreign Affair, A*

Who Lives? Who Dies? Who Cares? (video), 73, 84–87. *See also* Social conservative organizations

Women; African American, 160, 165–68, 318 nn.42, 47, 319 n.53; images of, 152, 194, 203, 205, 210, 275, 281–86, 317 n.34, 327 nn.6, 9, 329 nn.37, 45; as immature, 258–64; Jewish, 172–73, 260, 270–71, 275, 281–86, 290–92, 317 n.34; as mothers, 83, 85, 87, 99, 109–13, 115–20, 125, 130–35, 160,

Women (*cont.*)
162–68, 173–74, 194–95, 203, 205,
232–33, 243, 296 n.8, 311 n.24, 313
n.53, 313 n.54, 314 nn.56, 57, 318 n.47,
330 n.62; as national symbols, 29, 47–
49; Nazi, 6, 19, 82, 213–47, 248–52,
331 nn.71, 72, 332 n.85, 333 nn.2, 4; as
political actors, 10, 12, 25, 60–64,
125–30, 135–37, 233–39, 248–51,
278–80, 339 n.79; as victims, 49–51,
59–64, 67, 87, 103, 158–62, 262–63;
white, 158–62, 198–201, 235–37, 319
n.54. *See also* Family values rhetoric;
Feminazi; Feminism; Sexuality: lesbianism; Nationalism: nationalist
melodrama
Wright, Geoffrey. See *Romper Stomper*
Wylie, Philip, 128, 130–32, 313 nn.53, 54,
314 n.57

Žižek, Slavoj, 1, 4

Andrea Slane, formerly Assistant Professor of Film Studies at Old Dominion University, is currently enrolled in the
Faculty of Law at the University of Toronto.

Library of Congress Cataloging-in-Publication Data
Slane, Andrea.
A not so foreign affair : fascism, sexuality, and the cultural
rhetoric of American democracy / Andrea Slane.
Includes bibliographical references and index.
ISBN 0-8223-2684-1 (cloth : alk. paper)
ISBN 0-8223-2693-0 (pbk. : alk. paper)
1. National socialism in motion pictures.   2. National so-
cialism and motion pictures.   3. Motion pictures—
Political aspects.   I. Title.
PN1995.9.N36 S58 2001   791.43'658—dc21   2001017231